fourth edition

THREE GENRES

The Writing of Poetry, Fiction, and Drama

STEPHEN MINOT
Trinity College
Hartford, Connecticut

PRENTICE HALL   Englewood Cliffs, New Jersey 07632

Library of Congress Cataloging-in-Publication Data

MINOT, STEPHEN.
   Three genres.

   Bibliography: p.
   Includes index.
   1. Creative writing.   I. Title.
PN145.M5 1987   808'.02   87-19330
ISBN 0-13-920430-X

Editorial/production supervision and
   interior design: Arthur Maisel
Cover design: George Cornell
Manufacturing buyer: Ray Keating

 © 1988, 1982 by Prentice Hall
A Division of Simon & Schuster
Englewood Cliffs, New Jersey 07632

Printed in the United States of America

10   9   8   7   6   5   4

ISBN 0-13-920430-X 01

Prentice-Hall International (UK) Limited, *London*
Prentice-Hall of Australia Pty. Limited, *Sydney*
Prentice-Hall Canada Inc., *Toronto*
Prentice-Hall Hispanoamericana, S.A., *Mexico*
Prentice-Hall of India Private Limited, *New Delhi*
Prentice-Hall of Japan, Inc., *Tokyo*
Prentice-Hall of Southeast Asia Pte. Ltd., *Singapore*
Editora Prentice-Hall do Brasil, Ltda., *Rio de Janeiro*

to Ginny

CONTENTS

PREFACE FOR STUDENTS

People write poetry, fiction, and drama for a number of different reasons. For some, it is one of the best ways of understanding literary writing. Just as those who have played a particular sport become better spectators, those who have written poems, short stories, or a play know what to look for in published work. They are apt to see more and as a result enjoy reading more. It is a resource which stays with you for life.

Others write because they hope it will become an avocation. They don't expect that it will ever become their true vocation, but they want to continue writing and perhaps to publish from time to time. They are like those who take up a musical instrument seriously but without any intention of becoming a professional musician. Such individuals may have to set aside their creative work for long periods, but many return to writing whenever their schedule permits.

Then there is that small group of writers who are deeply committed to a particular genre and are determined to make it their central concern. They may have to enter other fields to earn income—especially at first. But they identify themselves as *poets, writers,* or *dramatists.* They have to fashion an individual lifestyle which will allow time for writing. They also allot a portion of each day to reading contemporary fiction, poetry, or drama in a close, professional way. Once out of school, they attend readings and conferences. In short, they are immersed in their art—not just their own work but the best of what is being published as well.

In school and college, however, the largest group is made up of those who really don't know how important writing will become. They are open to what may develop. Some may begin with high expectations and discover that after graduation they will be readers rather than writers. Students in courses dealing with more than one genre may find that they have a talent in an area they hadn't expected. Writers, unlike ballet dancers, don't have to start at an early age. Anything is possible at any stage. There is no way of predicting how much talent and commitment will develop until one makes an initial effort.

This book is designed for individuals in all four areas. It can be used in a creative writing class, in an informal writers' group, or by individuals working on their own.

I do, however, have one word of warning: You will not make full use of this book if you simply read it the way you might a history text. It is very important to keep applying the analysis of writing to literary samples and to your own work as well. Here are some specific suggestions which will help you draw the most from this text:

- In the poetry section, there are a number of references made to poems which are printed in Chapter 11, "Poems for Study." Since these poems are used repeatedly to illustrate different aspects of verse, they are conveniently grouped in that concluding chapter. *Take the time to turn to the poem in question each time.* Read it over carefully and see how the analysis applies. In this way you will understand the concepts much better and in the process will acquire an increasingly deep understanding of what that poem has to offer.

- Although I have limited the literary terms to those that are really useful in the practical business of analyzing and discussing poetry, there are a number which may be unfamiliar to those who have not studied verse. *Try to use these terms in your discussions.* If you need a quick review at some later point, *use the Glossary-Index* at the back of the book. These terms will help you to keep your analysis precise, and they will soon become a useful part of your active vocabulary.

- There are four stories in the fiction section and two complete plays in the drama section. Read them carefully as you come to them, but *don't hesitate to reread specific scenes whenever they are analyzed in detail.* As with poems, you will come to know these works well if you make the effort to review them regularly.

- In all three sections, try to *apply concepts and specific terms to literary samples not printed in this text.* Remember that your goal is not merely to acquire terms but to gain and understand literary concepts and to apply them to other work—including your own.

All this will take you a little more time than it would simply to read a textbook from beginning to end. But creative writing is not a skill which can be mastered in ten easy lessons. It is a slow process of growth—growth both in your understanding of what literature has to offer and your ability to create new work with your own individual stamp.

Preface for Teachers

With the appearance of this, the fourth edition, *Three Genres* will have been in print 23 years. Although generally used in small classes and seminars, it has been read by over 100,000 student writers so far. Some of you who have adopted it for your writing courses were introduced to earlier editions when you yourselves were undergraduates. Many of your students today were not born when the first edition appeared.

My concern here, however, is not for past performance but for the present and the future. Although contemporary literature is not subject to the rapid fluctuations in style which influence music and art, it nonetheless is never static. A textbook which is dominated by stylistic patterns and literary selections from the 1960s will not meet the needs of those writing today.

How does a writing text stay young? The answer lies partially in the author's attitude but equally in the readers' response. With regard to the first, I am more actively involved as a free-lance writer now than I was when I wrote the first edition. Although my schedule no longer allows me to teach full time, I return to the classroom periodically so as not to lose contact with today's students. My commitment to my own writing requires a continuing process of self-education. As a result, I see *Three Genres* not as a definitive statement but as a perpetually evolving examination of the creative process.

The other side of this equation is equally important. Teachers in 47 states have used this text in every conceivable sort of institution. They write and advise. I take all of these comments seriously for these individuals are the ones who have first-hand experience with each new edition.

As a fellow teacher, I too have had mixed feelings about new editions. Just when you get used to certain works and have all your marginal notes in place, a revision appears and you have to start all over again. And your students, hard pressed by the cost of textbooks, must invest in new copies.

New editions are essential, however, just as are new lecture notes and revised syllabuses. Since the technique of preparing a new edition is rarely explained in print, let me outline at least briefly what it entails.

Two years in advance, I review the text and read over the file of unsolicited letters from teachers and students that have been sent to me through the publisher. From these I prepare a questionnaire for teachers about what worked in class, what was confusing, and how the respondents would feel about certain specific revisions. These questions, along with a more general set prepared by the publisher, are sent by Prentice Hall to four teachers in significantly different types of institutions in different parts of the country.

The detailed responses—with names and institutions carefully removed—are sent to me. On the basis of these and other more informal suggestions, basic decisions are made about which works to retain and which to replace. Permissions have to be secured for each new work, and permission fees are negotiated—sometimes at considerable length.

Then the actual revision process begins. It takes me about a year to prepare the manuscript. Almost every page requires some changes and certain chapters are entirely new. It then takes the publisher a year to go through the production process—edited manuscript, galleys, page proofs, and finally the printing. A month after the new edition has been distributed, the file for the edition after that is begun.

Why so many changes? They result partly from shifts in what is current and partly from an effort to find literary samples that best illustrate aspects of contemporary writing. Just as one's course is revised on the basis of personal teaching experience, *Three Genres* is altered in response to a network of teachers throughout the country.

In the poetry section of this fourth edition, for example, I was very pleased to add a metered poem, "The Pardon" by Richard Wilbur, which many teachers have found to be highly successful in class. On the nonmetrical end of the scale, I added free-verse poems by Sharon Olds and Nikki Giovanni. I also added a previously unanthologized poem by Chase Twichell because I believe her work is among the best now being published. The sonnet is now represented by a work with contemporary phrasing and details, one of John Berryman's remarkable and rarely anthologized works. Such examples should give students a good idea of the range of styles and approaches available in contemporary poetry.

In the fiction section I was pleased to obtain permission to use Bobbie Ann Mason's story "Graveyard Day." It not only provides excellent examples of subtle symbolic suggestion, but it also represents a style which has come into prominence only recently—a combination of the present tense and heavy use of dialogue at the expense of exposition and dialogue. And Robert Fox's "A Fable" adds an example of gentle satire not represented in the text before.

The long search for a contemporary, nonrealistic play involved reading 280 scripts. The standard I applied was that it should resemble Edward Albee's *The Sandbox* which was included in the second edition and then dropped partly for reasons of expense. The final decision to return once again to the Albee play was based partly on my continuing admiration but was made largely because of reports from many teachers at different institutions that it was an ideal companion piece to the more traditional work of William Saroyan, *Hello Out There*.

My thanks to all those who wrote with suggestions—both positive and negative. Now, looking ahead, I invite teachers, students, and individuals working on their own to write to me care of Prentice Hall, Englewood Cliffs, NJ 07632. Let me know what was helpful in this fourth edition and, equally important, what was not. Because of forwarding, my reply may take months, but I do answer every correspondent. In a very real sense, this text is a collaboration between author and you the readers.

1 WHAT MAKES A POEM A POEM?

The four characteristics of poetry: the use of the *line*, the *sound* of words, *rhythm*, and *compression* of statement; *sophisticated* poetry distinguished from *simple*; the use of poetic *conventions* to achieve true *individuality.*

Yes, but is it really a poem? This question keeps coming up whenever we discuss poetry—particularly contemporary work. But we rarely take the time to answer it. Defining poetry seems difficult because the genre includes such an astonishing variety of forms and approaches—from lengthy Greek epics to three-line haikus, from complex metrical schemes to the apparent formlessness of some free verse.

In spite of all this variation, however, there are certain basic characteristics shared by poetry of all ages. These not only help to distinguish poetry from prose, they suggest special assets which have drawn men and women to this genre in almost every culture since before there were written languages. As readers, we have come to expect these qualities unconsciously. When they are missing, we may sense the lack without knowing exactly what is wrong. As writers of poetry, we depend on them. Regardless of what stage we have reached, they remain four areas of special concern.

The Four Characteristics of Poetry

The first of these characteristics is *line length*. Poets determine the length of each line they write; it is a part of the art form itself. This is in sharp contrast with prose, in which the author has no control over the length of the line. Prose lines are determined mainly by the size of the page, and if the manuscript is retyped or printed, the length of the lines may well be changed by the typist. Line length is as external to the literary form of prose as the color of the paper.

The arrangement of short lines on a page sends a signal to readers from the very outset. It suggests that this will probably be a concentrated bit of writing which will have to be read more slowly than prose. Perhaps it will require some study. Conscientious readers shift to a lower gear when they confront a poem.

Line length is even more significant for the poet than it is for the reader. When we write prose we usually move from beginning to end, consciously or unconsciously following a logical outline. With a story, for example, the outline may be a sequence of events—the plot. With essays we follow—or *should* follow—a sequence of logically related ideas. But when we shift to writing poetry, we are liberated from that kind of controlling structure. Instead, our attention is apt to turn to visual aspects: short lines or long lines? Stanza breaks or one solid block of print? In addition, the creative process itself tends to move line by line. Our imagination begins to focus on one visual image after another, prompted by memory. We are guided more by association than by logical sequence, particularly in early drafts. The final version will probably have a structure of some sort, but the line which came first may have ended up as the fifth or the last, and the original ending may now be buried in the middle.

The importance of the line in poetry actually preceded the written word. Epics like the *Iliad* and the *Odyssey* were apparently memorized and recited before they were written, and the rhythms of spoken lines were an essential aid to memorization. So was rhyme. This theory has been further supported by the discovery of lengthy Yugoslavian epics which even today have been memorized by individuals who can neither read nor write.

As soon as poetry was recorded on the page, there was less need for memory aids. But it has never lost its roots in the spoken language nor its reliance on line length. In the case of metered verse, the length of the line is absolutely essential. Meter is based on a specific number of stressed and unstressed syllables in each line, so the length of the line is determined in advance by the metrical scheme the poet has chosen. It is a structuring of natural speech rhythms, just as formal dance steps are agreed-upon patterns drawn from improvised dancing.

Free verse, like free-style dancing, has no such guiding structure, so the lines may vary in length. But those variations can be extremely important. They are often used to control the pace of reading, to emphasize a key image, to establish rhythms, and sometimes even to give the printed poem as a whole a significant shape.

Control of line length is an absolute distinction which differentiates all poetry from all prose. The three other characteristics of poetry, however, are not as absolute as this. One can find poems which may not make use of them all. But they are the qualities we associate with the genre and which give us that seemingly intuitive sense that a particular work is indeed a poem. Like the use of the line, these characteristics continue to be major concerns for poets at any stage of development.

The most noticeable of these is the *heightened use of sound.* We think of rhyme first because ending two lines with the same sound is an unmistakable device. Jingles, nursery rhymes, and simple ballads almost always rhyme in an obvious way. But as we will see, rhyme can be muted in ways to keep it from becoming obtrusive. In addition, there are two other ways to link words by sound: by matching the initial letter ("*green* as *grass*") or through internal syllables which echo each other ("*trees* and *leaves*"). The paired sounds, of course, must appear in words that are close enough together so that the reader can hear the linkage.

"Fern Hill" by Dylan Thomas is a good example of an unrhymed poem which nonetheless ripples with sound linkages. The poet is describing with dreamlike phrasing his memories of his childhood on a beautiful farm. Here are the first three of 54 lines. I have circled several of the linkages in sound.

> And once below a time I lordly had the trees and leaves
>
> Trail with daisies and barley
>
> Down the rivers of the windfall light.

The poem is printed in its entirety on page 104. You may wish to turn to it now and discover for yourself how intricate sound linkages can be even in poetry that is not rhymed.

Prose also appeals to the ear. Often it is achieved by repetition of words and phrases. When this is done with restraint, we call it "poetic prose" or a "lyrical passage." But when it is overdone it becomes obtrusive. Readers may complain that the style has become pretentious or "frilly." Remember that we usually read prose more rapidly than poetry and sometimes we resent impediments to the flow of ideas in an essay or the development of plot in a story or novel. Each genre has its own special assets, and they are not easily transferred from one to another.

The third of these four characteristics of poetry is the use of *rhythm*. In simplest terms, rhythm is a systematic variation in the flow of sound. All speech varies the flow of sound, of course; otherwise it would be a steady hum. But the key word here is "systematic." Here are two lines taken from Richard Wilbur's "The Pardon":

$$\overset{\cup}{\text{Well,}} \overset{/}{\text{I}} \overset{\cup}{\text{was}} \overset{/}{\text{ten}} \overset{\cup}{\text{and}} \overset{/}{\text{very}} \overset{\cup}{\text{much}} \overset{/}{\text{afraid.}}$$

$$\overset{\cup}{\text{In}} \overset{/}{\text{my}} \overset{\cup}{\text{kind}} \overset{/}{\text{world}} \overset{\cup}{\text{the}} \overset{/}{\text{dead}} \overset{\cup}{\text{were}} \overset{/}{\text{out}} \overset{\cup}{\text{of}} \overset{/}{\text{range}}$$

There are five stressed syllables (/) in each line and five unstressed ($\cup$). Rhythm which takes on a traditional pattern like this is called *meter;* I will return to metrics in Chapter 6. These lines are unusual in their regularity, but I use them here simply as an example of how language can be infused with a regular rhythmical system without making it sound artificial.

Although metrics have dominated British and American poetry until recently, there are nonmetrical rhythmical techniques which also have long histories. Samples of what we now call *free verse* can be found as far back as the Song of Songs, one of the books of the Old Testament.

Nonmetrical rhythms can be created in many ways. Some poets develop a recurring pattern based on the number of syllables in each line. The haiku is about the shortest form of this, with five syllables in the first line, seven in the second, and five in the third. "Fern Hill" by Dylan Thomas is a much more complex example, and I will return to both it and the haiku in Chapter 7. Other poets arrange long and short lines on the page in such a way as to highlight certain phrases or even trip the reader. The poems by Denise Levertov and E. E. Cummings in Chapter 11 are good examples. I will be analyzing these techniques in greater detail in the chapter on free verse. I mention them here simply as an overview of the range of rhythmical techniques available to the poet.

It is also possible to create rhythms in prose. We hear it most often in political oratory and in traditional sermons. But because prose writers do not control the length of the line, prose rhythms are generally limited to repetitions in sentence structure, words, or phrases. Poets have many more rhythmical techniques at their disposal, and most make use of them.

The fourth and most subtle characteristic of poetry is *compression*. Poems usually say a lot in a few words. They achieve this through language which suggests much more than the immediate, surface meaning. As a result, readers may have to give a complex poem several readings to enjoy it fully. The resistance some feel to reading a new poem comes from the realization that it will probably take more work than does a short story or an article. With practice, however—and it does take practice—this more densely packed genre offers the reader special pleasures which are well worth the effort.

When we turn to writing poetry, we may have to spend hours, often spaced over several days, going through draft after draft to achieve this density. The process may seem slow, but the reward comes when we have the feeling that we have said more in a few lines than a prose writer could have done in pages.

Because poems are concentrated does not mean they necessarily have to be short. Epic poems like the *Iliad* and *Beowulf* deal with the mythic and historical events that unify a culture, and they are written in metered verse. In spite of their length, however, they are still more concentrated, more powerful than prose. One cannot read them at the same rapid pace as a contemporary novel.

We still produce "epics" today—works that deal with major historical events and help to define our culture; but they are more likely to be produced as novels or films. Perhaps as a result, poets have turned increasingly to personal experience and the subtleties of private emotions. Even when they are making blunt social or political statements, they frequently draw on their own lives, creating impact through language charged with overtones.

As you start out to write poetry, then, the most fertile sources to consider will be your own feelings and experiences. What is important to you can be shared with others if you are truly honest. But poetry isn't simply a collection of feelings spilled out on the page like journal entries. Useful as journals are, their entries are more like grocery lists than a carefully prepared meal. A poem is an art form in itself, as is a painting or a musical composition. It is a verbal and auditory art which makes special use of the line, the sound of words, the rhythms of language, and the impact of genuine insight. These are not only the recurring characteristics of poetry, they are the special assets of the genre which poets keep working to develop. They form the core of the chapters that follow.

Sophisticated versus Simple Poetry

What is a *good* poem? This question invites a second: good for what? If a poem is intended for a mass market—as greeting cards are—it should have a positive message and be phrased in unvaried metrical lines with a regular rhyme scheme. Both the sentiments and phrasing should be familiar, not fresh or startling. To be "good," a mass-market poem should soothe, not probe.

Poems that are sometimes called literary, however, are intended for readers who ask for an entirely different set of characteristics. These poems attempt to share personal experience and feelings honestly, to comment in a fresh manner on what it is to be human. They often probe deeply and occasionally contain disturbing insights. The language is fresh and sometimes demanding. They may create unusual rhythms. Some such poems emphasize language itself, playing with words in complicated ways; others are more concerned with image and statement. Many assume that the reader has some previous familiarity with the genre and is willing to work a little.

There are problems with calling this kind of work literary. For one thing, the term seems a bit pretentious when applied to contemporary work. Besides, we then face the problem of defining *literary*. Our problems are compounded when we call it "good" poetry. It seems like a value judgment and implies that popular, mass-market poetry is "bad." It is as subjective as calling classical music "good" and popular music "bad." Too often, the terms lead to lengthy and pointless arguments.

The best solution is to borrow two terms from the language of science. To a biologist, simple forms of life are *simple* and complex forms are *sophisticated*. Thus, the bird is not better in any objective sense than the jellyfish, but it is far more sophisticated in that its potential as a living creature is greater.

In writing—as in nature—*simple* and *sophisticated* represent a scale with an infinite number of points between. The clever, comic verse of someone like Ogden Nash is certainly more sophisticated than most nursery rhymes, but less sophisticated than the poems of, say, Dylan Thomas. The works of an individual poet will also vary. Just because someone is able to write highly sophisticated work that is dense in meaning and complex in treatment does not mean that he or she can't also write comic verse or light, satiric pieces as well.

Should all poetry be sophisticated? Of course not. Millions enjoy not only greeting cards but volumes of simple verse. Others take pleasure in relatively simple ballads and inspirational poetry. Mass-market magazines publish simple verse as "fillers." Writing verse like that is an honest craft which requires practice. There are books to help those who want to succeed at it, but this is not one of them.

Sophisticated writing—poetry, fiction, and drama—is the subject of this text. Such work is by definition complex, but it is not necessarily cluttered or obscure. There are technically complex poems in which the intricacies of meter or repeated refrains become a kind of game; but these may end up being less sophisticated as poetry than a three-line haiku which manages to convey a wide range of suggestion. Complexity of meaning is not always achieved by complex language or metrical schemes.

Joyce Kilmer's "Trees" has been used many times in battles over what is and what is not "good" poetry. Let's sidestep that argument and take an objective look at what makes it a good example of highly popular simple verse. Here are the first three of its six stanzas:

I think that I shall never see
A poem lovely as a tree.

A tree whose hungry mouth is pressed
Against the earth's sweet flowing breast;

A tree that looks to God all day
And lifts her leafy arms to pray; . . .

What can we say objectively about these six lines? First, they clearly come from a poem. The length of the lines has been set by the writer, and some kind of regular rhythm can be heard simply by reading it aloud. In addition, the intentional use of sound is unmistakable: the lines are grouped in pairs which end with the same sounds to form rhyming couplets.

We can also say objectively that it is relatively simple verse. As with nursery rhymes, there is great regularity to the rhythm and to the rhyme. Without knowing anything about meter, one can detect four distinct beats to each line, and every rhyme is an exact matching of sound landing on a stressed syllable. This regularity creates a singsong effect.

As for the suggestion, that too is on a fairly simple level. Since trees are generally regarded as beautiful, the poet is repeating a commonly held view, a *truism*, rather than presenting a fresh concept or experience. Seeing the tree as a praying figure is somewhat hackneyed. We can't say that the poem is "bad" since it has given pleasure to millions of readers. But we can say that both the poetic techniques and the assertion it makes are on a simple level.

By way of contrast, here is a two-line poem by Ezra Pound:

In a Station of the Metro

The apparition of these faces in the crowd;
Petals on a wet, black bough.

If this were printed in a solid line like prose, we would probably assume that it was merely a fragment—perhaps from a journal—and skip over it quickly. But because it is presented with a title and in two lines, we are assured at the outset that this is a poem and that it is intended to be read with some care. As with "Trees," its very shape on the page has influenced the way we will read it.

How seriously should we take it? After a single reading it is clear that this is not a comic jingle, nor is it a conventional statement about the beauty of nature. Something more sophisticated is going on. Perhaps, though, it is just a descriptive poem. Saying "just" suggests that such poems are not as sophisticated as those that have some kind of contrast or conflicting emotion. If this poem were, as it seems at first, merely a quick verbal snapshot of faces in the Metro (the Paris subway), then it would be more sophisticated than a jingle but not the kind we need to spend much time on.

But what is being suggested with that word "apparitions"? These faces have appeared suddenly, almost like ghosts. In what way might they resemble "Petals on a wet, black bough"? Faces seen in the windows of a black subway car come to mind. The car has abruptly arrived at the station and the faces inside remind the poet of petals.

Are there any more overtones? Petals that have been torn from blossoms by a rainstorm and plastered on the limb of a branch are being swept along by events over which they have no control. Does this apply to the passengers? The wording of the poem suggests that it does. This is how they appeared to the poet.

It would be a mistake to push the poem beyond this. There is nothing here to suggest forces of evil against good; the poet isn't calling on the passengers to rebel. Nor are we told that this is beautiful or pitiful. It is more as if the poet has seized our arm and said, "Hey, look at that!"

Except for this: The poet has not only caught our attention the way one might in conversation, he has created the scene as well. The suddenness of the "apparition," the fragile quality of those petals torn loose by the rainstorm, and the impact of the subway car highlighted by those three stressed syllables at the end—"wet, black bough"—all these help us to share both the visual impression and his reaction to it.

There is no rhyme in this poem, but like the lines from "Fern Hill" quoted earlier, it has a number of linkages in sound. "Crowd" and "bough" echo the same vowel sound in what is known as a *slant rhyme*. The second line has two linked pairs: the *e* sound in "petals" and "wet" and that heavy *b* in "black" and "bough." Unlike most prose passages, these lines are linked together not only with meaning but with sound.

The essential difference between these two poems is that Kilmer makes a conventional or commonplace assertion about trees in general, while Pound gives us a unique insight drawn from a very specific scene. In addition, the two poems represent a difference in technique which often distinguishes simple from sophisticated work: Kilmer employs rigid metrical and rhyme schemes, while Pound mutes both the rhythms and the sound linkages so that they do not become obtrusive. Even with the sonnet, a metered and rhymed form I will turn to in Chapter 9, rhythm and sound can be kept in the background.

Simple verse has its function. It soothes. Often it marks an occasion like an anniversary or a birthday in a simple, positive way. Who wants to be told they are impossible to live with at fifteen or getting cranky at 60? Sophisticated poetry, the subject of this text, has more complex and intricate rewards: It gives pleasure through fresh insights and subtle use of form. When it speaks to us, we don't throw it away after the first reading. We savor it.

Conventions versus Individuality

Anyone who hopes to write sophisticated poetry wants to be fresh and original. Is there a danger, then, that studying the works of others and the long
tradition of the genre will stifle our individuality? Actually, the opposite is
true. Those who are not familiar with what the genre has to offer are apt to
settle on just one approach and begin repeating themselves. Finding one's
own unique voice requires being familiar with a wide range of poetic conventions.

An artistic *convention* is any pattern or device that is used in a large
number of works. In popular music, for example, it is helpful to distinguish
blues from blue grass and rock from jazz. Artists distinguish realists from
impressionists, surrealists, and minimalists. Within each category there are
usually subdivisions. Being familiar with basic terms makes conversation about
music or art more precise and enjoyable even for the casual listener. Those
who compose music or paint, however, need to know a few more.

It is the same with poetry. Some terms describe the form. We will be
examining the characteristics of the sonnet, villanelle, and a technique called
syllabics, among others. Other terms refer to type—narrative, lyric, and the
like. Basic classifications like these are valuable for anyone who wants to read
poetry with enjoyment. When we turn to writing poetry, however, we have
to go a bit further. It helps to know how to use meter and the free-verse
technique of spacing lines on the page, for example. Rhyme is an important
technique even if you later decide not to use it, and so are those more muted
effects achieved by linking words through similar-sounding syllables.

When poetry (some would prefer *verse*) is rigidly bound by conventions such as unvaried meter and blatant rhyme, stock themes, and overly
familiar metaphors, we say it is conventional and simple. By *conventional* we
mean that the conventions have become too rigidly used, too obvious. But
all poetry—even the most sophisticated—is based on conventions. They are
for the poet what notes, measures, and phrases are for the musician.

Our first task as poets, then, is to master the basic conventions of the
genre. Only in this way can we achieve freedom as writers, for only when
we are at ease with a particular technique are we free to decide whether to
use it.

Take, for example, the various systems of creating rhythm. Which is
"best," rhythm of stress, meter, or free verse? Best for what? And for whom?
Practicing poets base their decisions partly on personal preference and partly
on the needs of a particular poem. They can do this only when they are at
home with each system.

The first step toward sophisticated work is to master the craft of
poetry. The second is learning how to mute that craft so that the technique
you use is not obtrusive. This is when you begin to use the language of poetry
to reflect what is unique in yourself: your specific insights and reactions. Soon

you will find yourself going beyond mere mastery of conventions to develop your own "voice" as a poet.

The following nine chapters deal with the conventions of verse and with the ways poets use these techniques to create work that is sophisticated and unique. When you have drawn as much as you can from this kind of analysis, let other poets be your teachers and work to develop your own true individuality.

2 THE SOURCES OF POETRY

Poetic sources contrasted with those for prose; the dangers of *abstractions;* five *basic sources* for poetry: personal *experience, mixed emotions* (ambivalence), the lives of *other people,* using the *senses* (sight, sound, smells, taste, and touch), the pleasure of *language as language; getting started.*

Most of the writing assigned in school and in college is either analytical or persuasive. It deals with abstractions in what we hope is a logical way. This kind of writing is important to master partly because it is the sort one is most likely to do after graduation—committee reports, applications, recommendations, and the like. In addition, writing clearly helps one to think clearly.

After so much training in analytical writing, it is natural enough to start composing a poem as if it were a little essay written in short, melodic lines. But this is a serious mistake. The way in which a poem comes to the mind and is developed is entirely different from the way we write prose. This is more than a matter of technique; the actual *process* of creativity differs. This distinction between the generative process in the two genres is so fundamental that it is worth examining closely right at the start.

Suppose, for example, you planned to write a paper on the plight of the high-school dropout. Your first step would probably be to gather facts from newspaper and magazine articles. A good deal of the material might be statistical—dropout rates, unemployment figures, crime rates, and the like. You would then probably focus your paper with a thesis statement, a sentence that represents your primary theme or central concern. Most writers find it helpful to write an outline at this stage, listing major and minor points. The actual writing expands on these points and works toward a conclusion about dropouts in general.

This entire process is abstract and analytical. It begins with an abstract concept and ends with a generalized conclusion. If the paper has specific examples, their function is secondary—merely to illustrate the points being made.

The genesis of a poem is much more likely to be specific and particular. Although there is no rigid pattern, poems today tend to be rooted in an experience—a person, a specific place, something seen. Rarely do poems start with a broad abstraction like *truth, beauty,* or even a social problem like *dropouts.* This starting point, or poetic kernel, often springs from the poet's private life. It holds the reader's attention the way an intensely personal conversation does; it is an honest moment of sharing. If there is some kind of conclusion at the end, it need only be implied. The poem maintains its vitality through specifics, not generalities.

Returning to the problem of dropouts, here is how Gwendolyn Brooks treats the subject in a poem entitled "We Real Cool: The Pool Players. Seven at the Golden Shovel."

We real cool. We
Left School. We

Lurk late. We
Strike straight. We

Sing sin. We
Thin gin. We

Jazz June. We
Die soon.

No statistics here. No abstract tables showing the relationship between dropouts and unemployment or early death. All that would be appropriate for an essay in prose, but it would defeat the effectiveness of a poem. The poet hasn't tried to *prove* anything about those who leave school early, but she has made us *feel* something about their plight.

How has she achieved this? Partly through diction—word choice. There are no long, abstract words here; in fact, they are all just one syllable long. The effect sounds like street language. In addition, the rhythm and rhyme echo chants that we associate with street games. She avoids *end rhymes* (rhyming words coming at the end of the lines), perhaps because they might have made the poem sound too conventional. Instead, she has muted the sound linkages by using *internal rhyme*—rhymed words falling within each line. The conclusion in the last line comes as a jolt, jarring us just as news about the death of a young friend might.

These seven pool players may be a composite of many different people the poet has known or seen, but that lengthy subtitle gives us the feeling that we are listening to seven young men at a specific place called the Golden Shovel. This is not an abstract statement decorated with "poetic" rhythm and rhyme. Those one-syllable words, the chantlike rhythm, and the rhyme all contribute to give us the illusion of street language.

Yet this is not a tape recording of actual speech either. Why not? Because what we say in daily speech tends to be rambling and lacks this kind of compression. Without focus, conversations are quickly forgotten. Recordings of them are surprisingly boring. This poem has the *illusion* of street language, yet it is also a highly compressed statement which sets the reader up for that last jolt: "We / Die soon." It is an artistic creation, but as in most sophisticated poems, the artistry is muted.

The Danger of Abstractions

An abstract word is a concept or state of being. It may be enormously important, but it exists only in the mind. The opposite of *abstract* is *concrete.* Stinginess is an abstraction, but the character named Scrooge in Charles Dickens' story *A Christmas Carol* is concrete. Death is an abstraction, but the seven pool players in Gwendolyn Brooks' "We Real Cool" are concrete, and the implication of early death is made more comprehensive for us through them.

Abstractions are essential for any kind of analytical thought. We cannot design a rocket without talking about the abstraction thrust. We cannot vote intelligently without understanding the concepts of Republican and Democratic. We can't even discuss a poem without understanding abstractions like rhythm and compression. But there is a significant difference between analyzing a poem and writing one. Basing a poem on a general abstraction almost guarantees that the result will be conventional and unconvincing. Watch out for topics like *love, death, nature, peace, war, brotherhood, hypocrisy, God, beauty, justice, prejudice, liberty,* and *truth.* These are all important concepts, but when treated in the abstract they sound devoid of real feeling no matter how strong your convictions may be. *Love* in the abstract, for example, sounds like a greeting card or the simplest song lyric until it is seen in terms of an actual relationship. Poems about nature or beauty in the abstract tend to become truisms, echoing what we all feel without adding to our experience. Even attacks on injustice or prejudice sound like empty slogans until they are given life through specific instances.

Where should one look for subject matter? Begin with what is close to you. You know your life better than anyone. Second, take a close look at your own mixed emotions. They may surprise you. Third, consider the experiences of other people as Brooks did in "We Real Cool." Fourth, rely on your senses—what you have seen, heard, felt, smelled, tasted, and touched. Finally, remember that it is fun to play with language itself. These represent five important sources for poetry. Each is worth careful consideration.

Personal Experience

Poets rely heavily on personal experience. Often, the type of experience is vivid and visual. We have already seen how Ezra Pound caught a single visual impression in a station of the Paris subway system. And Gwendolyn Brooks appears to have been responding to seven specific pool players whom she saw or knew. If you turn to the poems printed in Chapter 11, you will see that this sense of sharing an experience with the poet applies to many of them.

Denise Levertov's "Merritt Parkway" (p. 99), for example, describes the motion of cars on a superhighway. From a reader's point of view it is not important that she has in mind a particular parkway just north of New York City. The "dreamlike continuum" and the "slurred sound" apply just as well to a California freeway. But it is important for a poet to know that something as mechanical and apparently unpoetic as the Merritt Parkway can serve as a poetic source.

Or take Maya Angelou's "This Winter Day" (p. 99), which describes a simple kitchen scene as she makes soup. The first stanza is as follows:

> The kitchen in its readiness
> white green and orange things
> leak their blood selves in the soup.

She is not writing about kitchens in general. This has the unmistakable sense of a personal experience examined closely with language that startles us. A familiar scene—like Levertov's superhighway—is being described in a way that helps us to see it more vividly than we would have without the poet's help.

Occasionally the experience is dramatic. Take, for example, these opening lines of Ann Z. Leventhal's "Pilot Error" (p. 112):

The phone rings on a Sunday afternoon.
"There's been an accident," Juliet's
husband says. I go on folding laundry,

matching every corner, every seam
exactly, caressing terry velvet

Through the next five stanzas the poem develops the extraordinary contrast between the shock of personal tragedy and the mind's numbed response—the desperate clinging to routine.

Earlier I warned against writing about love in the abstract. This does not mean, however, that aspects of love between two people cannot be used effectively. The subject has real potential if the experience is genuine and if contrasting emotions are presented through specific incidents. Here, for example, is the opening from Adrienne Rich's "Like This Together," the first of six stanzas.

Wind rocks the car
We sit parked by the river,
silence between our teeth.
Birds scatter across islands
of broken ice. Another time
I'd have said "Canada geese,"
knowing you love them.
A year, ten years from now,
I'll remember this,
this sitting like drugged birds
in a glass case—
not why, only that we
were here like this together.

The poet is not here concerned with Love in the abstract; she is dealing with a specific relationship between two people at a specific moment in time. She recalls the scene through very precise memories—the feel of a car shuddering in the wind, the look of that icy river. And then she develops the *unique* quality of that relationship at that particular stage: the chill of the landscape, the couple sitting "like drugged birds / in a glass case . . ." There is love here, but it is a part of a complex set of emotions and its future is uncertain.

The sources of contemporary poetry tend to be personal and specific. It takes a little courage and a good deal of personal honesty to find material which will lend itself to poetic statement. But it is important to remember that we all have in our own lives more than enough experiences with which to work.

Mixed Emotions

In simple verse, love is pure and hate is nonexistent. In life, emotions are rarely that simple. They become mixed in complex ways. Sophisticated poetry often deals with the complexities of our feelings.

Ambivalence refers to our capacity to have two conflicting emotions about a person or thing at the same time. This is more than a simple alternation of feelings. Ambivalent feelings occur simultaneously. We like to think that our feelings of love are unalloyed and our distaste for certain things is never tinged with desire or longing, but sadly this is rarely true. Genuine love can be mixed with mistrust or even hate at the very same instant; courage is often laced with fear; what we think of as happy memories are sometimes seasoned with regret; and some of our worst experiences may have elements of pleasure.

Our tendency is to deny these inconsistencies in ourselves and others. Look at greeting card verse. Not a hint of mixed feelings there. But when we deal honestly with the rich complexity of experience, we have to deal with mixed emotions, with ambivalence.

The tone of Gwendolyn Brooks' poem "We Real Cool" is not pure disdain. There is a mix of sad compassion with harsh condemnation. Adrienne Rich's poem "Like This Together" does not describe a pure love. It is a highly complex relationship which is described with greater complexity and detail as the poem continues. Dylan Thomas' "Fern Hill," also included in Chapter 11 (p. 104), describes what appears to be an idealized view of childhood, but it ends with a melancholy recognition of the fact that we are indeed mortal. For all the joy he feels in the memory of those vivid childhood days, he is at the same time distressed at the inevitability of death.

Writing sophisticated poetry which shares genuine feelings is sometimes embarrassing, even painful. Remember, though, that your readers expect honesty. A poem written on the page or read aloud rises above the level of casual conversation. If well done, the poem takes on a life separate from that of the poet.

There are three questions that help to keep poetry genuine, honest, and insightful.

- Did I really feel that?
- Was that all I felt?
- Have I found the specific details that will help my reader to share the same feelings?

Emotions that most naturally generate poetry do not have to be intense, but they do have to be genuine and fairly complex.

Other People

Important as you are to yourself and your poetry, you are not the only source for poetic composition. There are other people.

No one—not even an orphan—is raised in isolation. We all have people in our lives who are important to us. We have parents or foster parents, and many of us have siblings, cousins, aunts, and uncles. There are friends, acquaintances of all ages, and people we barely know who have made an impression on us.

Brooks' "We Real Cool" is one of those poems that seems unmistakably based on real people. Even if she did not know the seven young men at the Golden Shovel personally, she has seen people like that and listened to them talk. This personal familiarity helps to give the poem a sense of authenticity.

Anthony Hecht's "Lizards and Snakes" (p. 97) is another good example. It is a *narrative poem* in that it tells a story. Unlike prose fiction, however, it is a highly compressed account. It is written in the first person and appears to be a childhood experience involving a persona (probably, but not necessarily, the poet himself) and his friend Joe. But the core of the poem deals with his Aunt Martha, whose religious beliefs are vivid and intense.

Parents, grandparents, sisters, brothers, aunts, and uncles have all been subjects of poems. Because there is an infinite variety of relationships between members of the same family, the subject will never be exhausted.

Sharon Olds' poem "The Guild" (p. 108) is a dramatic example. The poem begins with a description of her grandfather who used to sit "in the darkened room in front of the fire, / the liquor like fire in his hand. . . ." We then see that his companion is a "college boy with / white skin, unlined, a narrow / beautiful face. . . ." This young man, "the apprentice" in drinking, is identified at the end of the poem as the narrator's father.

This is a dark portrait, but it is vivid and memorable. The title, "The Guild," reminds us of the way in which destructive traits can be passed on from generation to generation as if from "master" to "apprentice."

Poems about relatives and friends don't have to be this dark, but they cannot be entirely sweet and laudatory without becoming sentimental. The best way to guard against sentimentality is to select those relationships in which you can recognize and describe some degree of ambivalence.

The Five Senses

Regardless of whether you draw material from your own life or the lives of others, it is important to make use of your five senses: seeing, hearing, touching, smelling, and tasting. Some people do remarkably well with one or more sense impaired. A much larger group have been graced with all five but don't use them fully. They don't stop to look at a scene carefully, don't linger to listen, say, to the sound of cars on a highway. They avoid the feel of a cow's tongue and ignore a subway's rocking motion, and they may try to stay clear of unfamiliar smells and tastes. Poets, on the other hand, draw heavily on all five senses.

Sight is by far the most frequently used sense in poetry. While writers of fiction look for a sequence of events, poets more often start with a visual impression. The poems we keep returning to in Chapter 11 provide excellent examples. Even before you study them in detail, you can see how many of them begin not with an abstraction but with a specific visual detail known as an *image*.

Sometimes the visual scene is broad, as in Dylan Thomas' "Fern Hill." Although the phrasing is dreamlike ("About the lilting house and happy as the grass was green"), the origin is clearly the farm on which he was raised. The poem is filled with precise visual details—wagons, apple trees, daisies, barns, foxes, horses, owls, and the like.

Conrad Kent Rivers also uses visual images from his childhood in "The Still Voice of Harlem" (p. 105), although the scene is urban and the tone is a mix of bitterness and hope.

But those are big scenes. More often, poets avoid such a wide focus, preferring instead specific places that have lingered in their memories for some reason. This is the origin of Robley Wilson's "On a Maine Beach" (p. 103).

> Look, in these pools, how rocks are like worn change
> Keeping the ocean's mint-mark; barnacles
> Miser on them. . . .

Written in Iowa, the poem draws on an earlier summer. It doesn't indulge in generalities about the Maine coastline the way travel ads usually do; instead it focuses on specific details, drawing a pattern from them. Almost every line contains a precise visual image which the poet eventually uses to link this scene with broader, more abstract suggestions. I will return to this poem in a later chapter on images, but it would be useful to read it now as an example of how a relatively simple experience can serve as the genesis for a highly sophisticated poem.

Occasionally sounds may also serve as sources for the poet. In "Fern Hill," for example, the boy imagines that calves "sang" to his horn like a pack of hunting dogs, and he hears the foxes bark "clear and cold," and the sound of distant church bells mingled with that of the brook is described with the phrase, "The sabbath rang slowly"—all this in one stanza!

In using sounds, the poet has to go further than generalities. "The roar of traffic" doesn't give the reader enough to work with; besides, the metaphor is worn out with overuse. The poet tries to recall those specific elements that created the general effect—the sounds of pneumatic drills, police whistles, car and truck horns, and the like. Or if the scene is in the country, he or she may try to isolate exactly how the wind sounds in a pine grove or through wheat fields.

It is annoying when the sound that actually initiated a poetic sequence is sufficiently overused to be considered a cliché. Brooks babbling, gulls crying, and wind whistling in the rigging have all reached the level of song lyrics. That is the end of the line. If the sound is truly an individual experience, one can include it in the early drafts and decide later whether to delete the image altogether or to revitalize it, as Howard Moss did in "Local Places," where what might have been a babbling brook became "the stream's small talk at dark."

The other senses—touch, smell, and taste—serve less frequently as sources for the poet, but they are worth considering. They may come as mild reactions like the feel of grit on a cafeteria table, the coarse lick of a cow, the smell of a pine grove in August, the taste of potato chips combined with the smell of sweat or the exhaust of a diesel bus.

Often taste and smell are linked with visual images as in Maya Angelou's "This Winter Day" (p. 98). Right there in her kitchen she describes "green and orange things" which "leak their blood selves in the soup" creating "an odor at my nose" which "starts my tongue to march. . . ." Read that poem when you're hungry!

In addition to simple sensations, there are heavy ones to consider: the sharp pain of a knife wound or of childbirth; or the sounds an injured man makes.

A specific sense impression is called an *image.* An image can be used directly or as a simile, metaphor, or symbol. More about that in Chapter 4. I am concerned here with how you as a poet must not only keep your eyes open but keep your other senses alert and receptive to every stimulus about you.

The Pleasures of Language

This final source of poetry is in some ways the most significant. All writers have to be aware of how they use words, but poets often take a special pleasure in fresh and ingenious phrasing. Because poems are read more deliberately, poets can push language into new configurations.

Returning to Wilson's poem "On a Maine Beach" (p. 103), we see barnacles that "miser" on the rocks and, later, snails that spend their lives "pinwheeling." Here he has made new verbs of familiar nouns—a liberty that would be confusing in prose. In the context of the poem, however, we understand what they mean. His verbal ingenuity is similar to the liberties Dylan

Thomas takes in "Fern Hill" (p. 104). Out of context, it is hard to imagine a "lilting house" or a fire "green as grass." This is phrasing we rarely see in prose. But as we read the poem over carefully in its entirety, the lines themselves teach us to make sense of such language: His childhood home lingers in his memory like a lilting tune, and the fire in the fireplace was as lively as youth which, we are informed elsewhere, is like green shoots of new growth.

Sometimes a whole poem can be centered on a single play of words. The narrator in Robert Frost's "Canis Major" (p. 108), for example, considers himself "a poor underdog"; but as he looks up at the constellation known as Canis Major, the great dog, he feels like barking with "the great Overdog" there in the night sky.

Wit, ingenuity, fresh phrasing are to poetry what yeast is to bread. Without them, you are apt to serve up something heavy and inedible. Take a quick look at E. E. Cummings' "Buffalo Bill's," a semicomic poem which points out how even a man who can shoot pigeons "onetwothreefourfive . . . just like that" is himself subject to death. The theme is ultimately serious, but the phrasing and the lively use of the line produce a kind of linguistic comedy.

Nonfiction prose is apt to be utilitarian. We have to do this kind of writing so much we sometimes forget that language can also be fun to write. One of the special pleasures of writing poetry comes from the fact that your readers will move through your work more slowly and more deliberately than they would prose. As a poet, you can be more ingenious, more inventive. There is, of course, an obligation in this too: It is hardly fair to give readers a jumble, hoping they will discover a meaning that is not really there. But if you honestly want to share your work with a reader, writing poetry is a time to play around with language, give it a twist, look for the unexpected.

Getting Started

Where should you begin? Keeping a journal is a good first step. A journal differs from a diary in that it is not a simple record of the day's events. A poet's journal is more apt to include the kinds of material I have described in this chapter. You don't have to write a lot at any one time. Twenty minutes a day will give you plenty to look over at the end of each week. Here are some suggestions to start filling those empty pages.

Recall briefly some of the most vivid experiences you have had in the past year. Why do they stick in your mind? Can you remember and record specific details that no one else would have noticed?

Which are the three most memorable experiences from your childhood? Did they change your attitude? Did they help you to see things in a different light? Read over Richard Wilbur's "The Pardon" (p. 107). Did you experience anything like this?

What about your feelings toward members of your family? Any mixed emotions there? (Remember that this is a *private* journal!) How about relatives? Friends? Look closely and be honest. Which of these people have influenced you? Can you recall any special insight into the lives of any of these people?

Turning to the five senses, list very briefly a few of the objects you saw today that you might remember twenty years from now. What aspect seems memorable? Try the same for last summer. Reach back to visual impressions from childhood.

Now turn to sound. Music may come to mind first, but don't forget the voice or laugh of a particular person; the sounds of mechanical objects like a car, truck, or old refrigerator; or natural sounds like wind or rain. Describe these with fresh language—no babbling brooks or howling gales.

Now try the same for memorable sensations of touch, taste, and smells. If memories flood back, make lists. If they come slowly, describe them in greater detail.

When you are in a less introspective mood, try fooling around with language a bit. Here is an exercise to get you going: Carefully draw these two shapes at the top of a fresh page in your journal:

If each shape had a name, which one would be Kepick and which Oona? Now think of them as a couple. Which is the girl? Assume that one of them is a brand of gasoline and the other a type of oil. Which is which? Suppose one is a melon and the other a lemon? And now listen to them: one is a cymbal and the other a violin. Too easy? One is a saxophone and the other a trumpet; one is the wind and the other a dog's bark. It is an odd and significant fact that nineteen out of twenty people will give identical answers. This is the "language" of association, of connotation, which is the special concern of the poet both consciously and subconsciously.

Thinking of them once again as a couple, give each of them four more nonsense names. Now try a few lines of very free verse describing Oona and Kepick, using their other names as adjectives or verbs. (Surely you think of

Oona looking feenly in the shane, but what happens when Kepick kacks his bip and zabots all the lovely leems?)

There is no end to this. It won't lead directly to sophisticated poetry, but it does help to link language with music. The two should not be confused, but poems often have as much to do with sound, rhythm, and overtones as they do with making a pronouncement.

Keep your journal going. Make a point of writing *something* in it every day for a month. Even if it doesn't produce finished poems, it will serve as a reservoir from which to draw material. And it will keep you thinking like a poet.

3 THE LANGUAGE OF POETRY

The level of usage: language that is *appropriate* to the speaker and the subject; the four *primary dangers* in poetic diction: *clichés, hackneyed language,* sweeping *generalities,* and *archaisms;* achieving vitality through *concrete nouns, forceful verbs, contemporary language,* and *compression.*

There is no such thing as a good poem poorly expressed. No matter how insightful or compelling the theme may be, the poem itself will fail if the language is dull or conventional.

To some degree, this applies to all types of writing, but in a poem the manner of expression is inseparable from what is being expressed. We can analyze the language of a poem as if it were a separate entity, but remember that as you write, the questions of how you express yourself and what you wish to say become merged.

Levels of Usage

When we speak, we adopt different levels of usage without thinking. While giving a prepared address to an audience, for example, our phrasing tends to be more formal and our vocabulary more selective than it will be ten minutes later chatting with friends in the cafeteria. This isn't dishonest; it is merely a matter of using the type of language that meets the occasion.

As we have seen, poetry often deals with personal feelings and insights, so it frequently uses a vocabulary that is more varied and phrasing that is denser in implication than what we might use in a casual letter to a friend. But this doesn't justify using needlessly long words or outdated phrases. That will turn your readers off just as quickly as it would to speak to them in language that sounds stuffy or old-fashioned.

A poet's task is to find the *appropriate* words and phrases, not fancy ones. What is appropriate for one poem may not be for another. Ask yourself these two questions: Who is speaking in this poem and what is his or her mood?

In some cases, the persona or implied speaker of a poem is clearly not the poet. As we saw in the last chapter, the persona in Gwendolyn Brooks' poem "We Real Cool" appears to be one of seven young people who play pool at a place called the Golden Shovel. The language is appropriate for them. In the case of Anthony Hecht's "Lizards and Snakes," the persona appears to be a young man. We don't know for sure whether the poet was writing about himself, but that isn't important. What we do know is that the persona is young enough to enjoy playing practical jokes. He recalls slipping a lizard in his Aunt Martha's knitting box with this easygoing line: "It broadened her life, as Joe said. Joe was my friend." At the end of the poem, we learn how deeply Aunt Martha believes in the devil not by being told directly but through her own words: "I can see him plain as a pikestaff." We come to understand both the young man and his Aunt Martha from what they say and how they say it.

Many poems, of course, do not use the first person and may not have a clearly defined persona. But mood and personality are often reflected by an *implied* speaker. Here are the opening lines of two poems. The first is from "What the Mirror Said" by Louise Clifton (p. 106).

> listen,
> you a wonder.
> you a city
> of a woman.
> you got a geography
> of your own.

Like "We Real Cool," this poem echoes the simple, direct language of speech. One word of warning, however: Don't try colloquial speech or street language unless it comes from your own personal experience. Attempting to echo other people's speech often sounds patronizing and unconvincing. But if it is a part of your own life, it may well be a rich source.

Now contrast Clifton's level of usage with that in this opening stanza from "The Bay at West Falmouth" by Barbara Howes (p. 108):

> Serenity of mind poises
> Like a gull swinging in air,
> At ease, sculptured, held there
> For a moment so long-drawn-out all time pauses.
>
> The heart's serenity is like the gold
> Geometry of sunlight. . . .

The level of usage here is further from everyday speech. It is more complex and intricate. Which approach you prefer is a personal matter; what concerns us as poets is how the level of usage reflects an unidentified persona and a particular mood. Effective language is that which is appropriate to the tone of the poem and to the persona.

Does this mean that anything goes? Hardly! The most sincerely felt theme can be lost if the phrasing is not fresh. Here are four areas that seem to give the most trouble.

The Cliché

We have all been warned against clichés since grade school. Yet they remain a temptation—particularly when we are tired and careless. It is important to understand what a cliché is and why it is so damaging to any kind of writing, especially a poem.

The cliché, as George Orwell points out in "Politics and the English Language," is actually a dying metaphor; that is, an expression that was once fresh enough to create a clear picture in the reader's mind but has now lost its vitality through constant use. The normal function of both metaphors and similes (discussed in greater detail in the next chapter) is to clarify an abstract word (*serenity*, for example) by linking it with a concrete one (like *gull*). But when comparisons like this are used over and over, they lose all visual impact. Thus, "sharp as a tack" has become dull; "free as a bird" no longer takes flight; "clean as a whistle" sets readers wondering whether they are to picture one of those bright, shiny referee's whistles or the sound of someone whistling. And as Orwell points out, "to toe the line" (literally to place one's toe on a line) has strayed so far from the original metaphor that it is now often seen in print as "to *tow* the line."

When a metaphor or simile finally "dies," it becomes built into the language as a single word which no longer appeals to a visual comparison. For example, to be baited like a badger has created a new verb, to *badger*, but most of us have forgotten that the badger was originally the victim, not the tormentor. The meaning is the same as to *hound* someone into doing something, but the original image was just the opposite. We accept these new verbs, *badger* and *hound*, without seeing them as metaphors. The same applies to *cliché* itself and to *stereotype*, both of which were originally printers' terms for metal plates of print. They are now useful nouns. No harm in this. What does the damage to poetry are those phrases that are both wordy and too familiar to provide a mental picture. They are excess baggage.

There are three different ways of dealing with clichés that appear in a first draft. First, one can work hard to find a fresh simile or metaphor which will force the reader to see (hear, taste, and so on) the object being used in the comparison. Or one can drop the comparison completely and deal with the subject directly. Finally, one can twist the cliché around so that it is reborn in some slightly altered form. This technique is often seen in comic verse, but it can be highly effective in serious poetry as well.

For example, if you discover that you have allowed "blood red" to slide into your verse, you can avoid this ancient cliché with such alternatives as "balloon red," "hot red," or "shouting red," depending on the overtones you wish to establish. If none of these will do, go back to just "red."

A good way to improve your skill in dealing with clichés is to apply these techniques to "mother nature," "strong as an ox," "wise as an owl," and "where there's smoke, there's fire."

Hackneyed Language

This is a general term which includes not only the cliché but the far broader areas of phrases that have simply been overused. Whereas clichés usually consist only of conventionalized similes and are easily identified, hackneyed language also includes direct description that has been seen in print too long to provide impact. A seventh-grader can compile a list of clichés as readily as names of common birds; but only one who has read literature extensively can identify that which is literarily hackneyed. This is one reason why vocabulary lists are no substitute for wide and varied reading.

Certain subjects seem to generate hackneyed language like maggots. Take, for example, sunsets. The "dying day" is a true cliché, but perfectly respectable words like "golden," "resplendent," "magnificent," and even "richly scarlet" all become hackneyed when used to describe a sunset. It is not the word itself that should be avoided—one cannot make lists; it is the particular combination which is limp from overuse.

In the same way, smiles are too often "radiant," "infectious," or "glowing." Trees tend to have "arms" and frequently "reach heavenward." The seasons are particularly dangerous: Spring is "young" or "youthful," suggesting virginity, vitality, or both; summer is "full blown"; and by autumn many poets slide into a "September Song" with only slight variations on the popular lyrics. Winter, of course, leads the poet to sterility and death, terms that too often describe the quality of the poem as well.

Our judgment of what is hackneyed depends somewhat on the age. That which was fresh and vivid in an earlier period may have become shopworn for us. Protesting "But Pope used it" does not make a metaphor acceptable for our own use. Standards of fresh language, however, are far less tied to period than many believe. It is difficult to find lines in, say, Shakespeare's sonnets which would even today be considered hackneyed. Conversely, many of the conventions he attacked as stale and useless have continued in popular use and reappear like tenacious weeds in mass-market poetry.

In "Sonnet 130," for example, he protests that

> My mistress' eyes are nothing like the sun;
> Coral is far more red than her lips' red. . . .
> And in some perfumes is there more delight
> Than in the breath that from my mistress reeks.

The poem is directed not so much at his mistress as at those poets of his day who were content to root their work in conventions which were even then thoroughly stale. Yet more than 300 years later poetry is produced (more often by the greeting card industry than by students) in which eyes sparkle like the sun, lips are either ruby or coral red, and breath is either honeyed or perfumed.

Remember that your task as a poet is to find fresh insights. If you are dealing with seasons, don't announce that spring is a time for growth. We know that. There are other aspects of spring, however, that are worth considering. Here is what T. S. Eliot saw in that season and described in the opening of "The Waste Land."

> April is the cruellest month, breeding
> Lilacs out of the dead land, mixing
> Memory and desire. . . .
> Winter kept us warm, covering
> Earth in forgetful snow, feeding
> A little life with dried tubers

Not only is he telling us that in some ways winter is "kinder" by keeping the ground covered, he is suggesting that sometimes memory and desire awaken aspects of ourselves which we would rather forget. Both are reversals of the simple sentiments we see so often in simple verse.

Abstractions and Sweeping Generalities

In the chapter on the sources of poems, I warned against beginning with a broad, abstract principle like love, death, nature, and the like. It is equally dangerous to allow a poem that was originally inspired by some genuine experience or personal reaction to slide into generalities. Last stanzas are particularly vulnerable. There is a temptation to "explain" one's poem in a concluding stanza that too easily turns into a truism.

If the origin of a poem is a specific love, try to deal with the details as precisely as possible. There will be, of course, aspects that would mean nothing to another reader without a great deal of background explanation, and these should be avoided. But if the relationship is dealt with honestly, the reader will be able to draw universals from the specifics you provide.

Adrienne Rich's "Like This Together" (p. 101) is a particularly good example. The relationship she describes is unique, but most of us have at some period felt the desperate need to "hold fast to the / one thing we know." She has defined an aspect of love, but she has done it by sharing with the reader the personal details of an apparently real relationship.

The same is true of death. Treating the subject in the abstract almost always seems empty of real feelings. Before the concept becomes poetically manageable, we have to find a set of images that will make the familiar abstraction fresh and convincing.

Robley Wilson, Jr. is concerned with death in his poem "On a Maine Beach" (p. 103). After describing the life rhythms of creatures like snails and barnacles living in rock pools, he concludes with these lines: "Beach rhythms flow / In circles. Perfections teach us to die."

Richard Wilbur deals with death even more directly in his poem "The Pardon" (p. 107). Here are the first two of six stanzas.

> My dog lay dead five days without a grave
> In the thick of summer, hid in a clump of pine
> And a jungle of grass and honeysuckle-vine.
> I who had loved him while he kept alive
>
> Went only close enough to where he was
> To sniff the heavy honeysuckle-smell
> Twined with another odour heavier still
> And hear the flies' intolerable buzz.

That opening line announces the topic unmistakably. But there is nothing abstract about it. We are thrust into a personal experience and are given concrete details—sight, sound, and smells. If you turn to it now and read the poem in its entirety you will see how Wilbur develops important abstract concerns toward the end. But the poem remains rooted in specifics.

Other abstractions like patriotism, liberty, and peace contain the same dangers death does; in addition, they have a special tendency to attract clichés. It is hard not to be influenced by unimaginative political orators. The best solution is to select a single specific example of the abstraction and concentrate on that. If it is social injustice that concerns you, pick one person you know and one incident that occurred to that individual. If you help readers to share your feelings about that event, you will have done more than any generalized statement about Truth and Justice could possibly have done.

If you start out writing "Life is . . ." or "Love is . . ." *stop!* Ask yourself, What made me feel like that? What specific event or experience brought that to my mind? Work with that and you will reach your readers.

Archaic Diction

This is the last in the list of four threats to fresh language. Quite often it takes the form of time-honored but dated contractions such as "o'er" and "oft" as substitutions for "over" and "often." But there are other words that now have the same musty quality: "lo!" "hark!" "ere," and even "O!" are the most frequently used.

The majority of poets writing today need no such warning, and some may be surprised that it must be included here. Yet the practice is still seen in writing classes and in some of the less distinguished poetry journals.

Sometimes the temptation to use archaic words comes from a determination to write perfectly metered poetry. Meter is the subject of Chapter 6, but I should point out here that the rhythms one creates from a metrical line should never be so regular as to dominate the choice of words. Mature use of meter allows substitutions and variations. There is no need to use "lo!" "hark!" and "ere" just to make the line go "ta-*tum*, ta-*tum*, ta-*tum*" like a toy drum.

More often, archaisms slip in because the writer understandably admires poets from former centuries. There is nothing wrong with studying poetry of earlier periods; indeed, for every hour of work on your own composition you really should spend an hour reading the poetry of others. But remember that language changes. You will benefit richly from studying the sonnets of Shakespeare, the ballad as refined by Coleridge, the lyrics of Wordsworth; but don't forget that they were writing with the language of their day just as you should be doing. You can learn a great deal about the *use* of language without imitating the words themselves.

These, then, are the four practices that most frequently defeat the goal of fresh diction: clichés, hackneyed language, sweeping generalities, and archaisms. They are not absolute taboos. Each may, in certain cases, be used to create a particular effect—especially in verse that echoes daily speech. In most cases, however, stay clear of them all.

Achieving Vitality in Language

Avoiding these four danger areas is an important first step, but true vitality in language requires a positive effort too. Here are some recommendations which with practice will become second nature.

- Look for phrasing that will catch the attention of your readers. Give them fresh insights and new ways of looking at the familiar. Remind yourself of how tired your readers probably are of the utilitarian prose in newspapers, magazines, and, yes, even textbooks. Try to give them something interesting to savor in every line. It doesn't have to be sensational, just a new metaphor or an original phrase.

- Find nouns that are solid, specific, and visual. Don't write about "life" and "mortality" if you can suggest something about these abstractions through a rock pool with barnacles and snails. Avoid "women" if "Aunt Martha" is your true subject. Don't even settle for "bird" if "gull" is what hovers in your mind's eye. Take a second look at every adjective in your first draft and see if selecting a different noun will do the job: Replace "big hills" with "mountains" if that's what you see; scratch out "howling wind" if "gale" will do.

- Find verbs that are specific. The right verb rarely needs to be modified. Birds that "fly suddenly" are not as memorable as those that "scatter." Vegetables that "add their colors to the soup" are bland compared with those that "leak their blood selves in the soup." Move slowly through the poems printed in Chapter 11 and circle the verbs. Notice how many of them provide a kind of impact we rarely achieve in the rush of daily speech or even in utilitarian prose writing.

- Use the language of your own age, and adapt it to your persona, the implied narrator of your poem. There is no such thing as "poetic language"; there is only language that is appropriate for a particular poem.

- Compress. Compress. Compress. Occasionally you will find wordy poems in print, and you will even find poems that read like prose in short lines. But one of the special attributes of this genre is its capacity to say more and imply more in each line than prose can in a paragraph. The only way to achieve this is to weed out those do-nothing phrases and lines. What is left will have impact and vitality.

Sophisticated poetry stimulates the reader in some way—intellectually, spiritually, or emotionally. To achieve this goal, the language must be fresh and every line should work toward that end.

4 IMAGES

*The image defined; using all five senses; images used to create
similes and metaphors; the importance of vehicle and tenor in
every figure of speech; the value of image clusters; the image as
symbol; playing with images in journal writing; shifting to
serious work.*

In its purest sense, an image in poetry is any significant piece of sense data.
Although we tend to think of images as objects seen, the term also covers
sounds heard, textures felt, odors smelled, and objects tasted.

As I pointed out in Chapter 2, sense perception is a major source of
poetic creation. For this reason alone, the image becomes one of the most
significant elements in the construction of a poem. But images are also the
foundation of similes, metaphors, puns, hyperboles, and other types of figurative language as well as symbolic suggestion.

Because the term *imagery* is used so frequently in connection with
similes and metaphors, it is sometimes used interchangeably with these terms.
In this text, however, *image* is used to refer to an object seen or perceived by
the other senses regardless of whether that word is used literally or as a part
of a figure of speech.

Images, then, tend to be concrete nouns—objects that are specific and have shape and weight. But there is no sharp line between words that are concrete and those that are abstract. It all depends on how vividly we can perceive the object.

"Serenity," for example, is not an image. It is an abstraction which, like all abstractions, cannot be seen or heard. It is a concept. "Bird" is more concrete, though it is still rather general. "A gull" is more specific, and "a gull swinging in air, / At ease, sculptured, held there. . . ." is a fully developed image. This is taken from Barbara Howes' poem "The Bay at West Falmouth" (p. 108). Turn to it now and see how this first image—the gull in flight suggesting "serenity of mind"—is followed by a second image in which she compares "the heart's serenity" with "the gold geometry of sunlight."

There is another good example of imagery in Anthony Hecht's poem, "Lizards and Snakes" (p. 97). The idea of evil is highly abstract, but "the devil" presents a picture that has been used for centuries to suggest evil. The trouble with "devil" as an image, however, is that it has been used so much. It has become a kind of visual cliché and so has lost impact. So when Hecht wants us to see what Aunt Martha sees, he has her describe a terrible vision without using the word "devil" at all: "Look how he grins / And swings the scaly horror of his folded tail."

Using All Five Senses

When we think of images, visual details come to mind first. Poets depend heavily on what they see. But don't neglect the other four senses. Sounds, for example, can be highly effective. Chase Twichell begins her poem "Rhymes for Old Age" (p. 111) with a vivid auditory image:

> The wind's untiring saxophone
> keens at the glass.

The verb *to keen* is not widely used, so if you are not familiar with it, take the time to look it up. Its overtones contribute to the mournful sound of the wind. This is, incidentally, a good illustration of why one has to spend a little extra time with the first reading of a sophisticated poem.

Sometimes auditory images like this one are repeated several times in the same poem. We are so used to eliminating redundancies from prose that we forget how effective repetition can be in poetry. When used with care, a repeated word or phrase can have the effect of a recurring phrase in music.

Here are six lines from Robert Frost's "Mowing" which make use of a scythe's "whispering." I have marked them here as if in pencil.

There was never a sound beside the wood but one,
And that was my long scythe (whispering) to the ground.
What was it it (whispered?) I know not well myself;
Perhaps it was (something) about the heat of the sun,
Something, perhaps, (about the) lack of sound—
And that was why it (whispered) and did not speak.

In the next seven lines, not one reference is made to sound—either directly or metaphorically. But the image returns again with this final line:

My long scythe (whispered) and left the hay to make.

You have to be careful about the word *sound*, of course. Song lyrics and popular verse have long made use of "sounds in the night," "sounds of the street," and "sounds of the sea." But if you can link the word "sound" with something specific which we can hear—like Frost's "scythe whispering to the ground"—the image will have vitality.

Images of touch, smell, and taste are often used in conjunction with each other and with visual details. The poem "Local Places" by Howard Moss provides a fine example. The following stanza is the first of five, and I have circled some of the images.

auditory (The song you sang) you will not sing again,

Floating in the spring to all your local places,

Lured by archaic sense to the wood

visual   To watch (the frog jump from the mossy rock,)

auditory To listen to (the stream's small) talk at dark,

touch   Or to feel (the springy pine-floor) where you walk—

If your green secrecies were such as these,

visual   The mystery is now (in other trees.)

Three of the five senses are used in this single stanza. Only taste and smell are missing, and one of these appears in the next stanza with the phrase, "To perfume aridness." These images of sight, sound, touch, and smell are not mere decorations. They are the basic materials from which the poem is constructed.

Images as Figures of Speech

To this point, I have been describing images used simply as descriptive details—things seen, heard, felt, smelled, and tasted. Images also serve as the
concrete element in almost any figure of speech.

Figurative language most commonly takes the form of the *simile* and
the *metaphor*. These are both comparisons, the simile linking the two elements
explicitly with "like" or "as" and the metaphor implying a relationship. Here
are three similes from three different poems included in Chapter 11. I have
circled the image that completes the simile.

- From Adrienne Rich's "Like This Together":

  . . . sitting like drugged birds
  in a glass case

- From Robley Wilson's "On a Maine Beach":

  . . . rocks are like worn change

- From Dylan Thomas' "Fern Hill":

  Now as I was young and easy under the apple boughs
  About the lilting house and happy as the grass was green

It should be clear from these examples that similes are not simple comparisons.
When we compare, for example, a starling with a grackle, we imply that *in
most respects* the two objects are similar. But when Rich compares the couple
sitting silently in the car with "drugged birds" in a "glass case," she certainly
does not want us to picture them as beaked and feathered. They are alike
only in certain respects—in this case, their dulled mood and their isolation from
the natural world outside the car. As with most similes, the area of similarity
is far narrower than the area of differences. Its impact depends on how sharply
it can make the reader see a new relationship.

Similarly, when Wilson writes that beach rocks are "like worn change,"
he is suggesting that only in very specific ways can the two be compared. It
is less of a visual comparison than it is a way of describing their value as
objects from which we can learn a lot. This is not like saying that the rock
pools one finds in Maine are like those one can find on the coast of Oregon.
That would be a simple comparison.

A *metaphor* may be thought of as a simile that doesn't use "like" or
"as." But there are more subtle differences which are worth keeping in mind.
Similes are explicit; the relationship is clearly stated. But in a metaphor, the
comparison is implied. It doesn't make sense literally, but we understand

what the intent is. The metaphor may demand more of the reader, but it often has greater impact.

It doesn't make literal sense, for example, to refer to a house as "lilting," a word normally applied to melodies, not objects. Yet this is the word Dylan Thomas uses in the lines quoted earlier, and we understand his meaning through the context of the poem.

To analyze how a metaphor works, convert it to a simile. The result may be awkward, but it is a good technique to use with your own work as well as with published poems. In this case, the conversion comes out something like this: "A house as cheerful and merry as a lilting tune."

Notice how compressed the metaphor is compared with the corresponding simile. This is one of those cases where the metaphor is far more than just a simile with "as" left out. It is a kind of shorthand that provides a wide range of overtones with a minimum number of words.

Incidentally, the term *metaphorical language* is occasionally used to describe both similes and metaphors. For the sake of clarity, however, I will use the terms in their precise senses.

There are two more terms that are extremely helpful in analyzing figures of speech, including those in your own work. I. A. Richards has suggested *tenor* to describe the poet's actual subject of concern (often an abstraction) and *vehicle* as the image associated with it. Take, for example, the simile in the lines from "Fern Hill" quoted earlier: "Happy as the grass was green." The tenor or subject here is "happy" and "green grass" is the vehicle—with overtones of spring growth, vividness, intensity.

One advantage of being familiar with these terms is that they can help you identify and get rid of *mixed metaphors*. A mixed metaphor is one with two contradictory vehicles. For example:

> The wind's untiring saxophone
> hammers at the glass

The wind here is the tenor, and there are two vehicles that suggest characteristics of that tenor: the sound of a saxophone and the pounding of a hammer. Individually, each vehicle is effective in its own way, but together they are "mixed" badly since saxophones are rarely used as hammers.

One solution is the wording Chase Twichell uses in "Rhymes for Old Age" (p. 111).

> The wind's untiring saxophone
> keens at the glass.

This version also uses a double metaphor (that is, two vehicles applied to one tenor), but the vehicles are harmonious. A saxophone often produces a wailing sound, and the verb *to keen* means to wail for the dead. The two tenors work together, and that wail is appropriate to the theme of the poem, which is a lament for a woman close to death.

The term *figurative language* is used primarily to describe similes and metaphors. Most other figures of speech are specialized forms of the metaphor and are of more value to critics analyzing literature than for writers in the process of composition. Two, however, concern us here. They are techniques you may wish to use.

Hyperbole is usually defined as extreme exaggeration, but in most cases it is a metaphorical exaggeration as well. The persona in Lucille Clifton's "What the Mirror Said" (p. 106), for example, looks at herself and says, "Listen, . . . you a city of a woman." This cheerful bit of self-affirmation is not only an exaggeration, it is a metaphor. Converting it back to a simile, we end up with something like, "You're so complex and interesting, you're like an entire city."

Even the pun can be seen as a form of metaphor when one is able to separate the tenor from the vehicle. In Thomas' "A Refusal to Mourn . . . " he has a play on "grave":

> I shall not murder
> The mankind of her going with a grave truth. . . .

The tenor here is "solemn truth," and he has, in effect, added "*as if* spoken at the grave-side." He uses essentially the same device in "Do Not Go Gentle into that Good Night" with the line, "Grave men, near death, who see with blinding sight. . . ." Once again, we have only to convert the pun to a simile in order to see it as a part of a metaphorical construction.

Building Image Clusters

Although many images are used only once and then dropped, they may also appear as a series of related details. Since images are often used in similes and metaphors, they too become interlocked. When you read a new poem, look for such clusters or groups of related details even before you are entirely clear about the theme. If the book is your own, it is well worth the time to circle these clusters and identify them. If it is not, photocopy the poem and mark the copy. This kind of visual analysis is not only helpful in the process of understanding new work, it will help you to adopt the same techniques in your own work. Here is a copy of "On a Maine Beach" by Robley Wilson Jr., annotated with marginal notes indicating image clusters. An unmarked copy appears on page 103, and you may wish to read that first.

Look, in these pools how rocks are like worn change

Keeping the ocean's mint-mark; barnacles

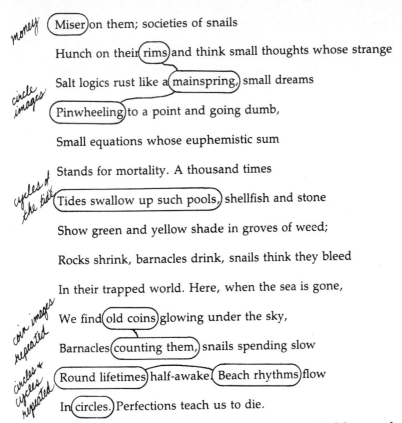

money   (Miser) on them; societies of snails

Hunch on their (rims) and think small thoughts whose strange

circle images   Salt logics rust like a (mainspring,) small dreams

(Pinwheeling) to a point and going dumb,

Small equations whose euphemistic sum

Stands for mortality. A thousand times

cycles of the tide   (Tides swallow up such pools,) shellfish and stone

Show green and yellow shade in groves of weed;

Rocks shrink, barnacles drink, snails think they bleed

In their trapped world. Here, when the sea is gone,

coin images repeated   We find (old coins) glowing under the sky,

Barnacles (counting them,) snails spending slow

circles & cycles repeated   (Round lifetimes) half-awake (Beach rhythms) flow

In (circles.) Perfections teach us to die.

The first of these image clusters is coins. The second has to do with circles and spirals. As the last line suggests, watching these cycles of living and dying within the rock pool helps us to see our own mortality in perspective. In this way, the life and death of the reader is included in the dominant image cluster of circles and cycles.

The Image as Symbol

A symbol is a metaphor in which the meaning (tenor) is implied rather than stated. Some are called *public symbols* because they are widely known and are almost a part of the language. "Madison Avenue" for example, suggests commercial values; "the flag" represents the country; "the cross" stands for the Christian church. These are so common that they can be used in cartoons.

Because public symbols are often hackneyed from overuse, poets usually construct their own. These are called *private symbols*, though of course they have to be introduced in such a way that the reader can understand the meaning. In Anthony Hecht's "Lizards and Snakes," for example, we are introduced to the lizard at the outset, but not until the end of the poem do we realize that for Aunt Martha the lizard suggests the devil and, by extension, death itself.

If the same image were treated as a simile, it might come out like this: "Death for Aunt Martha was like a horrible lizard." A metaphor would eliminate the word *like:* "She saw death, a horrible lizard." The version Hecht uses in the poem does not use the word *death* at all, but we understand that this is what Aunt Martha has in mind from the symbolic language she uses: "He can crack us like lice with his fingernail."

Wilson's "On a Maine Beach" provides another good example of a symbol. We have already seen how frequently he uses similes: rocks "like worn change," the "small thoughts of snails" which eventually "rust like a mainspring." But when we come down to "snails think they bleed / In their trapped world," we begin to see that these short-lived sea colonies are in a sense like our own lives. Nowhere does he say, "Our lives, like those of snails and barnacles . . . " The poem implies it instead. Why not state it directly? One good reason is that it would deprive the reader of the sense of discovery which echoes that of the poet when he first made that connection in his own mind. A symbol requires careful reading, but once grasped, it often provides a range of meaning far broader than a simile or metaphor.

In many poems, a central symbol unlocks the theme itself. If the rock pool in "On a Maine Beach" were not given symbolic meaning, the poem would be merely descriptive. As such, it might be pleasant to read, but it would be too *simple* in the literary sense to hold the interest of anyone who enjoys the sophisticated use of language. In the same way, "Lizards and Snakes" without its concluding symbol would be reduced to a humorous anecdote, and "Fern Hill" would turn into a sentimental and romanticized description of childhood. In each of those cases, the theme of the poem depends on a symbol.

Important as symbols are, however, don't feel that they are essential— particularly at first. It is much better to keep a poem relatively simple than it is to tack on a symbol as an afterthought. Examine your subject carefully and determine what it has meant to you. Try to get beyond the simple observation that you liked it or hated it. If at that point a symbol comes to mind, let it develop naturally. Revise the poem so that you can share this with your readers, being careful in the process not to make it so obvious that it becomes obtrusive. When symbols are shaped this way, they will seem like an organic part of the poem and may provide a far wider set of suggestions.

Playing Games with Images

When you first start working with similes and metaphors and their components, tenors and vehicles, they are apt to seem rather forbidding. It's hard to imagine playing games with them. But remember that although writing poetry is ultimately a serious and complex art, practicing in your own journal can be fun—as well as valuable.

Here, for a start, is a list of five images. Three of them are visual, one auditory, and one tactile.

1. A contented cat
2. A city street in August
3. A ballet dancer
4. The sound of good jazz
5. The warmth of an open fire

The simplest sort of conversion is to make each one into a vehicle for a simile. For example: "After winning the Pulitzer Prize, he looked like a contented cat."

Now that I have used a person as the tenor, try using the image to describe a section of a city or a segment of the society. Be careful to avoid clichés like *fat cats*.

After composing one simile with each image, try converting them to metaphors. In each case, remember, the item in the list is a vehicle and what you are providing is an appropriate subject, or tenor, such as the man who won the Pulitzer Prize.

Now reverse the process, using each item as the tenor. Try, first, to find an image that would serve as a vivid simile for a fat, lazy cat. Let your mind go free. How about a cat lying in the sun "like a pool of molasses"? Go through each of the others like this.

Next, convert these to metaphors. In some cases, there will be little difference except for the use of "like" or "as." But in other cases there will be a surprising boost of strength. Notice how often the metaphorical version will read more like a line of verse than did the simile.

Here is a different approach: Start with the abstraction and convert it into something we can see, feel, or touch through the creation of a simile or a metaphor. Be careful not to settle for a cliché or hackneyed phrase. As a general rule, if you have seen it in print or heard it in a song lyric, avoid it.

Here are some examples:

- *Beauty:*
  Beautiful as a brook in spring (simile)
  Beautiful as a lioness with cubs (simile)
  She stood there, a lioness protecting her cubs. (metaphor)
- *Anger:*
  Angry as a cornered cougar (simile)
  An avalanche of protest (metaphor)
  The letter was pure acid. (metaphor)

You can continue the process with qualities like *gentle, mean, ugly, lively.* Notice that the same abstraction (tenor) can be seen through quite different objects (vehicles). Just as there are many different kinds of beauty, so each state or quality has variations which can be suggested through vehicles as varied as brooks and lionesses.

For variety, try turning from highly abstract qualities to objects about which you may have strong feelings. See if you can find similes to complete these phrases:

> "The city I live in is like . . ."
> "The school I attend (attended) is . . . "
> "Being little in a room full of adults is like . . ."

When you feel at home with these figures of speech, you might want to try writing some *haiku.* This is a Japanese verse form which contains no rhyme or meter but is based entirely on line length. Traditionally the poem is three lines long with five syllables in the first line, seven in the second, and five in the third. Occasionally this pattern varies when the poems are translated from the Japanese, but it is helpful to try to maintain it. Haiku often make use of a metaphor, but occasionally they are intended to be more like a quick photograph or painting.

Here are two anonymous samples of the sort you might try in your journal:

> Her song seizes me,
> Takes me on a secret trip
> Through lands without time.

> Small town of my birth
> Nurtures its sons and daughters,
> Smothers those who stay.

Two haiku which have been translated from the Japanese appear on pages 106 and 107.

From Games to Serious Work

Poets never stop playing with language. But there is a difference between the random experimentation in a journal and the concentrated effort required for a poem you take seriously. Journal writing is for your own benefit, but a poem you ask others to read is on another level. Presumably it has been carefully revised. It is your best work.

In general, the more poetry you read, the more time you will spend on revising your own work. I will have more to say about this at the end of the poetry section, but for now consider this: A textbook like this can suggest what to look for in a poem, but it cannot substitute for careful reading of specific examples. This chapter has focused on various types of images and the ways in which they can serve to create similes, metaphors, and symbols. Before you go on to the next chapter, take some time to study the poems in Chapter 11 and perhaps others from an anthology. Circle the images you consider effective and determine for yourself whether they are used directly or as vehicles for similes or metaphors. Link image clusters. Identify those that have symbolic overtones. No good poem is ever spoiled by analysis.

Then apply the same objective view to your own work. Have you made the best possible use of images? No matter how penetrating or insightful your theme may be, your poem will depend on the effectiveness of your images.

5 THE SOUND OF WORDS

The oral tradition in poetry; *nonrhyming devices* of sound
including *alliteration, assonance, consonance,* and *onomatopoeia:*
the sound of *true rhyme* and its use in *rhyme schemes; muting*
sound devices; *training your ear.*

Poetry was recited aloud long before it was written down to be read on the
page. We are fortunate today to have such an enormous body of work available
in print, but the genre has never lost its roots in the oral tradition. The growing
popularity of readings and recordings and the introduction of poetry videos
are good indications of how poetry, far more than prose, continues to appeal
to the ear.

When we consider the sound of language, we're apt to think of rhyme
first because this particular device dominated the genre for so many centuries.
Some of the major poets of our own century have preferred rhymed to unrhymed verse. Robert Frost, Anthony Hecht, and Richard Wilbur are good
examples; they are all represented in Chapter 11.

But rhyme is only one way to make "music" with words. There are
a number of other techniques that are more common and generally less noticed. Sometimes they are so subtle that the casual reader is only aware that

the poem "sounds nice." For those who write, however, it is important to examine these devices closely in order to make good use of them.

Nonrhyming Devices of Sound

These nonrhyming techniques can be found in all types of writing and oratory. The following passage, for example, is actually prose in spite of its lyrical or "musical" quality. It comes from Dylan Thomas' "August Bank Holiday" and describes a summer day at the beach not through plot but, in the manner of poetry, through a succession of vivid images. The first paragraph is typical of them all. I have made marginal notations here to indicate some of the linking sounds.

> August Bank Holiday.—A tune on an ice-cream cornet. A slap of sea and a tickle of sand. A fanfare of sunshades opening. A wince and whinny of bathers dancing into deceptive water. A tuck of dresses. A rolling of trousers. A compromise of paddlers. A sunburn of girls and a lark of boys. A silent hullabaloo of balloons.

What makes this prose passage sound "poetic"? Primarily it is all those linkages in sound. Some make use of vowels (*a,e,i,o,u,* and sometimes *y*), and others link consonants. A number of the linking sounds occur at the beginning of words; others link syllables within words. Occasionally the word itself echoes the action or object it describes. Since these four techniques are widely used, it helps to be able to refer to them by name.

Alliteration is the repetition of consonants, particularly those at the beginning of words. There are three groups of these:

slap—sea—sand
wince—whinny (a similarity, not an identity of sound)
dancing—deceptive

Assonance is the repetition of similar vowel sounds regardless of where they are located in the word. Some good examples are:

W*i*nce—wh*i*nny
sunb*ur*n—g*ir*ls (similarity of sound, not spelling)
hullabal*oo*—ball*oo*ns

Consonance is the repetition of consonantal sounds. Since *alliteration* is used to describe similarity in initial sounds, *consonance* usually refers to sounds within the words. Often the two are used in conjunction. There are three sets of consonance in this passage:

> wince—whinny
> girls—lark
> silent—hullabaloo—balloons

Onomatopoeia is often defined as a word that sounds like the object or action it describes; but actually most onomatopoetic words suggest a sound only to those who already know what the meaning is. That is, we are not dealing with language that mimics life directly; it is usually just an echo. There are three good examples in Thomas' paragraph:

> slap of sea (the sound of a wave on the beach)
> whinny (an approximation of the horse's sound)
> hullabaloo (the derivation of this coming from "hullo" and "hello" with an echo of "babble")

Analyses like this tend to remain abstract and theoretical until one tries the technique in actual composition. Stop now and think of a scene, a friend, or a piece of music which comes to you with the soft, gentle contours you associated with the Oona figure in Chapter 2. Now try a paragraph of descriptive prose in which you make use of as many sound devices as possible. Remember that this is prose, so there is no need to worry about rhythm or a regular rhyme scheme. It might help to circle the linkages in sound. The point of this exercise is merely to help you find and use sound clusters.

Now, by way of contrast, think of a place, a person, or a piece of music that more closely resembles the sharp characteristics of the Kepick figure. Again, work out one or two prose paragraphs. This is to poetry what preliminary sketches are to a finished painting.

The Sound of Rhyme

A true rhyme scheme is one device that is the exclusive property of poets. Prose may contain scattered rhymes, but only when the writer controls the length of the line is it possible to have a rhyme *scheme* or system.

This is not to suggest, of course, that all poetry makes use of rhyme or even that it should. The choice is up to you. But the only way to determine exactly what rhyme has to offer is to master it at least enough to try it.

True rhyme can be defined in three short sentences: It is an *identity* in *sound* in accented syllables. The identity must begin with the *accented vowel* and *continue* to the end. The sounds preceding the accented vowel must be *unlike*.

Here are three examples of true rhymes.

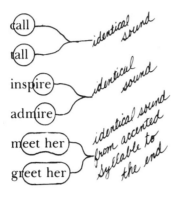

In that three-sentence definition I have italicized the key concepts that seem to give the most trouble. First, we are talking here about true rhyme as opposed to slant rhymes or off rhymes, which will be discussed shortly. True rhyme is not a general similarity in sound like assonance and consonance, it is an actual identity. Thus "ru*n*" and "co*me*" are not true rhymes because of the subtle difference in sound, nor are "see*n*" and "crea*m*."

Second, rhyme is a matter of sound, not spelling. "Girl" and "furl" rhyme, but "to read" and "having read" obviously do not. It is often necessary to repeat the final syllable aloud several times before one is sure whether the rhyme is true or not—as do composers when testing the relationship between chords.

Next, there is the matter of continuing identity which must begin with the accented vowel and run through to the end of each word. This is only a problem with two-syllable rhymes (known as feminine rhymes). In "running," for example, the accented vowel is *u* and the only words that rhyme with it end with *unning,* as in "sunning." The word "jumping" has the *u* sound, but the *mp* keeps it from rhyming with "running."

Finally, the sound that comes before that accented vowel must differ from its rhyming partner. Thus, "night" and "fight" rhyme since the accented vowel (*i*) is preceded by *n* in one case and *f* in the other. But "night" and "knight" do not. These are technically know as *identities*.

Since rhyme is based on the sound of syllables and has nothing to do with the division of words, the same principles apply when more than one word is involved in each rhyming end. "Bind me" and "find me" rhyme (the accented vowel is *i* in each case, and the rhyming sound is *ind me*), but neither rhyme with "kindly" because of the *l*.

Rules like these seem artificial when you first meet them; but like the rules of any new game, they become second nature once you get used to working with them. An easy way to check each pair of words you hope will rhyme is to ask these three questions:

1.   What is the accented vowel sound?
2.   Is the sound in each word identical from that vowel through to the end of each?
3.   Is the consonantal sound preceding that vowel different?

These three questions become automatic; one's eye moves first to that key vowel, then forward to the end of each word, then back to the preceding sound. And in each case the eye is translating what is seen into what would be heard if the word were sounded—a fact that makes it almost impossible to work with rhyme without muttering.

If you have the mechanics of rhyme clearly in mind, study the following table. By placing your hand over the right side of the page, you can test yourself by judging whether the pair of words on the left is a true rhyme or not, and what makes it so.

RELATED WORDS	ACCENTED VOWEL SOUND	ACTUAL RELATIONSHIP AND EXPLANATION
1. night fight	*i*	True rhyme (meets all three requirements)
2. night knight	*i*	An identity (preceding consonants are identical)
3. ocean motion	*o*	True rhyme (*cean* and *tion* have the same sound), also known as a *double* or *feminine rhyme* (see page 45)
4. warring wearing	*or* and *air*	Consonance or off rhyme (accented vowel sounds do not match)
5. lyrical miracle	*y*	Off rhyme (the *i* in "lyrical" does not match the *a* sound in "miracle")
6. track to me back to me	*a*	True rhyme (a triple rhyme)
7. dies remedies	*i* and *em*	Eye rhyme (similarity only in spelling)
8. bear bare	*a*	Identity (preceding consonants are identical)
9. balloon hullabaloo	*oo* and *u*	Consonance and assonance (vowel sounds do not match, nor do the endings)
10. then you see us; when you flee us	*e*	Quadruple rhyme—true (rare and usually appears forced—often comic)

For a less mechanical examination of rhyme, turn to the Anthony Hecht poem, "Lizards and Snakes," on page 97. You have already studied this poem for its use of image and symbol, but you may not have noticed that it is perfectly rhymed. The rhyme endings don't stand out because they occur on alternate lines—a rhyme scheme referred to as *abab*—and also because the poet has adopted an almost conversational tone. But every line is rhymed and all but two are true rhymes. Can you spot the exceptions? When looking for them, identify the accented syllable in each rhyming word.

Varieties of Rhyme Schemes

Most poets who use rhyme use it regularly in a recurring pattern—a *rhyme scheme*. The basic unit of that scheme is the *stanza*.

Stanzas in poetry are like paragraphs in prose. But in metered verse each stanza usually has the same number of lines. I will have more to say about stanzas and how they relate to meter in the next chapter; our concern here is limited to systems of sound.

The rhyming *couplet* is the shortest possible stanza and consists of two rhymed lines. Those pairs of rhymed lines are designated as *aa, bb, cc*. The pattern was popular in the eighteenth century, but it is rarely used today except for comic verse and greeting cards. One problem with couplets is that the paired rhymed endings are so obvious. Unless one is very skillful, they are apt to become monotonous.

It is primarily a matter of taste, but poets in our own century have tended to keep their sound relationships subtle and unobtrusive. As a result, those who use rhyme schemes often prefer three-line stanzas (known as *triplets* or *tercets*), or even more frequently the four-line stanza (*quatrain*).

Richard Wilbur uses quatrains in "The Pardon" (p. 107), and he rhymes every line in a system that is essentially *abba*. I say "essentially" since he uses a number of slant rhymes, which I will turn to shortly. But the third stanza uses true rhymes consistently and is the clearest example of the pattern used throughout:

Well, I was ten and very much afraid   (a)

In my kind world the dead were out of range   (b)

And I could not forgive the sad or strange   (b)

In beast or man. My father took the spade   (a)

Anthony Hecht also uses a regular rhyme scheme in "Lizards and Snakes." The stanzas are eight lines long, but if you examine them closely you will see that the rhyme scheme is like quatrains run together. The pattern is *abab, cdcd, efef.*

Longer stanzas and more complex rhyme schemes were popular in earlier centuries and are well worth careful study. But the trend today is toward relatively simple systems. The examples given here provide a wide range of options.

Muting Sound Devices

In simple verse, like nursery rhymes, greeting cards, and street chants, rhyme is often blatant. It tends to be regular, frequent, and stressed. When rhyme is used in sophisticated poetry, however, it is almost always muted. The sound of language remains important, but it is kept from becoming monotonous or obtrusive.

One way to mute rhyme is to use *run-on lines* occasionally. A run-on line is one in which the grammatical construction or the meaning continues to the next line. It is distinguished from the *end-stopped line*, which usually is concluded with a period or a semicolon. Rhyme is less noticeable when one's eye is moving rapidly to the next line.

Here, for example, are two rhyming lines from John Berryman's poem "I Lift" (p. 110). Notice how quickly one skips over the rhyming words *none* and *done.* The persona is sitting in an unfamiliar bar, thinking of a distant friend:

> . . . this bar you never graced, where none
> Ever I know came, where what work is done
> Even by these men I know not . . .

A more radical method of muting rhyme is simply to separate the rhyming lines. As I have already pointed out, rhyming couplets (*aa,bb,cc*) are far more obvious than lines that alternate the rhyme endings (*abab*). The rhyme is muted still further if you have certain lines unrhymed (*abcb*).

Here, for example, is a revised quatrain based on the second stanza of Robert Frost's "Canis Major." The poem deals with the constellation called Canis Major or the Great Dog, and the following has been rewritten as rhyming couplets:

> He dances upright
> Until dawn's first light
> All the way to the west
> He guards without rest.

Now here is how Frost actually wrote it. Notice how the rhyme is muted to prevent the singsong effect:

> He dances upright
> All the way to the west
> And never once drops
> On his forefeet to rest.

You can hear the difference even from a casual reading of these two versions. But you have to look more closely to see how it is achieved. Frost has muted his rhyme endings partly by reducing them from four to two and partly by separating them—*abcb*.

A third method of muting the sound relationships is by replacing true rhymes with *slant rhymes*. Slant rhymes (also called *off rhymes*) are similar but not identical in sound. Often they are a form of assonance that comes at the end of the line.

Robley Wilson's "On a Maine Beach" (p. 103) is actually rhymed, but it is easy enough to miss this fact on first reading. As with some recurring phrases in music, the effect is almost subliminal. But the pattern is unmistakable if you look closely.

To see the rhyme scheme, it helps to divide the poem into four groups of four lines each. These "stanzas" are for analysis only. Here is a list of the last words in each line with marginal comments:

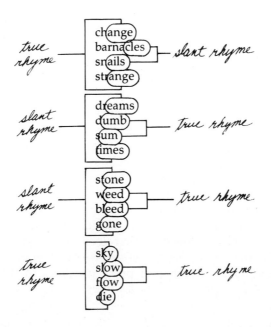

The rhyme scheme is partially hidden by the fact that the poet has not used stanza divisions. And even after we divide the lines for purposes of analysis, the true rhyme endings are separated by two apparently nonrhyming lines. The last "stanza," however, is made up of true rhymes in a pattern of *abba*, and when we look closely at the other lines we see that the scheme there is completed with slant rhymes.

In addition to this somewhat hidden rhyme scheme, Wilson has used alliteration (initial sounds), assonance (vowel sounds), and consonance (consonantal sounds) on almost every line. There are three pairs of these nonrhyming devices in the first two lines. Notice that unlike true rhyme endings, these sound linkages can be approximate.

Look, in these pools, how rocks are like worn change

Keeping the ocean's mint mark; . . .

And later there is a triple assonance:

Rocks shrink, barnacles drink, snails think they bleed

Some poets avoid rhyme altogether, but this does not mean that they necessarily ignore the sound of language. Dylan Thomas in "Fern Hill," for example, relies almost entirely on alliteration, assonance, and consonance in much the same way he did in the prose passage quoted at the beginning of this chapter. The only trace of a rhyme is seen (if you look hard) linking the third and the eighth lines in all but one stanza. These are slant rhymes and the gap is far too great to hear on first reading, but when they are added to the heavy use of other sound devices, they contribute to what we sense as the "musical tone" of the poem as a whole.

The number of sound connections is astonishing. Almost every line contains two or more words that are linked by sound. Yet the connections are muted enough so that we sense the general effect long before we see the mechanics of how he achieves it.

There has been a tendency in contemporary poetry to rely more heavily on images than on the sound of language. Adrienne Rich's "Like This Together" (p. 101) is an example. Other poems depend on a dramatic situation like a highly concentrated story, as does Ann Leventhal's "Pilot Error" (p. 112). But a significant number of poets continue to draw on the auditory aspect of the genre in one form or another.

Training Your Ear

It is hard to imagine a musical composer who doesn't spend a good deal of time listening to music. Yet some beginning poets are reluctant to read too much published poetry for fear of being influenced. Actually there is no danger of becoming imitative if one reads a wide variety of works; and only by reading—preferably aloud—can one begin to appreciate the ways in which poetry is written for the ear.

The best way to hear poetry is to read it slowly and aloud. But you can also "hear" a poem by mouthing the lines—a necessity if you are working in the library.

The analysis of the sound devices in Robley Wilson's "On a Maine Beach" is only a first step. Now that you know what to look for, turn to the complete poem on page 103 and read it through without stopping—preferably aloud. Then mark as many of the rhyme endings and the nonrhyming sound devices as you can find. After you have done this, read the poem aloud again. This sequence of reading, analyzing, and reading again is a good way to combine close study with general appreciation.

Next, turn to Chase Twichell's "Rhymes for Old Age" on page 111. It is similar to the Wilson poem in that it has a rhyme scheme highly muted with slant rhymes. In fact, there are only two pure rhymes. Although some of the connections are difficult to hear, the basic pattern for each stanza is *aba cbc*. Look closely and sound out the linked words. You can teach yourself how to identify the sound in poetry if you use the same sequence with this poem as you did with the Wilson poem: Read for pleasure, analyze carefully, and read again.

Another method of training your ear is to listen to records of poets reading their own work. Most large libraries have collections. If you have a cassette recorder, you may be able to make tapes for your own use. Repeated listening is valuable as well as pleasurable.

But don't be a passive listener for long. Whenever possible, study the poem in print and mark up a photocopy. Then go back to listening again. What you hear after analysis will almost always be richer in sound and more pleasurable as well.

Finally, practice sound combinations in your poetry journal. Don't limit yourself to those lines that might develop into finished poems. Let yourself go. Experiment with assonance, with alliterative runs, with light verse in rhyme. Try a few imitations of poets with pronounced styles.

Sound in poetry is partly a matter of knowing what you are doing—technique. But it is also a matter of hearing what you are writing—a sensitivity to spoken language. Good poetry requires both.

6 RHYTHMS OF STRESS

Rhythm as a *psychological need* in humans; *stressed words* within the spoken sentence; *stressed syllables* within English words; from simple stress to *meter; staying loose* with meter; *why metrics?*

Rhythm is a surprisingly basic need in human beings. Some babies thump their cribs rhythmically long before they are introduced to language. Young people throughout the world learn and enjoy schoolyard chants taught to them not by teachers but by older children, generation after generation. And in almost every culture people of all ages take pleasure in rhythmical music and dance.

Most poetry is rhythmical in some way. This is due partly to its close association with the spoken language and partly to its affinity with music. Song lyrics, after all, are a form of poetry, and the word *verse* refers both to poetry and to lines to be sung.

There are several different methods of creating rhythmical patterns in poetry. Rhythms of stress, the subject of this chapter, are based on the fact that certain words in a spoken statement and certain syllables within most words are given greater weight than others. Rhythms associated with free verse, discussed in the next chapter, are more generally based on how the poem is arranged on the page.

Rhythm of Stressed Words

Every time we speak, we stress some words more than others. Take, for example, this straightforward sentence:

I went to town to buy some bread.

Written on the page it looks like eight one-syllable words of even weight. But imagine how that same sentence might sound to someone who doesn't know any English.

i-WENT t'TOWN t'BUY s'mBREAD

The stressed words have muscled out the unstressed. This is one reason it is so difficult to learn a foreign language without help. But the frustrations of a language student become an asset for the poet. It is easy enough to construct lines in which there are, say, four stressed words. And this is essentially the system used in *Beowulf*, the Old English epic.

Here is a passage where Beowulf, the hero, pursues a sea monster (the "brine-wolf") to her underwater lair. Read the selection a couple of times and underline the stressed words.

Then bore this brine-wolf, when bottom she touched,
the lord of rings to the lair she haunted,
whiles vainly he strove, though his valor held,
weapon to wield against wondrous monster
that sore beset him; sea-beasts many
tried with fierce tusks to tear his mail

It is obvious that poets in this tradition never counted syllables. They were concerned only with having two stresses, a pause known as a *caesura*, and two more stresses in each line. They concentrated on this simple beat, and *Beowulf* it is so clear that one can pound on the table while the song is chanted or sung—which is probably just what the ancients did.

This is a simple system of rhythm. A much more subtle (and literarily *sophisticated*) use of stress was developed by Gerard Manley Hopkins. Like the poet of *Beowulf*, he based his rhythms on the spoken language, usually with a given number of stresses per line. He often paid no attention to the number of unstressed syllables, calling his method "sprung rhythm" in the sense of "freed rhythm."

Turn to his "Pied Beauty" on page 103. For a comparison with the

Beowulf passage, underline what you feel are the four stressed words in each line. The first line is clear enough, but others are not as pronounced. Stress is being used more subtly here.

From Stressed Syllables to Meter

Stressed words are easy to work with, but counting stressed and unstressed syllables provides a whole new range of possibilities. This is the basis of meter.

Historically, meter came to English verse when the French language was imposed on the Anglo-Saxons after the Norman invasion. It has been in use ever since. Although it has gone through considerable refinement over the centuries, remember that in essence meter is a way of structuring the natural rhythms of the spoken language. In some respects, it is to daily speech what dance is to the way we move about when not dancing.

Before we turn to the terminology, here is how a metrical rhythm is created. First, look at a slightly extended version of our simple prose statement:

I went to town today to buy some bread

If you pound out the rhythm in the tradition of an Anglo-Saxon poetry reading, it comes out like this:

> / 2 |3 4 |5 6 |7 8 | 9 /0 |
> I *went*|to *town*|*today*|to *buy*|some *bread.* |

This looks very much like our Anglo-Saxon line of stressed words, but in the case of "to*day*" we counted syllables rather than words. There are, in fact, ten syllables—five stressed and five unstressed. Since we are dealing with pairs of syllables, the pattern can bridge words as in the following line:

> ᴗ / |ᴗ / |ᴗ / |ᴗ / |ᴗ / |
> My fa|ther can|not gam|ble with|his health. |

Notice that we are not forcing anything on the language; we are only arranging the words so as to emphasize a natural spoken rhythm.

If we want to describe this particular rhythmical effect without using technical terms, we might say that it goes ta-*tum*, ta-*tum*, ta-*tum*, ta-*tum*, ta-*tum*. There are five pairs of unstressed and stressed syllables here.

How might we convert this to a line that reverses the pattern? That is, how can we arrange the syllables to sound like *tum*-ta, *tum*-ta? Here is one possible version:

$$\overset{/\quad \cup}{\text{Father}} \Big| \overset{/\quad \cup}{\text{cannot}} \Big| \overset{/\quad \cup}{\text{gamble}} \Big| \overset{\cup \quad \cup}{\text{with his}} \Big| \overset{\cup \quad /\quad \cup}{\text{illness.}} \Big|$$

There are two changes here: I have dropped the initial unstressed syllable, *my*, and I have added a syllable at the end by replacing *health* with *illness*. We still have ten syllables, but with one exception the pattern has changed to *tum*-ta.

This conversion shows how much depends on how we begin a line of metered verse. The pattern you start with is frequently (though not always) the scheme used throughout the line. None of this is possible in prose, of course. To achieve it you must have control over where each line begins and ends.

At this point, referring to metrical patterns as "ta-*tum*" and "*tum*-ta" becomes more cumbersome than learning a few terms. It is helpful, for example, to refer to each unit of stressed and unstressed syllables as a *foot*. The foot with which we began (ta-*tum*) is called an *iamb*. The iambic foot is by far the most popular in English.

A line with five feet is called *pentameter*. *Penta* comes from the Greek word for *five*, as in that five-sided building, the Pentagon. Iambic pentameter has been a favorite metrical scheme from Shakespeare to Robert Frost and Richard Wilbur.

Now that we have a basic metrical line and some terms to describe it, let's apply them to a pair of lines from Richard Wilbur's "The Pardon" (p. 107). The poem as a whole should be familiar to you by now, but this is a new aspect.

$$\overset{\cup \quad /}{\text{And death}} \Big| \overset{\cup \quad /}{\text{was breeding}} \Big| \overset{\cup \quad /}{\text{in}} \Big| \overset{\cup \quad /}{\text{his lively}} \Big| \overset{\cup \quad /}{\text{eyes.}} \Big| \; 5 \; iambs$$

$$\overset{\cup \quad /}{\text{I started}} \Big| \overset{\cup \quad /}{\text{in}} \Big| \overset{\cup \quad /}{\text{to cry}} \Big| \overset{\cup \quad /}{\text{and call}} \Big| \overset{\cup \quad /}{\text{his name}} \Big| \; 5 \; iambs$$

Actually, these lines are unusual in that there is no variation in that iambic pentameter pattern. Most other lines contain minor variations, an important aspect I will return to shortly. In spite of these variations, however, the basic metrical scheme applies to the poem as a whole. Other examples of iambic pentameter in Chapter 11 are Robley Wilson's "On a Maine Beach" and John Berryman's sonnet, "I Lift."

The *iamb* is the most popular foot in English partly because so many two-syllable words fall naturally into this pattern: ex*cept*, al*low*, dis*rupt*, a*dore*, and the like. In addition, there is a natural tendency for sentences to begin with an unstressed syllable—often with words like *a, the, but, he, she, I*. But there are three other types of feet which are also used as the basis for metered poems:

The *trochee* is the reverse pattern, which we achieved by beginning each foot with a stressed syllable: "Father cannot gamble . . . ." Trochees can be used as the basic foot for an entire poem, but more often they are used as a substitution for an iambic foot in an iambic poem. As we shall see, this can give a special emphasis to a word or phrase, particularly if it is done at the beginning of a line.

The *anapest* consists of three syllables—two unstressed followed by one stressed: ta-ta-*tum*. It has a lively, cheerful beat and perhaps for this reason was selected by Robert Frost for his lighthearted poem "Canis Major" (p. 108). Although he uses a number of substitutions in that poem, the basic scheme is anapestic:

I'm a poor | underdog, | *one anapest*
But tonight | I will bark | *two anapests*
With the great | Overdog | *one anapest*

The *dactyl* is, as you might suspect, the reverse of the anapest: *tum*-ta-ta, as in "*happily,*" "*merrily,*" and "*sing to me.*"

These basic four feet are common enough so that familiarity with them is sufficient to *scan* (analyze and classify) almost any sample of metered verse in English and related languages. And they will provide you with enough flexibility to write metered verse skillfully without studying some thirty other combinations used by classical poets.

Conscientious scanning occasionally requires familiarity with the *spondee*—two equally stressed syllables, as in "heartbreak"—and the *pyrrhic foot*—two equally unstressed syllables, such as "in the" or "and the"; but the practicing poet often reads these as softened versions of iambs or trochees.

As review, the following table shows the four basic metrical feet, with the stress pattern and examples of each.

TYPE OF FOOT	ADJECTIVE	STRESS PATTERN	EXAMPLES
iamb	iambic	ta-*tum*	except; she might
trochee	trochaic	*tum*-ta	asking; lost it
anapest	anapestic	ta-ta-*tum*	disappoint; lower down
dactyl	dactylic	*tum*-ta-ta	happily; sing to me

In addition to the types of feet, there is the matter of how many feet are used in each line. By far the most popular length in English is five feet, pentameter. Unrhymed iambic pentameter, known as blank verse, was used by Shakespeare in his plays; pentameter is also the line used in the sonnet, described in the next chapter. In our own century such poets as Robert Frost, Richard Wilbur, and Anthony Hecht have made extensive use of this line.

The four-footed line, *tetrameter*, is a close second. And *trimeter* is also used widely. Lines that are longer than pentameter and shorter than trimeter are used far less frequently, but for the purpose of clarity, here is a list of types:

Two feet to each line (rare and usually comic)	*dimeter*
Three feet to each line (fairly common)	*trimeter*
Four feet (sometimes combined with trimeter)	*tetrameter*
Five feet (most common in English)	*pentameter*
Six feet (less used in this century)	*hexameter*
Seven feet (rare)	*heptameter*
Eight feet (a heavy, very rare line)	*octometer*

Don't let the terms put you off. They are intended for your use. At this point, it would be helpful to try three lines of iambic tetrameter. Take some simple topic as if you were about to write a haiku and follow the iambic pattern: ta-*tum*, ta-*tum*, ta-*tum*. Don't worry about rhyme and don't feel you have to be profound. This is just to help you feel the rhythm.

Now try shifting those lines so that they are trochaic: *tum*-ta, *tum*-ta, and so on. Once you get the line started, the rest should follow somewhat more easily.

Next, shift the topic to something lighter and try a few lines of anapests: ta-ta-*tum*, ta-ta-*tum*. For example: "In a leap and a bound, the gazelle in delight welcomes spring!"

Most writers find the iamb the easiest to work with. The trochee has added punch, thanks to that initial stress in each line. The anapest usually has a lilting quality, as we saw in Robert Frost's "Canis Major" (p. 108). And the dactyl, least used of the four, tends to have some of the heavy quality of the trochee and the length of an anapest. Its main function is to serve as substitution for variation.

Iambs and anapests are similar in that they both end on a stressed syllable. This is called *rising* (or *ascending*) meter. Trochees and dactyls, on the other hand, end on unstressed syllables and therefore are *falling* (or *descending*) meters. This distinction becomes important when one begins to use substitutions for variety and special effects.

Staying Loose with Metrics

Until now, I have been working only with skeletal outlines. They may appear to be as far from the actual creation of lyrical poetry as the study of notes and clefs appears to be from musical composition. But the process of absorption is similar in these two cases. What appears at first to be a set of arbitrary rules eventually becomes—even for those who may then depart from them—an internalized influence.

When you first begin working with meter, there is a natural tendency to make it as perfect and blatant as possible. The result is apt to be like the dancer who is still counting out each step. As soon as possible, try to mute your meter—not by careless construction but by adopting the methods of poets you admire.

There are four ways of keeping your metrical rhythm from taking over a poem, and often you will find three or all four used in a single work.

The first and most commonly used method is to make sure that at least some of your words bridge two metrical feet. Contrast, for example, these two versions:

$$\overset{\cup}{\text{Tides}} \overset{\prime}{\text{drown}} \Big| \overset{\cup}{\text{such}} \overset{\prime}{\text{pools}} \Big| \overset{\cup}{\text{each}} \overset{\prime}{\text{day}} \Big|$$

$$\overset{\cup}{\text{Tides}} \overset{\prime}{\text{swal}}\big|\text{low} \overset{\cup}{\text{up}} \Big| \overset{\cup}{\text{such}} \overset{\prime}{\text{pools}} \Big|$$

There is nothing wrong with the first version, but each beat is a separate word. It may have been to avoid such regularity that Robley Wilson chose the second version for his poem "On a Maine Beach." The word "swallow" bridges the first and second feet, muting the impact of the meter.

A second method of muting meter is to use *run-on lines*. A run-on line, described briefly in the previous chapter, is one in which both the grammatical construction and the sense are continued into the next line. It is opposed to the *end-stopped line* in which there is a natural pause—usually with a comma or a period. Some end-stopped lines are more abrupt than others, of course; and the more pronounced such a pause is, the more it will emphasize the meter.

Run-on lines help to soften the impact of meter just as they mute rhyme endings. At the conclusion of Wilson's "On a Maine Beach," for example, the run-on line appropriately echoes the "beach rhythms" he is describing:

> Round lifetimes half-awake. Beach rhythms flow
> In circles. Perfections teach us to die.

Another technique of softening the impact of meter is rarely used but well illustrated in Anthony Hecht's "Lizards and Snakes" (p. 97). Instead of writing consistently in lines of pentameter or tetrameter, he alternates between these two. The first line has five feet and the next has four. A few of his lines even have six feet.

This is a risky approach since the reader is apt—at least unconsciously—to expect greater regularity. One reason it seems natural here is that the poet has consciously adopted an informal, conversational tone.

The fourth and by far the most frequently used method is called *substitution.* That is, the poet occasionally substitutes a different foot from the one which has been adopted for the poem as a whole.

In iambic verse, for example, it is often effective to place a trochaic foot at the beginning of the line to stress a particular word or phrase. Here is how John Berryman provides a special emphasis on an initial word by using a trochee rather than an iamb:

> Beasts in the hills their tigerish love are snarling.

Since we are used to an iambic pattern in this poem (in spite of many substitutions), the initial trochee has the effect of underlining *"Beasts."*

Exactly the same technique is used by Richard Wilbur in the final and most dramatic stanza of "The Pardon" (p. 107).

> Asking forgiveness of his tongueless head.

Robert Frost uses a different kind of substitution in "Canis Major" (p. 108). As we have seen, the final stanza is unmistakably anapestic dimeter—two anapests to each line. But at the start of that poem, it really isn't clear whether the basic foot is going to be iambs or anapests. There is a substitution in each line:

$$\breve{\text{The}} \ \acute{\text{Great}} \ | \ \acute{\text{O}}\breve{\text{ver}}\breve{\text{dog}}$$
$$\breve{\text{That}} \ \acute{\text{heav}}\text{|}\breve{\text{en}}\breve{\text{ly}} \ \acute{\text{beast}}$$

It is only after those initial lines that we see anapests taking over as the basic pattern of the poem.

How much substitution can a poem absorb? Anthony Hecht's "Lizards and Snakes" comes close to the limit. The poem is essentially iambic, but here is a line in which three of the five feet are non-iambic substitutions. Can you scan it and spot the variations?

> In the set of the jaw, a fierce pulse in the throat

The most logical way to scan this is to read the opening six words as two anapests. The other substitution is the trochee in "pulse in."

With so many variations, why do we call the poem iambic? Because *most* of the lines are largely iambic, with no more than one or occasionally two substitutions. When we come to a line like the one just quoted, we retain the memory of that iambic beat and assume that the poem will return to it, as indeed it does. If the poem contained very many lines with so few iambs, we would begin to conclude that it was unmetered.

Why Metered Verse?

There are ways of creating rhythm in poetry without using meter at all. These will be analyzed in the next chapter on free verse. But in spite of all these free-verse alternatives, a large number of poets in our own century prefer the structure meter provides. Robert Frost is widely quoted as having said that writing poetry without meter is "like playing tennis with the net down." In varying degrees poets like W. H. Auden, Anthony Hecht, X. J. Kennedy, Theodore Roethke, Robert Lowell, Richard Wilbur, and many others agree.

Why? Tastes vary just as they do in any art; but here are four reasons often given by poets themselves.

Some simply prefer to establish the rhythmical base in advance, seeing meter as a flexible structure which saves them from devising new rhythmical cues with each line. Second, the very process of revising so as to create a metrical pattern often leads to word choice and arrangement that one didn't consider at first. In this way meter can push a poet into exploring possibilities which might not have been tried with less structured systems.

Third, many like the opportunity of emphasizing or highlighting a word or phrase through the natural stress of a metrical foot or—stronger still—through substitution. We have already seen how trochaic substitution can emphasize a word at the beginning of a line. And in the case of Robert Frost's "Canis Major," an anapestic base with many iambic substitutions gives the poem a whimsical lilt which would have been impossible in prose. Substitution of feet has, in effect, the capacity of underlining a word or establishing a mood. This is a delicate control of language not available to the writer of fiction.

Finally, meter provides an identifiable rhythm from which one may depart and return again, a pleasure in itself which is somewhat like a jazz player who feels free to improvise around an established melody. Because metrical rhythms are regular, the poet can, in a sense, play with them. For some, this is an important aspect of writing poetry.

In any case, meter should not be thought of as some external system added to a poem for decoration. It is for many a basic part of the creative art, a way of making the poem do more than it could have otherwise.

7 RHYTHMS OF FREE VERSE

The visual patterns of typography; syntactical rhythms of Whitman and others; the use of syllabics and breath units; methods of developing a facility in the full range of rhythmical techniques.

Free verse abandons meter for other rhythmical devices, and it avoids regular rhyme in favor of looser sound systems. But it is not a revolution in poetry. It is not even new. It is a continuing tradition with some of its roots reaching back to the verse of the Bible.

Essentially, it refers to a wide variety of verse in which the rhythmical patterns are *not* based on stress or meter. In no way, however, does *free verse* imply an absence of rhythm. Even though the techniques are nonmetrical, a great deal of free verse is highly rhythmical.

Free-verse rhythms can be created in at least four different ways: typography (arrangement on the page), syntax (sentence structure), syllabics (syllables per line), and breath units. Varied as these techniques are, they do not represent separate, unrelated systems. They are often used in conjunction with each other.

Those who are just beginning to write free verse are sometimes tempted to establish a personal "style" by adopting a single rhythmical system and repeating it in poem after poem. This is limiting, however. Most accomplished poets vary their methods, particularly early in their careers. Variety helps one to grow. Dylan Thomas, for example, was equally at home with the rhyme and meter of a sonnet (described in Chapter 9) as he was with the syllabics and breath units of free verse. Once again, being familiar with a wide range of methods will give you the artistic freedom to choose what is best for a particular poem.

The Visual Patterns of Typography

This method of creating rhythmical effects is not strictly a matter of sound. Since it depends heavily on how the poem looks on the printed page, it is often called *visual rhythm.* But actually there is no clear separation between visual and auditory rhythms. The way a poem is arranged on the page is going to affect a reading in some way. *Typography,* then, refers to the arrangement of words on the page, but it is linked closely with the sound of a poem.

Turn now to Denise Levertov's free-verse poem "Merritt Parkway," on page 99. Read it a couple of times just for the sense of motion. The typography of the lines is clearly designed to suggest both the motion and our mood as we drive.

Although the structure is not formal as it is in the stanzas of metered verse, there are cues that establish form. Notice, for example, the phrase "keep moving—" which appears in the third line and again a little more than halfway through. In each case the words are used to introduce a new block of images—the first indented to the right and the second brought out to the left.

The images tend to be linked visually more than by the sound of the words, but notice how at the end the poet employs not only alliteration but onomatopoeia in the echo of cars sliding by on the highway:

in six lanes, gliding

north & south, speeding with

a slurred sound—

E. E. Cummings' poem "Buffalo Bill's" (p. 100) is an even more dramatic example of typography. Turn to it now and read it over several times for the pleasure of it. Then study it carefully, looking for the ways in which he controls the speed of your reading and provides elements of surprise.

There are two ways in which Cummings appears to speed up your reading of this poem: by running words together and by using long, fairly uncluttered lines which can be read as fast as prose. In some cases, however, this may only be an illusion of speed—particularly in the first reading. It often takes longer to puzzle out lines that are printed without spaces. But once one is used to the poem, these lines seem to ripple by as if they were moving.

> and break onetwothreefourfive pigeonsjustlikethat
> > Jesus
>
> he was a handsome man

Here the word "Jesus" appears to be linked syntactically with Buffalo Bill's shooting ability; but then it leaps forward to become linked with how handsome he was. It is essentially a visual trick, tripping our expectations through an unexpected shift in rhythm. Of course, the same device of syntactical ambiguity can be used in metered verse, but the effect is heightened here by hanging the word between the two lines.

Notice, too, the way he uses line length. In many cases it is clear that he has kept a line short to highlight a certain phrase or even a word. But remember that one cannot find a rational explanation for every typographical element. Like the brush strokes of a painter, a majority of decisions that go into a poem are intuitive.

One extreme form of typography is the "shaped poem" which molds the shape of the work into the object it is describing. This was particularly popular in the seventeenth century and is well illustrated by Herbert's "The Altar" and "Easter Wings," as well as by Herrick's "The Pillar of Flame," each of which resembles the object suggested in its title. More recently, contemporaries like Allen Ginsberg have published poems in the shape of atomic clouds and, with the aid of punctuation, rockets.

Shaped poetry—also called *concrete poetry*—does have certain limitations. As a poem begins to rely more and more on its shape, it generally makes less and less use of the sound of language, rhythms, or metaphor. Even the theme becomes simplified. It is as if concern for the visual effect overpowers all other aspects. One can, for example, repeat the word *death* all over the page in such a way as to resemble a skull. It takes time and patience to do this, but the result is more like a cartoon than a poem. In general, the more extreme experiments in shaped poetry are remembered more for their curiosity value than their literary worth.

Even nonpictorial use of typography has its drawbacks if used to an extreme. Sophisticated poetry depends at least in part on maintaining unity and flow. As you increase the rearrangement of words and lines on the page, the poem becomes more fragmented and, as a result, less of an organically unified work. This may be one reason why many poets, like Adrienne Rich and Ann Leventhal, use regular stanzas even though they are writing free verse.

Syntactical Rhythms

Syntax is sentence structure. Syntactical rhythm is achieved by repeating or balancing a particular grammatical element such as a question, phrase, or clause.

Walt Whitman made extensive use of syntactical rhythms. Here is a sample from his "Passage to India":

> Ah who shall soothe these feverish children?
> Who justify these restless explorations?
> Who speak the secret of impassive earth?
> Who bind it to us? what is this separate Nature so unnatural?
> What is this earth to our affections? . . .

This is rhythm by syntactical repetition. The repetition of the word "who" is only a cue; the full interrelationship among these quoted lines has to do with the echo of each question with the one which precedes it. The key verbs are "soothe," "justify," "speak," "bind," and "is." One can see from these highly varied verbs that the *statement* is not repetitious; it is only the *form*. Whitman has replaced rhythm of metrical units with rhythm of grammatical units.

Allen Ginsberg wrote "Howl" in 1959, 104 years after Whitman first published "Leaves of Grass," and his indebtedness is clear. Here he describes "the best minds of my generation":

> who bared their brains to Heaven under the El and saw Mohammedan angels
>   staggering on tenement roofs illuminated,
> who passed through universities with radiant cool eyes hallucinating Arkan-
>   sas and Blake-light tragedy among the scholars of war,
> who were expelled from the academies for crazy & publishing obscene odes
>   on the windows of the skull,
> who cowered in unshaven rooms in underwear, burning their money in
>   wastebaskets and listening to the Terror through the wall. . . .

Ginsberg is clearly influenced by Whitman, but both of them drew on a still earlier source, the Bible. Although Whitman's version was in English (the King James translation), and Ginsberg's was in the original Hebrew, both men were strongly influenced by the rhythmical patterns found there. Compare, for example, the selections quoted from these two poets with this passage from Job 38:34:

> Canst thou lift up thy voice to the clouds,
>   that abundance of waters may cover thee?
> Canst thou send lightnings, that they may go
>   and say unto thee, Here we are?

> Who hath put wisdom in the inward parts?
>   or who hath given understanding to the heart?
> Who can number the clouds in wisdom?
>   or who can pour out the bottles of heaven?

Here too, it is the entire syntactical unit that is repeated to achieve the rhythm. The repeated words are merely cues which signal the repeated form. For further examples, read over the rest of the Book of Job and review The Psalms. Then go back and study the complex system of syntactical rhythms in Genesis. Doing this makes one far more open to the rhythms not only of Whitman and Ginsberg but Ferlinghetti, Gregory Corso, John Ashbery, Amiri Baraka (LeRoi Jones), and many others writing today.

Syntactical repetitions do not have to be thundering to succeed. The technique used by Lisel Mueller in "Night Song" (p. 110) is similar to that used in the passage just quoted from Job, but the voice is a quiet one. Her repetitions are like those we are used to in song lyrics. Here is the first stanza:

> Among rocks, I am the loose one,
> among arrows, I am the heart,
> among daughters, I am the recluse,
> among sons, the one who dies young.

The simplicity of the form is deceptive. If you read the poem over as a whole, you will see how the speaker finally becomes a symbol of poets everywhere. "Among the bones you find on the beach," she concludes, "the one that sings was mine."

Both Mueller's poem and the earlier examples, by the way, demonstrate the close relationship between syntactical rhythms and typography. If we wrote out "Night Song" or the selection from Job in lines of prose, the rhythm would still be unmistakable just as it is in certain types of traditional oratory:

> Among rocks, I am the loose one; among arrows I am the heart; among daughters, I am the recluse; among sons, the one who dies young.

Because the poet controls the arrangement on the page, however, she can place each repeated phrase at the start of a new line. In this way, typography emphasizes the syntactical rhythms already there. This is one of the advantages poets have over writers of prose.

We think of syntactical rhythms as repeating whole syntactical units, as in the examples just given. But sometimes the effect can be achieved simply by repeating key words in a regular pattern. Lucille Clifton's poem "What the Mirror Said" appears to be a merry bit of self-affirmation almost without form. It is printed without marginal comments on page 106, but here are the first sixteen lines with the structure marked:

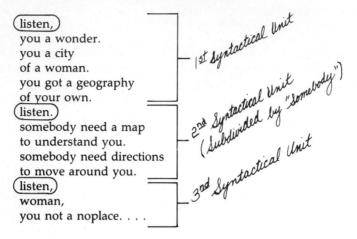

(listen,)
you a wonder.
you a city
of a woman.
you got a geography
of your own.
(listen.)
somebody need a map
to understand you.
somebody need directions
to move around you.
(listen,)
woman,
you not a noplace. . . .

1st Syntactical Unit

2nd Syntactical Unit
(Subdivided by "Somebody")

3rd Syntactical Unit

One of the pleasures of this poem is that it appears to be so spontaneous. But behind that apparent spontaneity there is a syntactical rhythm.

Syllabics and Breath Units

Syllabics and breath units are two more methods of creating rhythm in free verse. They are distinct and essentially unrelated to each other.

Syllabics, quite simply, involves counting syllables. A haiku, discussed briefly in Chapter 4, is one form of syllabics. It is an unrhymed and unmetered poem in which the first line has five syllables, the second has seven, and the third has five. Two contemporary haiku are printed on pages 106 and 107. Here are two more samples, each of which has been translated from the Japanese.

> After spring sunset
> Mist rises from the river
> Spreading like a flood

> Even with insects . . .
> Some are hatched out musical . . .
> Some, alas, tone-deaf

Like all types of syllabics, this form is partially visual and only faintly auditory. When we look at a haiku we recognize the shape even before we count syllables—just as we do the fourteen-line form of the sonnet. The shape creates certain expectations if we have read other haiku. We assume that probably there will be a single image (often from nature) and that the central concern may be merely a visual impression rather than a philosophical statement.

As for the sound, the predetermined pattern of line length does not affect our way of reading the poem out loud, as in the case of meter, but it does make our reading more deliberate. Often each line is a single visual unit or, as in the second poem, a single suggestion.

In general, however, the value of the form is not strictly visual or auditory. For many it is merely a recognizable way of concentrating a single impression or insight. The formal requirements are simple, yet the varieties of treatment are infinite. In Japan, where many nonpoets enjoy writing and reading haiku, it has been estimated that a million new haiku are published each year.

Syllabics for the practiced poet can become a far more complex form of expression. Dylan Thomas' "Fern Hill" is a fine example. It is clear that the poem is not metered. The lines do not scan and they are far too varied in length to fit any traditional stanza pattern. But you can read the poem many times (as I did) without realizing that it is meticulously composed in stanzas that have the same pattern of syllables.

To be specific, the first line of every stanza has fourteen syllables and so do all the second lines. The third line of every stanza has nine syllables, the fourth line regularly has six syllables, and the fifth line always has nine. Up to this point the system is absolutely regular.

The sixth line has fourteen syllables in every stanza but the first (which has fifteen); the seventh line also has fourteen in every stanza but—you guessed it—the last (which again has fifteen). The eighth lines are either seven or nine syllables, and the final lines are either nine or six. Even his variations take on a certain order.

This is an astonishingly complex system. Why on earth should he bother when a majority of his readers will enjoy the poem as if it were an essentially formless work? There are three possible answers, all speculative. First, one might argue that this hidden structure beneath apparent formlessness echoes the theme of the poem itself: I was "young and easy" in my childhood, he is saying, but because everyone is mortal and subject to aging and death—as sure as the tides—"I sang in my chains like the sea."

A second and less academic explanation is his obvious delight in working with form for its own sake. Here, after all, is a poet who in another poem adopted the bizarre rhyme scheme of *abcdefggfedcba*. One can read that poem a hundred times and not be aware of more than the central and apparently accidental couplet. But Thomas, like many poets, seems to have enjoyed working with ingenious systems.

Finally—and most significantly—hidden form has its effect even on readers who have not analyzed the system precisely. There is a certain sense of control in these stanzas which one senses even without counting syllables. This is probably the best reason for considering some type of rhythmical system even in an apparently free work.

Breath units are the loosest form of rhythm in poetry today. Essentially, the line is broken at the point where the reader might be expected to take a breath. Poets like Charles Olson defended this approach by arguing that it emphasizes the oral aspect of verse and provides greater freedom for the poet. Adrienne Rich's "Like This Together" (p. 101) and Ann Leventhal's "Pilot Error" (p. 112) provide examples. Each has the sense of a persona speaking aloud, the first in a reflective mood and the second in a state of shock.

Does all free verse contain some kind of rhythmical system? That depends on how broad your definition of *verse* is. *Prose poetry,* for example, is a hybrid form written in short lines but frequently without rhythm, sound linkages, or figurative language. In spite of the short lines, it frequently seems less like poetry than does the prose of, say, Dylan Thomas in "August Bank Holiday," quoted in Chapter 5. At best, it offers some kind of compression of statement, but more often it reads like a straightforward paragraph of prose.

Developing a Facility in Rhythm

These methods of creating rhythm in free verse are closely related to the metrical rhythms discussed in the last chapter. The goal is essentially the same. To see the relationship, it is helpful to take a single work and convert it into various rhythmical systems, both metrical and free.

Here, for example, is a sample of iambic pentameter, the first four lines from Shakespeare's "Sonnet 2":

> When forty winters shall besiege thy brow
> And dig deep trenches in thy beauty's field,
> Thy youth's proud livery so gazed on now,
> Will be a tattered weed of small worth held.

It is an unusual passage because there is not a single substitution. For this reason, it serves as a good base for rhythmical doodling. One might begin, for example, by converting it to iambic trimeter. There are many ways of handling this, but here is one:

> When forty winters shall
> Besiege thy brow and dig
> Deep trenches in thy face
> Thy youth's proud livery
> Will be a worthless weed.

The point of this exercise is not to improve on Shakespeare but to improve one's own ability to work with meter and one's inner *sense* of pentameter and trimeter. Line-length conversions are easy; shifting from iambic to trochaic requires a little more effort. It might come out like this:

> Forty winters shall besiege thy lovely
> Brow and dig deep trenches in thy beauty's
> Field and youth's proud livery loved so fully
> Soon will be a tattered weed of little worth.

The perceptive reader will notice that I have slurred "livery," a three-syllable word, to "liv'ry," two syllables; I also allowed an extra stressed syllable at the end of the fourth line. Keeping in mind that there is no one way to handle meter, you may be able to devise a more perfect rendering.

Moving from meter to visual rhythm, any number of possibilities might be tried. Here is one sample:

> When forty winters shall
>   besiege
>   starve
>   torment
> The rounded beauty of your brow,
>   then
> Your light step will
>   limp
>   pause
>   trembling before the last descent.

When we turn from typography to syntactical rhythms our attention shifts from the purely visual arrangement of lines on the page to the dramatic use of sentence structure. Remember the impact of rhetorical questions and repeated words and phrases as often seen in biblical verse and the work of Whitman and Ginsberg. Freely rendered, our Shakespearean passage might come out like this:

> Forty winters shall besiege thy brow
> Winters that will dig deep trenches in thy beauty's field
> Winters that will wither that proud young livery
> Winters that will leave a tattered weed of little worth

All this is doodling for your journal. You could continue with, say, the last four lines of Wilson's "On a Maine Beach" (p. 103) or any stanza from Adrienne Rich's "Like This Together" (p. 101). It should be fun, and if you apply some of the specific techniques described in this and the previous chapter, it should be useful as well.

In addition to composing in your journal, spend some time each day examining the rhythms of published poetry. Since most poetry contains rhythmical patterns of some sort, every anthology and literary quarterly can serve as a source for study. By combining exercises in your journal and extensive, careful reading, you will soon acquire a facility in poetic rhythms.

8 TONE

Tone as your *attitude toward your subject*: cheerful, reflective,
wry, somber, angry; *attitudes toward your persona*: close identity
versus critical; *tensions* in tone; varieties of *irony*; the caustic
tone of *satire*; *fine tuning* your tone.

"I want that."
    This looks like a clear statement. How could we mistake its meaning?
But if someone said that to us, would we respond just to the words or to
other factors, such as who the speaker is and what is the tone of voice?
    Suppose, for example, the speaker is a stranger on a dark street and
he is holding a gun. That's going to evoke one set of responses. But suppose
those same words were the joking comment of a friend on first seeing Fort
Knox. The whole meaning shifts.
    Now imagine a situation in which there is no threat and no humor
involved: The same words are said by a sobbing child in a supermarket,
pointing to a sugar-coated breakfast cereal you detest. And what happens to
the statement when it is the retort of someone who has just discovered her
tax rate has been doubled—"I want that like a hole in the head"?
    In spoken language we respond not only to the literal meaning of

words, the *denotation*, but almost always to an array of *connotations* which we gather from the circumstances and the tone of voice. Tone is equally important in poetry. It is the manner in which you reveal your attitude toward the subject of your poem and your relationship to your persona as well.

Your Attitude Toward Your Subject

When we refer to the tone of a poem we use such words as *comic, reflective, somber, wry,* and *angry.* Keep in mind, however, that there are really as many different shadings of tone as there are different tones of voice and that there are no sharp divisions between them. Like the names of colors, they are convenient segments of a spectrum.

Comic verse is often looked on as being unworthy of serious effort. Much of it, of course, is *simple* in the sense that it is written for special occasions (birthdays, anniversaries) or merely for a chuckle and is not intended for the kind of attention we give sophisticated poetry. Remember, however, that it is possible to introduce fairly complex notions through a comic voice.

Robert Frost's "Canis Major" (p. 108), for example, appears to be a rather slight little piece about the constellation of that name. The persona describes himself as "poor underdog," but his spirits are lifted as he looks up at the stars:

> But tonight I will bark
> With the great Overdog
> That romps through the dark.

What elevates this above the level of, most appropriately, doggerel, is the fact that most of us have taken on fresh spirits from looking up at the heavens on a clear night. The tone of the poem is comic, but the theme goes beyond the trivial.

The same is true of Lucille Clifton's "What the Mirror Said" (p. 106). The tone of this poem is comic. A woman looks in the mirror and compares herself with a whole country. She is so complex someone would have to have a map to understand her. We smile, but we are also aware that the speaker is a woman and is black. Just behind those comic lines lie two major social issues.

A *reflective tone* is a broad and inclusive category. In many cases, the poet has seen something he or she wishes to share with readers. "Look, in the pools, how rocks are like worn change" Wilson says at the opening of "On a Maine Beach" (p. 103). He goes on to describe the scene and also to draw an analogy from it. In the same way, Maya Angelou draws the reader into her kitchen in "This Winter Day" (p. 98) and points out how the vegetables she is cutting up "leak their blood selves in the soup." At the end of the poem she tells us that making soup is a kind of bulwark against the rain outside. Gerard Manley Hopkins is also in a reflective mood in "Pied Beauty" (p. 103). He lists a great variety of dappled things—skies, cows, trout, and the like, and gives thanks for their beauty. All three of these poems help us as readers to look more closely at the world about us. The tone in each case is reflective.

Somber tones often dominate student poems. Remember, though, that listening to a whiner isn't much fun, and reading complaints in verse can be just as bad. On the other hand, it is possible to be somber without being depressingly negative. Adrienne Rich's poem, "Like This Together" (p. 101) starts out with a rather dark image—the speaker and her friend sitting in a car by the river "like drugged birds / in a glass case." The poem is concerned with how the past is soon obliterated ("They're tearing down the houses / we met and lived in") and their energies are dissipated ("Susceptibilities . . . / sucking / blind power from our roots"). But what keeps this poem from being just a list of complaints is the affirmation at the end. The two of them will:

> hold fast to the
> one thing we know,
> grip earth and let burn.

Chase Twichell's "Rhymes for Old Age" (p. 111) is another good example of a poem in which the tone is somber without being depressing. The subject of the poem is an old woman who is close to death. Twichell has avoided sentimentality by using starkly clinical details; on the other hand, she has avoided cold detachment by showing deep compassion for the subject of her poem. Establishing just the right tone in a poem requires careful adjustment.

A *wry tone* is an excellent way to avoid self-pity. The character in John Berryman's "I Lift" (p. 110) has good reason to be depressed, but he adopts a wry tone similar to what he might use if speaking to a friend. He is alone in a strange bar and quietly drinks a toast to his friend who is miles away. He thinks of "beasts in the hills" in their "tigerish love," and blows on the gray ash of his cigarette: As the ash suddenly turns red, she joins him in his mind and "we have our drink together." This is a poem that deals with the melancholy mood of separation—a subject well worked over in song lyrics. Berryman has avoided sentimentality by understatement and, like Twichell, by using absolutely fresh language. The tone is just wry enough to avoid self-pity.

Anger and *protest* have long been expressed in poetry. Some of the strongest examples come from the Hebrew prophets. They tended to stand outside the mainstream of their own cultures and were highly critical of the societies of their day. Their language was blunt and direct. Take this brief example from Isaiah 3:24:

And it shall come to pass, that instead of sweet smell
    here shall be stink; and instead of a girdle, a rent;
And instead of well set hair, baldness; and instead of
    a stomacher, a girding of sackcloth;
And burning instead of beauty.
Thy men shall fall by the sword,
    and thy mighty in the war.

The following (Isaiah 33:1) is an attack on those in power. It is not far in spirit
and to some degree in technique from the attacks made in the 1960s by poets
like Allen Ginsberg, Gregory Corso, and others.

Woe to thee that spoilest, and thou wast not spoiled;
    and dealest treacherously, and they dealt not treacherously with thee!
When thou shalt cease to spoil, thou shalt be spoiled;
And when thou shalt make an end to deal treacherously,
    they shall deal treacherously with thee.

In this country, black Americans have struck the same note. For generations,
slaves identified themselves with the oppressed Jews of the Old Testament;
this link is reflected in the spirituals. The protest poetry of today, however,
is released from the sense of resignation that characterized many of the spirituals. In many respects, these are closer to the bitter sense of outrage that
is so much a part of the works of Isaiah, Jeremiah, and Ezekiel.

Clarence Major speaks for many black poets with this statement from
the introduction to his anthology, *The New Black Poetry*:

Our poetry is shaped by our experience in the world, both deeply personal
and social. . . . We constantly mean our poems to reshape the world; in this
sense all excellent art is social. . . .

Turn now to Conrad Kent Rivers' "The Still Voice of Harlem" (p. 105)
and study the pattern of tensions there. Notice how the harshness of life for
black Americans is contrasted with the sense of serenity within the "gardens"
of Harlem. Obviously this is not intended to suggest literally that life in Harlem
is easy; the "hope" is the sense of identity found there. This poem has many
parallels in biblical verse where the Jews looked to Israel as a source of identity—
the brutality of the world pitted against the solidarity of the group. The tone
is a complex mix of bitterness and hope.

When examining the tone in one of your own poems, be sure to ask
this crucial question: Is this what I *really* feel about the subject of this poem?
If you are even unconsciously trying to sweeten the tone, you may be moving
in the direction of sentimentality. And if you dramatize it beyond your real
feelings, you may end up with self-pity or melodrama. Such poems do not

ring true. Usually, the most appropriate tone to adopt is an honest reflection of how you feel about the subject.

You and Your Persona

When we discuss a poem, we never know for sure whether the speaker in the poem represents the poet or an imagined character. For this reason, it is best to refer to "the persona," "the speaker," or "the narrator."

As a poet, however, you have a choice as to whether you wish to place yourself in your poem, using *I* to introduce yourself and your feelings, or whether you wish to present your poem through a character who is someone else. This distinction is referred to as *distance*, a term we will return to in the section on fiction.

Since contemporary poetry is often personal, it is frequently set in the first person. This trend is reflected in the poems included in Chapter 11—poems with which you are now familiar. Robley Wilson's rock pool in Maine, Maya Angelou's kitchen on a rainy day, Ann Leventhal's terrible phone call when she learns that a relative has been killed in a plane crash: All these have the illusion of a recent experience. They may actually be fictionalized, so we refer to the speaker in each case as the persona, but the feeling we have is that the speaker and the poet are one.

Some poems increase the distance by having the persona or narrator recall an episode from the past. The narrator in Richard Wilbur's "The Pardon" describes the day he discovered the body of his dog. The insight and the language at the end of that poem are clearly those of an adult looking back. The same is true of the narrator's view of his childhood in "Fern Hill." Here too, the conclusion—". . . I sang in my chains like the sea"—is that of an adult who is well aware of his own mortality.

Then there are poems in which the first person, *I*, does not appear at all. Chase Twichell's view of the old and dying woman in "Rhymes for Old Age" does not identify the viewer, nor does Gerard Manley Hopkins' description of dappled things in "Pied Beauty." We can still refer to the assumed persona as compassionate in the first case and filled with pious awe in the other; but the existence of these "narrators" is only implied.

Finally, there are those poems in which the narrator is clearly someone other than the poet. In fact, the narrator in many cases is being presented in a critical way. We have already seen how Gwendolyn Brooks uses "we" in "We Real Cool" to describe a character who is one of the pool players at the Golden Shovel. The narrator reveals himself (we assume "he" perhaps unfairly) and his future without quite realizing how much he is saying. There is greater distance here between poet and narrator since she has chosen to present the poem through the words of a character clearly removed from herself, but this does not mean that she does not feel compassion for these characters.

Creating Tension Through Tone

If you study a sophisticated poem carefully, you will almost always find some sort of contrast, mixed emotion, or apparent contradiction in tone. These are the crosscurrents that help keep a poem from becoming static. They are ways of creating poetic tension.

Contrasts in attitude are common and fairly easy to identify. We have already touched on a few: Brooks' easygoing use of street language contrasted with the jolting prophesy at the end of "We Real Cool"; Hecht's merry anecdote played against the darkly dramatic image of the devil in "Lizards and Snakes"; Dylan Thomas' dreamlike description of an apparently ideal childhood played against a dark recognition of mortality in the last stanza.

Another poem that depends heavily on contrast throughout is "Pilot Error" by Ann Z. Leventhal (p. 112). Written in a stark, almost prosaic style without figurative language, the poem regularly repeats the contrast between the terrible news about the narrator's friend and the numbed response— folding laundry. The almost telegraphic style echoes that of a mind in a state of shock. In this poem the contrast is not held off until the last stanza as it is in the examples given earlier. Read it now and notice how the contrast between the unfolding story of the accident and the folding of linen is repeated in each of seven stanzas.

Ambivalence is an important concept in all three genres—poetry, fiction, and drama. It refers to the conflicting emotions we sometimes have toward a person or object—not alternating, but at the same time. We may, for example, love and hate an individual simultaneously; we may be fond of a particular place and long to get away at the same time. It is also possible to feel anger and compassion for someone, resentment and envy, even scorn and admiration.

The reason ambivalence in tone is so important is that it is one of the characteristics that distinguish sophisticated verse from simple. Who has ever seen a birthday card verse to a mother who is at the same time solicitous and a tyrant? Or, to be fair, a get-well card to dear old Dad, admitting the fact that it gives some satisfaction to see him flat on his back? Ambivalence in tone does not guarantee sophistication in a poem, but the lack of it may suggest that you have not probed your own feelings deeply enough.

Ambivalence is particularly appropriate when dealing with individuals who are close to you. Adrienne Rich, for example, develops a highly complex set of emotions in "Like This Together." It is a relationship both loving and distant, close yet separated like the houses that are being torn down and "cut in half . . . flayed."

Varieties of Irony

All forms of irony are based on a reversal of some sort. We expect a logical order in our world and are jolted when, say, the fire truck catches fire or the Olympic swimming champion drowns in his backyard pool. Since these involve our assumptions about the world around us, they are called examples of *cosmic irony*.

Irony can also appear in the form of a statement which unwittingly suggests future events either directly or indirectly. "I bring good news," the messenger in *Oedipus Rex* says, and the audience shudders, knowing that disaster is at hand. Since this is most closely associated with plays, it is called *dramatic irony*. More will be said about this in the chapters on drama.

The type of irony most frequently found in poetry is *verbal* or *conscious* irony. The terms are used interchangeably. It is verbal in that it is usually based on words rather than events, and it is conscious in that it is not a statement given by innocent speakers as in the case of dramatic irony.

Verbal irony often is achieved through the bringing together of elements we normally consider opposite in one way or another. There are several examples in these lines from Richard Wilbur's "The Pardon" (p. 107). The scene, you will remember, is the one in which the persona dreams he sees the ghost of his dog.

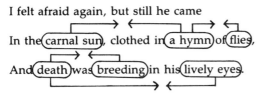

It is ironic to have a hymn associated with a "carnal sun" and a swarm of flies. It is equally ironic to think of death as "breeding." And there is a grim irony in those "lively eyes" of a dog which died some time ago.

There is another sample of irony in Chase Twichell's "Rhymes for Old Age" which you may have spotted in earlier readings of that poem. She describes the process of dying this way:

> One slips into it undressed,
> as into first love. . . .

When an ironic contrast is phrased in a way that makes it sound like a complete contradiction, it is called a *paradox*. John Donne, for example, in his sonnet "Death Be Not Proud" ends with these lines:

> One short sleep past, we wake eternally,
> And death shall be no more; Death, thou shalt die.

On one level it is illogical to say that death shall die, but as a description of eternal life, it makes sense metaphorically.

All these examples are contained in specific phrases. There are also broader ironic contrasts which are in some cases at the very heart of a poem as a whole. As we have already seen, "Fern Hill" appears to describe unending youth; yet the real concern of the speaker at the end of that poem is focused on the word "dying." And in Ann Leventhal's "Pilot Error" there is an unstated irony in the way the persona's apparently emotionless responses to terrible news reveals her true emotions.

Poets do not usually add irony to a poem the way a cook adds seasoning to a bland receipe—though the results may be similar. Instead, ironies suggest themselves either in the original conception or in the revisions.

But you can't be passive either. You should be willing to probe your own ambivalences honestly, looking for elements of hate in love, hidden longings in hatred, or subtle desires buried in fears. In addition, explore the possibilities of ironic contrasts in the material at hand. Just as the process of dying is in some ways like lovemaking, so also the kindness of a parent may in some ways be cruel; aspects of combat may seem peaceful; a motorcycle's roar may be a lullaby.

The Caustic Tone of Satire

Satire criticizes or ridicules through some form of exaggeration. In mild satire the exaggeration may be only a matter of selecting some characteristics and neglecting others. The tone may be a gentle kidding. At the other extreme, it may be wildly exaggerated and the tone vitriolic.

Satire and irony can, of course, be used independently from each other. All the examples of irony above are nonsatiric, and the first example of satire below does not use irony. But ridicule is particularly effective when it is presented "with a straight face." That is, the cutting edge of satire is sharpest when the poet gives the illusion of presenting an unbiased view. It is the tension between the poet's apparent honesty and the actual intent that makes satire almost invariably ironic. In fact, when satire is presented without irony the result often appears rather crude. Such is the case with Kingsley Amis' "A Tribute to the Founder." In this first of four stanzas, the intent to ridicule is clear, but because the material is presented directly rather than ironically the attack lacks subtlety:

> By bluster, graft, and doing people down
> Sam Baines got rich, but mellowing at last,
> Felt that by giving something to the town
> He might undo the evils of his past.

There is, of course, irony in the title since "tribute" is not intended literally. But the first line destroys all chance of sustaining subtlety. As soon as we see the words "bluster, graft, and doing people down" we know exactly where the poet stands, which is no sin in itself unless one asks more of poetry than one does of a good newspaper editorial.

William Jay Smith describes essentially the same sort of individual in his poem "American Primitive," and he also is satiric. But notice how different the effect is when irony is sustained.

> Look at him there in his stovepipe hat,
> His high-top shoes, and his handsome collar;
> Only my Daddy could look like that,
> And I love my Daddy like he loves his Dollar.

The lines flow like the ripple that runs silently down the length of a bull whip; and with his final word comes the "snap" which is sharp enough to make the most sophisticated reader jump. This is still fairly light verse, but the satire, sharpened with irony, draws blood. The tension here lies in the contrast between the *apparent* tone of sentimental tribute and the *actual* tone of cutting protest.

Moving further—much further—in the direction of subtlety and complexity, we have a third example of satire in Eliot's "The Love Song of J. Alfred Prufrock." The poem is an entire course in satire and deserves much more careful scrutiny than I can give it here. One brief selection from 131 lines will have to serve as appetizer.

Like the other two poems, this one aims its attack at an individual who represents a general type. Unlike the other two, the attack comes not from the poet directly but indirectly through what the character says about himself. If you read this selection carefully, you will see that he repeatedly veers from self-deprecation to self-defense, employing both in a pattern of self-deceit which almost deceives us, the readers.

> Should I, after tea and cakes and ices,
> Have the strength to force the moment to its crisis?
> But though I have wept and fasted, wept and prayed,
> Though I have seen my head (grown slightly bald) brought in upon a platter,
> I am no prophet—and here's no great matter;
> I have seen the moment of my greatness flicker,
> And I have seen the eternal Footman hold my coat, and snicker,
> And in short, I was afraid.

At first we may be tempted to see him as he sees himself: a man who recognizes the superficiality of his own society ("tea and cakes and ices"), has tried to rise above it ("wept and fasted"), is aware of his failure ("I have seen . . . my greatness flicker"), and is uneasy about death ("I was afraid").

But if we look more carefully, we see an aging man who has chosen to live in this particular society and has neither the strength nor the courage to leave it. He uses such absurd exaggeration ("wept and fasted") that we can't take him seriously. There is irony in the fact that he reveals his weaknesses through his defense of himself. He is being satirized through his own words.

Satire on television and in magazines like *Mad* and *National Lampoon* tends to be highly exaggerated and, like cartoons, obvious. It is one-shot entertainment. Satire in sophisticated poetry, however, is usually more subtle and frequently based on many aspects of character.

Fine Tuning Your Tone

When you are writing the first draft of a poem, tone may not be your primary concern. It will seem reasonable to address your subject with whatever attitude strikes you first. But as you begin to revise, consider the tone carefully. Slight shifts may be made fairly easily, and many times they will improve the poem dramatically.

In some cases you may find that your attitude is too serious. Look with particular care at poems that describe your feelings about those close to you.

Ask yourself, too, whether the poem in a sense plays only one note. That is, does it present only one side of your feelings? Would it be worth countering that feeling with a bit of its opposite? This may come in the form of an alternation—this side, but that side too—or simultaneously as the mixed emotions of ambivalence. This may require looking closely and honestly at your own feelings.

Irony and satire are often avoided because they tend to stress the intellectual portion of the poem—less feeling and more opinion. But if you find yourself writing a poem that criticizes a person or an institution, an ironic or satiric tone may be appropriate.

Although we have been examining tone as if it were a separate element, it is interwoven with the theme or statement of a poem. In the examples of how we might respond to the statement "I want that," the meaning was ambiguous until we knew what the tone was. In other words, tone was really a part of the meaning. In the same way, the meaning of a poem is often shaped by the signals you give to the reader regarding your attitude toward the subject. Your poem is not complete until you have established just the right tone.

9 From Units to Unity

Creating *internal structure*: related images, contrasts, narrative sequences, thematic unity; *visual structure*: recurrent stanzas, nonrecurrent stanzas, typography; the structure of *traditional verse forms*: haiku, ballad, sonnet, villanelle; *revising* to achieve effective unity.

Until now we have been examining aspects of poetry as if they were separate elements. This approach is necessary for analysis. But a poem, like any art object, is a single, unified creation. Without structure and some measure of unity, it would read like a journal-entry fragment—of more interest to the writer than to anyone else.

This chapter deals with the ways in which the various elements of a poem work together. Some of these, like imagery and theme, can be thought of as internal elements, and others, such as typography and traditional forms, are visual; but ultimately they are all interrelated and contribute to the unity of a poem. When we read a successful poem for pleasure, we are hardly aware of what went into its construction.

Internal Structure

When writing an essay, most of us select a topic and then outline the major points that will be covered. Logical order is important. When we turn to poetry, however, all that concern for logic feels out of place. In fact, it seems rather uncreative to spend much time on any kind of structure. After all, the work is often personal and usually much shorter than an analytical essay. We like to trust our natural feelings, our "poetic instinct."

As indeed we should—up to a point. But remember that even when we write with total disregard for structure, we are usually following some sort of organizational scheme quite unconsciously. The question to ask as the poem develops is whether this intuitive ordering can be improved.

A cluster of *related images* is the kind of structuring that is apt to occur quite unconsciously. If we write about tidal pools, snails and barnacles naturally come to mind. And if our subject is life on a farm, barns, cows, and fields will doubtless play a part just as they would if the topic came up in conversation.

But a *system* of related images requires a little more planning. Often it develops only after successive drafts. As I pointed out in the chapter on images, Robley Wilson's poem "On a Maine Beach" (p. 103) is organized around a series of related images. Remember that although it is written without stanza divisions, the rhyme scheme is based on a four-line unit as if the poem were written in quatrains. If you look closely you will see that each unit is dominated by certain key images: the rock pools, the mainspring, the tides, and, in the concluding four lines, old coins.

The organizational structure, then, is based partly on a series of closely related images, and each series is subtly reinforced with "stanzas" formed by a loose rhyme scheme. Overall unity is achieved both by the setting and by the final two lines, in which the roundness of pools and mainsprings are fused in the phrase "round lifetimes," and the motion of the tide is repeated in "beach rhythms."

Notice how when we discuss the pattern of images we have to examine these "stanzas" at the same time. This is a good example of how intermeshed content and form really are. The same is true of Adrienne Rich's "Like This Together." As I pointed out earlier, this free-verse poem is rich in visual images. What I'm concerned with here is the way those images are grouped by stanza. The topic for each of these six numbered stanzas is announced in the first or second line. Turn to the poem now (on p. 101) and circle what you feel these dominant images are. Then see how they shape the stanzas that follow.

The poem can be paraphrased by listing each of those key images: The narrator sits in (1) "the car" with her friend and is reminded of how they're (2) "tearing down . . . the city," but recalls that the two of them have (3) "certain things in common;" yet she finds (4) "our words misunderstand us." (5) "Dead winter" seems to characterize aspects of their relationship, and (6) "a severed hand" describes separation. These six sets of related images are drawn together in the end with her determination to "hold fast to the / one thing we know." In this way, a poem that seems like a rambling discourse is in fact organized through related images and pulled together with a single assertion at the end.

Providing a thematic or tonal *contrast* is a second method of organizing and unifying a poem. This technique, so common in essays, may play one view against another or—sometimes quite subtly—one mood or tone against another. You might think that divergent views or feelings would lead to *dis*unity, but they provide a clear structure and through this a sense of order. We have already seen how the apparently "cool" attitude of the narrator in Gwendolyn Brooks' "We Real Cool" is played against that harsh ending, "We / Die soon." The contrast is a miniature version of the one in "Fern Hill" where the idyllic view of the speaker's youth is brought up short at the end with the awareness of death.

The tonal contrast in Ann Leventhal's "Pilot Error" has already been examined as an example of poetic tension in the previous chapter. The terrible drama of a fatal plane accident is contrasted with the numbed response of the persona. But instead of withholding this contrast until the end of the poem, the poet uses it in each of the seven stanzas. The unity of the poem is drawn from the fusing of these two elements in the last stanza.

Narrative is as natural a structure for poetry as it is for prose. Story-telling was, after all, one of the original purposes of poetry. Epics like the *Iliad* and the *Odyssey* were long stories set in verse primarily to aid memorization. Unwritten epics have been recorded in Africa, India, Yugoslavia, and elsewhere. What we call the *literary ballads* of the nineteenth and twentieth centuries have their roots in poetry intended to be sung and often presented by individuals who could not read. Narrative sequence, like meter and rhyme, made the works easier to remember.

Anthony Hecht's "Lizards and Snakes" makes effective use of narrative sequence. It tells a story. It does other things also, but its primary organizational technique is to keep the reader wondering what will happen next.

In addition to plot, narrative poems often have a speaker who helps to unify the work. In the Hecht poem the identity of the narrator is not clearly defined. We know only that he and his friend, Joe, were a part of the action and he is now looking back after what appears to be a number of years.

"The Pardon" by Richard Wilbur (p. 107) is another good example. It begins with the summer day on which the persona finds the body of his dog. It continues through the burial. Much later the narrator has a nightmare that causes him to "beg death's pardon." This is a highly sophisticated poem with a complex theme, yet it is organized and unified with a relatively simple story line.

Unity of theme is just as important in a poem as it is in an essay. Think of it as a kind of gravitational force that keeps a poem from flying apart. Even when it is unseen—that is, unstated—it is felt. Thematic unity usually occurs naturally in a short piece, but you may have to pay more attention to it in longer works. As we have seen, both "Fern Hill" and "Like This Together" are relatively long poems that contain a number of divergent elements, but each is unified in the concluding lines.

Be careful, though, not to end a poem with an abstract summary. This may be very tempting, particularly if the theme is still a bit fuzzy in your own mind; but it is apt to oversimplify a successful poem and undercut its subtlety. Notice that in both of the poems cited, the concluding lines unify the poem not with a simple summary but through a fresh and powerful metaphor: "I sang in my chains . . ." in "Fern Hill" and "hold fast . . . grip earth" in "Like This Together."

Visual Structure

Whenever the lines of a poem are arranged in some kind of visual pattern, this is what readers notice first. The eye sees the shape of a poem even before it focuses on the first line. As I pointed out in earlier chapters, those white spaces between blocks of print help to establish rhythms both in metered poetry and in free verse. In addition, they can be used to highlight the organizational structure of a poem.

There are an infinite number of visual patterns available for the poet, but as we have already seen, they generally fall into three groups: the regular (recurrent) stanzas of metered poetry, irregular (nonrecurrent) stanzas of some free verse, and the more extreme forms of typography.

Stanza lengths in metered poetry tend to remain fixed in any one work. This regularity gives the reader a structure right from the start. Each stanza length has its own advantages and disadvantages.

Couplets, as I pointed out in the chapter on meter, are less popular today than they were in the past partly because they can easily become monotonous. It is hard to achieve a flow or unity with such short units. But remember that "We Real Cool" by Gwendolyn Brooks (p. 98) is not only written in couplets, it is also rhymed. How does the poem hang together? By echoing a street chant. For all those short units, it becomes a single, highly musical unit.

The triplet (three lines to a stanza) offers a larger unit. In "Pied Beauty" (p. 103), Gerald Manley Hopkins uses two triplets followed by a longer stanza. Each of the triplets concludes with an end-stopped line, emphasizing the stanza. The concluding half line, "Praise him," draws those distinct units together into a genuine unity.

The quatrain comes closer to the paragraph of prose in that one can use its four lines to present more of a complete idea or impression. It is not surprising that the narrative sequence of Richard Wilbur's "The Pardon" is based on quatrains. Although some are run-on stanzas (both the sense and the syntax continue unbroken into the next stanza), the four-line units remain the basic organizational structure.

The longer forms—quintet, sestet, septet, and octave—all share the advantage of providing a solid block of lines in which entire sets of images or extended metaphors can be developed. The variety of rhyme schemes and random rhyme endings in these long stanzas is practically limitless. Anthony Hecht's "Lizards and Snakes" (p. 97), for example, is printed as three octaves (eight lines). But the rhyme scheme divides each stanza in half as if it were made up of two quatrains.

Some of these stanza types serve not only as regularly recurring units but as components in more complex schemes. The triplet, for example, is the basic unit of the villanelle, just as the octave and sestet become subdivisions of the sonnet, forms I will turn to later in this chapter.

Regular stanzas are just as important in syllabics as they are in metered poetry. With syllabics, you remember, the number of syllables in each line matches the number in the corresponding line of the other stanzas. As we saw in Dylan Thomas' "Fern Hill," the length of the lines can vary freely, but each stanza must have the same number of lines. All this may seem cumbersome when described in the abstract, but if you read over "Fern Hill" once again just for the pleasure of it (an excellent antidote to close analysis), you will see how the anatomy of form is hidden in an effective poem just as it is in a painting.

Turning now to free verse, we can still find examples in which regular, recurrent stanzas are used as a basic organizing pattern. Lisel Mueller's "Night Song" (p. 110) is unmetered, unrhymed, and does not employ syllabics, but it too is written in regular quatrains. The rhythm, you will remember, is syntactical, based on the repetition of the phrase, "Among . . . , I am the . . ." But by dividing the poem into three end-stopped quatrains, Mueller has created four-line units that provide the structure she needs.

Adrienne Rich uses a somewhat looser structure in "Like This Together" (p. 101). As we have seen earlier, the poem moves from one image cluster to another. On first reading, it appears that these image clusters are grouped in six perfectly regular stanzas. But if you look closely (as fellow poets generally do), you will see that the length of these units varies from twelve to fifteen lines. Stanzas of unequal length—*nonrecurrent stanzas*—have some of the characteristics and functions of a paragraph in prose.

It is only one step from this to the loose typographical divisions in such poems as "Buffalo Bill's" by E. E. Cummings and "Merritt Parkway" by Denise Levertov. In such verse the word "stanza" is used rather freely to describe any group of lines set off by extra spacing. These are truly nonrecurrent in that they, like the prose paragraph, are not intended to echo each other in length or internal structure. They are merely divisions of thought, feeling, tone, or topic.

The *canto* is a longer division found in both metered and free verse. It usually consists of several stanzas, and the divisions are often signaled by printing numerals at the head of each. It serves somewhat the same function as the chapter does in fiction. The canto can be very helpful in longer poems to suggest a new setting, a new mood, or a new aspect of the theme. Sometimes it is possible to signal such shifts in the first lines in the same way that Adrienne Rich does in her stanzas.

The *refrain* is closely associated with lyrics written for singing. All but the simplest stanza forms depend on the written page for their identification, as do cantos. But the refrain can be detected easily by ear alone.

Refrains in ballads are a simple example. There, a line or two is repeated either after each verse (stanza) or at regular intervals such as every three verses. In Lisel Mueller's "Night Song" (p. 110) the recurring phrase is used as a refrain in almost every line, but if you look closely you will see subtle variations in each stanza.

Traditional Verse Forms

There are many verse forms that provide the poet with a certain pattern of meter, rhyme, syllables, refrains, or other structural elements. These are sometimes called *fixed forms*. While some poets find them restrictive, others find them a pleasure and even liberating in that the demands of the form may, like metered verse, suggest new directions in thought and phrasing.

Traditional verse forms need not be complex or demanding. The haiku, discussed in Chapter 7, is a simple system of syllabics in which the first line has five syllables, the second has seven, and the third has five. There is no meter involved and generally no rhyme.

Like many fixed verse forms, the haiku has a *convention* associated with it which one can make use of or ignore. The classical haiku dating from the eighteenth century in Japan often makes use of an image from nature and suggests one of the four seasons. But these conventions are not a part of the form, which specifies only the pattern of syllables in each line.

The *ballad* is a longer, looser form associated with narrative poetry and verse to be sung. The ballad stanza is a quatrain which alternates lines of iambic tetrameter with iambic trimeter. The rhyme scheme is *abcb*. Early ballads tended to be simple in plot with lively action reported by someone outside the story. Ballads today often follow those conventions.

Coleridge adapted the ballad form to develop a highly sophisticated poem in "The Rime of the Ancient Mariner." Although he allowed himself occasional variations in traditional ballad meter, here is a dramatic stanza that contains only one rather inconspicuous substitution.

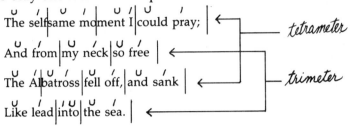

Although Coleridge used the ballad form to create a complex work, we still tend to think of ballads as entertaining stories set to verse, often with musical accompaniment. When selecting a verse form, it is generally a good idea to use one that harmonizes with the tone and subject matter you have in mind.

The *sonnet* is a metered and rhymed poem of fourteen lines, almost always in iambic pentameter. Unlike the ballad, it is not really long enough to tell a rambling story, but it has sufficient length to develop far more intricate statements than the haiku.

There are two types of sonnet. The *Elizabethan sonnet* is the form made famous by Shakespeare. It can be thought of as three quatrains and a final rhyming couplet: *abab, cdcd, efef, gg*. The first eight lines are referred to as the octave and the last six as the sestet. Often there is some shift of mood at the beginning of the sestet, providing poetic tension. In these cases, the unity of the poem is established with the resolution in the final rhyming couplet.

The *Italian sonnet* is also made up of fourteen lines of iambic pentameter, but it is usually arranged as two quatrains and two triplets: *abba, abba; cde, cde*.

One tends to associate the sonnet with earlier literary periods, but the form has such versatility that many contemporary poets have used it. John Berryman, for example, known primarily for his free verse, wrote 115 sonnets, all in the Italian form. "I Lift" (the title is taken from the first line) is printed without commentary on page 110. Read it now to catch the contemporary flavor of the phrasing. Then examine the structure by studying the annotated version below. Normally a sonnet is printed as a solid block or with a single break between the octave and the sestet, but I have divided the various rhyming units to highlight the construction.

quatrain

I lift—lift you five States away your glass,   (a)

Wide of this bar you never graced, where none (b)

Ever I know came, where what work is done   (b)

Even by these men I know not, where a brass   (a)

quatrain

Police-car sign peers in, wet strange cars pass,   (a)

Soiled hangs the rag of day out over this town,   (b)

A juke-box brains air where I drink alone,   (b)

The spruce barkeep sports a toupee alas—   (a)

triplet

My glass I lift at six o'clock, my darling,   (c)

As you plotted . . Chinese couples shift in bed,   (d)

We shared today not even filthy weather,   (e)

triplet

Beasts in the hills their tigerish love are snarling,   (c)

Suddenly they clash, I blow my short ash red,   (d)

Grey eyes light! and we have our drink together.   (e)

Although a lament for an absent love is an old, well-used theme, Berryman achieves originality through specific, contemporary details and a slightly blurred, as-if-intoxicated style. In general, the sonnet provides a form that lends itself to a great variety of themes and moods—from light to serious.

The *villanelle* is the most complex verse form I will discuss in this text. It has some of the intricacy of a crossword puzzle, but its repetitions have a haunting quality which can be highly effective.

The poem has nineteen lines divided into five triplets and a final quatrain. Like the sonnet, it is usually written in iambic pentameter. Simple enough so far. But unlike the sonnet, there are only two rhymes. The pattern is a somewhat demanding *aba, aba, aba, aba, aba, abaa*. As you can see, it is a good idea to select rhyme endings that are rich in choice. It is not considered dishonest to use a rhyming dictionary.

There is one more requirement: The first line is used as a refrain which is repeated to form lines 6, 12, and 18; and the third line is repeated to form lines 9, 15, and 19. This means that those two refrains appear alternately as the last line of each stanza until the end of the poem (lines 18 and 19), where they are used together as a couplet. The refrains are used like the chorus of a song to enhance unity.

"The Waking" by Theodore Roethke (p. 100) is a villanelle. The opening phrase, "I wake to sleep," is central. It suggests that life is a gradual waking followed by death, an eternal sleep. He goes on to say that with this in mind he will prolong this waking process as long as he can: ". . . take my waking slow." This key concept is, because of the villanelle form, repeated in the even-numbered stanzas: second, fourth, and sixth.

The other key concept is that one gains experience simply by moving through life toward inevitable death: "I learn by going where I have to go." This is repeated in the odd-numbered stanzas, three and five, as well as in the final stanza.

If you look at how these two key concepts are used, you will see how the seeming complexity of the form allows a poet to highlight certain themes. Form and content work together.

Here are the first two stanzas with annotations showing the meter and those two refrains that are repeated alternately in the other stanzas:

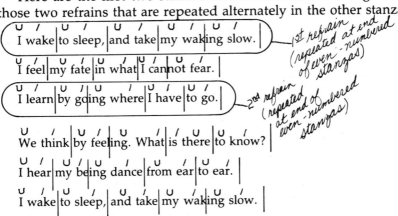

If you look carefully at the whole poem printed on page 100, you will notice that Roethke takes certain minor liberties with the form. Some of the rhymes, for example, are slant rhymes, and one of the refrains is subtly altered (without giving up the pentameter). But he is essentially faithful to the form, and if you enjoy this kind of challenge you will want to match his fidelity.

Why bother? The parallel with music is helpful here. Form in varying degrees gives structure, and a basic structure gives pleasure. It's as simple as that. Each composer or poet has a different view of the ideal balance between form and free flight, but most poetry, like most music, is based on recognizable units that contribute to a sense of overall unity.

Revising to Achieve Unity

Let your mind run free in those early drafts. Explore your emotions. Discover your own true feelings. Try different versions until it "sounds right." Just when you finally feel satisfied and a bit pleased with yourself, look over your work with a cool, critical eye.

Try to determine what is holding your poem together. Are there clusters of related images? Do they harmonize? Should they be trimmed or expanded upon? Is the structure of the poem as a whole based on some type of contrast? Are the divergent elements brought together into some type of unity? Perhaps the poem is essentially a narrative sequence. If so, how much of this story is essential? Have you left out important aspects? What is your true theme? Will readers be able to share it with you?

In some cases your poem will suggest two different meanings. This is an *ambiguity*. If it is merely a thematic confusion or an unresolved contradiction, the poem will fail. But if you can draw the two themes together so that they suggest a broader, more profound insight (as does Dylan Thomas in "Fern Hill"), then the ambiguity may be highly effective.

Next, take a close look at the visual aspect: What kind of cues have you given the reader? If it is a metered poem, have you made full use of the form? If it is a free verse, are there ways you can highlight the structure of the poem through breaks between the lines or indentations?

When you ask questions like these, you can begin to decide what to cut, what to add, and where to rearrange. You may find that there are extraneous elements left over from the experience itself that only clutter the poem. On the other hand, there may be aspects that are clear enough in your own mind but are not yet revealed in the poem. Keep reading your early drafts as if you were a stranger to the material: How are others going to react to what you have on the page? Will it really pull together for them? Yes, you want to be true to your feelings, but a poem is not entirely private property. It belongs in part to your readers. For their sake, make sure that the various elements coalesce to create a unified work of art.

10 DEVELOPING AS A POET

The *three requirements* of continuing development: *reading*
poetry critically, *writing* regularly, *evaluating* your own work
honestly; the *basic critical questions* that lead to effective
revision; drawing from the *fellowship of poets*.

Poetry won't support you financially, but it can enrich you in other ways. If
you make the effort, it can become an important and valuable part of your
life. Like playing the violin, painting, or any other artistic endeavor, a commitment to poetry is self-reinforcing: The more you do to expand your
abilities, the more it does to expand your life.

Developing as a poet is a continuing process and a complex one.
Publication is certainly a legitimate lure; but if it becomes the sole motive,
you may end up manufacturing a product to be sold. When you place that
much emphasis on the marketplace, you may neglect the development of
your own voice.

How do you nurture true development? There are three equally important aspects to the process. If you ignore any one, growth will probably
be hampered and eventually there will not be enough satisfaction to continue.
The first of these essentials is reading published poetry critically; the second

is writing regularly; and the third is learning how to evaluate your own work objectively. Each of these deserves careful consideration.

Reading Poetry Critically

Poets read the work of other poets. Serious poets read poetry seriously—that is, critically. This does not mean that they are necessarily critical in the negative sense—wonder, admiration, and sheer envy all have their place; but it does mean that they read analytically.

Is there a risk that you will become imitative? Not if you read widely. And consider the alternative: If you do not read other poets, you will end up imitating yourself, a sterile route. Besides, occasional imitation of poetry you admire is an effective form of study. Even if the result remains in your journal, the process brings you close to the original. When you return to your own work, you will draw on what you have learned.

When students tell me that they are "very serious" about poetry, I don't ask how much they have written; I ask what was the last volume of poetry they read and what poetry journal they subscribe to. This isn't intended as a put-down. It is merely based on what I have observed: Developing poets are readers even when they are not taking courses.

How do you find out what to read? If you are in school, take literature courses. Don't shun work written in earlier periods. It all has a bearing on your own work. If you are not taking classes, buy anthologies and read poetry journals. Find out what poets speak to you, then order collections of their work. Expensive? No more so than records and tapes of music or a dinner for two.

Reading critically requires a little more concentration than reading passively. It means applying what you have drawn from this and other analytical texts to what you are reading. It means marking up your own copy or photocopies of work printed in library books. It means commenting on these poems in your journal—not just likes and dislikes, but analytical aspects.

In short, when you read poetry critically you adopt those poets as your teachers. You will enjoy the works of some more than others, but you will learn from them all if you respond as a fellow poet.

Writing Regularly

Poets write regularly. Even when they have full-time jobs, they write regularly. Even when they have children or financial problems or are splitting up with their partners, they write. I have met poets who get up at 5 A.M. to write before going to work and others who reserve the late hours of the night for composition. But they write. Regularly.

True, a busy schedule does not allow for long blocks of time. But one of the blessings of poetry is that it doesn't necessarily require lengthy work sessions. Unlike a novelist, a poet can often recapture the mood of an unfinished poem in minutes and make good use of a spare half hour a day. Thirty minutes a day may be frustratingly brief, but for most it is more productive than having a whole day for work once a week. Poems are small, intense works, and they can take root in the chinks that exist even in a tight schedule.

For most poets, even writing incomplete or fragmentary work on a regular basis is ultimately more fruitful than waiting for a summer vacation. Fragments have a way of generating work that can be developed. Waiting for ideal working time generates nothing.

Evaluating Your Own Work

Neither reading carefully nor writing regularly will help you to develop as a poet if you don't learn to examine your own work objectively. Too many would-be poets maintain such faith in intuitive writing that they insulate themselves against change and growth.

Evaluating your own work starts with asking the right questions. It is often helpful to have the reactions of a fellow poet or a group, but make sure that you are turning to individuals who read poetry. Well-meaning friends may not know what questions to ask or how to advise. As a result, they tend to respond subjectively. "I like it," one may say. "It doesn't do much for me," another says. "Well," a third says, "it works for me. Sort of." Reactions like these will tell you more about the speaker than about your poem.

The kind of criticism that will be the most help to you as a practicing poet will be highly specific. It will focus on phrasing, on imagery, on rhythm. What you as writer need to find out is precisely what came through to the reader. In the process you may learn what didn't come through as well.

A helpful critic might say something like this: "Your three opening images are really dramatic and got me into the poem, but I lost track of them later. I don't see what you are doing with them. And I can't hear any sound devices in this poem." You may be tempted to use the well-worn defense, "That's the way I intended it." But resist that impulse! Ask yourself whether it might be possible to develop those opening images and whether you could do more with the sounds of the poem.

There is a distinct advantage to having your poem discussed by a group rather than evaluated by a single reader. No matter how specific and articulate your reader is, personal feelings may affect the critique. With a group you can weigh what is a chance misreading against what is a general impression. If several readers feel your poem is too static and needs some kind of tension in tone or attitude, that is worth more careful consideration than if only one had that feeling. This is not to say that you should blindly follow majority rule, but it is important to understand how your work is being perceived by a number of careful readers.

Valuable as group reaction is, the final decisions are yours alone. You have to be able and willing to ask yourself the kind of critical questions that will lead to improvement.

The Basic Critical Questions

Here are six questions often asked in writing classes by individual readers who know how to help a poet. They are also questions you will find helpful in analyzing your own work. I present them not as a simple checklist but as a description of the range of concerns that will be important to you as you revise. Eventually they will become internalized.

Each of these topics has been the subject of at least one chapter, though the order here has been changed slightly. The discussion of every poem will vary with the work and with the inclination of the group, but it is often helpful to begin with those aspects that strike the reader first—key images, for example. The more complex concerns, such as tone, unity, and theme, are sometimes best postponed until later in the discussion.

First, *are the images effective?* In a difficult poem, isolated images may be all that reaches the reader the first time through. These may be vivid visual details used for their own sake, or they may be vehicles for metaphors; but the poet needs to know what has really made an impression. It is mainly by listening to the reactions of others that you will be able to judge for yourself what is a fresh image and what is bland, flat, or too familiar.

Second, *is the diction fresh?* The concern here shifts to individual words and phrases. Make sure that all your readers have a copy of your work in front of them. They will be looking not only for clichés but for familiar phrasing, echoes from song lyrics, and conventional adjectives that are either unnecessary or poorly selected. If a reader says, "Some of your phrases seem sort of hackneyed," don't get sulky or defensive: ask "Which ones?"

Occasionally critics will tell you that your poem or a part of it seems "prosaic" or "prosy." This may come from using too much abstract language (references to "love" and "trust" when what you had in mind was a particular person); or you may be telling a story without focusing on key images. In either case, encourage your critic to identify specific lines so you can decide whether the problem lies in images, diction, or the degree of compression.

If you are working alone—as you probably will much of the time—you will have to serve as your own critic. These same questions become the basis of your own analysis.

Third, *are there sound devices?* True, some poems depend heavily on sharpness of image and do not make use of such techniques as rhyme, assonance, alliteration, consonance, and onomatopoeia. But if you choose that route, make sure that it is by conscious decision, not forgetfulness.

Occasionally the problem may be just the reverse: sound devices that are obtrusive. As was pointed out in Chapter 5, rhyming couplets can do this, particularly when they are emphasized with regular, end-stopped lines. Contiguous alliteration can also become blatant. Just how much is too much obviously is a matter of individual opinion, but if several readers express the same complaint, the line certainly deserves reconsideration.

Fourth, *does the poem make use of rhythm?* Here again it is important to urge your critics to be as specific as possible. If the poem is metered, where does the meter become monotonous and where, on the other hand, do the metrical substitutions become so numerous that the flow of reading is interrupted? Even if your critic is unable to scan metered poetry, he or she should be able to detect awkwardness in the rhythm. And if the poem is free verse, what rhythmical systems are being used? Don't instruct your critics: let them tell you what they have perceived in their reading.

Rhythm, of course, is closely connected with the sound linkages—rhyme, assonance, alliteration, and the like. You may find it valuable to read your work out loud to your group or, if you are working alone, to yourself. Some poets use cassette recorders for their own work. But it is still important to have copies to look at. As we saw in Chapter 7, some rhythms—particularly in free verse—depend on seeing as well as hearing the work.

Fifth, *what is the tone?* This may surprise you. Those choice samples of wit may have eluded your readers. And what you took most seriously may not have had the impact you intended.

Equally important, you will want to determine whether the tone has developed some kind of tension—one attitude or reaction played against another. If it does not, have you considered all the aspects of your subject? Did you honestly have such a clearly defined attitude? Is there really only one way of looking at the subject? Sometimes what you thought was a finished poem ends up being a portion of a longer, more complex poem involving some kind of contrast or ambivalence.

Sixth, *how is the poem constructed and how do those various parts achieve unity?* Frequently this will turn into a discussion of the poem's theme or central concern. This is important, of course, but it shouldn't obscure the question of how the elements of the poem are put together.

Unity, you remember, can be achieved by the way thoughts or feelings are arranged; it can be augmented by the visual patterns of the stanzas or free-verse typography. Or the poem may be drawn together through a traditional verse form. When we ask the familiar question, "What does this poem mean?" we run the risk of implying that a poem is a philosophical statement with a lot of verbal decoration. When examining a poem—especially your own—try to see the arrangement of elements and the unity of the whole.

Occasionally the tone or even the central theme of a poem may shift as you are working on it. There is no harm in this, but make sure that each line and every image in the new version really belongs there. This is particularly important when your attitude toward your subject has changed between, say, the third and fourth draft. Make sure that your original approach doesn't "show through" as an inconsistency in the later draft.

The Fellowship of Poets

When you take a course in creative writing, you usually draw a good deal from those who share your interests. That sense of fellowship keeps you going. But when you graduate you may feel strangely isolated. Whatever happened to all those who took poetry seriously? Rest assured, however, that there are tens of thousands of people who share your enthusiasms. Anyone who has judged a national poetry contest can tell you that the number of poets in this country is staggering. The problem is not numbers, it is placement. Poets are scattered across a very large country.

You have to make a special effort to bridge the gap between yourself and other poets. If there is a reading in the area, take the time to attend. Better yet, order the latest volume by the poet and study his or her work in advance. The reading will be far more meaningful if you do.

In addition, you may be able to find a poetry group whose members meet regularly to discuss their work. If it is a harmonious, supportive group, you can draw a good deal from it—both in critical insight and in your sense of worth. If you are tempted to start your own group, much will depend on the tone you set at the first meeting. You may wish to use the list of basic critical questions described in this chapter as an initial guide. The most helpful approach is to steer a middle course between excessive politeness on the one hand and potentially damaging bluntness on the other.

Finally, make use of poetry journals. They are edited and supported by people like yourself, and they depend on subscribers for survival. A very brief list of quarterlies appears in Appendix B. Use this as a start, reading sample copies in your local library. As soon as you find which ones you enjoy, subscribe. You will read the poetry much more carefully if you own your own copy, and you can mark up whatever poem you wish. The cost of two subscriptions will be less than a ticket to a rock concert or a trip to the supermarket, and what you get will last a good deal longer.

11 POEMS
FOR STUDY

Lizards and Snakes

ANTHONY HECHT

On the summer road that ran by our front porch
    Lizards and snakes came out to sun.
It was hot as a stove out there, enough to scorch
    A buzzard's foot. Still, it was fun
To lie in the dust and spy on them. Near but remote,   5
    They snoozed in the carriage ruts, a smile
In the set of the jaw, a fierce pulse in the throat
Working away like Jack Doyle's after he'd run the mile.

Aunt Martha had an unfair prejudice
    Against them (as well as being cold   10
Toward bats.) She was pretty inflexible in this,
    Being a spinster and all, and old.
So we used to slip them into her knitting box.
    In the evening she'd bring in things to mend
And a nice surprise would slide out from under the socks.   15
It broadened her life, as Joe said. Joe was my friend.

But we never did it again after the day
    Of the big wind when you could hear the trees
Creak like rockingchairs. She was looking away
    Off, and kept saying, "Sweet Jesus, please   20
Don't let him hear me. He's as like as twins.
    He can crack us like lice with his fingernail.
I can see him plain as a pikestaff. Look how he grins
And swinges the scaly horror of his folded tail."

This Winter Day

MAYA ANGELOU

The kitchen is its readiness
white green and orange things
leak their blood selves in the soup.

Ritual sacrifice that snaps
an odor at my nose and starts   5
my tongue to march
slipping in the liquid of its drip.

The day, silver striped
in rain, is balked against
my window and the soup.   10

We Real Cool

GWENDOLYN BROOKS

The Pool Players.
Seven at the Golden Shovel.

We real cool. We
Left school. We

Lurk late. We
Strike straight. We

Sing sin. We   5
Thin gin. We

Jazz June. We
Die soon.

Merritt Parkway

DENISE LEVERTOV

As if it were
forever that they move, that we
   keep moving—

       Under a wan sky where
     as the lights went on a star   5
         pierced the haze & now
   follows steadily
        a constant
  above our six lanes
  the dreamlike continuum . . .   10

And the people—ourselves!
  the humans from inside the
  cars, apparent
  only at gasoline stops   15
        unsure,
   eyeing each other

      drink coffee hastily at the
    slot machines & hurry
back to the cars
   vanish   20
   into them forever, to
   keep moving—

Houses now & then beyond the
sealed road, the trees / trees, bushes
passing by, passing   25
   the cars that
    keep moving ahead of
  us, past us, pressing behind us
        and
     over left, those that come   30
    toward us shining too brightly
moving relentlessly

  in six lanes, gliding
  north & south, speeding with
  a slurred sound—   35

The Waking

THEODORE ROETHKE

I wake to sleep, and take my waking slow.
I feel my fate in what I cannot fear.
I learn by going where I have to go.

We think by feeling. What is there to know?
I hear my being dance from ear to ear.   5
I wake to sleep, and take my waking slow.

Of those so close beside me, which are you?
God bless the Ground! I shall walk softly there,
And learn by going where I have to go.

Light takes the Tree; but who can tell us how?   10
The lowly worm climbs up a winding stair;
I wake to sleep, and take my waking slow.

Great Nature has another thing to do
To you and me; so take the lively air,
And, lovely, learn by going where to go.   15

This shaking keeps me steady. I should know.
What falls away is always. And is near.
I wake to sleep, and take my waking slow.
I learn by going where I have to go.

"Buffalo Bill's"

E. E. CUMMINGS

Buffalo Bill's
defunct
          who used to
          ride a watersmooth-silver
                              stallion   5

and break onetwothreefourfive pigeonsjustlikethat
                                        Jesus
he was a handsome man
                    and what i want to know is
how do you like your blueeyed boy   10
Mister Death

In a Station of the Metro

EZRA POUND

The apparition of these faces in the crowd;
Petals on a wet, black bough.

Like This Together

ADRIENNE RICH

1.
Wind rocks the car.
We sit parked by the river,
silence between our teeth.
Birds scatter across islands
of broken ice. Another time   5
I'd have said "Canada geese,"
knowing you love them.
A year, ten years from now,
I'll remember this—
this sitting like drugged birds   10
in a glass case—
not why, only that we
were here like this together.

2.
They're tearing down, tearing up
this city, block by block.   15
Rooms, cut in half,
hand like flayed carcasses,
their old roses in rags,
famous streets have forgotten
where they were going. Only   20
a fact could be so dreamlike.
They're tearing down the houses
we met and lived in,
soon our two bodies will be all   25
left standing from that era.

3.
We have, as they say,
certain things in common.
I mean: a view
from a bathroom window
over slate to stiff pigeons   30
huddled every morning; the way
water tastes from our tap,
which you marvel at, letting
it splash into the glass.
Because of you I notice   35
the taste of water,
a luxury I might
otherwise have missed.

4.
Our words misunderstand us.
Sometimes at night   40
you are my mother:
old detailed griefs
twitch at my dreams, and I
crawl against you, fighting
for shelter, making you   45
my cave. Sometimes
you're the wave of birth
that drowns me in my first
nightmare. I suck the air.
Miscarried knowledge twists us   50
like hot sheets thrown askew.

5.
Dead winter doesn't die.
It wears away, a piece of carrion
picked clean at last,
rained away or burnt dry.   55
Our desiring does this,
make no mistake, I'm speaking
of fact: through mere indifference
we could prevent it.
Only our fierce attention   60
gets hyacinths out of those
hard cerebral lumps,
unwraps the wet buds down
the whole length of a stem.

6.
A severed hand   65
keeps tingling, air still suffers
beyond the stump. But new
life? How do we bear it
(or you, huge tree)
when fresh flames start spurting   70
out through our old sealed skins,
nerve-endings ours and not yet ours?
Susceptibilities we still
can't use, sucking
blind power from our roots—   75
what else to do but
hold fast to the
one thing we know,
grip earth and let burn.

Pied Beauty

GERARD MANLEY HOPKINS

Glory be to God for dappled things—
   For skies of couple-colour as a brinded cow;
     For rose-moles all in stipple upon trout that swim;

Fresh-firecoal chestnut-falls; finches' wings;
   Landscape plotted and pieced-fold, fallow, and plough;   5
     And áll trádes, their gear and tackle and trim.

All things counter, original, spare, strange;
   Whatever is fickle, freckled (who knows how?)
     With swift, slow; sweet, sour; adazzle, dim;
He fathers-forth whose beauty is past change: 10
              Praise him.

On a Maine Beach

ROBLEY WILSON, JR.

Look, in these pools, how rocks are like worn change
Keeping the ocean's mint-mark; barnacles
Miser on them; societies of snails

Hunch on their rims and think small thoughts whose strange
Salt logics rust like a mainspring, small dreams   5
Pinwheeling to a point and going dumb,
Small equations whose euphemistic sum
Stands for mortality. A thousand times
Tides swallow up such pools, shellfish and stone
Show green and yellow shade in groves of weed;   10
Rocks shrink, barnacles drink, snails think they bleed
In their trapped world. Here, when the sea is gone,
We find old coins glowing under the sky,
Barnacles counting them, snails spending slow
Round lifetimes half-awake. Beach rhythms flow   15
In circles. Perfections teach us to die.

Fern Hill

DYLAN THOMAS

Now as I was young and easy under the apple boughs
About the lilting house and happy as the grass was green,
　　　　The night above the dingle starry,
　　　　　　Time let me hail and climb
　　　　Golden in the heydays of his eyes,   5
And honoured among wagons I was prince of the apple towns
And once below a time I lordly had the trees and leaves
　　　　　　Trail with daisies and barley
　　　　Down the rivers of the windfall light.

And as I was green and carefree, famous among the barns   10
About the happy yard and singing as the farm was home,
　　　　　　In the sun that is young once only,
　　　　　　Time let me play and be
　　　　Golden in the mercy of his means,
And green and golden I was huntsman and herdsman, the calves 15
Sang to my horn, the foxes on the hills barked clear and cold,
　　　　　　And the sabbath rang slowly
　　　　In the pebbles of the holy streams.

All the sun long it was running, it was lovely, the hay
Fields high as the house, the tunes from the chimneys, it was air 20
　　　　And playing, lovely and watery
　　　　　　And fire green as grass.
　　　　And nightly under the simple stars

As I rode to sleep the owls were bearing the farm away,
All the moon long I heard, blessed among stables, the nightjars   25
      Flying with the ricks, and the horses
        Flashing into the dark.

And then to awake, and the farm, like a wanderer white
With the dew, come back, the cock on his shoulder: it was all
      Shining, it was Adam and maiden,   30
        The sky gathered again
      And the sun grew round that very day.
So it must have been after the birth of the simple light
In the first, spinning place, the spellbound horses walking warm
      Out of the whinnying green stable   35
        On to the fields of praise.

And honoured among foxes and pheasants by the gay house
Under the new made clouds and happy as the heart was long
      In the sun born over and over,
        I ran my heedless ways,   40
      My wishes raced through the house-high hay
And nothing I cared, at my sky blue trades, that time allows
In all his tunefull turning so few and such morning songs
      Before the children green and golden
        Follow him out of grace,   45

Nothing I cared, in the lamb white days, that time would take me
Up to the swallow thronged loft by the shadow of my hand,
      In the moon that is always rising,
        Nor that riding to sleep
      I should hear him fly with the high fields   50
And wake to the farm forever fled from the childless land.
Oh as I was young and easy in the mercy of his means,
      Time held me green and dying
      Though I sang in my chains like the sea.

The Still Voice of Harlem

CONRAD KENT RIVERS

Come to me broken dreams and all
      bring me the glory of fruitless souls,
I shall find a place for them in my gardens.

Weep not for the golden sun of California,
      think not of the fertile soil of Alabama. . .   5
nor your father's eyes, your mother's body twisted
      by the washing board.

I am the hope of your unborn,
      truly, when there is no more of me. . .
there shall be no more of you. . .   10

What the Mirror Said

LUCILLE CLIFTON

listen,
you a wonder,
you a city
of a woman.
you got a geography   5
of your own.
listen,
somebody need a map
to understand you.
somebody need directions   10
to move around you.
listen,
woman,
you not a noplace   15
anonymous
girl;
mister with his hands on you
he got his hands on
some
damn
body!   20

After Spring

CHORA

After spring sunset
Mist rises from the river
Spreading like a flood

Even with Insects

ISSA

Even with insects. . .
Some are hatched out musical. . .
Some, alas, tone-deaf

The Pardon

RICHARD WILBUR

My dog lay dead five days without a grave
In the thick of summer, hid in a clump of pine
And a jungle of grass and honeysuckle-vine.
I who had loved him while he kept alive

Went only close enough to where he was   5
To sniff the heavy honeysuckle-smell
Twined with another odour heavier still
And hear the flies' intolerable buzz.

Well, I was ten and very much afraid.
In my kind world the dead were out of range   10
And I could not forgive the sad or strange
In beast or man. My father took the spade

And buried him. Last night I saw the grass
Slowly divide (it was the same scene
But now it glowed a fierce and mortal green)   15
And saw the dog emerging. I confess

I felt afraid again, but still he came
In the carnal sun, clothed in a hymn of flies,
And death was breeding in his lively eyes.
I started in to cry and call his name,   20

Asking forgiveness of his tongueless head.
. . . I dreamt the past was never past redeeming:
But whether this was false or honest dreaming
I beg death's pardon now. And mourn the dead.

The Bay at West Falmouth

BARBARA HOWES

Serenity of mind poises
Like a gull swinging in air,
At ease, sculptured, held there
For a moment so long-drawn-out all time pauses.

The heart's serenity is like the gold   5
Geometry of sunlight: motion shafting
Down through green dimensions, rung below rung
Of incandescence, out of which grace unfolds.

Watching that wind schooling the bay, the helter-skelter
Of trees juggling air, waves signalling the sun   10
To signal light, brings peace; as our being open
To love does, near this serenity of water.

Canis Major

ROBERT FROST

The great Overdog,
That heavenly beast
With a star in one eye,
Gives a leap in the east.

He dances upright   5
All the way to the west
And never once drops
On his forefeet to rest.

I'm a poor underdog,
But tonight I will bark   10
With the great Overdog
That romps through the dark.

The Guild

SHARON OLDS

Every night, as my grandfather sat
in the darkened room in front of the fire,

the liquor like fire in his hand, his eye
glittering meaninglessly in the light
from the flames, his glass eye baleful and stony,   5
a young man sat with him
in silence and darkness, a college boy with
white skin, unlined, a narrow
beautiful face, a broad domed
forehead, and eyes amber as the resin from   10
trees too young to be cut yet.
This was his son, who sat, an apprentice,
night after night, his glass of coals
next to the old man's glass of coals,
and he drank when the old man drank, and he learned   15
the craft of oblivion—that young man
not yet cruel, his hair dark as the
soil that feeds the tree's roots,
that son who would come to be in his turn
better at this than the teacher, the apprentice   20
who would pass his master in cruelty and oblivion,
drinking steadily by the flames in the blackness,
that young man my father.

Balances

Nikki Giovanni

in life
one is always
balancing

like we juggle our mothers
against our fathers   5

or one teacher
against another
(only to balance our grade average)

3 grains salt
to one ounce truth   10

our sweet black essence
or the funky honkies down the street

and lately i've begun wondering
if you're trying to tell me something

we used to talk all night   15
and do things alone together

and i've begun

(as a reaction to a feeling)
to balance
the pleasure of loneliness   20
against the pain
of loving you

I Lift

JOHN BERRYMAN

I lift—lift you five States away your glass,
Wide of this bar you never graced, where none
Ever I know came, where what work is done
Even by these men I know not, where a brass
Police-car sign peers in, wet strange cars pass,   5
Soiled hangs the rag of day out over this town,
A juke-box brains air where I drink alone,
The spruce barkeep sports a toupee alas—

My glass I lift at six o'clock, my darling,
As you plotted . . . Chinese couples shift in bed,   10
We shared today not even filthy weather,
Beasts in the hills their tigerish love are snarling,
Suddenly they clash, I blow my short ash red,
Grey eyes light! and we have our drink together.

Night Song

LISEL MUELLER

Among rocks, I am the loose one,
among arrows, I am the heart,
among daughters, I am the recluse,
among sons, the one who dies young.

Among answers, I am the question,   5
between lovers, I am the sword,
among scars, I am the fresh wound,
among confetti, the black flag.

Among shoes, I am the one with the pebble,
among days, the one that never comes,   10
among the bones you find on the beach,
the one that sings was mine.

Rhymes for Old Age

CHASE TWICHELL

The wind's untiring saxophone
keens at the glass.
The lamp sheds a monochrome
of stainless steel and linens,
the nurse in her snowy dress   5
firm in her regimens.

The form in the bed
is a soul diminished
to a fledgling, fed
on the tentative balm of spring,   10
sketch for an angel, half-finished,
shoulder blades the stubs of wings.

Darkened with glaucoma,
the room floats on the retina.
The long vowel of *coma*   15
broods in the breath, part vapor.
What has become of the penetralia?
Eau de cologne sanctifies the diaper.

Flood and drag, the undertow.
One slips into it undressed,   20
as into first love, the vertigo
that shrinks to a keepsake of passion.
Sky's amethyst
lies with a sponge in the basin.

Pilot Error
(For Juliet Leventhal Balgley 1914–1965)

ANN Z. LEVENTHAL

The phone rings on a Sunday afternoon.
"There's been an accident," Juliet's
husband says. I go on folding laundry,

matching every corner, every seam
exactly, caressing terry velvet   5
on Sunday, after the phone rings,

I stack the towels, make
of them four piles, four
pillars. "The plane went down,

Juliet's not expected . . . " I shake   10
out socks, press them flat together,
roll them into neat, tight fists.

"I'll get back to you," he says.
I go back to laundry, the white
sheets I pull from the line—day-   15

filled blanks—stiff, cool, I
stretch them wide across my breasts.
Juliet is not like her name, not

fourteen but fifty, and thickly warm
as the furnace that holds off winter.   20
The phone rings. I carry inside

my basket of clean and the phone talks
funeral, me asking when as if there is
still a clock and there is still time.

12 THE SCOPE OF FICTION

Fiction as a mix of *experience and invention; simple versus sophisticated* fiction as seen in *plot, character* and the *five narrative modes;* the *forms* of fiction: short-short story, story, novella, novel; differing *motives for writing* fiction and how they affect the results.

Fiction tells an untrue story in prose. This brief statement indicates just how broad the scope of this genre is. It also defines its boundaries. When a story is told in lines of verse, it becomes narrative poetry. When it is intended to be acted out on the stage, it is drama. And when it is purported to be factually true—that is, openly and consistently based on actual characters and events—we call it notification and describe it with terms like biography, autobiography, historical analysis, and the like.

Blending Experience and Invention

Fiction is "untrue" in the sense that it is at least partly made up. It is an artistic creation that stands on its own no matter how much it may make use of characters, events, and settings from life. When we write fiction, we are free to assume the existence of dragons, unicorns, or life on Mars without being called liars. A story or novel cannot be criticized for being "untrue"; it is judged on whether it *seems* true.

But fiction is also rooted in the actual world—and frequently in the life experiences of the author. A standard legal disclaimer states that "any similarity to persons or places is purely coincidental," but no one who writes fiction takes that seriously. A more honest statement would be that similarities to persons and places are frequent and intentional but generally fragmentary, inconsistent, and disguised with fanciful invention.

This uneven mix of personal experience and invention varies from story to story and within any one work from scene to scene. One character may be an exact likeness of the author's brother and another an almost complete invention. Or the basic incident may be autobiographical while the setting and characters are devised. The age of characters may be radically different from the models on which they were based, and sometimes the sex is reversed.

Once in a while you may have an experience that seems as if it would make a fine short story just as it is. In such cases there is an understandable temptation to use both events and characters directly, without change. Life really does imitate fiction on occasion, and it seems then as if you could capture the moment as if with a video camera. But be careful. If you begin to feel that your first responsibility is to record the episode exactly as it happened, you will start to include irrelevant details and find yourself unwilling to reshape the material. If you hear yourself resisting revision with the plea, "But this is how it really happened," it means that you have become a recorder of events, a reporter. No great sin in that, but you are no longer writing fiction.

To avoid this servitude to events, many authors make a point of altering some aspect of the situation right from the start so that their attention will remain focused on the story as an artistic creation rather than being bound to the original events. The fiction may still draw heavily from the experience, but it won't be limited to it.

At the opposite extreme are stories that are pure invention. Too often, such work is borrowed consciously or unconsciously from other stories, movies, or television. I'll have more to say about that in the next chapter. My point here is simply that drawing from your own life provides a sense of authenticity which we expect in sophisticated fiction.

Sometimes beginning writers avoid using their own experiences because they feel that their lives are too uneventful. Remember, though, that short fiction does not require high drama. Your life is filled with problem solving, minor achievements, betrayals, reversals, and discoveries. You know more about the details than anyone else. And the people you grew up with—friends and relatives—have revealed themselves in interesting ways from time to time. If you learn how to draw on material like this and how to reshape it, you will have discovered how to use one of the basic ingredients of fiction.

Simple versus Sophisticated Fiction

This distinction, described earlier in the poetry section, is crucial for anyone who writes fiction. Essentially, sophisticated works "do" more in the sense that they suggest more, imply a greater range of suggestions, and develop more subtle shadings of meaning than simple works do. This text is concerned with sophisticated writing, but that does not imply that such work is "better." It is simply "other" in the sense that the biologically simple crayfish is different from the far more sophisticated porpoise.

The span between the most simple and relatively sophisticated fiction is enormous. Compare a comic strip about adolescents like *Archie, The Jackson Twins,* or *Gil Thorpe* with a novel about adolescents like Knowles' *A Separate Peace* or Salinger's *Catcher in the Rye.* They are similar in that they are both samples of fiction as I have been defining it—they both tell untrue stories in prose. Further, they both have plot, characters, setting, and themes. And they share certain basic techniques: dialogue, thoughts, action, description, and exposition. They even use the same subject matter: that highly charged period between childhood and adulthood. And before one brands one as "good" and the other as "bad," remember that many intelligent adults read the comics in the morning paper, and *Catcher in the Rye* is still barred from some secondary schools as immoral and unacceptable.

But obviously they are utterly different forms of fiction. Archie as a fictional character is *simple;* so are the stories in which he appears. There is only a limited number of suggestions or implications that can be made from the highly conventional, monotonously repetitive types of situations in which he is placed. On the other hand, Holden Caulfield is a sophisticated character as is the novel in which we come to know him. It is important here to distinguish this literary use of *sophisticated* from its popular use, which describes merely personal characteristics. Mark Twain's Huck Finn, for example, is certainly unsophisticated as an individual, but the complexity and intricacy with which the author presents him is sophisticated.

As in the case of poetry, there are an infinite number of gradations between the simplest forms of fiction and the most sophisticated. Juveniles—stories and novels written for adolescents—are far more intricate in characterization and theme than comic strips. And gothic novels, for all their repetition of plots, have a certain sophistication of vocabulary. But none are intended to be very subtle or insightful compared with a literary novel. In the case of murder mysteries, most of the sophistication takes the form of ingenious plots, but thematically they tend to be fairly simple. They are for most enthusiasts "a quick read." For sophisticated work, one must turn to the literary journals, quarterlies, and the so-called "qualities" like *The Atlantic* and *The New Yorker*, though all of them vary their offerings from relatively accessible pieces to works that, like sophisticated poetry, may require some effort on the part of the reader.

How high should you aim? It would be a mistake to start out by attempting an extremely complex plot and intricate theme. If you have one or two interesting characters and a single, insightful event, you can write a story that is fresh and rewarding.

As you gain experience, you will want to examine what makes some works more sophisticated than others. There are two areas to consider. The first is the *content* of a story, the basic ingredients such as plot, characters, and the like. Second—and equally important to the practicing writer—is the *process* by which a story is presented, as seen in the five *narrative modes* available in fiction: dialogue, thought, action, description, and exposition.

Starting with plot, it is obvious that all fiction, whether simple or sophisticated, is developed through a sequence of actions. Simple fiction, however, not only reduces the complexity of the plot, but it usually avoids originality as well. Simple plots tend to be based on well-used conventions known in the magazine field as "formulas." The pleasure some people derive from, say, husband-tempted-by-widow-next-door-but-finally-returns-to-wife is not the excitement of a fresh experience but, rather, the anesthesia of the safely familiar.

Chapter 15 is devoted entirely to structure, from individual scenes to the construction of plot. The point to remember here, however, is that so-phistication in plot does not necessarily mean complexity. What one aims for is a situation and a sequence of actions that are fresh and subtly suggest a great deal to the reader. The determining factor is how much the reader discovers, not how many twists and turns the synopsis may take.

The same is true with characters. In simple fiction, the characters do a lot, but you never get to know much about them. It is possible to follow the adventures of a comic-strip character for twenty years and still not know her the way one comes to know the character Joanna in "The Nightingales Sing," which appears in this book as Chapter 18.

All fiction has setting, but in simple fiction it is often all too familiar: New York City pieces make use of Madison Avenue or Broadway, San Francisco scenes are "in the shadow of the Golden Gate," and Paris stories have a vista looking out onto the Eiffel Tower. "Originality" frequently takes the form of the exotic: a ski resort high in the Andes, a spy headquarters four hundred feet beneath the House of Parliament, a royal palace constructed entirely in glowing lucite on the planet Octo.

Sophisticated fiction, on the other hand, tends to avoid both the hackneyed and the bizarre. The setting is used as a way of increasing cred-ibility and placing the reader in the center of the story—regardless of whether it is based on an actual place or upon the dreamscape of the author.

Theme is another aspect of fiction that varies with the degree of sophistication. Simple themes suggest truisms that make no more impact on us than the background music in a restaurant. So-called detective magazines and their television counterparts reiterate endlessly, "Crime doesn't pay, but it's exciting to try." Many of television's situation comedies suggest repeatedly that "Nice girls eventually end up with nice boys, but only after being hurt." The fact that we know nice young women who have ended up with terrible husbands and fine young men who never married at all doesn't seem to weaken the popularity of this simple thematic concern. There are others that will be discussed in the next chapter.

Sophisticated fiction tends to have thematic concerns that suggest mixed feelings. Often this takes the form of ambivalence, a blending of love and hate for the same person at the same time. Further complexity is sometimes achieved with irony, a reversal of one's normal expectations.

Whenever you read fiction you evaluate the level of sophistication on the basis of elements like these either consciously or unconsciously. And when you write, they are concerns that will hold your attention at every stage.

In addition to the content of a story, you will want to examine the way the material is presented. For purposes of analysis, it is helpful to see every sentence in a story as presented in one of five different ways or *narrative modes:* dialogue, thoughts, action, description, or exposition.

I will develop the idea of narrative modes further in Chapter 23 because they are a helpful method of looking at a writer's style. I am concerned here with the matter of literary sophistication.

Dialogue and thoughts are two effective ways of suggesting character, and often they are used in tandem so that one sees a contrast between the inner and the outer person. In simple fiction, however, they are often stereotyped—predictable lines for predictable characters.

Action is the dominant mode for simple fiction—particularly adventure stories. But as we will see in the examples included in this text, sophisticated fiction makes significant use of action too. The difference is that as the story begins to gain a greater range of suggestion, the action necessarily must take on a more subtle role of implication. Put another way, action shifts from being an end in itself to being a means of suggestion.

The same is true of description. In a sophisticated story, almost every phrase devoted to describing characters, places, possessions, and the like contributes to the theme or to some aspect of characterization.

The last of these five narrative modes, exposition, is perhaps the most dangerous. In simple fiction it is used to point up the theme as one progresses through the story and, often, to sum it up directly at the end. "Down deep," we are told periodically, "Old Karl had a warm spot in his heart." And in case we missed it, we are given the clincher at the end: "Though his parting words were gruff, there was an undertone of kindness in the old prospector's voice. It was clear that he still knew the meaning of love."

Those who are used to sophisticated fiction grimace at this because it is a familiar convention. It is also close to the technique of the essay. A sophisticated story may use just as much exposition, but it will rarely label the theme that way. This is not because authors want to be evasive, but because the success of literarily sophisticated fiction depends on the degree to which readers have the feeling that they themselves have discovered the thematic suggestions in a story. It is similar to the way we make judgments about people and situations in actual life. We listen to what people say and watch what they do and then we come to conclusions. In fiction, of course, those lines of dialogue and actions are carefully selected by an author, but when we read we like the illusion of discovering significances on our own.

The Forms of Fiction

We talk about fiction as if it falls into four precise categories: the short-short story, the story, the novella, and the novel. These terms are handy, but they are far from precise. There is no sharp line between one length and the next.

When editors call for a *short-short story,* they usually mean a piece from 700 to 2000 words—from about three to eight pages of double-spaced, typed manuscript. Some short-short story contests, however, have a 1000-word limit. Short shorts, as they are called, frequently consist of a single scene with only two characters, though there is no rule about this.

There are two dangers in this form which one should guard against. The first is superficial characterization. With so little length, there is a temptation to settle for stock types rather than fully developed characters. To avoid this, you have to make full use of both action and dialogue to portray characters who are individualized and convincing. The other danger is the trick ending. These can be entertaining the way an anecdote is, but they tend to be a very simple sort of fiction and quickly forgotten. If possible, try to develop a story that has more to offer than a clever turn of events at the end.

The term *short story* usually refers to a work that is from 2000 to 6000 words—from eight to 24 pages. Within that span, the fifteen-to-twenty-page bracket is most frequently seen in print. Again, there is nothing rigid about these lengths, but there are factors that account for their popularity. When one starts writing fiction, the short-short seems appropriate, just as the short musical piece is the best for those learning to play the piano. But with practice many writers begin to feel that the shorter form limits their ability to develop character, interrelationships between characters, setting, and plot. The short-short form begins to feel constricting.

At the upper end of the scale, there are editorial constraints that limit the number of stories in the 30-to-40-page range. For a magazine editor to accept a story of this length means that two or three other stories will have to be rejected to make room. This means less variety in an issue. *The New*

Yorker and a few quarterlies will occasionally print a story of this length, and of course it can be included in a collection, but many authors hesitate to venture into an area in which the chances of publication are severely limited.

The *novella* is halfway between a story and a novel. It is often thought of as between 50 and 150 manuscript pages. Occasionally a magazine will include one or devote a special issue to several, but more often novellas are seen in published collections along with short stories by the same author. Since book publishers are usually unwilling to consider a novel manuscript of less than 200 or 250 pages, there is sometimes a temptation to pad a novella for submission, but too often the result is a thin novel without enough plot and richness of characterization to justify the length.

The *novel* form is really more than just a story that has been expanded beyond 250 pages—or it should be. The length allows an author to do interesting things with the plot and to develop subplots. One can introduce many more characters than in a story or novella, and some of them can change and develop over the course of time. The theme of such a work can be broader and more intricate than in the shorter forms. Of course, not all novels make use of all these assets, but taken together they do represent a substantive difference from the story form.

This is not to suggest that there is some sort of hierarchy, with the short-short designated for beginners and the novel as a goal for the experienced writer. Some excellent writers have worked with short stories exclusively, and some novelists have never even tried shorter forms. Others work with all lengths with equal commitment, just as a composer like Mozart shifted from a short work for the piano alone to a symphony with an equal respect for the opportunities within each form.

Three Motives for Writing Fiction

Both in the poetry section and at the beginning of this chapter I have stressed the fact that sophisticated writing is not "better" than simple works. We have all read well-respected literature—poetry and fiction—that we didn't enjoy; and we have all had times when a simple story, comic strip, or jingle was enjoyable. In this respect, "better" is a personal opinion.

But it should be clear by now that the concern of this book is for writing that is literarily sophisticated. Since this is a skill that takes a good deal of study and practice and does not promise early financial reward, it is important to ask yourself just why you are making the effort. Your motives will significantly affect how you develop as a writer.

There are many reasons for writing fiction, but they tend to fall into three distinct groups. Each has a different set of assumptions and results in a different kind of work.

First, there is the *private motive*. This leads to writing merely for the personal pleasure of the act without any regard for another reader. Often it takes the form of journal entries. Spontaneous and usually unrevised, writing like this is essentially a private act.

Many writers find it helpful to keep a journal regularly or to write from time to time "off the top of one's head." It is for the writer what sketching often is for the painter. But it is a mistake to ask a friend or a writing class to evaluate such work. There is really no way to judge it as "good" or "bad" or even "sophisticated" or "simple." It may be valuable as practice or enjoyable as a release, but it shouldn't be passed off as anything more than that.

Second is the *commercial motive.* In its pure form, commercial writing is the opposite of private writing since it is motivated entirely by outer rather than inner demands. It is writing for others. It is producing a product.

Commercial writers usually define their work as a craft rather than an art, and their primary goal is monetary reward. They produce entertainment. They study the market carefully and invest their time and energies in those areas that seem to have potential profit. Many spend more of their time writing nonfiction than they do fiction since the demand is greater.

The fiction produced by commercial writers tends to be conservative in theme and conventional in style mainly because that is what readers of many large-circulation magazines pay for. Like businesspeople, their goal is to supply what the market wants. Although there is a tendency for literarily-minded individuals to be scornful of such writers for shaping their fiction to meet the demands of a particular magazine or publisher, commercial writing is an honest profession that fills a need.

The third is the *literary motive.* Although it generates most of the fiction one reads in school and college, it is perhaps the most misunderstood. Writers in this area are like painters, sculptors, and composers who value the quality of the work they produce. Having an audience is obviously important, and being paid for one's efforts seems only fair; but making money is not the principle drive. Because of this, they do not generally tailor their work to meet the whims of the public, nor do they cater to commercial markets. They measure their efforts against what they consider to be the best fiction they have read.

Because literary writers require readers who have relatively sophisticated taste and experience, they must often (though not always) be content with a relatively small audience. Their novels may not be best sellers, and their short stories frequently appear in "little magazines" that have small circulations and cannot pay their contributors lavishly. Many have to do something else for their major source of income. But they have a special satisfaction in knowing that they are reaching readers who will spend time with their work and will react to it with some sensitivity. In addition, they are working in one of the few areas where they do not have to compromise. For many, this is very important.

The literary motive is sometimes difficult for nonwriters to understand. It helps, though, to compare the literary writer with the opera singer who knows that rock singers earn ten times as much. Opera continues not because its performers like being paid less but because this is what they do best and enjoy the most.

Every writer—like every artist in the broadest sense—is driven by a combination of all three motives. Those who are primarily concerned with sophisticated writing, however, share a respect for literature as something of value in itself. With this as a base, there is no end of possibilities for fresh creativity.

13 THE SOURCES OF FICTION

Sterile sources: the *"seven deadly sins"*; *fruitful sources*: drawing on *experience*, including family relationships, friends and acquaintances, moments of growth and discovery; the *metamorphosis of experience* to reshape experience into fictional form.

When a short story seems hackneyed, trite, or lacking in credibility, the fault often rests with the source from which it was developed. Like an omelet, fiction depends on fresh ingredients.

Unfortunately, our memories are cluttered with old plots, characters, and settings half recalled from what we have read and seen on television and in the movies. It is all too easy to draw on this material, often quite unconsciously. Like clichés, these conventional patterns can reduce a piece of writing to the simplest level. As soon as readers recognize the familiar ruts, they slip into that glazed half-attention with which one often watches an imitative television drama or listens to background music at a restaurant.

To guard against such borrowings, this chapter begins with what may be for some a rather discouraging list of prohibitions. It is followed by more positive suggestions for finding good material for fiction. Here, then, are the "seven deadly sins" of fiction which seem to do the most damage in the early stages of fiction writing.

The High-tech Melodrama.   A melodrama is any piece of fiction or drama that is overloaded with dramatic suspense. Unlike true drama, it is overdone. The competitive nature of television keeps many scriptwriters hovering on the border between drama and melodrama.

Everyone has a slightly different view of just where that line should be drawn; but regardless of labels, so-called suspense thrillers tend to have certain standard ingredients. Whether the protagonist is a solo detective, a cop, or a vice squad member, the props usually include both guns and late-model cars, and the plot turns out to be, at the mildest, some version of search-and-capture. More often, it's search-and-destroy. The high-speed chase is repeated as regularly as was the shoot-out in westerns of a decade ago. Replacing the magnum with a laser and moving the chase to another galaxy may be a challenge for the special-effect department, but the plot is remarkably similar, and the characters seem to speak the same lines. These scripts are referred to as *formula writing*.

All this can be good fun, but it is far from subtle. And when one borrows any portion of it for a fictional form as brief and essentially fragile as a short-short story, what was intended as high drama turns into inadvertent humor.

It is easy enough to avoid conscious borrowing, but unconscious influences can do damage as well. Remember that if you have watched five television dramas a week for four years (well below the national average), you have absorbed 1040 separate (but similar) plots, at least 3120 attempts at characterization, and the equivalent of 20,800 pages of dialogue. It is true that not much of this material was studied carefully, but the repetition of plot types, stock characters, and highly formal patterns of diction and syntax presented in a day-to-day sequence provide stiff competition for the literary fiction you have read during the same period.

It is not guns and uniforms by themselves that present the problem. If you have gone hunting, served on a police force, or been in the military, you should explore those experiences for fictional material that is genuine and manageable. The problem arises when you borrow material from scriptwriters who themselves are borrowing from a convention. Watch out for characters—male and female—who maintain their cool in times of stress and reveal nothing of themselves. Guard against that too-easy dichotomy between the good and the bad. Keep asking yourself: Where did I get this stuff? Is it really mine?

The Adolescent Tragedy.   The adolescent period is an excellent one for sophisticated fiction as long as you keep your material genuine and fresh in detail. But there are three dangerous pitfalls: lack of perspective, unconscious borrowing from slick and conventionalized fiction, and sentimentality.

Lack of perspective occurs when the experience is too fresh. In such cases, you find yourself *in* the story rather than *above* it. You cannot control it. This may well be your problem if you find yourself calling your fictional characters by the names of their nonfictional counterparts. Another sign is when you find yourself reluctant to change the plot because "that's not the way it happened."

To avoid this lack of perspective, make sure that enough time has elapsed between the event and your attempt to convert it into fiction. The more emotional the experience, the more time will be required to gain some measure of detachment.

Unconscious borrowing from slick fiction is sometimes as difficult to spot as influences from television. But it does happen. Those who do not read stories in the women's magazines may find themselves reaching back to conventionalized plots half-remembered from comics like *Mary Worth*. Whenever one detects the slightest borrowing from such sources, it is important to ask, "Where did the rest of this come from?" Not only the plot but types of characters, lines of dialogue, and even descriptive details may be contaminated.

Sentimentality, the third danger in writing about adolescents, may come from secondary sources like magazines and television or may just as easily come from the simple desire to move the reader. The difference between the sentimental story and one that is genuinely moving is a matter of sophistication. When a story is simple and rigged to short-circuit the emotions of the reader, we say it is sentimental. These are the stories in which the lonely, misunderstood little boy, the plain little girl with glasses, the cripple, the blind girl, the son of alcoholics are placed in some pitiable situation—any cold street corner will do, but a bombed-out village is better—simply to evoke tears.

But what if you really were the plain little girl with glasses or the son of alcoholics? The fact that the background is from life is never an excuse for fiction that *seems* like a sentimentalized treatment. Your job will be to find those unusual details or to explore ambivalences that will break the mold and convince the reader that this is a genuine experience.

The Poe Gimmick.   Edgar Allan Poe was a master of the strange, the bizarre, and the surprise ending. His stories remain popular, but they provide poor models for contemporary writers.

There are several reasons why warmed-over Poe is generally unsuccessful. The first is historical: Poe was working in a period when the modern short story as an independent genre was just being born. His tricks were fresh and truly surprised his readers. But today we expect more genuine characterization, more complexity of theme. Stories influenced by his work seem unconvincing.

Tricky and ingenious plots still have entertainment value, of course, and are still used in film and television dramas. You can see the Poe tradition in *Twilight Zone* reruns: The nearsighted book lover, for example, who is the sole survivor after World War III and discovers an undamaged library for his uninterrupted use. As he runs toward the treasured books he—you guessed it—trips and breaks his glasses.

The limitation of such stories is that plot dominates subtlety of theme and characterization. In some cases, most of the story is merely a buildup to the concluding scene or punch line. It can be as entertaining as a well-told joke, but there is little opportunity to develop characterization or anything more than the simplest theme.

In other cases Poe's tales created a dreamlike melodrama. "The Pit and the Pendulum" and "Ms. Found in a Bottle" are good examples. But while melodrama continues to have a certain popularity, it has been taken over by films. In general, contemporary fiction looks for insight rather than bizarre effects.

Mock Faulkner.   None of us can help being influenced by our favorite modern author, but excessive imitation—either conscious or unconscious—deprives us of our own voice at best and sometimes results in unintended satire. Hemingway's sparse style can be a problem, but Faulkner's opaque scenes of southern decadence and occasional violence simply self-destruct when imitated in short stories. My favorite example is an early attempt at fiction by a college sophomore who managed to pack into a single story a seduction, a rape, a case of incest, and a suicide—all in 2000 words. Grim as the subject matter and the author's intention were, the result was a hilarious burlesque.

The origin of that story was not Faulkner's work, but a corrupted memory of selected passages. There was no awareness of the intricate structure of a Faulknerian novel in which violence, when it does occur, is woven into the fabric of the entire work.

In addition, the author failed to understand the relationship between the length of a story and the degree of violence it can contain without spilling over into the area of melodrama. In long works one can prepare for a dramatic scene which would simply shatter a shorter piece.

By way of specific example, it is worth nothing Faulkner's "Dry September" and J. F. Powers' "The Eye." Both stories involve a brutal lynching. Both stories mute the degree of violence by refusing to describe directly the actual lynching scene. Neither author can be accused of literary cowardice. Inclusion of the lynch scenes in these two stories would have overloaded the circuit and the result would have been melodrama. Implying the horror can sometimes be more effective than describing it directly.

The Yuppie Gone Wrong.   This is one of the most common patterns in college writing courses. The protagonist is a young, upwardly mobile individual who has put career and love of material objects ahead of personal relationships and spiritual values. He drives a Porsche, has a Jacuzzi, lives in Silicon Valley or some mythical place with the same climate.

These are moral tales, starting with scenes of single-minded attention to professional advancement and ending with drink, drugs, or a bullet—sometimes all three.

The yuppie tragedy is the successor to an earlier model in which the protagonist is older, high in the corporate hierarchy, drives a Cadillac rather than an imported car, and works at a desk with three telephones. He is married—though unhappily—and has one child, just entering college. This hard-driving executive also sees his life crumble about him and, despite the affections of his secretary, takes his life in the standard manner.

It would be nice to think that such plots are inspired by novels like Theodore Dreiser's *An American Tragedy* or stories like F. Scott Fitzgerald's "Winter Dreams," both of which build convincing characters with some of these characteristics. But it seems more likely that the source is television.

In keeping with the times, the yuppie plot is occasionally refashioned with a young woman as unhappy protagonist. But if the original concept was hackneyed, the revised version will be no better. The problem with these stories is not that such characters don't exist but that the fictional version is based on an imitation which in turn is based on an imitation.

But suppose you knew a hard-driving individual who really did own a Porsche and tragically did commit suicide? It still would be a risky incident for fiction. Suicide is generally too big and complex a subject to handle convincingly in a short short. You may have to substitute some more subtle indication of a character's sense of defeat and despair. As for the other details, sometimes you have to revise life's events to keep them from echoing the conventions of simple fiction.

The Trials and Tribulations of the Incorruptible Writer.   The protagonist walks up and down the beach, planning a great novel. He resists the invitations of fun-loving friends and spurns an offer to join a major advertising firm. In the end, he sticks to his principles.

Or perhaps he is in New York and will not change a word of a novel he has already written. Or he is in Los Angeles and is torn between writing a great novel and being paid a fortune to write hack scripts.

I don't know where these come from—certainly not television—and I have to admire the spirit. But they make very poor fiction. They are literarily simple because they pit the good against the bad in a sadly unrealistic fashion. In some cases the hero is so wooden you can't help hoping he or she will "go Hollywood," make a fortune, and live happily ever after.

The Free-Flying Fantasy.   This is the last of the seven fictional sins. Although it is not derived from the traditions of commercial writing or television, it has a long and tired history and is perhaps the most dangerous item on our list.

In the 1920s it was called "automatic writing." Writers simply typed whatever came into their heads for three hours and saved the final fifteen pages as a "story." Occasionally they were published, but no one has republished them. They tended to be rather boring.

There was another flurry of interest in the late 1960s when it was defended as "literary tripping," an hallucinogenic voyage on paper. Again, it was generally more fun to write than to read.

This technique of aimless composition is not to be confused with *stream-of-consciousness* writing. The latter, made famous by James Joyce, is designed to give the illusion of entering the mind of a fictional character. It is presented as a part of a story, not as a display of the author's own psyche. It is a literary device.

Automatic writing, on the other hand, is very much a private act. It may be therapeutic and it may later suggest the beginnings of a short story, but by itself it belongs in your journal.

These, then, are seven of the most common causes for failure in short stories. They shouldn't discourage you. One of the primary functions of this text is to reduce the difficult period of trial and error in the creative process and to help you move on to the aspects of writing that are more intricate and individual. If you keep in mind how important it is to start with fresh and honest material, you will be ready to examine more fruitful sources.

Drawing on Experience

As I pointed out in the previous chapter, experience is the most reliable source for fiction. It is your best safeguard against work that is unconvincing. If personal experience is used selectively and honestly, it will provide a valuable sense of authenticity.

This is particularly true for those who are just beginning to write fiction. As you gain experience, you learn how to keep one foot in the circle of familiarity while reaching out with the other. Memories of a summer job on a construction crew, for example, might allow you to explore what it would be like to be foreman or, pushed further, a civil engineer in conflict with the foreman. Some of the more demanding moments of baby-sitting might serve as the basis for a story dealing with the life of a single parent. At the outset, however, it is wise to stay relatively close to the original experience.

Finding a good incident with which to work may come easily. But often it will not. Even experienced writers have dry periods. Since "waiting for inspiration" is just a romantic way of describing procrastination, it is important to learn how to look for material in a constructive way. Here are some areas that are worth exploring.

Family relationships are natural subjects for fiction. Everyone has had either parents or foster parents; everyone has experienced in some proportion that mixture of love and resentment that is a natural part of that relationship. And that instable balance is normally in constant flux. In very general terms, it is apt to be a progression from idealization through disillusionment to a new acceptance usually based on a fairly realistic evaluation. But this is a vast oversimplification, and stories based on a simple thematic statement of "The day I discovered my father was no saint" are apt to turn out thin and unconvincing. The writer has to probe deeper in order to discover and dramatize those unique shifts in attitude. Often it is some *specific* characteristic of, say, the father, altered in some slight but significant way, that lends itself to good fiction.

In addition to child-parent relationships, there are a variety of other intrafamily attitudes that also shift significantly: brother and sister, two sisters and a maiden aunt, two brothers and their cousin, a daughter dealing with a stepfather, the reactions of three brothers to their uncle. Relationships like these keep shifting in real life, and the shifts are remembered because something was done (action) or said (dialogue) or thought in such a way as to dramatize the change. To some degree you can use such relationships directly, but often you will have to metamorphose experience into something related but different—a process I will explain shortly.

Relationships between girls and boys and men and women are used repeatedly in fiction, and there are hackneyed situations that you should avoid. But in most cases you can find a safe path by asking these two essential questions: What *really* happened? And what was there about the action, the thoughts, the outcome that was truly unique? Of course there are those situations which at first glance seem too close to clichés to be credible or interesting. Occasionally lovers really do patch up quarrels while standing on the shore of Lake Placid under a full moon in June. But not often. You may have to douse the moon, change the name of the lake, and give the characters some uneasiness about that reconciliation if the story is to take on a sense of authenticity.

Some of the best relationships to examine are those with individuals who are much younger or older. The greater the gap in age, the more difficult it may be to enter the mind of the other individual. But you can always write the story from the point of view of the character who is about your own age.

A different way of stimulating your memory is to recall moments of intensity. Often these involve some kind of discovery about yourself or another person. As you examine the event (a good use for a journal), you may not really understand why the experience has remained so vivid in your memory. But you can be sure that if it is still clear there must have been some special meaning in it for you.

Such a memory may be fragmentary. Settings like a particular shopping plaza, a playing field or vacant lot where you used to play, a view from a car window, or a kitchen seen only once often stand out with extraordinary sharpness. They have remained for a reason.

Characters (not to be confused with "characters" who are held to be "unforgettable" by the *Reader's Digest*) may remain in your mind only from an overheard conversation or a quick glimpse: a subway attendant, a store clerk, a hitchhiker, or an auto mechanic. And incidents do not even have to be directly connected with the observer. They may involve an argument overheard in a supermarket; the smashing of a window; an automobile accident; or the playful flirtation of a girl and three boys on a beach, a park, or a parking lot.

One of the first things to do with such a memory-fragment is to recall every possible detail: the visual minutiae, the sounds, and the intricacies of your own feelings. From these you may discover why that particular experience remained in your memory while so many others drifted beyond recall. The final story may or may not include you as a character, and it will probably be far removed from the facts of the original episode, but it will have the advantage of being rooted in a genuine and personally significant experience.

Metamorphosis of Experience

Finding an episode that might serve as the basis for a short story is only the first step. Deciding which aspects to use, which to reject, and what to add is the next step. This radical reshaping of the original incident usually comes before one even begins writing. It is called metamorphosing experience.

Some metamorphosing may have already occurred unconsciously. The mind often works as a censor, weeding out what you don't want to reveal, reshaping memories for peace of mind. If you can, try to identify such changes and make sure they aren't hiding aspects of the experience that would add variety or insight to the fiction. Once again, ask yourself, "Is that how it *really* happened?" and "Is that how I *really* felt?"

Conscious metamorphosing, however, often moves you away from the experience and toward a unified story. Daily life, after all, is apt to be a continuing clutter of events. One of the functions of fiction is to transform this confusion into patterns that have order and relevance without appearing to be contrived. Metamorphosing is a process of cutting out that which is incidental, transforming that which is inappropriate, and adding new material. It precedes the actual writing. Don't confuse it with revising, an important step which comes after you have completed the first draft. Since the metamorphosis of experience determines the basic ingredients of a story, it is really the beginning of the creative process.

Suppose, for example, the original experience took place on a hot August day on which plans for a family picnic in the country were ruined when the car boiled over in the heart of the city's slums. The thematic elements that have kept the experience itself vivid in the writer's mind may consist of such varied details as a boy's first awareness of his father as a man hopeless in a crisis, a surprising insight into the instability of his parents' relationship, a recognition of a special bond between mother and daughter, the beginnings of social consciousness in the face of an economically repressed community, an introduction to racial distinctions, or an ironic contrast between the narrator's sense of high adventure and his parents' sense of disaster.

A good story can echo all of these themes. But the writer will probably want to focus on just one or two. Here is the first stage of the metamorphosis. If the father and the son are the focus, is there a need for the mother and the sister? Or if the important relationship is between daughter and mother, which of the other characters are really necessary? If social issues are the primary concern, is it necessary to include the tensions that existed between the two adults? This is partly a matter of selecting an aspect of the event and deciding which characters to use.

More radical, the final story may end with no children involved. This would swing the attention directly to the parents. Or the entire family might be dropped in order to build from some minor sequence of events observed while waiting for the car to be repaired. Occasionally all one retains is the flavor of the setting and a few individual details, such as a man's conversation with a woman leaning out of a fifth-floor window or an impatient cab driver waiting for his car to be repaired at the garage.

The first and primary reason for metamorphosing experience, then, is to sharpen the focus and to clarify the literary concerns such as theme, characterization, motivation, tone, and the like.

The second function of literary metamorphosis is the reverse: Occasionally the patterns of experience are too neat, too contrived for fiction. When the theme of a story is blatant, we are acutely aware of an author at work and no longer enter into the story as if it were an extension of experience. It becomes only a trick. And there is nothing to be gained by telling the reader that "it really happened that way." If, for example, the father in the story outlined above really was consistently irascible or without exception dependent on his wife's suggestions, he would become a "flat" character, a cliché of fiction. Variation and further insight would be needed not to clarify characterization but to make it more convincing. Or if the story ended up so obviously in the category of "The day I discovered father was not perfect," one might consider adding other thematic elements so that the reader won't have the feeling that the story has become an extended anecdote.

The third and final justification for these basic transformations is the experience that has not yet been emotionally digested. In many cases it takes us a year or more to recall intense personal experiences with enough objectivity and perspective to use them in fiction. When we are still involved in an experience, we have little ability to shape and refashion it.

In these cases, it is sometimes helpful to break the mold set by the experience itself. This is usually done through an initial metamorphosis of the story. Childhood experiences are sometimes converted in this way by dropping the child and seeing the story through the eyes of an adult; the original setting can be shifted to some completely different place; ages can be changed, even the sex of a character can be shifted; and, most basic of all, what originally came to mind as a minor or secondary theme can be developed as the primary theme of a story. Through this technique, the author can often reestablish control over a story that otherwise might have been only a journal entry.

Occasionally a story idea will come to you that needs no analysis and no radical overhaul. It may be fairly close to experience or it may have been metamorphosed unconsciously. When this happens, move ahead before you lose it!

But whenever you find it difficult to start a story, review the relationships you have had with members of your own family, classmates, people with whom you have worked—any vivid experience. When you have settled on an episode, see if it needs some kind of basic transformation. Decide which characters are important and what we are going to discover about them. Don't let the original experience limit you. Feel free to metamorphose the material from the very start.

When you consider the extraordinary variety of experiences stored in your mind and add to that the infinite number of variations you can devise for each, you can see how each new story is unique. This is the true meaning of *creative* writing.

14 A Story by Stephen Minot

Sausage and Beer

I kept quiet for most of the trip. It was too cold for talk. The car was getting old and the heater hadn't worked for as long as I could remember. My father said he couldn't afford to get it repaired, but he bought us a camping blanket which was supposed to be just as good. I knew from experience, though, that no matter how carefully I tucked it around me the cold would seep through the door cracks and, starting with a dull ache in my ankles, would work up my legs. There was nothing to do but sit still and wonder what Uncle Theodore would be like.

"Is it very far?" I asked at last. My words puffed vapor.

"We're about halfway now," he said.

That was all. Not enough, of course, but I hadn't expected much more. My father kept to his own world, and he didn't invite children to share it. Nor did he impose himself on us. My twin sister and I were allowed to live our own lives, and our parents led theirs, and there was a mutual respect for the border. In fact, when we were younger Tina and I had assumed that we would eventually marry each other, and while those plans were soon revised, the family continued to exist as two distinct couples.

But this particular January day was different because Tina hadn't been invited—nor had Mother. I was twelve that winter, and I believe it was the first time I had ever gone anywhere alone with my father.

The whole business of visiting Uncle Theodore had come up in the most unconvincingly offhand manner.

"Thought I'd visit your Uncle Theodore," he had said that day after Sunday dinner. "Wondered if you'd like to meet him."

He spoke with his eyes on a crack in the ceiling as if the idea had just popped into his head, but that didn't fool me. It was quite obvious that he had waited until both Tina and my mother were in the kitchen washing the dishes, that he had rehearsed it, and that I wasn't really being given a choice.

"Is Tina going?" I asked.

"No, she isn't feeling well."

I knew what that meant. But I also knew that my father was just using it as an excuse. So I got my coat.

The name Uncle Theodore had a familiar ring, but it was just a name. And I had learned early that you just do not ask about relatives who don't come up in adult conversation naturally. At least, you didn't in my family. You can never tell—like my Uncle Harry. He was another one of my father's brothers. My parents never said anything about Uncle Harry, but some of my best friends at school told me he'd taken a big nail, a spike really, and driven it into his heart with a ball peen hammer. I didn't believe it, so they took me to the library and we found the article on the front page of the *Herald* for the previous Saturday, so it must have been true.

But no one at school told me about Uncle Theodore because they didn't know he existed. Even I hadn't any real proof until that day. I knew that my father had a brother named Theodore in the same way I knew the earth was round without anyone ever taking me to the library to prove it. But then, there were many brothers I had never met—like Freddie, who had jointed a Theosophist colony somewhere in California and wore robes like a priest, and Uncle Herb, who was once in jail for leading a strike in New York.

We were well out in the New England countryside now, passing dark, snow-patched farm fields and scrubby woodlands where saplings choked and stunted each other. I tried to visualize this Uncle Theodore as a farmer: blue overalls, straw hat, chewing a long stem of alfalfa, and misquoting the Bible. But it was a highly unsatisfactory picture. Next I tried to conjure up a mystic living in—didn't St. Francis live in a cave? But it wasn't the sort of question I could ask my father. All I had to go on was what he had told me, which was nothing. And I knew without thinking that he didn't want me to ask him directly.

After a while I indulged in my old trick of fixing my eyes on the white lines down the middle of the road: dash-dash-dash, steady, dash-dash again. If you do that long enough, it will lull you nicely and pass the time. It had just begun to take effect when I felt the car slow down and turn abruptly. Two great gates flashed by, and we were inside a kind of walled city.

Prison, I thought. That's it. That's why they kept him quiet. A murderer, maybe. "My Uncle Theodore," I rehearsed silently, "he's the cop killer."

The place went on forever, row after row of identical buildings, four stories, brick, slate roofs, narrow windows with wire mesh. There wasn't a bright color anywhere. The brick had aged to gray, and so had the snow patches along the road. We passed a group of three old men lethargically shoveling ice and crusted snow into a truck.

"This is a kind of hospital," my father said flatly as we drove between the staring brick fronts. I had to take my father's word for it, but the place still had the feel of a prison.

"It's big," I said.

"It's enormous," he said, and then turned his whole attention to studying the numbers over each door. There was something in his tone that suggested that he didn't like the place either, and that did a lot to sustain me.

Uncle Theodore's building was 13-M, but aside from the number, it resembled the others. The door had been painted a dark green for many years, and the layers of paint over chipped and blistered paint gave it a mottled look. We had to wait quite a while before someone responded to the push bell.

A man let us in, not a nurse. And the man was clearly no doctor either. He wore a gray shirt which was clean but unpressed, and dark-green work pants with a huge ring of keys hanging from his belt.

"Hello there, Mr. Bates," he said in a round Irish voice to match his round face. "You brought the boy?"

"I brought the boy." My father's voice was reedy by comparison. "How's Ted?"

"Same as when you called. A little gloomy, maybe, but calm. Those boils have just about gone."

"Good," my father said.

"Funny about those boils. I don't remember a year but what he's had trouble. Funny."

My father agreed it was funny, and then we went into the visiting room to await Uncle Theodore.

The room was large, and it seemed even larger for the lack of furniture. There were benches around all four walls, and in the middle there was a long table flanked with two more benches. The rest was space. And through that space old men shuffled, younger men wheeled carts of linen, a woman visitor walked slowly up and down with her restless husband—or brother, or uncle. Or was *she* the patient? I couldn't decide which might be the face of madness, his troubled and shifting eyes or her deadened look. Beyond, a bleak couple counseled an ancient patient. I strained to hear, wanting to know the language of the place, but I could only make out mumbles.

The smell was oddly familiar. I cast about; this was no home smell. And then I remembered trips with my mother to a place called the Refuge, where the lucky brought old clothes, old furniture, old magazines, and old kitchenware to be bought by the unlucky. My training in Christian charity was to bring my chipped and dented toys and dump them into a great bin, where they were pored over by dead-faced mothers and children.

"Smells like the Refuge," I said very softly, not wanting to hurt anyone's feelings. My father nodded with an almost smile.

We went over to the corner where the benches met, though there was space to sit almost anywhere. And there we waited.

A couple of times I glanced cautiously at my father's face, hoping for some sort of guide. He could have been waiting for a train or listening to a sermon, and I felt a surge of respect. He had a long face with a nose so straight it looked as if it had been leveled with a rule. I guess he would have been handsome if he hadn't seemed so sad or tired much of the time. He worked for a paint wholesaler which had big, dusty offices in a commercial section of Dorchester. When I was younger I used to think the dirt of that place had rubbed off on him permanently.

I began to study the patients with the hope of preparing myself for Uncle Theodore. The old man beside us was stretched out on the bench full length, feet toward us, one arm over his eyes, as if he were lying on the beach, the other resting over his crotch. He had a kind of squeak to his snore. Another patient was persistently scratching his back on the dark-varnished door frame. Anywhere else this would have seemed perfectly normal.

Then my father stood up, and when I did too, I could see that what must be Uncle Theodore was being led in by a pock-marked attendant. They stopped some distance from us and the attendant pointed us out to Uncle Theodore. Then he set him free with a little nudge as if they were playing pin-the-tail-on-the-donkey.

Surprisingly, Uncle Theodore was heavy. I don't mean fat, because he wasn't solid. He was a great, sagging man. His jowls hung loose, his shoulders were massive but rounded like a dome, his hands were attached like brass weights on the ends of swinging pendulums. He wore a clean white shirt open at the neck and blue serge suit pants hung on suspenders which had been patched with a length of twine. It looked as if his pants had once been five sizes too large and that somehow, with the infinite patience of the infirm, he had managed to stretch the lower half of his stomach to fill them.

I would have assumed that he was far older than my father from his stance and his shuffling walk (he wore scuffs, which he slid across the floor without once lifting them), but his face was a baby pink, which made him look adolescent.

"Hello, Ted," my father said, "How have you been?"

Uncle Theodore just said "Hello," without a touch of enthusiasm, or even gratitude for our coming to see him. We stood there, the three of us, for an awkward moment.

Then: "I brought the boy."

"Who?"

"My boy, Will."

Uncle Theodore looked down at me with red-rimmed, blue eyes. Then he looked at my father, puzzled. "But *you're* Will."

"Right, but we've named our boy William too. Tried to call him Billy, but he insists on Will. Very confusing."

Uncle Theodore smiled for the first time. The smile made everything much easier; I relaxed. He was going to be like any other relative on a Sunday afternoon visit.

"Well, now," he said in an almost jovial manner, "there's one on me. I'd forgotten we even *had* a boy."

My face tingled the way it does when you open the furnace door. Somehow he had joined himself with my father as a married couple, and done it with a smile. No instruction could have prepared me for this quiet sound of madness.

But my father had, it seemed, learned how to handle it. He simply asked Uncle Theodore if he had enjoyed the magazines he had brought last time. We subscribed to *Life,* the news magazine, and apparently my father had been bringing him back copies from time to time. It worked, shifting the subject like that, because Uncle Theodore promptly forgot about who had produced what child and told us about how all his copies of *Life* had been stolen. He even pointed out the thief.

"The little one with the hook nose there," he said with irritation but no rage. "Stuffs them in his pants to make him look bigger. He's a problem, he is."

"I'll send you more," my father said. "Perhaps the attendant will keep them for you."

"Hennessy? He's a good one. Plays checkers like a pro."

"I'll bet he has a hard time beating you."

"Hasn't yet. Not once."

"I'm not surprised. You were always the winner." I winced, but neither of them seemed to think this was a strange thing to say. My father turned to me: "We used to play in the attic where it was quiet."

This jolted me. It hadn't occurred to me that the two of them had spent a childhood together. I even let some of their conversation slip by thinking of how they had grown up in the same old rambling house before my sister and I were born, had perhaps planned their future while sitting up there in that attic room the way my sister and I had, actually had gone to school together, and then at some point . . . But when? And how would it have happened? It was as impossible for me to look back and imagine that as it must have been for them as kids to look forward, to see what was in store for them.

"So they started banging on their plates," Uncle Theodore was saying, "and shouting for more heat. Those metal plates sure make a racket, I can tell you."

"That's no way to get heat," Father said, sounding paternal.

"Guess not. They put Schwartz and Cooper in the pit. That's what Hennessy said. And there's a bunch of them that's gone to different levels. They send them down when they act like that, you know. The doctors, they take a vote and send the troublemakers down." And then his voice lowered. Instinctively we both bent toward him for some confidence. "And I've found out—God's truth—that one of these nights they're going to shut down the heat *all the way. Freeze us!*"

There was a touch of panic in this which coursed through me. I could feel just how it would be, this great room black as midnight, the whine of wind outside, and then all those hissing radiators turning silent, and the aching cold seeping through the door cracks—

"Nonsense," my father said quietly, and I knew at once that it was nonsense. "They wouldn't do that. Hennessy's a friend of mine. I'll speak to him before I go."

"You do that," Uncle Theodore said with genuine gratitude, putting his hand on my father's knee. "You do that for us. I don't believe there would be a soul of us"—he swept his hand about expansively—"not a soul of us alive if it weren't for your influence."

My father nodded and then turned the conversation to milder topics. He talked about how the sills were rotting under the house, how a neighborhood gang had broken two windows one night, how Imperial Paint, where my father worked, had laid off a number of workers. My father wasn't usually so gloomy, but I got the feeling that he was somehow embarrassed at being on the outside, was trying to make his life appear less enviable. But Uncle Theodore didn't seem very concerned one way or the other. He was much more bothered about how a man named Altman was losing his eyesight because of the steam heat and how stern and unfair Hennessy was. At one point he moved back in time to describe a fishing trip by canoe through the Rangeley Lakes. It was like opening a great window, flooding the place with light and color and the smells of summer.

"Nothing finer," he said, his eyes half shut, "than frying those trout at the end of the day with the water so still you'd think you could walk on it."

He was interrupted by the sleeper on the bench beside us, who woke, stood, and stared down at us. Uncle Theodore told him to "Go blow," and when he had gone so were the Rangeley Lakes.

"Rangeley?" he asked, when my father tried to open that window again by suggestion. "He must be one of our cousins. Can't keep 'em straight."

And we were back to Mr. Altman's deafness and how seriously it hindered him and how the doctors paid no attention.

It was with relief that I smelled sauerkraut. That plus attendants gliding through with carts of food in dented steel containers seemed to suggest supper, and supper promised that the end was near.

"About suppertime," my father said after a particularly long silence.

Uncle Theodore took in a long, deep breath. He held it for a moment. Then he let it go with the slowest, saddest sigh I have ever heard.

"About suppertime," he said at the end of it.

There were mumbled farewells and nods of agreement. We were thanked for copies of *Life* which we hadn't brought; he was told he was looking fine, just fine.

We were only inches from escape when Uncle Theodore suddenly discovered me again.

"Tell me son," he said, bending down with a smile which on anyone else would have been friendly, "what d'you think of your Uncle Ted?"

I was overwhelmed. I stood there looking up at him, waiting for my father to save me. But he said nothing.

"It's been very nice meeting you," I said to the frozen pink smile, dredging the phrase up from my sparse catechism of social responses, assuming that what would do for maiden aunts would do for Uncle Theodore.

But it did not. He laughed. It was a loud and bitter laugh, derisive, and perfectly sane. He had seen my statement for the lie it was, had caught sight of himself, of all of us.

"Well," he said when the laugh withered, "say hi to Dad for me. Tell him to drop by."

Father said he would—though my grandfather had died before I was born. As we left, I felt oddly grateful that the moment of sanity had been so brief.

It was dark when we got back to the car, and it was just beginning to snow. I nestled into the seat and pulled the blanket around me.

We had been on the road about a half hour and were approaching our neighborhood by an odd route. My father finally broke the silence. "I could do with a drink."

This was a jolt because my parents never had liquor in the house. I knew about bars but had never been in one. I wondered if perhaps drinking was something men did—a kind of ritual.

"Sure," I said, trying to sound offhand. "It's fine with me."

"You like sausage?" he asked.

"I love sausage." Actually I'd never tasted it. My mother said you couldn't tell what they put in it.

"A little sausage and a cool beer is what we need." And after a pause, "It's a place I go from time to time. Been there since God knows when. Ted and I had some good times there back when. But . . . " He took a deep breath and then let it out slowly. "It might be best if you told your mother we went to a Howard Johnson for a hamburger, O.K.?"

"Sure, Dad."

We were on city streets I had never seen before. He finally parked in what looked like a dark, threatening neighborhood and headed for a place with neon signs in the window. I had to trot to keep up. As soon as we entered, we were plunged into a warm, humming, soothing, smoky world. The sound of music blended with voices and laughter. There was a bar to our right, marble tables ahead, booths beyond. My father nodded at a waiter he seemed to know and said hi to a group at a table; then he headed toward the booths with a sure step.

We hadn't got halfway before a fat man in a double-breasted suit came steaming up to us, furious.

"Whatcha doing," he said even before he reached us, "corruptin' the youth?"

I held my breath. But when the big man reached my father they broke out in easy laughter.

"So this is the boy?" he said. "Will, Junior—right?" We nodded. "Well, there's a good part of you in the boy, I can see that—it's in the eyes. Now, there's a girl too, isn't there? Younger?"

"She's my twin," I said, "Not identical."

The men laughed. Then the fat one said, "Jesus, twins sure run in your family, don't they!"

This surprised me. I knew of no other twins except some cousins from Maine. I looked up at my father, puzzled.

"Me and Ted," he said to me. "We're twins. Nonidentical."

We were ushered to a booth, and the fat man hovered over us, waiting for the order.

"Got sausage tonight?" my father asked.

"Sure. American or some nice hot Italian?"

"Italian."

"Drinks?"

"Well—" My father turned to me. "I guess you rate beer," he said. And then, to the fat man, "Two beers."

The man relayed the order to a passing waiter. Then he asked my father, "Been out to see Ted?"

"You guessed it."

"I figured." He paused, his smile gone. "You too?" he asked me.

"Yes," I said. "It was my first time."

"Oh," he said, with a series of silent nods which assured me that somehow he knew exactly what my afternoon had been like. "Ted was quite a boy. A great tackle. A pleasure to watch him. But no dope either. Used to win meals here playing chess. Never saw him lose. Why, he sat right over there."

He pointed to the corner booth, which had a round table. All three of us looked; a waiter with a tray full of dirty glasses stopped, turned, and also looked at the empty booth as if an apparition had just been sighted.

"And you know why he's locked up?"

"No," I whispered, appalled at the question.

"It's just the number he drew. Simple as that. Your Dad, me, you— any of us could draw the wrong number tomorrow. There's something to think about."

I nodded. All three of us nodded. Then the waiter brought a tray with the order, and the fat man left us with a quick, benedictory smile. We ate and drank quietly, lost in a kind of communion.

15 STRUCTURE: FROM SCENES TO PLOT

Fictional *scenes* compared with *episodes* of daily living; *scene construction* in "Sausage and Beer"; varieties of *plot patterns*: chronological, flashbacks, frame stories; *controlling the pace* through the rate of plot development; the *coherence* of plot; building toward a concluding *epiphany*.

Clocks move at a steady rate. And in one sense, so do our lives. Awake or asleep, we progress from birth to death at a steady pace.

But now take a moment to review what you did yesterday from the time you got up to the end of the day.

Notice how naturally that chronology turned into a list of identifiable events or episodes: getting dressed, eating breakfast, and, for students, attending classes, a coffee break with friends in the cafeteria, a conversation in the hall, and lunch. For nonstudents, the events would be different, but the rhythm from one unit of activity to the next is essentially the same. The point is that while the *clock* moves perfectly regularly, our *life* as we look back is recalled as a sequence of episodes.

These episodes have certain characteristics which every writer of fiction should consider. First, we often identify them by where they occurred—the setting. Second, we recall who was there—the characters. Third, such episodes remain clear long after we have forgotten what came just before and just afterward. Those unstructured periods of time that merely link one episode with the next (walking, waiting, driving, watching television, sleeping) tend to blend together and blur quickly.

Finally, we don't always remember these events in the order in which they occurred. Students complaining about bad teachers they have had are not necessarily going to start with kindergarten; football fans recalling dramatic games they have watched are not going to begin with the first one they attended; and a man recalling his love for a woman is not necessarily going to begin with the day he met her.

Fiction tends to imitate these patterns. What we call *episodes* in life become *scenes* in fiction. These are the basic units. And their arrangement is what we call *plot*.

Scene Structure in "Sausage and Beer"

A scene in a short story is not as clearly defined as in drama, but generally speaking it consists of an episode that is identifiable either because of the setting or the characters involved. The reader senses a transition from one scene to the next whenever the author changes the setting or alters the "cast of characters" by having one leave or arrive.

If you examine the scenes in "Sausage and Beer" you will see that there are six of them:

1. The narrator is being driven by his father to see the boy's uncle on a cold January day. (Includes a flashback—a scene within a scene—in which the father invites his son to visit his Uncle Theodore.)
2. A short scene outside the hospital building: It is set off by a description of the hospital and grounds.
3. The waiting room: Father and son wait for Uncle Theodore to appear.
4. The visit with Uncle Theodore: This begins with Theodore's arrival and ends with the conclusion of visiting hours. Notice that the setting hasn't changed, but there is a psychological break when Uncle Theodore appears.
5. A short scene in the car.
6. The important scene in the bar. Notice that this is not only a different setting, it is a different climate as well. The bar is warm and friendly.

Why six scenes? In blocking out the story, this is what emerged. Initially, the number of scenes should probably be determined by the way in which the story comes to you. But once the first draft is down on paper, take a close look at the number and length of your scenes. Occasionally you will have to add a new scene. But more often you will find that you can cut. In this particular story, a two-page flashback was cut just before the story was published in *The Atlantic,* and another page was cut from the second edition of this textbook. A few more cuts were made for this, the fourth edition. Stories, like poems, are never really finished.

There comes a point where a story cannot be cut further without doing damage. In terms of plot alone, this story could be reduced to a single scene—the one at the hospital. But too much would be lost. The earlier scenes establish the relationship between father and son while also providing suspense, and the concluding scenes shift the story from a simple initiation (the boy introduced to the disturbing reality of mental illness) to a kind of first communion in which a young man is welcomed into the fellowship of adult life with all its distressing ironies.

The answer to the question of why the story is in six scenes is not a simple matter of rules. It is judgment. More scenes would weigh the story down and less would begin to make it too sketchy, too simple. It is very helpful to have a rough idea of the scene pattern in advance—even a tentative outline. But it is equally important to be willing to make adjustments after the first draft, adding or cutting scenes where needed.

Varieties of Plot Patterns

The stories included in this volume all move chronologically from scene to scene. A majority of stories do—particularly those that are relatively short. But even in those cases, the writer is not bound to move relentlessly forward in time. The author—like the scriptwriter—is free to include glimpses of past action.

The *flashback* is a simple method of inserting an episode that occurred previous to the main flow (or *base time*) of the plot. The term "flashback," first used by film writers, describes more than a simple reference to the past seen through a character's thoughts or dialogue. A true flashback consists of a whole scene that took place previous to the main action of the story and is presented with setting and often dialogue.

Take, for example, the flashback that occurs in the opening scene of "Sausage and Beer." The father and son, you remember, are driving in silence, and the earlier incident is dropped in almost as if in brackets:

> The whole business of visiting Uncle Theodore had come up in the most unconvincingly offhand manner.
> "Thought I'd visit your Uncle Theodore," he had said that day after Sunday dinner. "Wondered if you'd like to meet him."
> He spoke with his eyes on a crack in the ceiling as if the idea had just popped into his head, but that didn't fool me.

Notice that the reader is informed of the fact that the story is moving back to an earlier time by the brief use of the past perfect: "*had* come up" and "he *had* said that day." This is a standard method of entering a flashback in past-tense stories, even though many readers are not consciously aware that they are being signaled by a shift in tense. In fact, many *writers* have used the technique without knowing that the *had* form is called the past perfect. Never mind the terminology, *had* is the cue for your reader. After one or two sentences, shift back to the simple past: "It was quite obvious" and "asked."

How do you come out of a flashback? The most obvious way is to identify the transition directly: "But that was hours ago" or "But that was when he was much younger." More often, authors simply make sure that the new paragraph starts with a bit of action or a line of dialogue that clearly indicates to the reader that the story has returned to base time, the events and setting of the primary plot line. In this particular flashback the reader should be set straight by the paragraph that begins: "We were well out in the New England countryside now."

The same principle is used when writing in the present tense. The shift is from present tense to simple past. There is a short flashback in Bobbie Ann Mason's "Graveyard Day," which appears on page 150. Waldeen is a divorced mother with a close friend named Joe:

> . . . Waldeen suspects Joe is bringing up the restaurant . . . to remind her that it was the scene of his proposal. Waldeen, not accustomed to eating out, studied the menu carefully, wavering between pork chops and T-bone steak. . . .

In that case, leaving the flashback returns us to another meal and the author gives no transitional phrase like "But that was a year ago now." Instead, she depends almost entirely on a return to the present tense, though a reference to her daughter, Holly, also helps to set the reader straight:

> During supper, Waldeen snaps at Holly for sneaking liver to the cat, . . . but Holly manages to eat three bites of liver without gagging.

Multiple flashbacks are sometimes used when the author wants to suggest a complicated set of clues leading to a symbolic or a literal trial. Joseph Conrad's *Lord Jim* is in this form; so is William Faulkner's well-known "A Rose for Emily." Such an approach tends to fragment the story line, of course, and it may be for this reason that it is usually found in longer works and ones that have a type of mystery or trial to maintain the story's unity and the reader's interest.

The *frame story* traditionally refers to a tale told by a character appearing in a larger work, such as the separate narrations within Chaucer's *The Canterbury Tales.* But by common usage it also refers to any story in which the bulk of the material is presented as a single, long flashback. It is possible to do this in the third person; but often a frame is achieved through the device of a narrator who recalls an incident that happened some time in the past.

"Sausage and Beer," for example, could have opened with the narrator looking back like this:

> As I stood with my wife waiting for the funeral to begin, I realized how little I had really seen of my father. It was as if he were a stranger until I was twelve. The turning point came one day when he took me to visit my Uncle Theodore.
>
> As I remember it, I had kept quiet for most of the trip. It was too cold for talk.

Notice the traditional use of the past perfect for a single sentence and then the simple past. And if the story were to have a complete frame, the ending might be rounded out with a return to the opening scene.

> Sitting there in the chapel, listening to the service intended to honor my father, I couldn't help feeling that he and I had experienced a more meaningful ritual there in that most secular bar years ago.

Such an ending seems wooden to me—a bit too obvious. But it does indicate how any story can be surrounded in a frame. Or, as an alternative, the frame can be left incomplete simply to avoid the danger of a needless summing up.

The use of the frame is well justified if there is a good reason for contrasting the attitude of the narrator at the time of the narration with that back when the event took place.

Controlling the Pace of Plot

Every reader is aware that some sections in a story move slowly or drag, while others move quickly. A writer, however, has to know *why* this has happened.

In part, the pace of fiction is controlled by the style—particularly the length and complexity of the sentence structure. This is discussed in Chapter 23. By far the greatest factor, however, is the *rate of revelation*. That is, a story seems to move rapidly when a great deal is being revealed to the reader; conversely, it slows down when the author turns to digression, speculation, description, or any type of exposition.

One can, of course, maintain a high rate of revelation simply by concentrating on what reviewers like to call an "action-packed plot." This is one of the recurring characteristics of many best sellers, adventure stories, and stories of "true romance." Extreme examples are seen in television drama series and the comics. What these stories sacrifice is the richness of suggestion and the subtleties of characterization.

When you write sophisticated fiction you have to be on guard against two dangers: If you maintain a consistently high rate of revelation, entertaining your readers with a lively plot, you may bore them for lack of significance. They will find your work superficial. But if you become philosophically discursive or heavily symbolic, you may also bore your readers by lack of drama. Because of this, most successfully sophisticated stories shift the pace throughout the work.

Openings are frequently given a high rate of revelation. It helps to plunge the reader into an ongoing situation or to present some kind of dramatic question. "Sausage and Beer" begins with the narrator driving with his father and wondering what his Uncle Theodore will be like. The question in the mind of the boy becomes the reader's concern too. It is similar in some ways to the opening of "The Nightingales Sing" (see page 172), which also opens with the protagonist, a girl in this case, being driven toward an unknown destination. In "Graveyard Day" (page 149) the opening is a minor dispute between mother and daughter. An ongoing conflict of some sort is a natural way to catch the reader's attention.

All three of these stories, however, provide description and exposition once the plot is in motion. Most readers experience a psychological inertia as they begin a new work. Once you help them overcome this reluctance to get started, you can afford to fill in the setting and provide background.

As a story develops, it is a good idea to continue alternating between the vitality of fresh plot development and the richness of description and exposition. In this way the pace of fiction often resembles that of a skater: After each forward thrust it glides a bit—but not too long.

As you read over your first draft, try to feel where the story loses momentum. If it is only slight, you have no problem. The forward motion of the narration should carry the reader. But if not enough happens for too long, the story will sag and you will need to revise.

On the other hand, too much emphasis on plot may make a story superficial—what we have been calling *simple.* In those cases you may wish to simplify the plot or reduce its impact. This is particularly important with short shorts—those under 2000 words. A fatal accident might be muted by allowing the character to survive; a divorce could be reduced to an argument.

Much depends on length. A short short, for example, may be based on a single scene and may move with essentially the same pace through to the end. The longer a story, the more natural it is to have multiple scenes. As the complexity increases, so does the importance of the pacing. There are no easy rules to follow, but one's sense of effective pacing will increase the more you read and the more you have a chance to hear others respond to your work.

The Coherence of Plot

A diary may list the events of a day with great accuracy, but this is not a plot. A fictional plot is a weaving together of events that are interrelated and work toward a conclusion. One event affects another, characters have an influence on one another, and elements that do not contribute to the whole—details left over from an actual experience, for example—are eliminated.

To what end? Short stories are rarely plotted with rising and falling action such as is common in traditional plays, but they do generally build toward what James Joyce called an *epiphany*. Although he used the term in a somewhat more limited sense, it has come to mean an important moment of recognition or discovery. It can take two different forms: Either the reader and the central character both learn something significant from the events of the story, or the reader alone makes such a discovery. Even stories that appear at first to be highly unstructured usually provide this important event.

In "Sausage and Beer," there are, I think, two such moments—one recognized by the boy and the other an insight perceived only by the reader. The first is given through the fat man at the bar who, in a serious moment almost at the end of the story, poses the question of why one or two brothers should live a normal life and the other should end up in a mental hospital. His answer is that it is just chance. We all run that risk. The boy and the reader come to realize this simultaneously.

The final sentence, however, offers an insight too complex for the boy to understand at this stage in his life. Father and son, having shared a difficult experience, are now sharing something like a communion—not a religious experience but a partaking of life itself.

The building of scenes and their arrangement as plot become more intuitive after you have written several stories. But there are ways you can speed this process. First, examine the scene construction of short stories in print. Mark in the margin where they begin and end. Study the transitions and the shifts in pace and in mood.

Second, study and question your own scene construction. Be on guard against two problem areas: the scattering of scenes that cover too broad a spectrum of time for the length of the story and, on the other hand, those long, talky, or highly descriptive scenes that sag for lack of development.

If the story seems too brief or thin or lacking in development, don't start padding the existing scenes with more explanation and longer sentences. Carefully consider whether the reader needs to know more about the characters or the situation through the addition of entire scenes. Conversely, if the story seems to ramble, don't think that the only solution is to remove a sentence here and a phrase there. Consider cutting or combining entire scenes.

Finally, ask yourself just what the reader learns from going through this experience. This shouldn't be a simple "moral" which the reader can shrug off as a truism, nor must it be a far-reaching philosophical or psycho-logical truth. What most authors aim for is a subtle sense of having achieved some insight either with the protagonist or independently.

This chapter corresponds roughly to the one entitled "From Units to Unity" in the section on poetry. A unit in fiction is different from one in verse, and the methods of creating an artistic whole vary as well. But the story resembles the poem (and the play as well) in that it is a construction of units; and like all art forms, the whole is greater than the sum of its parts.

16 A STORY BY BOBBIE ANN MASON

Graveyard Day

Holly, swinging her legs from the kitchen stool, lectures her mother on natural foods. Holly is ten.

Waldeen says, "I'll have to give your teacher a talking to. She's put notions in your head. You've got to have meat to grow."

Waldeen is tenderizing liver, beating it with the edge of a saucer. Her daughter insists that she is a vegetarian. If Holly had said Rosicrucian, it would have sounded just as strange to Waldeen. Holly wants to eat peanuts, soyburgers, and yogurt. Waldeen is sure this new fixation has something to do with Holly's father, Joe Murdock, although Holly rarely mentions him. After Waldeen and Joe were divorced last September, Joe moved to Arizona and got a construction job. Joe sends Holly letters occasionally, but Holly won't let Waldeen see them. At Christmas he sent Holly a copper Indian bracelet with unusual marks on it. It is Indian language, Holly tells her. Waldeen sees Holly polishing the bracelet while she is watching TV.

Waldeen shudders when she thinks of Joe Murdock. If he weren't Holly's father, she might be able to forget him. Waldeen was too young when she married him, and he had a reputation for being wild, which he did not outgrow. Now she could marry Joe McClain, who comes over for supper almost every night, always bringing something special, such as a roast or dessert. He seems to be oblivious to what things cost, and he frequently brings Holly presents. If Waldeen married Joe, then Holly would have a stepfather—something like a sugar substitute, Waldeen imagines. Shifting relationships confuse her. She doesn't know what marriage means anymore. She tells Joe they must wait. Her ex-husband is still on her mind, like the lingering aftereffects of an illness.

Joe McClain is punctual, considerate. Tonight he brings fudge ripple ice cream and a half-gallon of Coke in a plastic jug. He kisses Waldeen and hugs Holly. Waldeen says, "We're having liver and onions, but Holly's mad 'cause I won't make Soybean Supreme."

"Soybean *Delight*," says Holly.

"Oh, excuse me!"

"Liver is full of poison. The poisons in the feed settle in the liver."

"Do you want to stunt your growth?" Joe asks, patting Holly on the head. He winks at Waldeen and waves his walking stick at her playfully, like a conductor. Joe collects walking sticks, and he has an antique one that belonged to Jefferson Davis. On a gold band, in italics, it says Jefferson Davis. Joe doesn't go anywhere without a walking stick, although he is only thirty. It embarrasses Waldeen to be seen with him.

"Sometimes a cow's liver just explodes from the poison," says Holly. "Poisons are *oozing* out."

"Oh, Holly, hush, that's disgusting." Waldeen plops the pieces of liver onto a plate of flour.

"There's this restaurant at the lake that has Liver Lovers' Night," Joe says to Holly. "Every Tuesday is Liver Lovers' Night."

"Really?" Holly is wide-eyed, as if Joe is about to tell a long story, but Waldeen suspects Joe is bringing up the restaurant—Sea's Breeze at Kentucky Lake—to remind her that it was the scene of his proposal. Waldeen, not accustomed to eating out, studied the menu carefully, wavering between pork chops and T-bone steak and then suddenly, without thinking, ordering catfish. She was disappointed to learn that the catfish was not even local, but frozen ocean cat. "Why would they do that," she kept saying, interrupting Joe, "when they've got all the fresh channel cat in the world right here at Kentucky Lake?"

During supper, Waldeen snaps at Holly for sneaking liver to the cat, but with Joe gently persuading her, Holly manages to eat three bites of liver without gagging. Holly is trying to please him, as though he were some TV game show host who happened to live in the neighborhood. In Waldeen's opinion, families shouldn't shift memberships, like clubs. But here they are, trying to be a family. Holly, Waldeen, Joe McClain. Sometimes Joe spends the weekend, but Holly prefers weekends at Joe's house because of his shiny wood floors and his parrot that tries to sing "Inka Dinka Doo." Holly likes the idea of packing an overnight bag.

Waldeen dishes out the ice cream. Suddenly inspired, she suggests a picnic Saturday. "The weather's fairing up," she says.

"I can't." says Joe. "Saturday's graveyard day."

"Graveyard day?" Holly and Waldeen say together.

"It's my turn to clean off the graveyard. Every spring and fall somebody has to rake it off." Joe explains that he is responsible for taking geraniums to his grandparents' graves. His grandmother always kept the pot in her basement during the winter, and in the spring she took it to her husband's grave, but she had died in November.

"Couldn't we have a picnic at the graveyard?" asks Waldeen.

"That's gruesome."

"We never get to go on picnics," says Holly. "Or anywhere," She gives Waldeen a look.

"Well, okay," Joe says. "But remember, it's serious. No fooling around."

"We'll be real quiet," says Holly.

"Far be it from me to disturb the dead," Waldeen says, wondering why she is speaking in a mocking tone.

After supper, Joe plays rummy with Holly while Waldeen cracks pecans for a cake. Pecan shells fly across the floor, and the cat pounces on them. Holly and Joe are laughing together, whooping loudly over the cards. They sound like contestants on *Let's Make a Deal*. Joe Murdock wanted desperately to be on a game show and strike it rich. He wanted to go to California so he would have a chance to be on TV and so he could travel the freeways. He drove in the stock car races, and he had been drag racing since he learned to drive. Evel Knievel was his hero. Waldeen couldn't look when the TV showed Evel Knievel leaping over canyons. She told Joe many times, "He's nothing but a showoff. But if you want to break your fool neck, then go right ahead. Nobody's stopping you." She is better off without Joe Murdock. If he were still in town, he would do something to make her look foolish, such as paint her name on his car door. He once had WALDEEN painted in large red letters on the door of his LTD. It was like a tattoo. It is probably a good thing he is in Arizona. Still, she cannot really understand why he had to move so far away from home.

After Holly goes upstairs, carrying the cat, whose name is Mr. Spock, Waldeen says to Joe, "In China they have a law that the men have to help keep house." She is washing dishes.

Joe grins. "That's in China. This is *here*."

Waldeen slaps at him with the dish towel, and Joe jumps up and grabs her. "I'll do all the housework if you marry me," he says. "You can get the Chinese to arrest me if I don't."

"You sound just like my ex-husband. Full of promises."

"Guys named Joe are good at making promises." Joe laughs and hugs her.

"All the important men in my life were named Joe," says Waldeen, with pretended seriousness. "My first real boyfriend was named Joe. I was fourteen."

"You always bring that up," says Joe. "I wish you'd forget about them. You love *me*, don't you?"

"Of course, you idiot."

"Then why don't you marry me?"

"I just said I was going to think twice is all."

"But if you love me, what are you waiting for?"

"That's the easy part. Love is easy."

In the middle of *The Waltons*, C. W. Redmon and Betty Mathis drop by. Betty, Waldeen's best friend, lives with C. W., who works with Joe on a construction crew. Waldeen turns off the TV and clears magazines from the couch. C. W. and Betty have just returned from Florida and they are full of news about Sea World. Betty shows Waldeen her new tote bag with a killer whale pictured on it.

"Guess who we saw at the Louisville airport," Betty says.

"I give up," says Waldeen.

"Colonel Sanders!"

"He's eighty-four if he's a day," C. W. adds.

"You couldn't miss him in that white suit," Betty says. "I'm sure it was him. Oh, Joe! He had a walking stick. He went strutting along—"

"No kidding!"

"He probably beats chickens to death with it," says Holly, who is standing around.

"That would be something to have," says Joe. "Wow, one of the Colonel's walking sticks."

"Do you know what I read in a magazine?" says Betty. "That the Colonel Sanders outfit is trying to grow a three-legged chicken."

"No, a four-legged chicken," says C. W.

"Well, whatever."

Waldeen is startled by the conversation. She is rattling ice cubes, looking for glasses. She finds an opened Coke in the refrigerator, but it may have lost its fizz. Before she can decide whether to open the new one Joe brought, C. W. and Betty grab glasses of ice from her and hold them out. Waldeen pours the Coke. There is a little fizz.

"We went first class the whole way," says C. W. "I always say, what's a vacation for it you don't splurge?"

"I thought we were going to buy *out* Florida," says Betty. "We spent a fortune. Plus, I gained a ton."

"Man, those jumbo jets are really nice," says C. W.

C. W. and Betty seem changed, exactly like all people who come back from Florida with tales of adventure and glowing tans, except that they did not get tans. It rained. Waldeen cannot imagine flying, or spending that much money. Her ex-husband tried to get her to go up in an airplane with him once—a $7.50 ride in a Cessna—but she refused. If Holly goes to Arizona to visit him, she will have to fly. Arizona is probably as far away as Florida.

When C. W. says he is going fishing on Saturday, Holly demands to go along. Waldeen reminds her about the picnic. "You're full of wants," she says.

"I just wanted to go somewhere."

"I'll take you fishing one of these days soon," says Joe.

"Joe's got to clean off his graveyard," says Waldeen. Before she realizes what she is saying, she has invited C. W. and Betty to come along on the picnic. She turns to Joe. "Is that okay?"

"I'll bring some beer," says C. W. "To hell with fishing."

"I never heard of a picnic at a graveyard," says Betty. "But it sounds neat."

Joe seems embarrassed. "I'll put you to work," he warns.

Later, in the kitchen, Waldeen pours more Coke for Betty. Holly is playing solitaire on the kitchen table. As Betty takes the Coke, she says, "Let C. W. take Holly fishing if he wants a kid so bad." She had told Waldeen that she wants to marry C. W., but she does not want to ruin her figure by getting pregnant. Betty pets the cat. "Is this cat going to have kittens?"

Mr. Spock, sitting with his legs tucked under his stomach, is shaped somewhat like a turtle.

"Heavens, no," says Waldeen. "He's just fat because I had him nurtured."

"The word is *neutered!*" cries Holly, jumping up. She grabs Mr. Spock and marches up the stairs.

"That youngun," Waldeen says with a sigh. She feels suddenly afraid. Once, Holly's father, unemployed and drunk on whiskey and 7-Up, snatched Holly from the school playground and took her on a wild ride around town, buying her ice cream at the Tastee-Freez, and stopping at Newberry's to buy her an *All in the Family* Joey doll, with correct private parts. Holly was eight. When Joe brought her home, both were tearful and quiet. The excitement had worn off, but Waldeen had vividly imagined how it was. She wouldn't be surprised if Joe tried the same trick again, this time carrying Holly off to Arizona. She has heard of divorced parents who kidnap their own children.

The next day Joe McClain brings a pizza at noon. He is working nearby and has a chance to eat lunch with Waldeen. The pizza is large enough for four people. Waldeen is not hungry.

"I'm afraid we'll end up horsing around and won't get the graveyard cleaned off," Joe says. "It's really a lot of work."

"Why's it so important, anyway?"

"It's a family thing."

"Family. Ha!"

"Why are you looking at me in that tone of voice?"

"I don't know what's what anymore," Waldeen wails, "I've got this kid that wants to live on peanuts and sleeps with a cat—and didn't even see her daddy at Christmas. And here *you* are, talking about family. What do you know about family? You don't know the half of it."

"What's got into you lately?"

Waldeen tries to explain. "Take Colonel Sanders, for instance. He was on *I've Got a Secret* once, years ago, when nobody knew who he was. His secret was that he had a million-dollar check in his pocket for selling Kentucky Fried Chicken to John Y. Brown. *Now* look what's happened. Colonel Sanders sold it but didn't get rid of it. He's still Colonel Sanders. John Y. sold it too and he can't get rid of it either. Everybody calls him the Chicken King, even though he's governor. That's not very dignified, if you ask me."

"What in Sam Hill are you talking about? What's that got to do with families?"

"Oh, Colonel Sanders just came to mind because C. W. and Betty saw him. What I mean is, you can't just do something by itself. Everything else drags along. It's all *involved*. I can't get rid of my ex-husband just by signing a paper. Even if he *is* in Arizona and I never lay eyes on him again."

Joe stands up, takes Waldeen by the hand, and leads her to the couch. They sit down and he holds her tightly for a moment. Waldeen has the strange impression that Joe is an old friend who moved away and returned, years later, radically changed. She doesn't understand the walking sticks, or why he would buy such an enormous pizza.

"One of these days you'll see," says Joe, kissing her.

"See what?" Waldeen mumbles.

"One of these days you'll see. I'm not such a bad catch."

Waldeen stared at a split in the wallpaper.

"Who would cut your hair if it wasn't me?" he asks, rumpling her curls. "I should have gone to beauty school."

"I don't know."

"Nobody else can do Jimmy Durante imitations like I can."

"I wouldn't brag about it."

On Saturday Waldeen is still in bed when Joe arrives. He appears in the doorway of her bedroom, brandishing a shiny black walking stick. It looks like a stiffened black racer snake.

"I overslept," Waldeen says, rubbing her eyes. "First I had insomnia. Then I had bad dreams. Then—"

"You said you'd make a picnic."

"Just a minute. I'll go make it."

"There's not time now. We've got to pick up C. W. and Betty." Waldeen pulls on her jeans and a shirt, then runs a brush through her hair.

In the mirror she sees blue pouches under her eyes. She catches sight of Joe in the mirror. He looks like an actor in a vaudeville show.

They go into the kitchen, where Holly is eating granola. "She promised me she'd make carrot cake," Holly tells Joe.

"I get blamed for everything," says Waldeen. She is rushing around, not sure why. She is hardly awake.

"How could you forget?" asks Joe. "It was your idea in the first place."

"I didn't forget. I just overslept." Waldeen opens the refrigerator. She is looking for something. She stares at a ham.

When Holly leaves the kitchen, Waldeen asks Joe, "Are you mad at me?" Joe is thumping his stick on the floor.

"No. I just want to get this show on the road."

"My ex-husband always said I was never dependable, and he was right. But *he* was one to talk. He had his head in the clouds."

"Forget your ex-husband."

"His name is Joe. Do you want some juice?" Waldeen is looking for orange juice, but she cannot find it.

"No." Joe leans on his stick. "He's over and done with. Why don't you just cross him off your list?"

"Why do you think I had bad dreams? Answer me that. I must be afraid of *something*."

There is no juice. Waldeen closes the refrigerator door. Joe is smiling at her enigmatically. What she is really afraid of, she realizes, is that he will turn out to be just like Joe Murdock. But it must be only the names, she reminds herself. She hates the thought of a string of husbands, and the idea of a stepfather is like a substitute host on a talk show. It makes her think of Johnny Carson's many substitute hosts.

"You're just afraid to do anything new, Waldeen," Joe says. "You're afraid to cross the street. Why don't you get your ears pierced? Why don't you adopt a refugee? Why don't you get a dog?"

"You're crazy. You say the weirdest things." Waldeen searches the refrigerator again. She pours a glass of Coke and watches it foam.

It is afternoon before they reach the graveyard. They had to wait for C. W. to finish painting his garage door, and Betty was in the shower. On the way, they bought a bucket of fried chicken. Joe said little on the drive into the country. When he gets quiet, Waldeen can never figure out if he is angry or calm. When he put the beer cooler in the trunk, she caught a glimpse of the geraniums in an ornate concrete pot with a handle. It looked like a petrified Easter basket. On the drive, she closed her eyes and imagined that they were in a funeral procession.

The graveyard is next to the woods on a small rise fenced in with barbed wire. A herd of Holsteins grazes in the pasture nearby, and in the distance the smokestacks of the new industrial park send up lazy swirls of smoke. Waldeen spreads out a blanket, and Betty opens beers and hands them around. Holly sits down under a tree, her back to the gravestones, and opens a Vicki Barr flight stewardess book.

Joe won't sit down to eat until he has unloaded the geraniums. He fusses over the heavy basket, trying to find a level spot. The flowers are not yet blooming.

"Wouldn't plastic flowers keep better?" asks Waldeen. "Then you wouldn't have to lug that thing back and forth." There are several bunches of plastic flowers on the graves. Most of them have fallen out of their containers.

"Plastic, yuck!" cried Holly.

"I should have known I'd say the wrong thing," says Waldeen.

"My grandmother liked geraniums," Joe says.

At the picnic, Holly eats only slaw and the crust from a drumstick. Waldeen remarks, "Mr. Spock is going to have a feast."

"You've got a treasure, Waldeen," says C. W. "Most kids just want to load up on junk."

"Wonder how long a person can survive without meat?" says Waldeen, somewhat breezily. Suddenly, she feels miserable about the way she treats Holly. Everything Waldeen does is so roundabout, so devious, a habit she is sure she acquired from Joe Murdock. Disgusted, Waldeen flings a chicken bone out among the graves. Once, her ex-husband wouldn't bury the dog that was hit by a car. It lay in a ditch for over a week. She remembers Joe saying several times, "Wonder if the dog is still there?" He wouldn't admit that he didn't want to bury it. Waldeen wouldn't do it because he had said he would do it. It was a war of nerves. She finally called the Highway Department to pick it up. Joe McClain, at least, would never be that barbaric.

Joe pats Holly on the head and says, "My girl's stubborn, but she knows what she likes." He makes a Jimmy Durante face that causes Holly to smile. Then he brings out a surprise for her, a bag of trail mix, which includes pecans and raisins. When Holly pounces on it, Waldeen notices that Holly is not wearing the Indian bracelet her father gave her. Waldeen wonders if there are vegetarians in Arizona.

Blue sky burns through the intricate spring leaves of the maples on the fence line. The light glances off the gravestones—a few thin slabs that date back to the last century and eleven sturdy blocks of marble and granite. Joe's grandmother's grave is a brown heap.

Waldeen opens another beer. She and Betty are stretched out under a maple tree and Holly is reading. Betty is talking idly about the diet she intends to go on. Waldeen feels too lazy to move. She watches the men work. While C. W. rakes leaves, Joe washes off the gravestones with water he brought in a camp carrier. He scrubs out the carvings with a brush. He seems as devoted as a man washing and polishing his car on a Saturday afternoon. Betty plays he-loves-me-he-loves-me-not with the fingers of a maple leaf. The fragments fly away in a soft breeze.

From her Sea World tote bag, Betty pulls out playing cards with Holly Hobbie pictures on them. The old-fashioned child with the bonnet hiding her face is just the opposite of Waldeen's own strange daughter. Waldeen sees Holly secretly watching the men. They pick up their beer cans from a pink, shiny tombstone and drink a toast to Joe's great-great-grandfather Joseph McClain, who was killed in the Civil War. His stone, almost hidden in dead grasses, says 1841–1862.

"When I die, they can burn me and dump the ashes in the lake," says C. W.

"Not me," says Joe. "I want to be buried right here."

"*Want* to be? You planning to die soon?"

Joe laughs. "No, but if it's my time, then it's my time. I wouldn't be afraid to go."

"I guess that's the right way to look at it."

Betty says to Waldeen, "He'd marry me if I'd have his kid."

"What made you decide you don't want a kid, anyhow?" Waldeen is shuffling the cards, fifty-two identical children in bonnets.

"Who says I decided? You just do whatever comes natural. Whatever's right for you." Betty has already had three beers and she looks sleepy.

"Most people do just the opposite. They have kids without thinking. Or get married."

"Talk about decisions," Betty goes on. "Did you see *60 Minutes* when they were telling about Palm Springs? And how all those rich people live? One woman had hundreds of dresses and Morley Safer was asking her how she ever decided what on earth to wear. He was *strolling* through her closet. He could have played *golf* in her closet."

"Rich people don't know beans," says Waldeen. She drinks some beer, then deals out the cards for a game of hearts. Betty snatches each card eagerly. Waldeen does not look at her own cards right away. In the pasture, the cows are beginning to move. The sky is losing its blue. Holly seems lost in her book, and the men are laughing. C. W. stumbles over a footstone hidden in the grass and falls onto a grave. He rolls over, curled up with laughter.

"Y'all are going to kill yourselves," Waldeen says, calling to him across the graveyard.

Joe tells C. W. to shape up. "We've got work to do," he says.

Joe looks over at Waldeen and mouths something. "I love you"? Her ex-husband used to stand in front of the TV and pantomime singers. She suddenly remembers a Ku Klux Klansman she saw on TV. He was being arrested at a demonstration, and as he was led away in handcuffs, he spoke to someone off-camera, ending with a solemn message, "I *love* you." he was acting for the camera, as if to say, "Look what a nice guy I am." He gave Waldeen the creeps. That could have been Joe Murdock, Waldeen thinks. Not Joe McClain. Maybe she is beginning to get them straight in her mind. They have different ways of trying to get through to her. The differences are very subtle. Soon she will figure them out.

Waldeen and Betty play several hands of hearts and drink more beer. Betty is clumsy with the cards and loses three hands in a row. Waldeen cannot keep her mind on the cards either. She wins accidentally. She can't concentrate because of the graves, and Joe standing there saying "I love you." If she marries Joe, and doesn't get divorced again, they will be buried here together. She picks out a likely spot and imagines the headstone and the green carpet and the brown leaves that will someday cover the twin mounds. Joe and C. W. are bringing leaves to the center of the graveyard and piling them on the place she has chosen. Waldeen feels peculiar, as if the burial plot, not a diamond ring, symbolizes the promise of marriage. But there is something comforting about the thought, which she tries to explain to Betty.

"Ooh, that's gross," says Betty. She slaps down a heart and takes the trick.

Waldeen shuffles the cards for a long time. The pile of leaves is growing dramatically. Joe and C. W. have each claimed a side of the grave-yard, and they are racing. It occurs to Waldeen that she has spent half her life watching guys named Joe show off for her. Once, when Waldeen was fourteen, she went out onto the lake with Joe Suiter in a rented pedal boat. When Waldeen sees him at the bank, where he works, she always remembers the pedal boat and how they stayed out in the silver-blue lake all afternoon, ignoring the people waving them in from the shore. When they finally re-turned, Joe owed ten dollars in overtime on the boat, so he worked Saturdays, mowing yards, to pay for their spree. Only recently in the bank, when they laughed over the memory, he told her that it was worth it, for it was one of the great adventures of his life, going out in a pedal boat with Waldeen, with nothing but the lake and time.

Betty is saying, "We could have a nice bonfire and a wienie roast—what *are* you doing?"

Waldeen has pulled her shoes off. And she is taking a long, running start, like a pole vaulter, and then with a flying leap she lands in the immense pile of leaves, up to her elbows. Leaves are flying and everyone is standing around her, forming a stern circle, and Holly, with her book closed on her fist, is saying, "Don't you know *any*thing?"

17 VIEWPOINT: STRATEGIES OF PRESENTATION

The *means of perception* defined; *variations* in the means of perception; *first versus third person;* the *focus* of a story; *reviewing your options* in viewpoint, person, and focus.

Until now, we have been dealing with the ingredients of a story: where the material for fiction comes from and how that material can be shaped and woven into a coherent plot. This chapter is concerned with techniques of presentation. More specifically, it describes three areas of choice: *the means of perception*—who seems to be presenting the narrative? *person*—first or third? and *focus*—whose story is it? Although we shouldn't ignore the intuitive aspect of writing, these three areas offer different strategies that help us make the most of a developing story.

The Means of Perception

This term refers to the agent through whose eyes a piece of fiction appears to be presented. For example: "The boy looked at his grandfather, wondering if the old man had understood." Here the means of perception is the boy.

We know what he is wondering and so are "in his head." We don't know what the grandfather is thinking, and if the story continues in this vein we, like the boy, will not find out until the old man speaks or reveals his thoughts through his action.

Means of perception is synonymous with *point of view* and *viewpoint.* I will use them interchangeably. One disadvantage of these alternate terms, however, is that they are also used loosely to refer to attitude, as in the phrase ". . . from the British point of view." It doesn't matter which term you use as long as you remember that when applied to fiction it is a precise literary concept—and an important one.

Stories written in the first person are almost always limited to a single means of perception. The "I" who begins the story will, in almost every case, be our only source of information. Shifting from one narrator to another is possible, but it breaks the mood so severely that it is rarely done. What many beginning writers don't realize, however, is that the single means of perception is almost as common in third-person stories as well. In an anthology of fifteen or twenty stories by different authors, it is unusual to find even one that departs from this pattern.

This means that once the means of perception has been established—usually at the outset of a story—it is normally maintained through to the end. In our example of the boy and his grandfather, for example, it would be unusual to have the next line read, "Actually Grandfather did agree, but he knew that he could never tell the boy." It would be still more unusual by contemporary standards to have the author step in with an observation neither character could make, such as "Little did either of them realize that later that day they would both take a trip to the hospital." That's called *author's intrusion.* Although it was popular in the nineteenth century and is found occasionally in novels today, it is rare in short stories.

The primary advantage of limiting the means of perception to a single character is that it effectively draws the reader into the story. It increases the natural tendency to identify with a fictional character—a feeling that should not be confused with sympathy, respect, or even approval. It is the illusion of being someone else for a short period of time.

Another advantage, closely related, is that it allows the author to withhold information. "Sausage and Beer" is a good example. It is written in the first person, and one has the impression both at the beginning and at the end that we are listening to an adult recalling an experience from his childhood. The phrasing is not consistently that of a twelve-year-old boy, and the concluding image about a communion is clearly an adult reflection. But if you look at the body of the story, you will see that the means of perception is generally limited to the boy. In the opening scene, for example, we don't know where we are going any more than the boy does. It would spoil the suspense if the narrator said, "Actually we were driving to a mental hospital to visit my father's twin brother." The reader learns that in gradual stages, just as the boy does. The limited means of perception is in this case a way of heightening dramatic interest through withheld information.

In a first-person story like "Sausage and Beer," the means of perception is clearly identified from the outset with the word "I." In third-person fiction, however, we can't be sure who it will be until we are given a glimpse into the mind of a character. Usually this happens within the first half page. In "Graveyard Day" by Bobbie Ann Mason (previous chapter), we don't know at first whether we are going to see this story through the mother's eyes or the daughter's. Using "m.o.p." as a handy abbreviation for *means of perception*, here are some of the questions that might flash through the mind of someone reading this story for the first time:

appears to be the m.o.p.? (Holly), swinging her legs from the kitchen stool, lectures her mother on natural foods. Holly is ten.

or is it Waldeen? → (Waldeen) says, "I'll have to give your teacher a talking to. She's putting notions in your head. You've got to have meat to grow."

must be Waldeen → Waldeen is tenderizing liver, beating it with the edge of a saucer. Her daughter insists that she is a vegetarian. If Holly had said Rosicrucian, (it would have sounded just as strange to Waldeen.)

On the basis of this brief glimpse into Waldeen's mind we unconsciously assume that this story will probably be written from Waldeen's point of view. Technically it would be possible for the author to break this pattern at any point and give us Holly's thoughts or, later, enter Joe's mind. Shifts like this do occur in novels, but they are rare in contemporary short stories. Because of this, most readers will assume that Waldeen will be the means of perception through to the end—as indeed she is.

Readers are used to this convention even if they have not analyzed it. Notice how automatically our expectations would shift if the last line of the opening passage were revised so that it gave us the daughter's thoughts rather than the mother's:

> Holly couldn't imagine how her mother could go on eating meat when she knew perfectly well how bad it was for the system.

Merely by changing this one sentence we would cause most readers to assume that the entire story will be seen through Holly's eyes.

It may seem at first that the single means of perception is limiting. How is the author to reveal the thoughts of other characters? The answer is fairly simple: the same way we determine what our friends are thinking. After all, we can't hear their thoughts either—much as we might like to. Instead, we listen to what they say and observe what they do. If what they say doesn't seem to agree with what they actually do, we have to make a judgment.

How can we be sure that Joe McClain really loves Waldeen? We look for the same sort of evidence Waldeen does. We note that when he comes for supper he always brings "something special, such as a roast or dessert." She decides on past evidence that Joe "is punctual, considerate." Later we see how Joe gently persuades Holly to "eat three bites of liver without gagging." Given Holly's feelings, that's some achievement!

He *seems* warm, reliable, and loving, but how can we be sure? That's what Waldeen wonders too. She recalls the Ku Klux Klansman she saw on TV who put on an act to show "what a nice guy" he was. The memory makes her uneasy, but she decides that Joe McClain isn't like this. The slow process of judgment she is going through is matched by our own slow process of evaluating Joe. After all, she *has* been married to someone who seemed fine at first—and he even had the same first name.

The crucial point is this: By withholding direct access into Joe's mind, the author has put us in the same position as her protagonist. We, like her, want to make a decision. And when in the end Waldeen makes that "flying leap" into the pile of leaves, we too should make that leap of faith, accepting Joe as a good bet for Waldeen.

Variations in the Means of Perception

Although most contemporary fiction limits the means of perception to a single character, some long stories and a good many novels do not. Since this approach is usually reserved for longer works, it is not represented in this text. One of the best examples is "The Short Happy Life of Francis Macomber" by Ernest Hemingway. This frequently anthologized story is unusual in that the point of view shifts not only from character to character but at one point even enters the mind of a wounded lion.

Such an approach is sometimes described as a *limited omniscient point of view* because although there appears to be a narrator who knows all, our view of individual scenes is limited to that of a single character. In most stories of this type lengthy sections of the story are given first to one and then to another character. A fully omniscient viewpoint sounds like someone telling a story aloud and frequently commenting on the action and the characters. The process is not as popular as it was in the nineteenth century because the illusion of reality is broken for the reader every time the voice of the author is used. But varieties of the technique can be found in the works of a few novelists like John Fowles, Margaret Drabble, and Milan Kundera.

Another variety in point of view is what may be called the reportorial style. In such works the author, like a journalist, does not enter the mind of any character. Normally this tends to distance the material, making it read like a newspaper account. Or it may echo the tone of a fable or parable in which the thematic suggestion is more important than characterization or verisimilitude. In earlier periods, such work often presented a serious moral message such as the parables from the Bible; today they are more likely to be satiric in tone.

"A Fable" by Robert Fox is a good example. It appears on page 198, and I will discuss it in more detail in the chapter that follows it. By way of introduction, however, "A Fable" is, as its title implies, a modern fable or parable with a gently satiric tone. By concentrating on theme rather than characterization, it becomes an illustrated message with a light touch.

If this objective, reportorial style interests you, look up Shirley Jackson's frequently anthologized story "The Lottery." Unlike "A Fable," it is dark, dramatic, and ominous in theme. She does not enter the minds of her characters partly because she is dealing with a social issue, not individual characters, and partly because the detached voice of a journalist helps to keep the story from becoming melodramatic. This reportorial style, however, does have a limited application, and perhaps for this reason it is unusual in contemporary American fiction. There are good reasons why the single, clearly defined means of perception is generally preferred.

First versus Third Person

When children first start telling stories they often devise a mixture of autobiography and fantasy. Without thinking of technique they tend to select the first person.

"And I went down behind Mr. Syke's house where the woods are and I saw a little pond and right next that pond lying down was a blue lion and I *ran*."

Everything is here: a setting, a sequence of action, a climax with a protagonist pitted against a beast (at the age of five, stories are apt to be epic and archetypal), an emotional response, and a resolution. But the decision to use "I" rather than "she" or "he" has been made unconsciously. This makes sense for a child of five, but it is too random a choice for someone who is trying to write a literary short story for adult readers.

Fiction that is based on one's own personal experience should not necessarily be presented in the first person. It may be better to use the third person just to maintain some objectivity over your material. In the same way, an event that happened to someone else should not automatically be handled in the third person. You may be able to increase the sense of authenticity by imagining yourself in that situation and by writing as if it had really happened to you. The best rule of thumb is this: Don't choose between first and third person on the basis of where the material came from; instead, try to determine which will be more natural for you in the writing and, in addition, has the greatest potential of developing into an effective story.

Surprising as it may seem, one of the most effective uses of the first person is to criticize or satirize the narrator. Readers tend to trust first-person narrators, and you as writer can achieve an effective irony if you can expose your protagonist through what he or she says or does. Sometimes this can be gentle. Those who have read *Gulliver's Travels* usually recall Swift's satire of the Lilliputians and other strange creatures who echo the foibles of our own society; but there is a more subtle satiric level in Gulliver himself. As the first-person narrator, he unwittingly reveals conventional middle-class views through his descriptions and reactions.

Consider this technique when dealing with a character who takes a situation too seriously. It is sometimes possible to allow the reader to smile at characters even though they are the all-too-serious narrator. A good example of this is seen in a story by Sherwood Anderson called "I'm a Fool." It concerns a young man who is a far greater fool than he ever suspects, not because of what he has done but because of the melodramatic way in which he tells it. Here again, the author has not selected the first person to reveal his inner convictions or secret life but to gain a new dimension by allowing the reader to learn more about the character than the character understands. This fictional technique is similar to the irony in T. S. Eliot's poem, "The Love Song of J. Alfred Prufrock," which I discussed in Chapter 8.

Another use of the first person that is well worth considering is in stories of reminiscence. "Sausage and Beer" is essentially this type. As I pointed out earlier, there is at least the implication of an adult narrator who recalls an incident from his childhood. Although the bulk of the story is presented through the boy's perceptions, certain insights and the conclusion seem to come from that adult narrator.

Although the older narrator is only hinted at in "Sausage and Beer," it would be possible to develop such a character by giving him a clearer identity. Compare these two openings. The first is the published version of the story, and the second extends that first-person approach so that you have a clearly identified adult narrator.

A

I kept quiet for most of the trip. It was too cold for talk. The car was getting old and the heater hadn't worked for as long as I could remember.

B

I was a fairly talkative child at twelve. Conversation was as important to me then as now. But whenever I drove somewhere with my father, we seemed to lapse into an almost unbroken silence. And on this particular trip it was too cold for talk.

The second version is still in the first person, but the adult narrator has been highlighted. He identifies himself before beginning his reminiscence. Even if the rest of the story is told mainly from the boy's point of view, the reader will recall that adult. As I described in the chapter on structure, this is known as a frame story. Whether you return to that adult narrator at the end or not depends on how much you want to emphasize his role in the story.

Stories of reminiscence in the first person are not limited to situations in which an adult narrator recalls incidents from childhood. The approach can also be applied to incidents that occurred only a year or even a month before. The length of time is not as important as how much change in attitude or understanding has taken place.

A third use of first-person narration is to give the illusion of a storyteller speaking out loud. This as-if-spoken style is achieved by phrasing that echoes the spoken language. Returning to that same opening, it might sound like this:

> Cold? You don't know what that word means until you've spent an hour in a car without a heater. And being driven by a father who won't say a word to his own son doesn't help, believe me.

Echoing the sound of spoken language is mainly a matter of word choice and phrasing. Very few authors indulge in phonetic spelling like "goin'" for "going" and "'em" for "them" because it so easily becomes obtrusive. You can suggest a regional or foreign accent perfectly well through phrasing without altering the spelling of a single word. To achieve this, listen carefully to the way language is actually used and adopt some of the characteristic phrases you hear.

Another valuable method of learning how to create the illusion of the spoken language is to study examples in fiction. You will find good models in such widely anthologized stories as Sherwood Anderson's "I'm a Fool," William Faulkner's "Spotted Horses," and Eudora Welty's "Why I Live at the P.O." Keep in mind, however, that they represent a technique that is not widely used. Some authors feel that it is awkward maintaining the illusion of a nonstop talker. In addition, the technique depends as much on a good ear for dialogue as music depends on a good ear for tone.

Although the "I" of first-person stories is most often the protagonist, don't ignore the possibility of presenting a story through the eyes of a minor character. Children, for example, sometimes reveal more than they understand about their parents. In such a story, either parent might be the true protagonist. Or a first-person narrator might be beginning a new job and unfold a story that is focused on two other individuals.

For all the advantages of first-person writing, it is the third person that has a slight edge in contemporary fiction. This may be due to the fact that so many stories have originated with one or more personal experiences. Adopting the third person is an effective way of metamorphosing that material. It gives you as author a chance to look at both the characters and the action more objectively.

Perhaps the most important reason for the popularity of third-person fiction, however, is its flexibility. Whereas the first person sets the author squarely within the mind of a single character, the third person can fluctuate between a kind of neutral style and that which is truly an echo of first-person narration. In the following passage, for example, the means of perception remains with the boy, but there is a shift away from the neutral view toward the boy's own speech.

> He had been kept after school again. It was a simple matter of writing "Good boys do not cheat" fifty times and then cleaning up the classroom, but it took the length of the afternoon. Now he was in a hurry to get home because the shadows were long and it would be dark and scary soon. The short cut was through crazy old Mr. Syke's back lot—"Old Mr. Syke is higher than a kite" they used to chant, though no one had ever seen him actually drunk. He slipped through the hedge, down across the corner of the lawn, and under the trees. The air was still. He walked fast and held his breath. A few more feet and he would be past the pond where. . . . But there it was again, the enormous blue lion. It lay calmly by the edge of the pond, its paw dangling in the water. "Run" he thought, and he was running.

This is no longer a story written by a child. We have factual material at the very beginning which, though known by the character (and therefore in harmony with the means of perception), is told in neutral terms. Then the passage begins to echo the phrasing of what might be the boy's own telling. The first hint of this is the word "scary" which is borrowed from his own vocabulary. And we are then prepared to accept Mr. Syke as "crazy." All this leads us to a quick and natural acceptance of the blue lion.

Here the third person borrows some of the objectivity of the clinical report and some of the subjectivity of first-person narration. It avoids the cold detachment of a psychologist's statement which would humorlessly place "crazy old Mr. Syke" and "blue lion" in quotation marks to indicate that these are not the "truth." And it avoids a slavish adherence to a child's vocabulary which, particularly in longer pieces, becomes difficult to maintain.

The popular notion that the first person provides a sense of immediacy or realism that cannot be achieved in the third person is not justified. As readers, we enter a story using *he* or *she* just as easily as one that begins with *I*. But the decision of which to use should not be made carelessly. Your choice will be made partly from what feels right from the beginning, but consider the alternative before you become locked in to your first approach. It is a good idea to convert a sample paragraph from first person to third or the reverse fairly early in the writing.

One excellent way to maintain flexibility is to study the opening scene of a published story and then to write out a version in which only the person is changed. Here, for example, are three different openings for Bobbie Ann Mason's "Graveyard Day." Can you recall which is hers? Before making a simple choice of which you think is best, try to analyze how the alternative approaches would change the story as a whole.

> *A*
>
> I sit on the kitchen stool, swinging my legs, and lecture my mother on natural foods. My name is Holly and I'm ten.

> *B*
>
> Holly, swinging her legs from the kitchen stool, lectures her mother on natural foods. Holly is ten.

> *C*
>
> I'm doing my best to get supper ready while Holly sits on the kitchen stool, swinging her legs, lecturing me on natural foods. Holly is ten.

The Focus of a Story

The focus of a work of fiction answers the question, "Whose story is it?" In determining the focus, we are selecting who is truly the central character. In "Graveyard Day," for example, the focus is clearly on Waldeen. She is the one who must deal with memories of a bad marriage, and she is the one who must decide whether to marry once again. We are given some background and a good deal of her thinking. But most important, it is her dilemma that sustains the story and her impulsive act at the end that closes it.

Be careful not to confuse the focus of a story and the means of perception. In this case, as with a majority of stories, the means of perception is the central character as well. But it is possible to present a story through the perceptions of a secondary character. It is worth examining how this could be done in "Graveyard Day," not because such a revision would improve the story, but because it helps to clarify the difference between the focus of a story and the means of perception.

It might seem that by shifting the means of perception to Holly we would have to abandon those insights into Waldeen's mind—her inner thoughts. Take for example, the passage that describes Waldeen's reactions to her first husband, Joe Murdock. Here is the printed version:

> Waldeen shudders when she thinks of Joe Murdock. If he weren't Holly's father, she might be able to forget him. Waldeen was too young when she married him, and he had a reputation for being wild.

One way to reveal that in a story written from Holly's point of view would be simply to convert the thought into some very honest dialogue between mother and daughter:

> "Frankly, Holly, I shudder when I think of your father. If it weren't for you, I might be able to forget him. The thing is I was just too young when I married him, and he had sort of a reputation for being wild."

If that seems out of character, Holly could have picked up this same information from a variety of sources. Here is a version in the first person which, like the previous one, keeps the means of perception with Holly but maintains the focus of the story on Waldeen.

> Mum has this thing about my father. She shudders if I just mention his name. She probably figures that if it weren't for me, she could just forget about him. She told Joe she was just too young when she got married and it seems he had sort of a reputation for being wild.

These different versions demonstrate how one can maintain the same focus in a story while you shift the means of perception. There are times, however, when experimenting will convince you that it is the focus of the story that should be changed. If you are working with a story like this, for example, you might decide that you really want to make Holly the main character.

Shifting the focus from one character to another is a major undertaking, so consider it early—preferably while you are still in the planning stage and before you have even begun the first draft. If "Graveyard Day" were to be made Holly's story, more about her relationship with her father and with Joe McClain would be needed. The story's concern would have to center on her, and the resolution at the end would have to be hers. It would end up being an entirely different story, of course, but such radical transformations do occur in the early stages of writing.

In some stories the focus may be placed on two characters almost equally. This is rare, however. Even when it is the relationship that dominates a story, one side of that relationship is usually treated in greater depth. In "Sausage and Beer," for example, the developing bond between son and father is important; but essentially the focus is on the son, who also serves as the means of perception.

It might have been possible in that story to have shifted the focus to the father without changing the means of perception. In such a story, the speculations on the part of the boy would be reduced to a minimum. And the dialogue of the father would have to be increased considerably so that we could learn much more about his innermost feelings.

Such a story, for example, might begin by having the father talk to his son about duty and responsibility and how it was time for the boy to learn that relatives had to be visited no matter how unpleasant the experience. He might give examples of how illness—even the insanity of close friends— never bothered him. In that final scene, however, the father might reveal himself as utterly shaken by the experience of seeing his brother once again. The story would then focus not on the boy (though still told by him), but on the contrast between what the father said he felt and what his true feelings were.

Reviewing Your Options

When a story idea first comes to you, it will probably be a mix of personal experience and invention. Let it run through your head like a daydream. Don't concern yourself at this early stage about the means of perception, person, and focus. If you analyze too much too soon, you may lose the feel of the story.

There will come a point, however, when you feel you have enough to work with. This is when some writers like to take a few notes about plot and characters so they won't lose the original concept. This is also when you should consider some alternative strategies of presentation. Metamorphosing a story by altering the point of view, person, or focus at this stage may save you hours of rewriting later.

Begin by reviewing the means of perception. Make sure that the story is being presented through the right character. In most cases, that character will be the protagonist; but as we have seen, he or she could be an observer. It is well worth spending a few moments imagining your story through the eyes of other characters. The technique is the same as the one I used for the opening of "Graveyard Day." Even if you decide not to shift your original viewpoint, the exercise may well give you new insights into your characters.

When you have finished your first draft, take another look at how you have handled the means of perception in both the opening and closing. Stories with long, rambling introductions in the nineteenth-century manner seem dated today mainly because such passages are generally from the author's point of view. Contemporary fiction has reduced the author's role, especially in openings and closings. Readers expect to enter the mind of a character almost from the start.

In particular, guard against openings in which you as all-knowing author give away too much: "It was a beautiful August day on Lake Placid, and there was little to suggest that before sunset Laura and Harry would learn much about the vicissitudes of weather and perhaps a bit about themselves as well." This is an exaggeration, but the principle is important: When you introduce a story in your own voice as author, you are apt to reveal too much. Remember too that for many contemporary readers, a story hasn't really begun until a particular character is doing something, thinking something, or saying something. With these points in mind, you may find that your first paragraph or even the first half page can be cut.

Conclusions present the same kind of problem. Here again there is a temptation to step in as author and explain the story. If done too blatantly, you will be stating what the story should have shown through action and dialogue. Take a look at the ends of the stories you have just read. In "Graveyard Day," Waldeen pulls off her shoes and takes "a long, flying leap" into the pile of leaves, a leap that informs us that her indecision about marrying Joe has ended, that she has decided to take that flying leap into matrimony in spite of the risks.

This symbolic act does not come without preparation. Just previous to that scene she recalls through a flashback going out on a rented pedal boat with a young man. She was fourteen at the time and they remained out there for the entire afternoon, "ignoring the people waving them in from the shore." Recently she and this old friend had laughed over it, and he described the episode as "one of the great adventures of his life." Mason is careful not to end her story with an author's summary like, "Waldeen realized that marriage, too, might be a great adventure and was worth a flying leap." Instead, she shows us this through action.

Significant action is also used in "Sausage and Beer." A concluding paragraph of exposition from the adult narrator's point of view might lay it all out like this: "My father and I both realized how brutally random chance rules all of our lives, how even twins must travel in utterly different directions. In this shared understanding we discovered for the first time that we had much in common." Technically, this is from the narrator's point of view, speaking as an adult, but it has the ring of author's intrusion. To avoid that kind of labeling, the theme is suggested through action and the setting: father and son sharing a booth in a bar that is as warm and friendly as the earlier scenes were cold and forbidding.

Sometimes a line of dialogue rather than action is used to conclude a story. But whether it is action or dialogue, the means of perception remains the character, not the author. There are exceptions, but even these rarely identify the theme directly. Instead, they highlight some related aspect of the story. In essays, we expect the theme to be clear and explicitly stated. But with fiction it is important to give the reader a sense of discovery as if this were a personal experience.

Important as the means of perception is, try to resist the temptation to play with a bizarre point of view just for effect: the adventure story that assures us the hero will live because it is presented in the first person, until we discover at the end that it is a note written in a bottle; the first-person account of an over-supervised little girl who turns out to be a happy little dog; the brother-sister story that turns out in the last sentence to concern two robots. Remember that a literary trick, like a cartoon, may give momentary pleasure, but it is soon forgotten. Since sophisticated fiction is rooted in characterization and thematic insight, it has a lasting quality. Even if one is just beginning, this is a goal.

Shifting a story from third person to first or the reverse is not as radical a transformation as changing the means of perception. But it is more than changing "I" to "he" or "she." If you have any doubts about which approach is most appropriate for a particular story, try a half page each way and see which feels right. To a large degree, this is an intuitive choice.

Changing the focus, on the other hand, is major surgery. It is a terrible feeling to be working on what you hope is a final draft and to decide that the story really should be centered on a different character. To avoid this, consider focus right at the start. Have you turned the spotlight on the right character? Or should you consider shifting the emphasis so the story deals with a different character? This is of particular concern in stories that deal with couples—husband and wife, two lovers, parent and child, roommates. Which has the more interesting character? Which has the more complex problem to solve? Often a story that started out with a version of yourself as a protagonist may end up with the focus shifted to someone else.

Viewpoint, person, and focus are fundamental. They determine *how* a story will be told just as plot determines *what* will be used. Trust your first inclination to get you started. But then review each factor to make sure you have made the best possible choice.

18 A Story By Elizabeth Parsons

The Nightingales Sing

Through the fog the car went up the hill, whining in second gear, up the sandy road that ran between the highest and broadest stone walls that Joanna had ever seen. There were no trees at all, only the bright-green, cattle-cropped pastures sometimes visible above the walls, and sweet fern and juniper bushes, all dim in the opaque air and the wan light of an early summer evening. Phil, driving the creaking station wagon with dexterous recklessness, said to her, "I hope it's the right road. Nothing looks familiar in this fog and I've only been here once before."

"It was nice of him to ask us—me especially," said Joanna, who was young and shy and grateful for favors.

"Oh, he loves company," Phil said, "I wish we could have got away sooner to be here to help him unload the horses, though. Still, Chris will be there."

"Is Chris the girl who got thrown today?" Joanna asked, remembering the slight figure in the black coat going down in a spectacular fall with a big bay horse. Phil nodded, and brought the car so smartly around a bend that the two tack boxes in the back of it skidded across the floor. Then he stopped, at last on the level, at a five-barred gate that suddenly appeared out of the mist.

"I'll do the gate," said Joanna, and jumped out. It opened easily and she swung it back against the fence and held it while Phil drove through; then the engine stalled, and in the silence she stood for a moment, her head raised, sniffing the damp, clean air. There was no sound—not the sound of a bird, or a lamb, or the running of water over stones, or of wind in leaves; there was only a great stillness and a sense of height and strangeness and the smell of grass and dried dung. This was the top of the world, this lost hillside, green and bare, ruled across by enormous old walls—the work, so it seemed, of giants. In the air there was a faint movement as of a great wind far away, breathing through the fog. Joanna pulled the gate shut and got in again with Phil and they drove on along the smooth crest of the hill, the windshield wipers swinging slowly to and fro and Phil's sharp, red-headed profile drawn clearly against the gray background. She was grateful to him for taking her to the horse show that afternoon, but she was timid about the invitation to supper that it had led to. Still, there was no getting out of it now. Phil was the elder brother of a school friend of hers, Carol Watson— he was so old he might as well have been of another generation and there was about him, still incredibly unmarried at the age of thirty-one, the mysterious aura that bachelor elder brothers always possess. Carol was supposed to have come with them but she had developed chickenpox the day before. However, Phil had kindly offered to take Joanna just the same, since he had had to ride, and he had kept a fatherly eye on her whenever he could. Then a friend of his named Sandy Sheldon, a breeder of polo ponies, had asked him to stop at his farm for supper on the way home. Phil had asked Joanna if she wanted to go and she had said yes, knowing that he wanted to.

Being a good child, she had telephoned her family to tell them she would not be home until late.

"*Whose* place?" her mother's faraway voice had asked, doubtfully. "Well, don't be late, will you, dear? And call me up when you're leaving, won't you? It's a miserable night to be driving."

"I can't call you," Joanna had said. "There's no telephone."

"Couldn't you call up from somewhere after you've left?" the faint voice had said. "You know how Father worries, and Phil's such a fast driver."

"I'll try to." Exasperation had made Joanna's voice stiff. What earthly good was *telephoning?* She hung up the receiver with a bang, showing a temper she would not have dared display in the presence of her parents.

Now, suddenly, out of the fog great buildings loomed close, and they drove through an open gate into a farmyard with gray wooden barns on two sides of it and stone walls on the other two sides. A few white hens rushed away across the dusty ground, and a gray cat sitting on the pole of a blue dump cart stared coldly at the car as Phil stopped it beside a battered horse van. The instant he stopped, a springer ran barking out of one of the barn doors, and a man appeared behind him and came quickly out to them, up to Joanna's side of the car, where he put both hands on the door and bent his head a little to look in at them.

"Sandy, this is Joanna Gibbs," said Phil.

Sandy looked at her without smiling, but not at all with unfriendliness, only with calm consideration. "Hello, Joanna," he said, and opened the door for her.

"Hello," she said, and then forgot to be shy, for, instead of uttering the kind of asinine, polite remarks she was accustomed to hearing from strangers, he did not treat her as a stranger at all, but said immediately, "You're just in time to help put the horses away. Chris keeled over the minute we got here and I had to send her to bed, and Jake's gone after one of the cows that's strayed off." He spoke in a light, slow, Western voice. He was a small man about Phil's age, with a flat freckled face, light-brown, intelligent eyes, and faded brown hair cut short all over his round head. He looked very sturdy and stocky, walking toward the van beside Phil's thin New England elegance, and he had a self-confidence that sprang simply from his own good nature.

"Quite a fog you greet us with," said Phil, taking off his coat and hanging it on the latch of the open door of the van. Inside in the gloom four long, shining heads were turned toward them, and one of the horses gave a gentle, anxious whinny.

"Yes, we get them once in a while," said Sandy. "I like 'em."

"So do I," said Joanna.

He turned to her and said, "Look, there's really no need in your staying out here. Run in the house, where it's warm, and see if the invalid's all right. You go through that gate." He pointed to a small sagging gate at a gap in the wall.

"All right, I will," she answered, and she started off across the yard toward the end gable of a house she could see rising dimly above some apple trees, the spaniel going with her.

"Joanna!" Sandy called after her, just as she reached the gate.

"Yes?" She turned back. The two men were standing by the runway of the van. They both looked at her, seeing a tall young girl in a blue dress and sweater, with her hair drawn straight back over her head and tied at the back of her neck in a chignon with a black bow, and made more beautiful and airy than she actually was by the watery air.

"Put some wood on the kitchen fire as you go in, will you." Sandy shouted to her. "The woodbox is right by the stove."

"All right," she answered again, and she and the spaniel went through the little gate in the wall.

A path led from the gate, under the apple trees where the grass was cut short and neat, to a door in the ell of the house. The house itself was big and old and plain, almost square, with a great chimney settled firmly across the ridgepole, and presumably it faced down the hill toward the sea. It was conventional and unimposing, with white painted trim and covered with gray old shingles. There was a lilac bush by the front door and a bed of unbudded red lilies around one of the apple trees, but except for these there was neither shrubbery nor flowers. It looked austere and pleasing to Joanna, and she went in through the door in the ell and saw the woodbox beside the black stove. As she poked some pieces of birchwood down into the snapping fire, a girl's voice called from upstairs, "Sandy?"

Joanna put the lid on the stove and went through a tiny hallway into a living room. An enclosed staircase went up out of one corner and she went to it and called up it, "Sandy's in the barn. Are you all right?"

"Oh, I'm fine," the voice answered, hard and clear. "Just a little shaky when I move around. Come on up."

Joanna climbed up. Immediately at the top of the stairs was a big square bedroom, papered in a beautiful faded paper with scrolls and wheat sheaves. On a four-posted bed lay a girl not many years older than Joanna, covered to the chin with a dark patchwork quilt. Her short black hair stood out against the pillow, and her face was colorless and expressionless and at the same time likeable and amusing. She did not sit up when Joanna came in; she clasped her hands behind her head and looked at her with blue eyes under lowered black lashes.

"You came with Phil, didn't you?" she asked.

"Yes," said Joanna, moving hesitantly up to the bed and leaning against one of the footposts. "They're putting the horses away and they thought I'd better come in and see how you were."

"Oh, I'm fine," said Chris again. "I'll be O.K. in a few minutes. I lit on my head, I guess, by the way it feels, but I don't remember a thing."

Joanna remembered. It had not seemed possible that that black figure could emerge, apparently from directly underneath the bay horse and, after sitting a minute on the grass with hanging head, could get up and walk grimly away, ignoring the animal who had made such a clumsy error and was being led out by an attendant in a long tan coat.

She also remembered that when people were ill or in pain you brought them weak tea and aspirin and hot water bottles, and that they were usually in bed, wishing to suffer behind partly lowered shades, not just lying under a quilt with the fog pressing against darkening windows. But there was something here that did not belong in the land of tea and hot water bottles— a land that, indeed, now seemed on another planet. Joanna knew this, though she did not know what alternatives to offer, so she made no suggestions but just stood there, looking with shy politeness around the room. It was a cold, sparsely furnished place and it looked very bare to Joanna, most of whose life so far had been spent in comfortable, chintz-warmed interiors, with carpets that went from wall to wall. In this room, so obviously untouched for the past hundred years or more, was only the bed, a tall chest of drawers, a wash-stand with a gold and white bowl and pitcher, two plain painted chairs, and a threadbare oval braided rug beside the bed. There were no curtains at the four windows, and practically no paint left on the uneven old floor. The fireplace was black and damp-smelling and filled with ashes and charred paper that rose high about the feet of the andirons. Joanna could not make out whether it was a guest room, or whose room it was; here and there were scattered possessions that might have been male or female—a bootjack, some framed snapshots, a comb, a dirty towel, some socks, a magazine on the floor. Chris's black coat was lying on a chair, and her bowler stood on the bureau. It was a blank room, bleak in the failing light.

Chris watched her from under her half-closed lids, waiting for her to speak, and presently Joanna said, "That was really an awful spill you had."

Chris moved her head on the pillow and said, "He's a brute of a horse. He'll never be fit to ride. I've schooled him for Mrs. Whittaker for a year now and ridden him in three shows and I thought he was pretty well over his troubles." She shrugged, and wrapped herself tighter in the quilt. "She's sunk so much money in him it's a crime, but he's just a brute and I don't think I can do anything more with him. Of course, if she wants to go on paying me to ride him, O.K., and her other horses are tops, so I haven't any kick, really. You can't have them all perfect."

"What does she bother with him for?" asked Joanna.

"Well, she's cracked, like most horse-show people," said Chris. "They can't resist being spectacular—exhibitionists, or whatever they call it. Got to have something startling, and then more startling, and so on. And I must say this horse is something to see. He's beautiful." Her somewhat bored little voice died away.

Joanna contemplated all this seriously. It seemed to her an arduous yet dramatic way of earning one's living; she did not notice that there was nothing in the least dramatic about the girl on the bed beside her. Chris, for her part, was speculating more directly about Joanna, watching her, appreciating her looks, wondering what she was doing with Phil. Then, because she was not unkind and sensed that Joanna was at loose ends in the strange house, she said to her, suddenly leaving the world of horses for the domestic scene where women cozily collaborate over the comforts of their men, "Is there a fire in the living room? I was too queasy to notice when I came in. If there isn't one why don't you light it so it'll be warm when they come in?"

"I'll look," said Joanna. "I didn't notice either. Can I get you anything?"

"No, I'll be down pretty soon," Chris said. "I've got to start supper."

Joanna went back down the little stairs. There was no fire in the living room, but a broken basket beside the fireplace was half full of logs, and she carefully laid these on the andirons and stuffed in some twigs and old comics and lit them. The tall flames sprang up into the black chimney, shiny with creosote. As they roared up, she sat on the floor and looked around the room. It was the same size as the bedroom above it, but it was comfortable and snug, with plain gray walls and white woodwork. A fat sofa, covered with dirty flowered linen, stood in front of the fire. There were some big wicker chairs and four little carved Victorian chairs and a round table with big bowed legs, covered with a red tablecloth; a high, handsome secretary stood against the long wall opposite the fire—its veneer was peeling, and it was filled with tarnished silver cups and ribbon rosettes. A guitar lay on a chair. There were dog hairs on the sofa and the floor was dirty, and outside the windows there was nothingness. Joanna got up to look at the kitchen fire, put more wood on it, and returned to the living room. Overhead she heard Chris moving around quietly, and she pictured her walking about the barren, dusty bedroom, combing her short black hair, tying her necktie, folding up the quilt, looking in the gloom for a lipstick, and suddenly a dreadful, lonely sadness and longing came over her. The living room was growing dark too, and she would have lit the big nickel lamp standing on the table but she did not know how to, so she sat there dreaming in the hot golden firelight. Presently she heard the men's voices outside and they came into the kitchen and stopped there to talk, one of them rattling the stove lids. Sandy came to the door and, seeing Joanna, said to her, "Is Chris all right?"

"Yes, I think so," Joanna said, "She said she was, anyway."

"Guess I'll just see," he said, and went running up the stairs. The spaniel came in to the fire. Joanna stroked his back. His wavy coat was damp with fog and he smelled very strongly of dog; he sat down on the hearth facing the fire, raised his muzzle, and closed his eyes and gave a great sigh of comfort. Then all of a sudden he trotted away and went leaping up the stairs to the bedroom, and Joanna could hear his feet overhead.

Phil came in next, his hair sticking to his forehead. He hung his coat on a chair-back and said to Joanna, "How do you like it here?"

"It's wonderful," she said earnestly.

"It seems to me a queer place," he said, lifting the white fluted china shade off the lamp and striking a match. "Very queer—so far off. We're marooned. I don't feel there's any other place anywhere, do you?"

Joanna shook her head and watched him touch the match to the wick and stoop to settle the chimney on its base. When he put on the shade the soft yellow light caught becomingly on his red head and his narrow face with the sharp cheekbones and the small, deep-set blue eyes. Joanna had known him for years but she realized, looking at him in the yellow light, that she knew almost nothing about him. Before this, he had been Carol's elder brother, but here in the unfamiliar surroundings he was somebody real. She looked away from his lighted face, surprised and wondering. He took his pipe out of his coat pocket and came to the sofa and sat down with a sigh of comfort exactly like the dog's, sticking his long thin booted feet out to the fire, banishing the dark, making the fog retreat.

Sandy came down the stairs and went toward the kitchen, and Phil called after him, "Chris all right?"

"Yes," Sandy said, going out.

"She's a little crazy," Phil said. "Too much courage and no sense. But she's young. She'll settle down, maybe."

"Are she and Sandy engaged?" Joanna asked.

"Well, no," said Phil. "Sandy's got a wife. She stays in Texas." He paused to light his pipe, and then he said. "That's where he raises his horses, you know—this place is only sort of a salesroom. But he and Chris know each other pretty well."

This seemed obvious to Joanna, who said, "Yes, I know." Phil smoked in silence.

"Doesn't his wife *ever* come here?" Joanna asked after a moment.

"I don't think so," Phil answered.

They could hear Sandy in the kitchen, whistling, and occasionally rattling pans. They heard the pump squeak as he worked the handle and the water splashed down into the black iron sink. Then he too came in to the fire and said to Joanna, smiling down at her, "Are you comfy, and all?"

"Oh, *yes*," she said and flushed with pleasure. "I love your house," she managed to say.

"I'm glad you do. It's kind of a barn of a place, but fine for the little I'm in it." He walked away, pulled the flowered curtains across the windows, and came back to stand before the fire. He looked very solid, small, and cheerful, with his shirt-sleeves rolled up and his collar unbuttoned with the gay printed tie loosened. He seemed to Joanna so smug and kind, so, some-how, sympathetic, that she could have leaned forward and hugged him round the knees—but at the idea of doing any such thing she blushed again and bent to pat the dog. Sandy took up the guitar and tuned it lazily.

As he began playing absent-mindedly, his stubby fingers straying across the strings as he stared into the fire, Chris came down the stairs. Instead of her long black boots she had a pair of dilapidated Indian moccasins with a few beads remaining on the toes, and between these and the ends of her breeches legs were gay blue socks. The breeches were fawn-colored, and she had on a fresh white shirt with the sleeves rolled up. Her curly hair, cropped nearly as short as a boy's, was brushed and shining, and her hard, sallow little face was carefully made up and completely blank. Whether she was happy or disturbed, well or ill, Joanna could see no stranger would be able to tell.

"What about supper?" she asked Sandy.

"Calm yourself," he said. "I'm cook tonight. It's all started." He took her hand to draw her down on the sofa, but she moved away and pulled a cushion off a chair and lay down on the floor, her feet toward the fire and her hands folded like a child's on her stomach. Phil had gone into the next room and now he came back carrying a lighted lamp; it dipped wildly in his hand as he set it on the round table beside the other one. The room shone in the low, beneficent light. Sandy, leaning his head against the high, carved back of the sofa, humming and strumming, now sang aloud in a light, sweet voice.

> "For I'd rather hear your fiddle
> And the tone of one string
> Than watch the waters a-gliding,
> Hear the nightingales sing."

The soft strumming went on, and the soft voice, accompanied by Chris's gentle crooning. The fire snapped. Phil handed round some glasses and then went round with a bottle of whisky he had found in the kitchen. He paused at Joanna's glass, smiled at her, and poured her a very small portion.

> "If I ever return,
> It will be in the spring
> To watch the waters a-gliding,
> Hear the nightingales sing,"

The old air died on a trailing chord

"That's a lovely song," said Joanna, and then shrank at her sentimentality.

But Sandy said, "Yes, it's nice. My mother used to sing it. She knew an awful lot of old songs." He picked out the last bars again on the guitar. Joanna, sitting beside him on the floor, was swept with warmth and comfort.

"My God, the peas!" Sandy said suddenly in horror, as a loud sound of hissing came from the kitchen. Throwing the guitar down on the sofa, he rushed to rescue the supper.

Joanna and Chris picked their way toward the privy that adjoined the end of the barn nearer the house. They moved in a little circle of light from the kerosene lantern that Chris carried, the batteries of Sandy's big flashlight having turned out to be dead. They were both very full of food, and sleepy, and just a little tipsy. Chris had taken off her socks and moccasins and Joanna her leather sandals, and the soaking grass was cold indeed to their feet that had so lately been stretched out to the fire. Joanna had never been in a privy in her life and when Chris opened the door she was astonished at the four neatly covered holes, two large and—on a lower level—two small. Everything was whitewashed; there were pegs to hang things on, and a very strong smell of disinfectant. A few flies woke up and buzzed. Chris set the lantern down on the path and partly closed the door behind them.

There was something cozy about the privy, and they were in no particular hurry to go back to the house. Chris lit a cigarette, and they sat there comfortably in the semi-darkness, and Chris talked. She told Joanna about her two years in college, to which she had been made to go by her family. But Chris's love was horses, not gaining an education, and finally she had left and begun to support herself as a professional rider.

"I'd known Sandy ever since I was little," she said. "I used to hang around him when I was a kid, and he let me ride his horses and everything, and when I left college he got me jobs and sort of looked after me."

"He's a darling, isn't he?" Joanna said dreamily, watching the dim slice of light from the open door and the mist that drifted past it.

"Well, sometimes he is," said Chris. "And sometimes I wish I'd never seen him."

"Oh, *no!*" cried Joanna. "Why?"

"Because he's got so he takes charge too much of the time—you know?" Chris said, "At first I was so crazy about him I didn't care, but now it's gone on so long I'm beginning to see I'm handicapped in a way—or that's what I think, anyway. Everybody just assumes I'm his girl. And he's got a wife, you know, and he won't leave her, ever. And then he's not here a lot of the time. But the worst of all is that he's spoiled me—everybody else seems kind of tame and young. So you see it's a mixed pleasure."

Joanna pondered, a little fuzzily. She was not at all sure what it was that Chris was telling her, but she felt she was being talked to as by one worldly soul to another. Now Chris was saying, "He said that would happen and I didn't care then. He said, 'I'm too *old* for you, Chris, even if I was single, and this way it's hopeless for you.' But I didn't care. I didn't want anybody or anything else and I just plain chased him. And now I don't want anything else either. So it *is* hopeless. . . . I hope you don't ever love anybody more than he loves you," said Chris.

"I've never really been in love," said Joanna bravely.

"Well, you will be," Chris said, lighting a second cigarette. The little white interior and their two young, drowsy faces shone for a second in the flash of the match. "First I thought you were coming here because you were Phil's girl, but I soon saw you weren't."

"Oh, *no!*" cried Joanna again. "He's just the brother of a friend of mine, that's all."

"Yes," said Chris, "he always picks racier types than you."

Racy, thought Joanna. I wish *I* was racy, but I'm too scared.

"I've seen some of his girls, and not one of them was as good-looking as you are," Chris went on. "But they were all very dizzy. He has to have that, I guess—he's so sort of restrained himself, with that family and all. I went to a cocktail party at his house once, and it was terrible. Jeepers!" She began to laugh.

Vulgarity is what he likes, then, said Joanna to herself. Perhaps I like it myself, though I don't know that I know what it is. Perhaps my mother would say Chris and Sandy were vulgar, but they don't seem vulgar to me, though I'm glad Mother isn't here to hear their language and some of Sandy's songs.

She gave it up, as Chris said with a yawn, "We'd better get back."

As they went toward the house it loomed up above them, twice its size, the kitchen windows throwing low beams of light out into the fog. Still there was no wind. In the heavy night air nothing was real, not even Chris and the lantern and the corner of a great wall near the house. Joanna was disembodied, moving through a dream on her bare, numb feet to a house of no substance.

"Let's walk around to the front," she said, "I love the fog."

"O.K.," said Chris, and they went around the corner and stopped by the lilac bushes to listen to the stillness.

But suddenly the dampness reached their bones, and they shivered and screeched and ran back to the back door, with the bobbing lantern smoking and smelling in Chris's hand.

When they came in, Phil looked at them fondly. "Dear little Joanna," he said. "She's all dripping and watery and vaporous, like Undine. What in God's name have you girls been doing?

"Oh, talking," said Chris.

"Pull up to the fire," Sandy said. "What did you talk about? Us?"

"Yes, dear," said Chris, "We talked about you every single second."

"Joanna's very subdued," remarked Phil, "Did you talk her into a stupor, or what?"

"Joanna doesn't have to talk if she doesn't want to," said Sandy, "I like a quiet woman, myself."

"Do you now?" said Phil, laughing at Chris, who made a face at him and sat down beside Sandy and gave him a violent hug.

Joanna, blinking, sat on the floor with her wet feet tucked under her, and listened vaguely to the talk that ran to and fro above her. Her head was swimming, and she felt sleepy and wise, in the warm lamplight and with the sound of the bantering voices which she did not have to join unless she wanted to. Suddenly she heard Phil saying, "You know, Joanna, we've got to start along. It seems to me you made a rash promise to your family that you'd be home early and it's nearly ten now and we've got thirty miles to go." He yawned, stretched, and bent to knock out his pipe on the side of the fireplace.

"I don't want to go," said Joanna.

"Then stay," said Sandy. "There's plenty of room"

But Phil said, getting up, "No, we've got to go. They'd have the police out if we didn't come soon. Joanna's very carefully raised, you know."

"I *love* Joanna," said Chris, hugging Sandy again until he grunted. "I don't care how carefully she was raised, I love her."

"We all love her," Sandy said. "You haven't got a monopoly on her.

Come again and stay longer, will you, Joanna? We love you, and you look so nice here in this horrible old house."

They really do like me, thought Joanna, pulling on her sandals. But not as much as I like them. They have a lot of fun all the time, so it doesn't mean as much to them to find somebody they like. But I'll remember this evening as long as I live.

Sadly she went out with them to the station wagon, following the lantern, and climbed in and sat on the clammy leather seat beside Phil. Calling back, and being called to, they drove away, bumping slowly over the little road, and in a second Chris and Sandy and the lantern were gone in the fog.

Joanna let herself in the front door and turned to wave to Phil, who waved back and drove off down the leafy street, misty in the midnight silence. Inland, the fog was not as bad as it had been near the sea; but the trees dripped with the wetness and the sidewalk shone under the street light. She listened to the faraway, sucking sound of Phil's tires die away; then she sighed and closed the door and moved sleepily into the still house, dropping her key into the brass bowl on the hall table. The house was cool and dark downstairs except for the hall light, and it smelled of the earth in her mother's little conservatory.

Joanna started up the stairs, slowly unfastening the belt of the old trench coat she had borrowed from Phil. The drive back had been a meaningless interval swinging in the night, with nothing to remember but the glow of the headlights blanketed by the fog so that they had had to creep around the curves and down the hills, peering out until their eyes ached. Soon after they had left the farm they had stopped in a small town while Joanna telephoned her family; through the open door of the phone booth she had watched Phil sitting on a spindly stool at the little marble counter next to the shelves full of Westerns, drinking a Coke—she had a Coke herself and sipped it as the telephone rang far away in her parents' house, while back of the counter a radio played dance music. And twice after that Phil had pulled off the road, once to light his pipe, and once for Joanna to put on his coat. But now, moving up the shallow, carpeted stairs, she was back in the great, cold, dusty house with the sound of Sandy's guitar and the smell of the oil lamps, and the night, the real night, wide and black and empty, only a step away outside.

Upstairs, there was a light in her own room and one in her mother's dressing room. It was a family custom that when she came in late she should put out her mother's light, so now she went into the small, bright room. With her hand on the light-chain she looked around her, at the chintz-covered chaise longue, the chintz-skirted dressing table with family snapshots, both old and recent, arranged under its glass top, at the polished furniture, the long mirror, the agreeable clutter of many years of satisfactory married life. On the walls were more family pictures covering quite a long period of time— enlargements of picnic photographs, of boats, of a few pets. There was Joanna at the age of twelve on a cowpony in Wyoming, her father and uncle in snow goggles and climbing boots on the lower slopes of Mont Blanc heaven knows how long ago, her sister and brother-in-law looking very young and carefree with their bicycles outside Salisbury Cathedral sometime in the early thirties, judging by her sister's clothes. The world of the pictures was as fresh and good and simple as a May morning; the sun shone and everyone was happy. She stared at the familiar little scenes on the walls with love—and with a sympathy for them she had never felt before—and then she put out the light and went back along the hall.

In her own room she kicked off her sandals and dropped Phil's coat on a chair. A drawn window shade moved inward and fell back again in the night breeze that rustled the thick, wet trees close outside; her pajamas lay on the turned-down bed with its tall, fluted posts. Joanna did not stop to brush her teeth or braid her hair; she was in bed in less than two minutes.

In the darkness she heard the wind rising around Sandy's house, breathing over the open hill, whistling softly in the wet, rusted window screens, stirring in the apple trees. She heard the last burning log in the fireplace tumble apart, and a horse kick at his stall out in the barn. If I'd stayed all night, she thought, in the morning when the fog burned off I'd have known how far you could see from the top of the hill.

For in the morning the hot sun would shine from a mild blue sky, the roofs would steam, the horses would gallop and squeal in the pastures between the great walls, and all the nightingales would rise singing out of the short, tough grass.

19 CHARACTERIZATION

Characterization as an *illusion* based on three elements:
consistency of behavior and attitudes, *complexity*, and
individuality; techniques of developing these qualities
including *direct analysis*, significant *action*, *dialogue*, *thoughts*,
and *physical description*; *blending* these various techniques.

Characterization, like all aspects of fiction, is illusion. When we as readers feel that a fictional character is "convincing," "vivid," or "realistic," it is not because that character resembles someone familiar; the illusion we have is of meeting and coming to know someone new.

It is not necessary, for example, to have known a professional horse trainer to appreciate and understand Chris in "The Nightingales Sing." We don't have to be parents to respond to Holly, the ten-year-old daughter in "Graveyard Day," and to wince at her self-righteous insistence on her own views. Nor is it necessary to have known mental patients to have the illusion of having just met one in "Sausage and Beer." In each case, our sense of having been introduced to a person is based not on familiarity but on the way that character is revealed in the fiction.

Consider for a moment the full range of characters you feel that you have "met" through fiction. Stories and novels have allowed you to cross the barriers of age, nationality, social class, sex, and race. The illusion of reality is in no way dependent upon having known an old Caribbean fisherman, a nineteenth-century Russian countess, or a British country squire.

This "willing suspension of disbelief" has enormous power. How is it achieved? There are three elements involved: consistency, complexity, and individuality.

In practice, of course, making a character "come alive" on the page is not at all this mechanical. Most writers borrow heavily from people they have known and then metamorphose the details in a variety of ways, both consciously and unconsciously. This is the way they find those hundreds of minute details that go into a finely drawn character. But the reason for this dependence on experience is that it is the most natural way to develop consistency, complexity, and individuality.

Consistency

In real life we come to expect a certain consistency in our friends—patterns of behavior, outlook, dress, and the like. In spite of variations, some people tend to be naturally generous or constitutionally sloppy or ambitious.

In addition, these characteristics tend to be interlocked. If a man is an insurance executive, we don't expect him to be politically radical or to have a long black beard or to speak in incomplete sentences prefaced with "like," or to race his Honda on Sunday afternoons. It might be nice if he did, of course; and making such a contradiction plausible could be the start of a story. But that comes under the heading of *complexity*, which I shall turn to shortly. The point here is that consistency of character is one of the basic assumptions we make about people in real life, and it is also the fundamental assumption upon which fictional characterization is built.

In simple fiction, consistency is pushed to the point of predictability— and monotony. We know, for example, that Dick Tracy will never under any circumstances take a bribe or punch a sweet little old lady in the nose. It is most unlikely that Blondie will turn junkie. And Tarzan is not going to start wearing a suit. For many readers, these rigid conventions destroy the illusion of credibility; yet for others it is so effective that they send letters and presents to these fictional characters in care of their local paper, utterly confusing art and life.

In sophisticated fiction, it is the minor characters who are the most consistent. The heavyset owner of the bar in "Sausage and Beer" has some important lines, but he is what E. M. Forster calls a "flat character," one who is there merely to serve a function and so is not developed. He is completely consistent. In "The Nightingales Sing" more is made of Phil, but he is without significant contradictions.

A certain degree of consistency is necessary in major characters as well. Joanna in "The Nightingales Sing" has some conflicting needs and outlooks, which we will turn to shortly, but there is an underlying consistency which we as readers come to depend upon. Her youth and her genuine naiveté are clearly established, and whatever she does on this occasion must be within those limits. Our credulity would be stretched to the breaking point if she turned out to be a heroin addict or an undercover agent.

Complexity

To achieve complex characterization, you have to develop more than one aspect of a character. You can do this by establishing a pattern, countering it in some way, and then showing how both elements are a part of the whole character.

You will have to go beyond the stereotypes of film and television, of course. We are all familiar with the hard-driving businessman who has a suppressed longing for simple pleasures and the man-hating woman who turns out to be secretly in love. To achieve real complexity don't settle for the formula of the character who is "this but secretly that."

Take Joanna in "The Nightingales Sing," for example. In some respects she is a romantic young woman looking forward to new experiences and what she imagines to be the excitement of adulthood. She sees Chris' life as an "arduous yet dramatic way of earning one's living" even though *we* see Chris as a woman who has not only been thrown by a horse but who is forlornly involved with a married man, a relationship that clearly has no future. Joanna would like to be "racy" like Phil's other girls, and in the final scene she wistfully wonders what it would have been like to have spent the night there.

Yet on the other hand, she is also cautious. Although she is exasperated with her mother on the telephone, she does go back to the familiar security of her house and her room with those photographs from her childhood. She has taken one step toward adulthood and then retreated—though we know from her dreamy vision at the end of the story that she will soon enter the adult world.

The story, then, is not about a naive girl in a circle of older, more sophisticated people. It deals with a protagonist who is at the same time a girl who has led a sheltered life and a young woman looking forward eagerly to what she believes will be the excitement of adult life. We see this pattern in the vacillation of her attitude. Most readers of either sex and any age will recognize this ambivalence even if they have never known people like this.

Chris is also presented in a fairly complex manner even though the focus of the story is not placed on her. In part, she is a tomboy who loves horses and riding. She values her independence highly. Yet on the other hand she is very fond of a married man who has told her there is no future in the relationship. We assume that she will go on loving Sandy just as she loves riding spirited horses who will, from time to time, throw her.

Developing one or two characters in a complex manner is about all you can do in a short story. Secondary characters tend to be presented more simply. For instance, the two men in this story are credible, but they are not presented in detail.

In "Sausage and Beer," the complexity in Uncle Theodore takes the form of alternation: He appears at first to be quite sane and then reveals himself to be hopelessly out of contact with the real world. When, at the end of the visit, the boy assumes that a polite lie will do as well for a mad uncle as it does for other relatives, Theodore has an unnerving moment of lucidity.

More basic to the development of the story, however, is the complexity which I hope is apparent in the father. Before the visit, he is austere and distant. He is not the kind of man who confides anything. But visiting the hospital is an ordeal he shares with his son. After that he invites the boy to share a private corner of his life. The bar is where he once played chess with his brother, and it has apparently been a place of solace for him in recent years. There he reveals the warmer, more compassionate side of his nature.

The complexity of Waldeen in "Graveyard Day" is all the more surprising in view of how simple and straightforward she appears at first. Initially we see her as a cheerful but occasionally exasperated single parent. Through all her apparently aimless chatter, however, we gradually see that she is dealing with a serious and genuine question: How can she (or anyone) be sure that what seems like a good relationship is solid enough and deep enough to last? Joe asks, "But if you love me, what are you waiting for?" Her answer shows her true maturity. "That's the easy part," she says. "Love is easy."

Through the course of the story she wrestles with the question of whether she should take another chance. The fact that the man she loves has the same first name as her former husband suggests that she may just be trading one bad marriage for another. But in the end she has enough evidence to let go of her doubts. That's when she takes that leap into the leaves—a leap into the future.

Complexity, then, involves adding at least one other aspect to a character's original pattern. If the variation is too slight, the character may seem hackneyed and dull or inconsequential. But if the change is too great or is unconvincing, readers will feel that the character lacks consistency. "I just don't believe anyone would behave like that," they say, and the story has failed. Balancing complexity of character development with consistency is often a major concern as one revises.

Individuality

Some characters are memorable and some are not. Occasionally we recall a particular character long after the plot has been forgotten. In other cases we have to ask questions like, "Wasn't there a father in the story somewhere?" or, "I remember the fight, but what was it all about?" The characters who stick in our memory are those that have a high degree of individuality.

To some degree, individuality is simply a function of complexity. A many-sided character who remains credible is apt to seem individual or unique. But there is another factor as well, and this is the element of the unusual.

If you write about two typical college students who share a typical college room, it is quite likely that the reader will lose interest even if these characters are based on individuals you know. And if you present a family that on the surface resembles those which appear so often in television sitcoms and in commercials, it is unlikely any of those characters will linger in your reader's memory.

Often it is the unlikely occupation, the unusual commitment, the striking disability that serves to make a character vivid and memorable. An uncle in a mental hospital is more distinctive than a perfectly rational one who merely joins the family for dinner. A woman who is a professional horse rider is going to arouse more interest in fiction than one who has no professional commitment. Imagine how much would be lost if Chris in "The Nightingales Sing" were merely a close personal friend of Sandy without a distinctive occupation.

Be careful, however, not to push the search for individuality too far. There comes a point when it turns artificial and unconvincing. An inconsequential tale about two college roommates is not going to be improved by being metamorphosed into an inconsequential tale about two hunchbacks living in an abandoned fun house. Individuality for its own sake becomes a *gimmick,* a contrived and superficial attention getter.

The most effective examples of individuality are credible and add to our understanding of character. In "The Nightingales Sing," the fact that Chris is deeply committed to the world of horses and will go on riding them— even a hopeless "brute of a horse"—no matter how often she is thrown tells us a lot about her. It helps us to understand how she can go on being committed to Sandy no matter how much that relationship may hurt her. Her profession as a committed rider has not been selected merely for effect, it is used to reveal aspects of her character.

Individualization can be achieved with a relatively minor detail. In "Graveyard Day," for example, Joe McClain has an odd hobby. He "doesn't go anywhere without carrying a walking stick, although he is only thirty." It is strange enough so that it "embarrasses Waldeen to be seen with him." Distinctive as this characteristic is, it seems at first like an arbitrary detail thrown in just for effect. Since there is very little in this story that is arbitrary, however, we should take a close look at this particular detail.

Our first clue is his pride in a stick that belonged to Jefferson Davis, president of the Confederacy during the Civil War. Later in the story we learn that Joe's great-great-grandfather was killed in the Civil War and is buried in that very cemetery. And Joe announces that he would like to be buried there himself. These are scattered and minor details, but as we put them together we begin to see a picture of a man who values tradition and continuity. We begin to trust Joe McClain. His quirky fondness for walking sticks is an effective way of individualizing him, but it is also linked with a series of details through which we (and Waldeen too) come to understand him.

Direct Analysis of Character

Consistency, complexity, and individuality are the goals one works for in creating fictional characters. The techniques one uses to achieve these goals are more numerous. In addition to direct exposition, one can use a character's actions, dialogue, thoughts, and physical details. Each of these deserves a close look.

The direct approach is tempting because through exposition you can include a great deal of material very quickly. Suppose, for example, "The Nightingales Sing" had begun this way:

> Joanna was young and shy but growing restless with her safe, protected life. The future looked exciting and romantic to her though just a bit scary too. It seemed to her that Chris and Sandy held the key to a wonderful life.

This little paragraph unfolds a great deal of information which the reader of the original version has to gather over the course of several pages. But what appears to be an advantage also has liabilities you should consider.

First, an opening like this is apt to deprive the reader of the sense of discovery. The language of exposition, remember, is closer to that of the case history and newspaper article than it is to fiction. If you review the actual opening of the story you will see how carefully the element of mystery is created: "Through the fog the car went up the hill . . . up the sandy road that ran between the highest and broadest stone walls that Joanna had ever seen." Where are they going and what will it be like? Both Joanna and the reader wonder.

Exposition also tends to slow the pace no matter where it appears. Joanna's character is occasionally commented upon through exposition, but these passages are brief and scattered throughout the story. In this way the plot is kept moving by action and dialogue.

The greatest danger of using too much exposition, however, is the risk of laying out the theme. In stories like "The Nightingales Sing," theme and character are merged, and if the author analyzes her protagonist in detail she will be explaining the theme itself. If this happened the story would begin to resemble a case history or feature article and the reader would lose the sense of discovery so necessary in good fiction.

This is not to say that direct analysis of character is to be avoided at all costs. It can be a useful way to reveal some minor aspect which simply isn't worth the space it would take to imply through action or dialogue. Such passages are rarely found in introductions. Instead they usually appear as unobtrusive comments in the body of the story. In "The Nightingales Sing," for example, this editorial comment is slid in early in the story: "Being a good child, she had telephoned her family to tell them she would not be home until late." That first phrase is from the author's point of view. It is so brief that the suggestion is almost subliminal: In some ways Joanna *is* still a child. Longer samples of exposition analyzing character are occasionally found in the novels of certain authors like Margaret Drabble, but it is an approach that is more associated with the nineteenth century than with contemporary work.

The Use of Significant Action

"The Nightingales Sing" is a gentle story in terms of action. At the conclusion, the protagonist decides *not* to stay. Yet the story is filled with examples of subtle action that reveal character in a number of ways.

We see something of Joanna's exasperation with her parents through the way she hangs up the receiver; we see her desire to help and be a part of this new world from the way she lays and lights the fire—significantly burning old comics. When she feels an impulse to hug Sandy, we see her turn and pat the dog instead. And when she returns to the familiarity and comfort of her family, she follows the old custom of putting out her mother's light.

These are minor touches, but they work together to create a portrait of Joanna. And our view of Phil, while sketchy, also comes to us in part through action. The author devotes an entire paragraph to describing the spaniel—coming in, sitting by the hearth, giving a sigh of comfort, then suddenly trotting away. This might seem like needless action until soon afterward we see Phil sit down "with a sigh of comfort exactly like the dog's . . . making the fog retreat." Phil's ability to "make the fog retreat"—making the strange seem less threatening for Joanna—is seen toward the end when he lends her his coat.

Fiction, then, does not have to be highly dramatic to reveal character through action. The slightest movement or gesture can tell us a good deal.

And as we have seen in Joanna's case, even a decision not to do something is a decision and may help us to understand a character in depth.

"Graveyard Day" makes so much use of dialogue that it is easy to miss the significance of the action. But there are a number of small details that help to develop aspects of character. We get to know Joe a little better from the way he conscientiously scrubs the gravestones. It is one of the little ways in which we see his sense of duty, his concern for family. Later, the two women play cards. The game they choose is hearts. We learn that Betty "loses three hands in a row" but Waldeen "wins accidentally." Out of context, this looks like a rather blatant symbol, but it is so carefully buried in the story that we are apt to skip over it. Even if we don't notice it consciously on first reading, it contributes to our gradual realization that this time Waldeen will also be a winner at love.

On a broader level, Joe's willingness to have a picnic in his family's graveyard shows a certain flexibility. A more rigid individual might reject the idea on the grounds that he wouldn't get the job done. Yet the fact that he takes this responsibility seriously is shown in the way he insists that his friend C.W. work hard in the raking. From a fictional point of view, having the picnic in a graveyard is more memorable than if it were placed on some routine hillside; in addition, it is carefully used to reveal Joe's character and aspects of theme as well.

The most dramatic use of action in the story occurs when Waldeen finally leaves caution and indecision behind and leaps into the leaves. As I have already pointed out, this is prepared for by memories of an impulsive "adventure" with a friend years ago. It was also prepared for much earlier by Joe's complaint "You're just afraid to do anything new, Waldeen. . . . You're afraid to cross the street." In her leap into the leaves she has finally given up that caution.

We think of action as essentially a matter of plot. But this is only true of the simplest forms of fiction. In sophisticated work, action continually reveals aspects of character as well.

The Use of Dialogue and Thoughts

Dialogue, like action, often serves to inform the reader and advance the plot. A boy being driven to see his uncle is told that they are entering "a kind of hospital"; a girl asks if someone named Chris was the one who was thrown by a horse and in the process informs the reader of that fact; a woman asks "Couldn't we have a picnic at the graveyard?" and the plot moves in that direction.

But dialogue is also one of the most effective methods of revealing character. As a start, every line should be "in character," which is to say it should appear appropriate for the speaker. But my concern here is the way dialogue can be used to introduce new aspects of a character as well.

Joanna in "The Nightingales Sing" is a good example. Take a close look at how she reveals her rather naive and romantic notions about this house and those who use it.

"It's wonderful," she says to Phil, who replies that to him it seems like a "queer place." Undaunted, she tells Sandy, "I love your house." This pleases him, but he then describes it as "a barn of a place." Later Joanna responds to the song Sandy sings with "That's a lovely song"—though by this time she has begun to understand the tone of these people and she is described as shrinking at her own sentimentality.

These little exchanges seem to the casual reader to be snatches of routine conversation such as a hidden tape recorder might have picked up; yet actually they have been designed by the author to give readers not only insights into Joanna's attitude but further understanding of Phil and Sandy as well.

Chris is a secondary character, but she is developed in considerable detail. Almost all we learn about her is revealed through what she says. Here, for example, is the passage in which she describes her feelings about the horse that threw her:

> "He's a brute of a horse. He'll never be fit to ride. . . . he's just a brute and I don't think I can do anything more with him."

She goes on to admit that she probably will go on riding him and adds, "He's beautiful."

This is a fine example of *ambivalence,* which I described in the section on poetry: a simultaneous blending of two opposing feelings. This quotation alone would tell us a good deal about Chris and why she continues in a vocation that has already done her damage. But add to that the dialogue in which she describes her feelings about Sandy:

> "Sometimes I wish I'd never seen him. . . . He's got so he takes charge too much of the time. . . . But the worst of all is that he's spoiled me—everybody else seems kind of tame and young. So you see it's a mixed pleasure."

Now she has revealed two "mixed pleasures," and while Joanna is not able to make much of what she has heard, we as readers are able to see the complication of Chris' life and her needs. None of this has been stated by the author through exposition; it has all been revealed through dialogue.

Some stories rely even more heavily on dialogue. "Graveyard Day," like many of Bobbie Ann Mason's stories, contains a lot of dialogue which on first reading seems as aimless and inconsequential as casual conversation often is. But her characters keep revealing themselves through what they say.

Waldeen, for example rambles on about how Colonel Sanders was on the television show *I've Got a Secret,* and how his secret was that he had a million-dollar check in his pocket for selling his fried chicken chain, but now he continues to work for it and he "can't get rid of it," and the man who bought it is still called the "Chicken King" even though he has since sold it. All this appears so pointless that even Joe doesn't understand what she is getting at. "What's that got to do with families?" he asks.

Her response is a real insight into the inner struggle she is dealing with through most of the story:

> "What I mean is, you can't just do something by itself. Everything else drags along. It's all *involved.* I can't get rid of my ex-husband just by signing a paper. . . ."

Waldeen is never clearly analytical about what is going on in her head, but she expresses herself in vivid ways. In fictional terms, the lines of dialogue are not wasted. They continually work to reveal aspects of character.

Thoughts are merely internalized lines of dialogue. Normally they are presented without quotation marks. Quite often they counter or amend what a character has just said. Or they may simply be a reaction that is not stated out loud. When Joanna hears about the kind of women Phil usually goes out with, here are her thoughts:

> Vulgarity is what he likes, then, said Joanna to herself. Perhaps I like it myself, though I don't know that I know what it is.

Notice how close it is to spoken dialogue. It even seems natural to describe it as something she "said to herself."

Another passage appears as the next-to-last paragraph and draws the story together in ways Joanna herself doesn't yet understand:

> If I'd stayed all night, she thought, in the morning when the fog burned off I'd have known how far you could see from the top of the hill.

There are, incidentally, five conventions connected with dialogue which readers generally expect. If you are going to create the illusion of a real character through your use of dialogue, it helps to handle the mechanics smoothly so they don't become distracting.

First, most stories use quotation marks about that which is said out loud and none around thoughts. You will find occasional exceptions, but such stories run the risk of confusing readers. Second, most writers indent the first line of speech of each new speaker. This may appear to waste paper, but readers are used to it both in fiction and in drama. In exchanges between two characters, the reader does not have to be told each time which one spoke. It is a convenient signal.

Third, "she said," "he said," and "I said" are used more like punctuation marks than phrases and for this reason are repeated frequently. The prohibition against redundancy just doesn't apply to them. And trying to find substitutions like "she retorted," "he sneered," "she questioned," "he hissed" is obtrusive and sounds amateurish. In general, keep these identification tags simple. There is usually no reason for adding adverbs like "said angrily" or "said excitedly." Let the phrasing itself suggest the mood.

Finally, as I have suggested earlier, dialogue is rarely aided by phonetic spelling. If you are trying to catch the flavor of spoken language, try to find appropriate phrasing rather than tinkering with conventional spelling.

It is also possible to refer to thoughts or dialogue without actually quoting directly. If the phrasing comes close to actual quotation, it is called *indirect discourse*. This indirect treatment can be used both for dialogue and for thoughts. In "Graveyard Day," for example, Waldeen has just told Joe that she has bad dreams. As she looks for juice in the refrigerator she reflects on those dreams:

> What she is really afraid of, she realizes, is that he will turn out to be just like Joe Murdock [her first husband]. But it must be only the names, she reminds herself. She hates the thought of a string of husbands, and the idea of a stepfather is like a substitute host on a talk show. It makes her think of Johnny Carson's many substitute hosts.

If Mason had dropped those two phrases "she realizes" and "she reminds herself," this passage would become exposition from the author's point of view. Read it through that way and see how it changes the effect.

Or the passage could be handled in the first person as directly quoted thoughts. Notice how close it comes to spoken dialogue.

> Maybe what I'm really afraid of is that he'll turn out to be just like Joe Murdock. But it must be just the names. I really hate the idea of a string of husbands.

The differences between these approaches are largely a matter of tone. What concerns us here is that no matter how these thoughts are presented, they provide an insight into what is bothering her and, underlying that, her personality. It is one more example of the way she balances a basically warm and loving nature with caution.

There are times, of course, when dialogue has to be skipped over entirely. Occasionally one has to account for routine conversations that have no direct bearing on the story. Whole blocks of trivial conversation can be condensed with a brief phrase like: "They greeted her warmly," "They talked of other matters for over an hour," or "They lingered at the door, saying their goodbyes." Far better to use summaries like these than to weigh your story down with conversation that is only padding.

When you do use dialogue, however, try to make every line reflect the character of the speaker and, whenever possible, provide new insights.

The Use of Physical Details

There has been a steady decline in the use of physical description of characters in the past century. Today, some stories leave such detail entirely up to the reader. "Graveyard Day," for example, does not provide a single visual detail about any of the five characters. Readers form their own pictures on the basis of dialogue and action.

The other two stories do provide some physical details, though not at the beginning. Most authors today avoid blocks of description of any sort in the opening because it is a slow way to start a story. Instead they bury brief details after the story is well under way.

Here is the description of Uncle Theodore in "Sausage and Beer":

> He was a great, sagging man. His jowls hung loose, his shoulders were massive but rounded like a dome, his hands were attached like brass weights on the ends of swinging pendulums.

When a fictional character is based on a person you know, should you describe the model directly? The answer is simple: If doing so is inhibiting, don't. Like devising new names for your characters at the outset so as not to be bound to the actual model, metamorphosing physical descriptions sometimes helps to give you greater freedom.

In the case of Uncle Theodore, the actual uncle was tall, lean, and rather distinguished looking. But the father in the story had been described in essentially those terms, and it was important to have these twins strikingly dissimilar in appearance as they were in their fates. For this reason, the description of Uncle Theodore was based on the memory of a stranger I saw for only an instant in a hotel lobby.

Joanna in "The Nightingales Sing" is described in a highly unorthodox switch in the means of perception—the kind I have urged you to avoid! She is seen through the eyes of the two men:

They both looked at her, seeing a tall young girl in a blue dress and sweater, with her hair drawn straight back over her head and tied at the back of her neck in a chignon with a black bow. . . .

Helpful as these descriptions are, neither of them is essential. The stories would not be badly damaged without them. Keep that in mind before you load a short story down with a page of physical description.

Of equal importance—greater in some cases—are all the surrounding details: what a character wears, the house she or he lives in, the furnishings, the car, the cigarette or pipe, the ring. Every possession from the largest to the smallest can contribute to characterization.

When we think of Chris and Sandy, for example, we think of that house, which is as sparse and cut off from society as they are. Our impression of Phil is influenced by our associations with men who smoke pipes and also from the comparison with the carefully described spaniel. To create an individualized character, it helps to link that character with individualizing physical objects.

Blending the Techniques

When we analyze how characters are revealed in fiction, the process seems enormously complex. The same is true when we explain any artistic technique in abstract terms, whether it be dance, music, or some aspect of painting. Actual practice requires a blend of unconscious decision making along with conscious knowledge of craftsmanship.

The best way to develop what we think of as an "intuitive" ability to create believable characters in fiction is to read as much as possible. After an initial reading of a story for pleasure, go back over it and examine as a fellow writer just what the balance is between consistency and complexity. How is the character individualized? And how is the character revealed? Can you find samples of direct analysis on the part of the author? Could they have been avoided? How much has action contributed to your understanding? Or were dialogue and thoughts employed to a great extent? Exactly how much of a description were you given and how much is your impression based on the objects associated with that character? This is *active reading*—not for course credit but for your own development.

When you turn to the actual process of starting to write a new story, consider your characters carefully before you even outline the plot. Do you really know them? If you keep a journal, you may want to use it to record significant facts about the major characters in a new story: What kind of childhoods did they have? What kinds of parents? Where do they live and how do they spend their days—school? job? waiting for something to happen?

What kind of music do they like and what kinds of people do they enjoy? You should be able to write a page or so about the protagonist of any new story. You may not use more than half of the details you devise, but it helps if you have far more information about a character than is needed. Conversely, there is no kind of action, dialogue, or thoughts that can successfully reveal a character who is not yet fully formed in your own mind.

Finally, after having completed your first draft, you may wish to review your work from the point of view of craft to make sure your characters are consistent yet complex, and that they have individuality. It is at this point that you may wish to adjust the ways in which you have revealed your characters. Try to be as objective with your own work as you were when examining published stories.

In many cases the literary sophistication of a story is developed more from characterization than from complexity of plot. For this reason, those goals of consistency, complexity, and individuality will continue to be major concerns for as long as you write fiction.

20 A STORY BY ROBERT FOX

A Fable

The young man was clean shaven and neatly dressed. It was early Monday morning and he got on the subway. It was the first day of his first job and he was slightly nervous; he didn't know exactly what his job would be. Otherwise he felt fine. He loved everybody he saw. He loved everybody on the street and everybody disappearing into the subway and he loved the world because it was a fine clear day and he was starting his first job.

Without kicking anybody, the young man was able to find a seat on the Manhattan bound train. The car filled quickly and he looked up at the people standing over him envying his seat. Among them were a mother and daughter who were going shopping. The daughter was a beautiful girl with blonde hair and soft looking skin, and he was immediately attracted to her.

"He's staring at you," the mother whispered to the daughter.

"Yes, mother, I feel so uncomfortable. What shall I *do*?"

"He's in love with you."

"In love with me? How can you tell?"

"Because I'm your mother."

"But what shall I do?"

"Nothing. He'll try to talk to you. If he does, answer him. Be nice to him. He's only a boy."

The train reached the business district and many people got off. The girl and her mother found seats opposite the young man. He continued to look at the girl who occasionally looked to see if he was looking at her.

The young man found a good pretext for standing in giving his seat to an elderly man. He stood over the girl and her mother. They whispered back and forth and looked up at him. At another stop, the seat next to the girl was vacated and the young man blushed, but quickly took it.

"I knew it," the mother said between her teeth. "I knew it, I *knew* it."

The young man cleared his throat and tapped the girl. She jumped.

"Pardon me," he said. "You're a very pretty girl."

"Thank you," she said.

"Don't talk to him," her mother said. "Don't answer him; I'm warning you. Believe me."

"I'm in love with you," he said to the girl.

"I don't believe you," the girl said.

"Don't answer him," the mother said.

"I really do," he said. "In fact, I'm so much in love with you that I want to marry you."

"Do you have a job?" she said.

"Yes, today is my first day. I'm going to Manhattan to start my first day of work."

"What kind of work will you do?" she asked.

"I don't know exactly," he said. "You see, I didn't start yet."

"It sounds exciting," she said.

"It's my first job but I'll have my own desk and handle a lot of papers and carry them around in a briefcase, and it will pay well, and I'll work my way up."

"I love you," she said.

"Will you marry me?"

"I don't know. You'll have to ask my mother."

The young man rose from his seat and stood before the girl's mother. He cleared his throat very carefully for a long time. "May I have the honor of having your daughter's hand in marriage?" he said, but he was drowned out by the subway noise.

The mother looked up at him and said, "What?" He couldn't hear her either, but he could tell by the movement of her lips, and by the way her face wrinkled up that she said, what.

The train pulled to a stop.

"May I have the honor of having your daughter's hand in marriage!" he shouted, not realizing there was no subway noise. Everybody on the train looked at him, smiled, and then they all applauded.

"Are you crazy?" the mother asked.

The train started again.

"What?" he said.

"Why do you want to marry her?" she asked.

"Well, she's pretty—I mean, I'm in love with her."

"Is that all?"

"I guess so," he said. "Is there supposed to be more?"

"No. Not usually," the mother said. "Are you working?"

"Yes. As a matter of fact, that's why I'm going into Manhattan so early. Today is the first day of my first job."

"Congratulations," the mother said.

"Thanks," he said. "Can I marry your daughter?"

"Do you have a car?" she asked.

"Not yet," he said. "But I should be able to get one pretty soon. And a house, too."

"A house?"

"With lots of rooms."

"Yes, that's what I expected you to say," she said. She turned to her daughter. "Do you love him?"

"Yes, mother, I do."

"Why?"

"Because he's good, and gentle, and kind."

"Are you sure?"

"Yes."

"Then you really love him."

"Yes."

"Are you sure there isn't anyone else that you might love and might want to marry?"

"No, mother," the girl said.

"Well, then," the mother said to the young man. "Looks like there's nothing I can do about it. Ask her again."

The train stopped.

"My dearest one," he said. "Will you marry me?"

"Yes," she said.

Everybody in the car smiled and applauded.

"Isn't life wonderful?" the boy asked the mother.

"Beautiful," the mother said.

The conductor climbed down from between the cars as the train started up, and straightening his dark tie, approached them with a solemn black book in his hand.

21 NARRATIVE TENSION

Tension defined; techniques of creating tension: *dramatic conflict* between or within characters, *curiosity* aroused by means of a *dramatic question,* using *suspense* and *shock;* the tensions of *irony* and *satire* as illustrated by "A Fable."

A

Waldeen is preparing supper while her daughter, Holly, sits on the kitchen stool, swinging her legs. Waldeen has recently been divorced, but now she is seeing Joe McClain. He comes over for supper almost every night.

B

Waldeen is tenderizing liver, beating it with the edge of a saucer. Her daughter, Holly, insists that she is a vegetarian. Waldeen is sure this new fixation has something to do with Holly's father, Joe Murdock, from whom Waldeen is divorced. Waldeen shudders when she thinks of Joe Murdock.

It is easy enough to *feel* the difference between these two passages. But stop for a moment and see if you can analyze precisely what it is that makes passage A so bland compared with passage B even though they introduce the same story. Here is another pair of introductory paragraphs.

A

> Joanna went with Phil, a brother of a friend of hers, to visit a couple who lived in the country. Although she had not met them, she was assured that they loved company and would enjoy meeting her. It was a long drive.

B

> Through the fog the car went up the hill, whining in second gear, up the sandy road that ran between the highest and broadest stone walls that Joanna had ever seen. Phil, driving with dexterous recklessness, said to her, "I hope it's the right road. Nothing looks familiar in this fog."

The first version in each pair is a factually correct description of the situation at the beginning of "Graveyard Day" and "The Nightingales Sing" respectively. Although accurate, they will strike most readers as flat and undramatic. The second version in each pair seems more dynamic and charged with dramatic interest.

That sense of vitality, however, is created in different ways. The second introduction to "Graveyard Day" suggests potential conflict between Waldeen and her former husband as well as between her and her daughter. There is no way of knowing whether either conflict will be developed, but they create interest. In the case of "The Nightingales Sing," passage B provides no hint of conflict, but the setting is strange and threatening. One can imagine it as the opening of a television drama. Our attention is held primarily through curiosity: Where are they going and will they get lost?

An inclusive term that explains the energy generated in both of these more dynamic versions is *tension*. The two paragraphs marked B are condensed versions of the actual openings, and each contains the tensions that launch those works. Developing tensions like these is essential if one hopes to catch the reader's attention and hold interest at the very outset.

But tension is not limited to openings. It is the recurring force that maintains the sense of forward motion throughout a story or novel. You can develop tension at any point by arousing your readers's sense of curiosity or by providing conflict. Or you can use suspense or shock. You can also create tension in more subtle ways through the use of irony and satire. Since it is tension that provides the energy and vitality in fiction, each of these approaches deserves a close look.

Dramatic Conflict

Conflict is found in all types of narrative including plays, films, and some types of poetry. We call it "dramatic" partly because it is associated with plays, but mainly because it gives the sense of being vivid or striking.

On its simplest level, dramatic conflict is the mainspring of simple fiction and drama. Adventure stories and television thrillers pit characters against each other with great regularity. Occasionally an individual faces a group or, less often, some aspect of nature. The conflict in such works tends to be simple, straightforward, and not complicated with inner debate. The plots are remarkably similar.

With associations like these, it is no wonder that some novice writers unconsciously avoid all forms of conflict and keep their characters passive or isolated. But there is no need to avoid conflict in even the most sensitive fiction. It will serve you well and will add essential vitality to your fiction as long as you make sure it is reasonably subtle, insightful, and appropriate to the length of your story.

Sophisticated fiction often combines some type of visible, external conflict with inner conflict. If you return once again to "The Nightingales Sing," you will see that combination perfectly illustrated. Although the conflict is not hinted at in the opening, it is developed as the story unfolds and becomes the primary theme.

As I have already pointed out, a part of Joanna is being drawn forward into an adult world that seems exciting and rewarding; yet another part is cautious and willing to return, at least for the present, to the protective and sheltering life her family has provided. If this were her only chance to escape her protected environment, her return home at the end of that story might seem like a defeat. But the ending suggests that she is eagerly looking forward to entering the adult world with all its risks.

In addition to this inner debate, there is an outer conflict that adds a sense of vitality to the story. Chris, the professional rider, has just been thrown by "a brute of a horse." She is convinced he is unmanageable, but she won't quit. Her will is clearly pitted against that of the horse. Later we learn that sometimes she wishes she had never met Sandy. She tells Joanna, ". . . he's got so he takes charge too much of the time." But she won't leave him either. We come to understand Chris' conflict with Sandy more fully through what she said earlier about her struggle with that horse. These conflicts are the type Joanna will face when she finally leaves the protection of her home and enters the harsher realities of adult life.

An analysis like this is necessary to show how different types of conflict can be used within the same story. But I should make it clear that this does not describe how one goes about writing a story. One doesn't sit down with a determination to combine an inner conflict with an outer one. One begins with a character in a particular situation. A plot unfolds—part experience, perhaps, and part invention. It is usually midway in the writing or perhaps after the first draft is completed that a careful literary analysis of what you have done can be enormously helpful.

Just suppose, for example, that you are in the middle of a similar story in which a relatively inexperienced young woman visits an older couple. Let's assume that in the first draft the older couple simply explains to the young woman that the life they lead isn't really as perfect as it seems. It is quite possible that the story would strike you as a bit too talky, perhaps even dull and lacking in momentum. If you have not read a fair number of short stories and had not analyzed the ways in which dramatic conflict can be added to energize a scene, you might well be tempted to give up and abandon the story. But if you are familiar with the need for conflict, you will be more apt to identify your problem and devise a solution—in this case by having the older couple illustrate some of the strains of adulthood rather than merely talk about them.

With this in mind, let's take a close look at the use of conflict in "Graveyard Day." There are two initial conflicts in that story, and I have made use of both in the somewhat condensed version of the opening that appears as B at the beginning of this chapter. The first is the recurring dispute between mother and daughter. Although it runs through the entire story, it is always treated lightly. The other is the more complex relationship Waldeen has with her former husband. She wants to forget him, but she can't seem to get him out of her mind. This is not resolved until the very end of the story.

Closely related to the inner conflict Waldeen feels regarding her former husband is an outer one with Joe McClain: He wants her to marry him and she resists his proposals, wanting more time to decide. If this were the only conflict, the story would be reduced to the simplest level no matter how convincing the characters were. It is the intermeshing of conflicts—some external and some internal—that gives the story its individuality and its vitality.

One word of warning: When working with internal conflict, be careful not to rely too heavily on your protagonist's thoughts. Long passages in which characters "debate" with themselves begin to sound like explanatory essays. "Graveyard Day" is a good demonstration of how to keep a character's thoughts brief and fragmentary. The illusion of reality is preserved when readers have to put the pieces together themselves.

In addition, don't forget that you can often imply an inner conflict through action, dialogue, or even description. In "Nightingales," for example, the harsh reality of adult life that Joanna longs for is dramatized in that stark, unadorned house she visits. It is contrasted with her parents' home, which is described as "comfortable, chintz-warmed." At the end of the story we are shown family photos on the wall in which "the sun shone and everyone was happy." These descriptions go beyond an intellectual understanding of the conflict she faces; they help us to *see* it.

Arousing Curiosity

It takes time to develop conflict in a story. But you can arouse the reader's curiosity in the very first paragraph. Both "Sausage and Beer" and "The

Nightingales Sing" open with the protagonist being driven to some unknown spot. In the second story the sense of mystery is increased with the fog, the high stone walls, and the "dim . . . wan light" of early evening. Phil is not even sure they are on the right road.

This element that arouses curiosity is called the *dramatic question* (also the *hook*). Occasionally it is sustained until the very end. A detective story, for example, is one long dramatic question with the answer as a conclusion. Literary short stories, however, usually shift from one dramatic question to another to keep the technique from turning the work into a suspense thriller.

In "Sausage and Beer," for example, the initial question is "Where are they going?" This is partially explained and is replaced by the larger question, "Who is Uncle Theodore?" In the concluding scenes, there is once again a question of where they are going.

There is also a series of quietly dramatic questions in "The Nightingales Sing." Once we learn that Phil and Joanna are about to visit Chris and Sandy, there are a number of questions that arouse our curiosity just as they do Joanna's: Why does this couple live like this, and why does Chris keep on riding when obviously there are dangers involved? These questions are somewhat diffuse, but they are the elements that keep the reader in the story.

Sometimes a dramatic question is posed early in a story and sustains itself right through to the end. "Graveyard Day" uses this approach. In the opening scene we learn that Joe McClain wants to marry Waldeen but that she had told him that they must wait. "Her ex-husband is still on her mind, like the lingering aftereffects of an illness." The reader wonders: Will she change her mind? Should she?

The entire story is energized by these questions. And when she finally pulls off her shoes and takes that flying leap into the leaves, she has left indecision behind and the story is over.

Depending on a single dramatic question has its risks. If the reader has the feeling that there are only two possible outcomes, the result will seem too predictable. We see this sometimes in the sports story that poses the too-simple question, Will they win or lose? Or the mountain-climbing story that asks, once again, Will they make it to the top or not? One solution is to find a conclusion that is not quite one or the other. They lose the game but preserve their sense of honor. The climbers make it to the top but for complex reasons the victory brings no sense of satisfaction.

Mason uses a different approach. Although the basic question of whether Waldeen will accept Joe's proposal is repeated at various points, it is never highlighted in the manner of a sports story. In fact, some readers may be initially uncertain as to what is holding the story together. When Waldeen finally takes that leap into the leaves, however, she not only shows us that she has thrown off that indecision, she reveals just how preoccupied she has been with the possibility of remarriage. The resolution not only answers the dramatic question, it clarifies it as the central concern of the story.

Suspense is simply a heightened form of curiosity. It too uses a dramatic question, but the volume has been turned up. Since it takes time to build suspense convincingly, it is rarely found in contemporary short stories. Even in novels, suspense is frequently limited to specific scenes rather than becoming the primary energizing force. So-called suspense thrillers will, of course, continue to be popular, just as will television dramas of the same sort. The difficulty with suspense in sophisticated fiction is that it tends to overpower all other literary elements. Characterization, thematic suggestion, and tonal subtlety are apt to be sacrificed.

If you have a compelling plot, however, don't shy away from suspense. Just make sure it doesn't cause you to settle for stereotyped characters and win-or-lose plots. If you feel the story sliding in that direction, remember that because suspense is merely an intensified form of curiosity, it can always be muted to the point where other literary elements have a chance.

Shock is also used to create tension, but it cannot be sustained. It is generally a single flash. If you use it as the climax of the story, be sure you have led up to it carefully. If you hit readers with a shocking conclusion for which they were not prepared at least unconsciously, they will shrug off the whole story as a piece of sensationalism. Try instead to create the sense of inevitability—without predicting the exact outcome.

Since shock can all too easily dominate a short story, many authors prefer to mute it, creating what might be thought of as a minor jolt. In "Sausage and Beer," for example, there is the moment when the boy has just made a polite but absurdly untrue statement, "It's been very nice meeting you," and the uncle reacts with "a loud and bitter laugh, derisive, and perfectly sane."

Irony and Satire

Irony provides tension in quite a different way. While conflict is developed between and within characters, and curiosity is generated by heightening the reader's desire to find out, irony plays the author's apparent intent against the actual meaning. As we will see, this seemingly unrelated technique is also a form of tension which provides energy and vitality in fiction.

Before we can use irony effectively, it helps to be able to identify examples and understand how it works. Actually there are three different but closely related kinds of irony that appear in fiction and drama.

Verbal irony occurs when characters make statements that are knowingly different or even the opposite of what they really mean. In casual conversation we sometimes call it *sarcasm*, though sarcasm is generally hostile and critical. Irony can take the form of simple understatement, as when someone describes a hurricane as "quite a blow." Stronger irony can be a full reversal of meaning, as if the same character, while watching his house being washed away in the storm, says "Great day for a sail."

Verbal irony in fiction occurs most often in dialogue. It suggests a character who is wry and given to understatement. As such, it is one more way dialogue can help define character. It is also possible, however, to use verbal irony in passages of exposition. As I have already pointed out, author's intrusion is not widely used in contemporary writing, but it is always possible to adopt a wry tone when one does step into a story. Elizabeth Parsons is using a touch of irony when she writes of Joanna: "Being a good child, she had telephoned her family. . . ." In one sense Joanna *is* a child, but describing her as just that is ironic in view of the fact that so much of the story deals with her emerging adulthood.

The most interesting use of verbal irony, however, is when it becomes the voice of an entire story. This is often the case with satire and is perfectly illustrated in "A Fable" by Robert Fox. I will return to that shortly.

Dramatic irony is similar except that the character making the statement does not understand that it is ironic. It is called *dramatic* because it has been used in plays since the time of Sophocles, but it is also used in fiction. A more descriptive term is *unconscious irony* since the character is not aware of it.

It lends itself to a character's thoughts just as well as to dialogue. There is a good example toward the end of "The Nightingales Sing," when Joanna is about to leave.

> They really do like me, thought Joanna. . . . But not as much as I like them. They have a lot of fun all the time, so it doesn't mean as much to them to find somebody they like.

Her notion that they "have a lot of fun all the time" is highly ironic. *We* know life is not easy for Sandy and Chris because Chris made that clear. But even though Joanna has heard everything we have, she still has a romantic notion of what life can be like for adults.

More often, unconscious irony occurs in spoken dialogue. At the very end of "Graveyard Day" when Waldeen has taken that leap into the leaves, her daughter Holly looks down with the stern disapproval of a rather rigid parent and says, "Don't you know *anything*?" At ten, Holly seems convinced that she knows just about everything and her mother nothing. But the story as a whole has suggested that the reverse is true.

Unconscious irony is often used in comedy—sometimes subtly and often blatantly. It is a natural comic device to have characters say things that have a significance only the reader understands. On a more serious level, it can be highly effective in first-person stories in which narrators are not fully aware of how much they are revealing about themselves.

The third type of irony is sometimes called *cosmic* or the *irony of fate,* though it may take the form of a very minor event. It refers to any outcome that is the opposite of normal expectations. One often hears it used in a careless way to describe anything unexpected ("Ironically, the weaker team won.") True irony, however, is a real reversal. It is ironic for a composer like Beethoven to lose his hearing or for an Olympic swimmer to drown in his own bathtub.

Life occasionally provides ironic twists that are too blatant for fiction. Bad enough that America's first major toxic-waste disaster should actually occur in something known as the Love Canal, but what story writer would have dared call the culprit the Hooker Chemical Corporation?

Ironic reversals in fiction tend to be muted so they don't become obtrusive. One occurs in "Sausage and Beer" in the scene from which I quoted earlier—the visit with Uncle Theodore. Although one might expect that bizarre behavior would be the most disturbing aspect of such an experience, it is actually Theodore's one moment of lucidity that jolts the boy. And in "Graveyard Day" there is an ironic twist in the fact that the cemetery, normally a place for mourning, turns out to be the place in which Waldeen can finally let go of the past and joyfully leap into a new phase of her life. The "graveyard" of the title has been life-enhancing.

Some ironic details are so brief and fleeting that one can easily miss them. When Waldeen's marriage was breaking up, for example, her husband, "unemployed and drunk . . . snatched Holly from the school playground and took her on a wild ride around town." That's when he bought her an *All in the Family* Joey doll. So much for family spirit.

Irony provides tension in fiction because there is a strain between what is said and what is meant or between what occurs and normal expectations. The reader is caught off balance, jolted.

Satire is almost always rooted in irony. Essentially it is exaggeration for the purpose of ridicule. The writer usually adopts a solemn or serious tone when in fact he or she is making fun of the topic at hand. Occasionally the technique is reversed and a serious subject is treated as if it were high comedy. Either way, there is always a tension established between the apparent tone and the true intent.

Many readers are introduced to simple satire through magazines such as *Mad Magazine* and, later, *National Lampoon.* Neither these nor the satiric sketches one often sees on television are very subtle. In fiction there is a greater range and greater subtlety.

In this volume, "A Fable" by Robert Fox provides a fine example of both irony and satire. The author maintains an ironic tone throughout. On the one hand the story appears to be the most reasonable sequence of events imaginable. A young man is on the subway looking forward to his first day of his first job. This sounds as if it will be a conventional and realistic story.

At some point we realize that something weird is happening, yet the reasonable, almost bland tone continues.

At what point do we realize that this is also satire? Perhaps as early as when the mother informs her daughter that this total stranger is in love with her. "How can you tell?" asks the daughter. "Because I'm your mother" is the answer. If not there, surely when the young man says to this young woman he has just met, "I'm so much in love with you that I want to marry you." As soon as we see that the author's intent is to ridicule something or someone, we know we are dealing with satire.

We *feel* that it is satire even before we are sure exactly what is being ridiculed. Unlike satiric pieces in *National Lampoon,* this little story doesn't reveal its intent in the title. But when we get to the end, we realize that we have been through an entire ritual: meeting a young woman, falling in love without knowing her, receiving approval of a parent who has no evidence whatever, uttering truisms like "Isn't life wonderful," and being married as the spectators routinely applaud. It is the American courtship ritual in bizarre exaggeration, yet told straight-faced.

Where is the tension in this story? It certainly is not in conflict. The daughter agrees to marriage at once and the mother is almost instantly won over. There is some degree of curiosity as we wonder what is going on, but this is not what one would describe as a gripping plot. The true tension of the story lies in the pull between the matter-of-fact tone of narration and the bizarre exaggeration of the way we select our partners for life.

A *fable* is a very short tale intended to teach a lesson. It is similar to a parable except that it is less frequently religious and occasionally deals with animals rather than humans. The form is not in the mainstream of fiction, of course, and contains none of the subtleties of characterization and theme we have been discussing. But it was given a rebirth in this century with George Orwell's political satire, *Animal Farm.* Fox's tight little narrative provides a fine model for those who might be interested in experimenting with non-realistic fiction, with an ironic voice, and with satire.

If this approach interests you, keep in mind that there are two dangers in the writing of satire. The first is lack of focus. Decide in advance just what kind of person, institution, or tradition you wish to ridicule. Keep your satiric attack precise and detailed.

The other danger is a matter of excess. If the exaggeration becomes extreme, you will find the piece turning into slapstick. Such work may, like cartoons, be very funny, but also like cartoons may be quickly forgotten. If you want to study some light but durable satire, read the novels of J. P. Marquand or Peter DeVries. For heavier, more biting satire, try George Orwell's *Animal Farm* or Joseph Heller's *Catch-22.*

Satire is often avoided on the unfounded assumption that a story must be either wholly satiric or strictly literal. This is unfortunate. Frequently a story can be intensified or enlivened by turning the satiric ridicule on a secondary character, an aspect of the society, or some institution involved in the plot. If the level of satire is kept light, there is not apt to be any damaging break in the tone of an otherwise nonsatiric story.

Casual readers often sense the lack of tension without being able to identify it or suggest a remedy. "It doesn't grab me," they say; or, "It seems kind of flat." These are not literarily precise statements, but they are worth taking seriously. Better yet, try to evaluate your own first draft before anyone else reads it. Does it have the energy, the vitality needed to hold a reader who might have other things to do?

If not, see if there is the potential for at least implied conflict between two individuals or between one and a group. Or is the story better suited for an internal conflict within a single character? Check to make sure that you have aroused the reader's curiosity early in the story and have provided a few dramatic questions to maintain interest. And if you have made use of suspense or shock, make sure you haven't overdone it.

If the story is critical of particular types of people or institutions or traditions, should it be presented with irony or even pushed into satire? Remember that in doing this, the story will become less penetrating in character development since satiric characterization stresses surface appearance; but it may create the result you want.

When starting a new story, tension will not be your first concern. Plot, character, and theme are quite enough to deal with at that stage. But once you have the basic framework clearly in mind, make sure you have provided enough tension to give your story a sense of vitality and life.

22 ORIENTATION: PLACE AND TIME

The impact of *immediate surroundings* as seen through specific
visual details; the *geographic setting:* "real" versus imagined
places; *time:* historical period, season, and hour of day or
night; *revising* the orientation: metamorphosing, heightening,
and muting of details.

Orientation is the sense of being somewhere specific. This starts with the
immediate surroundings, but it may also include broader factors such as what
country one is in, what region. In terms of time, it may involve the historical
period, the season, or the time of day.

Stories vary in the degree to which they stress orientation and in
which aspects are emphasized, but even the most dreamlike fantasies provide,
as do dreams themselves, details that help readers to place themselves. Without such details the characters tend to remain detached and unconvincing.
And the story itself may not provide that sense of authenticity readers need
if they are to become absorbed in the work. Setting is a major factor in creating
the illusion of reality.

The Impact of Immediate Surroundings

"Where am I?" is the stereotyped cry of those who are regaining conscious-ness. It is also the instinctive question of readers who have just begun a new story or novel.

The parallel is more significant than one might think at first. When readers begin a new work of fiction, they let go of their immediate surround-ings and enter a new consciousness, a new world. It is natural for them to feel disoriented until they know where they are. For this reason, most stories establish the immediate setting early. Like a stage set, the surroundings help to place readers in the story. A particular house, a room in that house, a field, a beach, a factory assembly line—these and countless other settings not only help to start a story and make the opening scene come alive, but they may contribute to characterization and the theme as well.

The key to making the immediate surroundings vivid and convincing is *specifics*. Just as poems depend on the freshness of images, fictional scenes depend on precise, carefully selected visual details.

Here are two descriptive passages. The first is brief and provides few details. There would be nothing wrong with such a description if the setting was not going to be used extensively. But the story, "Sausage and Beer," does make prolonged use of that room, so the version actually used (passage B) includes details that amplify each aspect.

A

It was a large, sparsely furnished room. A number of people wandered about, but it was hard to tell whether they were patients or visitors.

B

The room was large, and it seemed even larger for the lack of furniture. There were benches around all four walls, and in the middle there was a long table flanked with two more benches. The rest was space. And through that space old men shuffled, younger men wheeled carts of linen, a woman visitor walked slowly up and down with her restless husband. . . . Or was she the patient?

In the second passage, "large" is amplified with a phrase designed to help the reader feel it. The word "space" is repeated for effect. "Sparsely furnished" is made visual with specific examples. And the simple assertion that it was hard to tell which were the patients is dramatized by picturing a particular couple. This is not merely a matter of adding words; it is a careful selection of visual details designed to draw the reader into that room.

How much description should you provide? Much depends on whether the setting is going to be used in a significant way. Rambling descriptions of surroundings that are incidental merely slow the story. If, on the other hand, the setting you are dealing with is intended to reflect a character's personality, create a mood, or provide a contrast with some other scene, you have good reason to provide details. The waiting room in "Sausage and Beer" is worth describing not only because it introduces the boy to the unfamiliar world of the mentally ill, but also because it is later contrasted with the warm and happy world of those who, by chance, are not afflicted.

One might think that a short, satiric work like Fox's "A Fable" would need no setting at all. It is, after all, more concerned with thematic suggestion than fully developed characterization. It could have begun with no mention of the subway: "A young man was on his way to work." But by adding the subway-car setting, the action is placed in a context. The car is not described with any detail, but it provides, in dreamlike fashion, an audience to applaud the couple and a clergyman for the ceremony. On a deeper level, it adds to that equally dreamlike sense of fast-forward motion through time.

Longer stories can afford more detail. At the end of "The Nightingales Sing" the author wishes to portray the traditional and safe world Joanna came from. She does it by devoting a paragraph to the mother's dressing room. Joanna looks around her (the scene is presented through her eyes, not the author's) and here is a list of the details she sees:

> a chintz-covered chaise lounge
> a chintz-skirted dressing table
> family snapshots under a glass top
> polished furniture
> a long mirror
> more family photos on the wall including scenes of:
>> picnics
>> boats
>> a few pets
>> Joanna on a cowpony in Wyoming
>> her father and uncle in climbing gear
>> her sister and brother-in-law outside Salisbury Cathedral

All that in one paragraph! And this is the very point at which the story is rapidly moving to a conclusion. Yet the paragraph manages to absorb all these details and does not slow the momentum of the story because it is providing us with a vivid glimpse of her childhood environment, a world she is returning to for a while longer, and presumably will later leave for good. The passage is a dramatic display of a whole way of life—dramatic not because the plot is advancing but because our understanding is. This descriptive passage tells us just why Joanna found the stark, almost Spartan surroundings at Sandy's old farmhouse so inviting.

Fiction does not always make extensive use of the immediate surroundings. "Graveyard Day," for example, relies so heavily on dialogue that one doesn't even get a glimpse of Waldeen's house. But there is one small passage that suggests far more than it appears to at first reading. It describes the cemetery, a central image in the story:

> The graveyard is next to the woods on a small rise fenced in with barbed wire. A herd of Holsteins grazes in the pasture nearby, and in the distance the smokestacks of the new industrial park send up lazy swirls of smoke.

By the end of the story, you remember, this graveyard comes to suggest continuity with the past which Joe values so. It is where his great-great-grandfather and his grandmother were buried and where he wants to be buried eventually. Such values are rare in a country where few people live near their parents, much less their grandparents, and landmarks of the past are constantly being lost in the name of progress. So the graveyard in this story is not simply placed in a meadow, it is surrounded by barbed wire as if threatened, and if we doubt that rural spot could ever be lost in the name of economic development, we are shown the smokestacks of the "new industrial park" in the distance. This descriptive passage is brief, but it subtly adds to the theme of the story.

Where in the World?

Some stories are set in a particular geographic region or a specific city. This type or orientation is not all necessary, but it can add a valuable new dimension to fiction. If you decide to take advantage of this approach, your first question will be one of tactics—whether to identify an actual state or city or to create your own imagination.

In some respects, there is a fallacy in the question. Since all fiction is only an illusion, you don't have a choice between a "real" location and one of your own creation. All fictional settings are imaginary, and everyone's use of, say, New York or Los Angeles is going to be a product of imagination.

Your true choice, then, is not, "Shall I set this story in a real city?" but "Shall I use the name and certain characteristics of a real city in the exercise of my imagination? Will it help readers see what I want them to see?"

There are two good reasons for drawing on a known city and naming it. First, it can serve as a geographic shorthand for the reader. There are aspects of our larger cities like New York, San Francisco, and Chicago that are known even by those who do not live there. In addition, using a real city can be a convenience for you as a writer *if* you know the area well. It will save you the trouble of making up your own map.

But there are a couple of dangers as well. Unless you are really familiar with the city you are using, you may begin to depend on scenes and details you have unconsciously absorbed from other stories and from television. Students who have never been to New York, for example, are apt to fall back on such standard conventions as a rainy night on Forty-Second Street, poodles on Park Avenue, hysteria on Madison Avenue, rumbles on either the lower East Side or the South Bronx, and general perversion in the Village.

The same is true for Paris. If in blind ignorance the author spices a story with shots of the Eiffel Tower, cancan dancers, and prostitutes with hearts of gold, the fiction is bound to reflect the television programs and musical comedies from which this material was taken.

To avoid this, make sure you know the city well if you are going to name it, and try to focus your attention not on the most obvious aspects of the city but on districts and details that will seem authentic to your readers without being reminders of hackneyed stories and films.

Another problem with using a specific place is that you may find it difficult to metamorphose your material. That is, your fiction may become locked into the town or city. This is particularly common when the events have been taken from recent experience.

Perhaps for this reason, a majority of published stories are set in towns or cities that are linked to but not identified directly with real-life locations. John Updike describes this in his foreword to *Olinger Stories:*

> The name Olinger is audibly a shadow of "Shillington," the real name of my home town, yet the two towns, however similar, are not at all the same. Shillington is a place on the map and belongs to the world; Olinger is a state of mind, of my mind, and belongs entirely to me.

In this spirit, John Updike has used Olinger, Pennsylvania, in eleven short stories. The names and ages of the protagonists vary, but essentially they are the same boy. The approach is similar to that of Sherwood Anderson's in *Winesburg, Ohio.* On a broader scale, Faulkner blended historical and fictional elements this way in his stories and novels set in his imaginary Yoknapatawpha County, Mississippi.

None of the stories included in this volume are linked with a specific town or even a state, but two contain references that place them in a particular part of the country. In "Sausage and Beer" the father and son are described as driving "well out in the New England countryside." Why New England? Partly because the author is familiar with it, but also because the bleak, snowy landscape helps to dramatize the chilly relationship between father and son. Later it provides a contrast with the warmth of the bar scene at the end of the story. The precise location is not important, but the New England climate does play a significant role in that story.

The exact geographic setting in "Graveyard Day" is also left vague, but a number of details suggest that the story is placed in a South-Central state. Although this is not stressed, it adds to our understanding of both character and theme. Initially there is no hint of where the action is taking place, but soon there are references to Kentucky Lake and to catfish. We are then informed directly that the setting is about equidistant from Florida and Arizona. In addition, Joe McClain is particularly proud of his cane, which belonged to Jefferson Davis, the Confederate leader. Much later in the story we learn that Joe's great-great-grandfather was killed in the Civil War and is buried in this very cemetery. Discovering that this story is set in the South does not affect our reading in any major way, but it does contribute to our view of Joe McClain. Although he is not rich (he works on a construction crew), he is the fifth generation of McClains to have lived in this very town. He is no snob, but we can see from his attitude about this cemetery that he does take his heritage seriously. Because of these details we see him as more trustworthy and reliable than we would have otherwise. As with "Sausage and Beer," identifying the geographic area has added to the resonance of the story.

Some fiction makes much more direct use of specific regions. There was a particular interest in this approach toward the end of the last century, and it became known as *local color* writing. Mark Twain, Bret Harte, and Sarah Orne Jewett are the best-known authors to have used local color. A number of less-known writers, however, gave the term a bad reputation by concentrating on regional dialects and customs in a patronizing manner.

True regionalism is flourishing today. Every area of the country is producing short fiction that draws heavily on local attitudes, values, and culture. There are several anthologies of short fiction that reflect these concerns. Writers with distinctly regional or ethnic backgrounds should consider drawing on those traditions.

Good regional writing depends on two elements: personal familiarity and respect. You really have to know what you are writing about if you are going to do justice to the people of a specific region or culture. It is important to write from the inside, not as an outside observer. And even though you may see their weaknesses and vulnerabilities, you have to have a basic respect for them if you are going to avoid a patronizing tone. This is the true distinction between local color writing in its worst sense and genuine regionalism. If you spend some time in New Mexico as a tourist, for example, you may gather some excellent material for a story about tourists in New Mexico, and you certainly can draw on the physical characteristics of the area, but that doesn't mean that you are equipped to depict the life of a Navaho living on the reservation.

The Uses of Time

A story or novel exists in time as well as in space. Time includes historical period, the season, and the hour of the day. As writer, you can ignore any one of these without disorienting a reader, but don't forget that any one of them can also be used to make a real contribution.

Most short stories are set in the same historical period as the one in which they are written. This is partly because it takes time to establish the atmosphere of an earlier period, time that one can't easily spare in so short a form. In addition, if you move back to the nineteenth century it is difficult to avoid sounding like historical romances and so-called costume gothics with their recurring plots and stereotyped characters.

There are, however, two ways of using an earlier historical period effectively without running the risk of echoing formulaic fiction. Both are approaches in which the writer maintains some personal link with the earlier time. First, it is sometimes possible to develop good fiction from extensive conversations with elderly people such as grandparents or others in that generation. Thanks in part to portable tape recorders, there has been a growing interest in oral history of the immediate past. If your subject is willing, material gathered in this manner can provide the basis of fiction that has the true ring of authenticity.

You do have to pick your subject carefully. Some people are more articulate than others. Some enjoy recalling their past, but others do not—often for good reason. If your informant is agreeable, let him or her do plenty of talking. Occasionally you will have to ask questions in order to clarify certain facts, but try not to be directive.

Interviews are a particularly effective source if your subject's childhood was significantly different from our lives today. Be very careful, however, not to sound patronizing or, even with the best intentions, sentimentally admiring. Since you are using borrowed material, your safest route is to maintain a fairly neutral tone. Let the story and its characters speak for themselves.

Be careful, too, not to turn your story into a simple anecdote. Anecdotes depend primarily on a turn of events, a clever little plot. This may be entertaining in conversation, but if it is turned into fiction it runs the risk of trivializing the subject. To guard against this, concentrate on characterization. If you focus on the ambivalences of your protagonist, you will add depth which anecdotes normally lack.

The other use of the past applies only to those writers who are themselves old enough to remember when life was different. The accumulation of memory is one of the compensating benefits of age, and that layering of experience is an excellent source for fiction. One word of caution, however: Be careful not to lay undue emphasis on the differences between the period being described and the present day. If you draw too much attention to how inexpensive things were, for example, the reader may begin to view the material as quaint. Try instead to recreate the period; help the reader to share it.

The *time of year* is another aspect of time that is well worth considering. If the season has no real significance in a story, you can ignore it without the reader even noticing. But occasionally it helps to fix a story in a specific season and make use of it. "Sausage and Beer," for example, makes use of winter. The opening paragraph starts the story with the fact that "It was too cold for talk." The heater does not work. And at the hospital Uncle Theodore tells about his nightmarish theory that some night the hospital will shut off the heat and freeze the patients to death. It is not until the end of the story that this pattern of cold is broken. When father and son enter the bar together the boy discovers a "warm, bubbling, sparkling, humming . . . bit of cheerful chaos." The cold of a New England winter serves as a contrast with the warmth of friendship and, particularly, the newfound relationship between father and son.

Season can also be used as a method of metamorphosing a personal experience into something manageable. An episode that occurred in the heat of midsummer can sometimes be shifted to January merely to remove it from the confines of experience. Or an event that happened to take place in autumn might lend itself to spring and at the same time give you some sense of freshness and objectivity over your material. You must, of course, be on guard against the clichés of season. A first love that ends with a paragraph about the spring buds on the apple tree is as hackneyed as the story about an old couple that ends with the fallen leaves of November. Seasons can be enormously valuable—but only when they are used with subtlety and originality.

The *time of day* also has its share of clichés. A surprising number of stories begin with protagonists waking and wondering where they are. Fewer— but still too many—use the old film ending: watching the sun go down and "looking forward to another day."

In spite of these dangers, the time of day can often serve to orient the reader and to provide the writer with a system to organize the plot. "The Nightingales Sing," for example, starts with the "wan light of early summer evening" (season as well as time), and continues to the late evening with her parents asleep and Joanna musing sleepily what it would have been like if she had stayed. The mystery of that foggy evening and the vision of the next day help to suggest her sense of uneasiness in the face of a new experience and her naive view of what the future will hold. References to evening and morning, then, are not either casual or incidental; they have symbolic suggestion.

Even if you are not making specific use of the time of day, keep track of it in your own mind. This will help you to avoid careless errors in which a character refers to the morning coffee break one moment and quitting time five minutes later.

Carelessness in time sense can lead to another type of error which often takes this form: Two characters meet, sit down and talk for what in fact is only two minutes of dialogue, and then they part saying "It's been great to be able to talk this over with you." Since serious conversations are rarely that brief, be sure to provide some reference to the rest of their talk with a phrase like, "She kept on arguing, but her heart was not in it," or "The conversation turned to milder topics."

Whether you make direct use of the time of day depends on whether it is useful to the story. But remember that whatever scene you develop exists in the fictional time of the story, and the reader will expect it to be consistent.

Revising the Orientation

Revising aspects of place and time usually comes early in the writing of a story. It may, as I have pointed out, take the form of fundamental metamorphosing of the original experience. As the story develops, however, such sweeping changes become more and more difficult. A basic sense of geographic and seasonal setting tends to permeate a story so that revisions become much more elaborate than, say, changing a Nebraska farmhouse into a Chicago apartment or replacing the references to a winter scene with details about summer. If one has used place and season prominently, they become a part of the "feel" of the story. For this reason, it is best to make sure that the place and the season of a story are right before one has invested many hours of work.

Still, minor revisions of these details often go on through successive drafts. Heightening often is the result of chance. One selects a season, perhaps, because that is when the experience took place; and then various implications and suggestions come from the material and demand development. The use of cold as a vehicle to suggest separation and isolation in "Sausage and Beer" evolved in just this way.

In other cases, sharpening the visual details of a story is demanded because the action has gone on in a non-place. A surprising number of unsuccessful stories are placed in some ill-defined urban area which conveniently allows the protagonist to dodge city traffic one minute and, when the plot demands it, to be wandering "in the outskirts of town" the next. If you find yourself doing this, shift the story to a specific town or city that you know even if you do not use the name.

Muting aspects of setting may be necessary if you feel your use of place or season has become hackneyed. The kinds of clichés that damage fiction have already been described, but I should stress here that it is easy even for experienced writers to borrow from overworked conventions. Sometimes it is due to the fact that the experience has, infuriatingly, echoed a fictional cliché. There is no cosmic law that forbids life from imitating the worst in fiction. Occasionally a beautiful woman and a handsome man really do fall in love while strolling by the Eiffel Tower in Paris on a lovely June day. They may even live happily ever after. But who is going to believe it? Leave that plot to the musical comedy writers. If you really have had such a marvelous experience, find aspects of it that are further from the conventional pattern. This may involve moving the story to another setting or another season or both.

Occasionally the setting has to be revised because it has begun to resemble a literary convention. Stories about migrant workers tend to sound like John Steinbeck: hitchhiking stories often pick up the smells and sounds of Jack Kerouac's *On the Road* or motorcycle films; scenes involving city gangs frequently use standard details, including switchblades and leather jackets. One often has to mute these details and stress ones that the reader will see as if for the first time. Once again, be careful not to assume that details from your own life will necessarily be convincing as fiction. If you present a setting that your reader will associate with another author or a film, song lyric, television commercial, or musical comedy, your story will be damaged by the association. Muting those details and highlighting other elements will be necessary, and usually you can do this without losing your original conception.

It is important to understand that a sense of place, historical period, season, and time of day are not adornments to a story. They are part of what you see and feel as you write; they are also the primary means by which your readers are going to enter your story and experience it as if they were physically present. It is this sense of being there that makes fiction an "as-if-real" experience.

23 Literary Concerns: Theme, Tone, Symbol, and Style

Theme described as a cluster of related concerns; *tone* as a variable regardless of the subject matter; *symbolic elements* used to broaden the range of meaning; *style:* a product of *diction, syntax,* the balance of *narrative modes,* and *tense.*

In a broad sense, of course, this entire text deals with literary concerns. But the title of this chapter refers to four abstract concepts that are at the heart of literary composition.

On a simple level, each of these is used quite unconsciously. All fiction except the freest sort of journal entry has a theme of some sort. And it is always written with some kind of tone, usually reflecting the emotion of the writer at the time of the experience or shortly thereafter. Symbolic details can be stumbled upon accidentally, and style is present in every line of writing whether the author is aware of it or not.

On a more sophisticated level, however, these are four concerns with which experienced writers grapple all their lives. These are not concepts merely to be learned; these are continuing concerns.

Theme: The Central Concern

As I pointed out in the poetry section, theme is often overemphasized. Certain stories—like certain poems—can't be summed up neatly in a single, complete sentence. Others may be primarily studies in character. But some type of theme is essential in every kind of story.

It is theme that distinguishes fiction from an aimless journal entry or a shapeless fantasy. If you do not provide a degree of thematic unity, your readers are apt to respond with questions like, "But what's the point?" or "What are you getting at?"

There are usually several themes, one of which can be called primary. Because of this, some critics prefer *central concern*, a term I will use interchangeably with *theme*. *Central concern* serves as a reminder that we are not dealing with something as logically specific as a thesis or as ethically concerned as a moral. It is also a reminder of why having some type of theme is important. After all, what is a story that has no concern at all?

Like almost every other aspect of literature, the theme can be simple or highly sophisticated. Fiction for the very young repeats such themes as "It's terrible being the littlest (ugliest, weakest, stupidest), but with luck you can be the hero of the day." This is no more demanding than the themes that still appear with fair regularity in women's magazines and on television: "Nice girls win out eventually," "Crotchety old grandfathers are sometimes just lonely old men," and "Newly marrieds face problems that we mature readers solved two and three years ago."

Sophisticated fiction usually has a cluster of related concerns. This is true of even very short pieces like "A Fable" by Robert Fox. Like most works of satire, the characters in this brief story represent types rather than portraying fully developed individuals. In this respect it is similar to a political cartoon. But words offer a greater range of suggestion than do graphics.

Fox's central concern is the ritual quality of courtship: The way individuals happily enter into the complex responsibility of marriage without really knowing each other. The prospective bride and groom are convinced that they are in love even though they have known each other only for minutes.

But the naive couple is not the only concern. The mother goes through a series of familiar responses as if being viewed at fast-forward speed. First she is all-knowing, telling her daughter that the young man is obviously in love. How does she know this? "Because I'm your mother." Then she tells her daughter to "be nice." But when the daughter *is* nice and the relationship becomes serious, the mother is furious. "I *knew* it," she says between clenched teeth.

Her rage is short-lived, however—less than a minute actually. When the young man asks if he can marry the girl, the mother poses all the essential questions: Does he have a job? a car? a house? Are they in love? "Well then," she says, "Looks like there's nothing I can do about it." She has gone through just about every maternal response in record time!

As for friends and relatives, they all applaud on cue though they haven't the slightest notion of whether this is a good marriage or not. Finally the conductor, a total stranger, steps up to join the couple in holy matrimony.

The central concern, then, is the way couples decide to get married. But the author is also poking fun at mothers, at friends of the family, and perhaps even at the *pro forma* attitude of some clergymen.

Longer, nonsatiric stories that develop characters with some depth rather than working with types have a still greater range of thematic suggestion. But the pattern is often the same: a dominant concern which provides thematic focus and then a cluster of related themes.

This would seem to be the case in "Sausage and Beer." Although authors are not always the best judge of their own writing, I can at least describe what I hope emerges in that story. The first thematic concern is the notion that when one discovers just how much of life is determined by pure chance, one is initiated into adulthood. The future, one learns, can't be predicted and may well be unfair. We see this in a lighthearted way from the fact that the boy and his twin sister once naively planned their future, assuming they would eventually marry each other. But this option was not open to them. On a more serious level, the boy learns that his father and his Uncle Theodore, also twins, once "planned their future . . . the way my sister and I had," but that they also had no real control over their destinies. In their case, chance determined that one of them would lead a normal life and the other not. The waiter at the end of the story highlights this aspect of the theme.

But in the writing of the story, a second major concern began to take shape and may have to some degree taken over as the central concern. This might be described as the need to reach others and the difficulty we all have in this effort. In the case of Uncle Theodore, contact with the real world is sporadic—like a light with a bad electrical connection. In the case of father and son, however, the progression is from polite distance to a kind of communion.

In some stories different characters suggest different but related themes. Our first concern in "Graveyard Day" is for Waldeen and the choice she faces: Should she accept Joe's proposal of marriage or is the risk too great? She is haunted by the fact that her first husband was also called Joe and by the realization that he and others (the K.K.K. member on TV, for example) often talk about love when they don't really mean it.

She finally overcomes her doubts because of a number of factors. As I have already pointed out, Joe gives every indication that he is responsible, as seen by his attitude toward the cemetery and, more specifically, his grandmother's grave. Waldeen's first husband wouldn't even bury the family dog! She is also impressed that Joe has deep roots in the area. She imagines herself buried there with earlier generations of McClains as a kind of honor—"as if it symbolizes the promise of marriage." She may also be influenced by the fact that Betty resists marriage merely because she doesn't want to spoil her figure. And the graveyard is a continuing reminder that life is short. Notice that Joe's ancestor (also named Joe) was only 21 when he died. With all that in mind, Waldeen finally abandons her indecision and takes that flying leap.

Drawing all that together, we can say that the theme of the story deals with making decisions. How do we trust our inclinations? How do we trust others? That's quite enough for one story. But what about Holly? Why is she included in this story? To some degree, she is justified simply as a gently satiric touch. That's a matter of tone, which I will return to shortly. But her primary function as a character is thematic: She is the exact inverse of her mother. While Waldeen is filled with indecision, Holly is absolutely certain about everything. So here is another theme: Uncertainty is a condition of adulthood; absolute certainty is only for kids.

What about Betty and C.W.? Every thematic element we have looked at so far could be handled without this additional couple. Are they really necessary? Notice that as a couple they also are indecisive about marriage. Betty, we learn, wants to marry C.W. but "she does not want to ruin her figure by getting pregnant." For her, the continuity of families is not important. When the two women are playing cards Waldeen tries to explain her feelings about this cemetery and being a part of it. Betty says, "Ooh, that's gross" and "slaps down a heart." Waldeen isn't about to slap down a heart in either sense.

Betty and C.W., then, become foils—characters who set off or enhance other characters by contrast. They are similar, but their values do not run as deep. As we compare those two couples, another thematic suggestion comes to mind: the strength a couple can draw from continuity with the past and a concern for the future.

The trouble with close analysis of an intricate story like this is that it can become profoundly discouraging for a beginning writer. It may seem like an impossible task to include such ingenious details and still produce a story that appears on first reading so natural and almost casual. But keep in mind that you are looking at a final draft. This is a work that, like most published stories, probably went through a long process of revision. Many of those ingenious little details, which contribute only in a subliminal way on first reading and which one identifies only after successive readings, actually weren't there in early drafts.

At this point, let me remind you once again how stories really are written. As I have pointed out before, you start out with a character in a situation. You create a scene. You add other scenes. You rough out a draft that captures your original conception. *Then* you look at it with the critical eye of one who has read fiction.

It helps to have a fairly clear idea of your central concern before starting to write a story. But it is also important to stay flexible and to allow shifts in emphasis to occur as you write. This is one reason why it is so important to review early drafts as objectively as possible. Often you will find passages or even entire scenes that are left over from when you had a different notion of what your central concern would be.

Revisions will also be necessary to avoid having so subtle a theme that no one can understand what the story is about. It helps, of course, if you have a conscientious reader or, better yet, a group that will discuss your work. But often you will have to make judgments on your own. If highlighting an obscure theme seems wise, think twice before you do so with a paragraph of exposition. Try instead to find a line of dialogue, a specific action, or perhaps even a new scene that will help your readers see for themselves what you had in mind.

Occasionally, the theme of your story may strike you as too obvious or lacking in depth. It will not help simply to "fuzz it up." Try instead to amplify and broaden the thematic suggestions. It may be possible, for example, to have a second or third character demonstrate other aspects of the same theme. Or an additional scene may provide a broader perspective.

The point to remember is that any sophisticated story generates a number of concerns only one of which is seen as the core of the work. Your task is to develop that central concern without becoming blatant. It is this type of fine tuning that usually makes the revisions take far more time than the first draft.

Varieties of Tone

We remember experiences with the coloring of the emotion we felt at the time. We remain embarrassed at awkward moments that occurred years before; we continue to smile at comic events; and we remain bitter toward those who hurt us. If you are writing a story that is at least partially based on personal experience, it will seem natural to present it with the emotional response you still feel.

This is reasonable, but remember that what you are writing is fiction, and you should be able to shift the tone if you feel that such a change would improve the story. Most of the time such changes take the form of light touches to stories that have become too heavy, too close to melodrama.

Be on the alert when working with a personal experience you recall with strong emotions—deep sorrow, strong anger, and the like. It may be that what are sincere emotions will appear sentimental or superficial in a short story if presented without relief. The same applies to experiences that were charged with excitement and fear. If you are not careful, they can become conventional thrillers. Remember that a story—particularly a relatively short one—is a rather delicate art form. Think of it as an electrical wire that cannot take too heavy a surge of voltage without burning out. By "burning out" I simply mean appearing ridiculous. It is not a pleasant experience to have readers respond to a scene you thought was moving or dramatic with chuckles and comments like, "Oh, come on now!"

The solution may be to back off from the material a bit. Look at your protagonist with a slightly detached attitude. See if there aren't some aspects of the situation that could be treated either lightly or at least with a hint of a smile. When you do this, you are establishing *distance* between you and your material.

In my own story, for example, I made a conscious effort to keep the asylum scene from turning excessively dark by working in some of the simple, humdrum complaints that the mad share with anyone living in an institution. Uncle Theodore's little worries about fellow patients were invented for this purpose. This is one of those cases in which the actual experience had to be softened to keep the scene from becoming melodramatic.

It is always possible and often advisable to add light elements to serious fiction. In "The Nightingales Sing," for example, what might have been a heavy-handed, earnest talk between Joanna and Chris is given a light, near-comic twist by having it take place in a privy. And imagine what "Graveyard Day" would be like if handled without a sense of humor. We might end up with a story that could be described this way: A distraught mother tries to deal with an opinionated daughter, memories of a bad marriage, and an insistent suitor who would rather clean up an old graveyard than go on a picnic. All those elements are there, but the story is kept buoyant partly through the cheerful personality of Waldeen and partly through a series of comic touches like Joe's odd habit of not going anywhere without a walking stick. In addition, there are Holly's dogmatic pronouncements. From her opening "lecture" on vegetarianism to the very end she is a comic satire of many ten-year-olds. That last line of hers—" 'Don't you know *anything*?' "— adds that quick flash of unconscious irony I pointed out earlier. Her mother, we would all agree, knows a good deal more about life then most.

Keep in mind that you as author determine what the tone will be. Even when a story is based fairly directly on a personal experience, treat it as fiction and consider carefully just what kind of tone would be the most effective. The darkest experiences often have lighter elements that can be developed. If not, feel free to invent them. Touches of humor and irony can add yeast to work that would otherwise be heavy.

Occasionally, the tone should be shifted in the other direction. Genuinely comic stories (a rare species!) should never be made serious, but some first drafts are simply too light, too lacking in tension, too kind to the characters. You may have to take a closer look at your characters and see if you can dig deeper, present more honest insights. You may have to provide dialogue or perhaps a whole new scene to develop such a character more fully.

Finally, consider tonal consistency. As I have explained, some variation is often helpful, but having an apparently cheerful story end in disaster is risky. The story may seem to fall apart and become unconvincing. To a certain degree, the tone you set at the beginning establishes expectations in the reader. If you plan to have a strongly dramatic ending, it is often wise to provide a touch of harshness at the opening to prepare the reader. Even a small detail will suffice. Traditionally this is called *forewarning*. A more contemporary phrase is a *pre-echo*. In either case, it prepares the reader—at least unconsciously—for the darker tone to come.

Symbolic Elements

A symbol, as I explained in the poetry section, is any detail (usually an object or an action) that takes on a range of meaning beyond and larger than itself. This larger meaning is implied, not stated. Herein lies a problem for many.

English teachers from the seventh grade on spend a good deal of time pointing out symbols both in poetry and fiction. This continues in college. For many students, the whole notion of literary symbols begins to sound artificial, contrived, and, worst of all, academic. Since for some this resentment lingers long after graduation, a few reassurances might help.

First, symbols are not a necessary ingredient in fiction. Excellent stories and novels—sophisticated works in the best sense—are written without even the hint of a symbolic detail. Second, symbols are not the invention of teachers. They have been a special concern of writers in every age. The reason that we—myself included—keep pointing them out is that they give us pleasure, and we all like to share our pleasures. Astronomers point out constellations that are difficult for others to see at first; musicians explain harmonies that are difficult to hear; teachers and writers point to symbols. Finally, very few stories are ruined if one does not at first see symbolic elements. Few works depend on them utterly. It's just that fiction becomes more meaningful if one can respond to the added dimension. It is possible to identify and enjoy a symphony that is played on the piano alone, but listening to how it sounds with a full orchestra is a far richer experience.

With all that in mind, let's take another look at some of the stories you have read in this volume. In the case of "Sausage and Beer," I have already discussed the culminating symbol without identifying it as such. At the end of the story the waiter brings the tray with sausage and beer and leaves the father and son with a "benedictory smile." This simple act takes on some of the overtones of communion in certain Christian services. The bread and wine used in such rituals is echoed in the concluding scene as well as in the title of the story. Recognizing this symbol is not essential to an understanding of the story, but it should add another range of overtones or *resonance* for those who make the connection.

In the same way, "The Nightingales Sing" can be read simply as a girl's first glimpse of life outside the security of a protective childhood home. Many sophisticated stories don't do much more than that. But Parsons has also infused the story with symbolic suggestions which expand and develop that basic theme.

The first of two dominant symbols in that story is the old farmhouse Chris and Sandy share. To Joanna it seems almost threateningly strange at first. It "looms" out of the fog. Inside, it is "sparsely furnished" and strikes her as "very bare." The house and its two straightforward, rather blunt oc-cupants give Joanna the feeling that she is "on another planet." Yet she is drawn to the house. She sees it as "austere and pleasing." And she is in much the same way drawn to these new friends who "instead of uttering the kind of asinine, polite remarks she was accustomed to hearing from strangers . . . did not treat her as a stranger at all."

This new world, sparse in furnishings and direct in manner, is con-trasted with the environment she was raised in, a home filled with "the agreeable clutter of many years of satisfactory married life." When she returns home we are given all those visual details I listed in the previous chapter: the chintz-covered furniture, family photos, and the like.

When we compare the two places, they take on larger implications. She has been given a glimpse of the somewhat harsh yet enticing world of adulthood, is drawn to it, then returns to the comforts of childhood. As she drifts off to sleep, however, she hears "the wind rising around Sandy's house . . . and a horse kick at his stall . . . ," and wonders whether if she had stayed all night "I'd have known how far you could see from the top of the hill." She, like that restless horse of her dream, is almost ready to break out, to leave the protection of childhood and accept the risks of adulthood.

Granted, one may not see all this on first reading. And that is all the casual reader will give it. Why, then, should an author bother? Because sym-bolic suggestion can add a resonance even for a hasty reader. A symbol does not have to be identified precisely to have an effect. It must, however, be constructed precisely. Because of this, writers have to study fiction more carefully than hasty readers. They have to look closely at symbolic elements just as a would-be dancer has to analyze carefully what to others appear to be the effortless motions of a ballerina. Creative and performing artists always have to work harder than their audiences.

In addition to these major symbols, there are many minor symbolic details worth noting. We have already seen how the "brute of a horse" that threw Chris is associated with Sandy, who makes other men seem "tame" yet who "takes charge too much of the time." She won't quit either of them. In addition, there is the use of chill and warmth. It would have been easy enough for the author to have stated that Joanna's cheerful, naive presence brought warmth into that old farmhouse, but Parsons *shows* it by having her lay the fire and light it, warming the room. And what does she use for kindling? Some "old comics"—echoes of childhood. Finally, Joanna's emerging sexuality is seen in her sleepy musings of what it would be like at Sandy's house in the morning: "the roofs would steam, the horses would gallop and squeal . . . and all the nightingales would rise singing. . . ."

The symbolic elements in "Graveyard Day" are even less obvious because the story has the illusion of being loosely structured and filled with random dialogue. Actually, many of the apparently casual details have a function, and the graveyard itself is rich in symbolic suggestion.

The first we hear about it is when Joe explains that "he is responsible for taking geraniums to his grandparents' graves." A minor detail, but it is the beginning of our understanding of how deeply committed Joe is to that cemetery. Much later Waldeen asks why the graveyard is so important, and Joe says " 'It's a family thing.' " When she gets there, Joe's grandmother's grave looks to her like "a brown heap."

None of this by itself would suggest a symbol, but then Waldeen realizes that "If she marries Joe . . . they will be buried here together." She actually picks out the spot and imagines the headstone among "the brown leaves," an echo of how the grandmother's grave appeared to her earlier. That's when she herself has the feeling that "the burial plot, not a diamond ring, symbolizes the promise of marriage." Clear enough? But there's more: At the end of the story she takes a flying leap, landing in the "immense pile of leaves, up to her elbows." If we're reading carefully, we recall the "brown heap" of the grandmother's grave, the fact that generations of McClains are buried here, and her notion that this is the "promise of marriage." In that leap she has symbolically entered both the past and the future of this McClain clan. In short, she has accepted Joe's proposal.

A word of warning for those who are just beginning to write fiction: This kind of elaborate symbolic suggestion is not often used in short-short stories. And as I pointed out before, it is not a necessary part of fiction, regardless of length. These examples, however, do provide a possible direction to move in as one gains confidence.

Keeping these qualifications in mind, here are some closely related guidelines which may help if you decide to develop symbols in your own work. First, don't be blatant. When readers recognize an unmistakable symbol, the illusion of reality breaks and the story seems contrived. Second, watch out for symbols so widely known that they defy all attempts to use them subtly. Adam and Eve and symbolic crucifixions turn up in every fiction-writing contest and do not win awards. Third, unless you are writing satire, think twice before you let a story depend utterly on a symbol. Such works often end up sacrificing credible characterization for the sake of that central abstract idea.

To put this more positively, move cautiously and let the story suggest to you what might be made symbolic. Whenever possible, develop your symbolic material from the events, the setting, and the characters of the story itself. The goal is to have symbolic details serve the story, not dominate it.

Elements of Style

All fiction has style. You can't compose without it any more than you can write your name without revealing—for better or for worse—your handwriting. But it is important to examine just what your style is and then to judge whether it is the best possible approach for a particular story.

Essentially, there are four factors that determine your prose style in fiction: *diction* (word choice), *syntax* (sentence structure), the *balance of narrative modes*, and *tense* (present or past).

Diction, your choice of words, is a more significant factor in English than in most other languages because there is such a radical difference in sound and tone between those words that came to us from the Norse and Anglo-Saxon and those from the Greek or Latin. To cite an extreme example, contrast your reaction to these two samples:

> Edgar got in the boat and gripped the seat, sweating like an ox. He hated the sea.

> Julius entered the vessel and embraced the cushions, perspiring profusely. He detested the ocean.

In the first, the nouns and verbs are without exception of Anglo-Saxon or Old Norse origin. In the second, every noun and verb is of Latin origin. Except for the articles and the conjunctions, these could be two different languages, each with its distinctive sound, and each with its own tone. Past generations were taught that words of Latin and Greek derivation were "elegant" and "refined," and some of that prejudice remains. You should feel free to use whatever the language has to offer, but remember that your choices will affect your style.

None of us has the time to look up the derivation of every word we use, but we all have a built-in awareness of the distinction between these two verbal heritages. One is dominated by short, abrupt sounds that imply simplicity, roughness, and in some cases obscenity; the other is characterized by longer words, smoother sounds, and a sense of elegance or even pomposity.

Aside from the derivations, there are the subtle distinctions between short words and long ones, harsh ones and smooth ones, crude ones and those that sound elegant. As with nonfiction writing, you will want to choose an appropriate *level of usage*. If the story is being narrated by a city dweller who is street-wise, your choice of words is going to be dramatically different than it would be if you were writing a third-person story in a neutral style. And of course the diction of each line of dialogue should be appropriate to the character who is speaking.

Fiction is not written word by word, however. When it is going well, let it flow. The time to take a close look at your diction is when you read over the completed first draft. Decide what effect you want and revise it carefully.

Syntax is the second factor that determines style. Long, elaborate constructions have one effect; short sentences with few added phrases have another.

Here are the opening paragraphs of two stories you have read. Try to read them as if for the first time and see if you can identify how your reactions differ.

A

The young man was clean shaven and neatly dressed. It was early Monday morning and he got on the subway. It was the first day of his first job and he was slightly nervous; he didn't know exactly what his job would be. Otherwise he felt fine. He loved everybody he saw.

B

Through the fog the car went up the hill, whining in second gear, up the sandy road the ran between the highest and broadest stone walls that Joanna had ever seen. There were no trees at all, only the bright-green, cattle-cropped pastures sometimes visible above the walls, and sweetfern and juniper bushes, all dim in the opaque air and the wan light of an early summer evening.

If these were nonfiction passages, the first would be criticized as choppy and the second as rambling and overmodified. But fiction writers are allowed greater latitude. The only true limit is effectiveness, and these two passages are effective even though they are at opposite ends of a scale.

The first selection consists of five sentences. Since the semicolon is a full stop, the paragraph actually reads as if there were six sentences. Although the second selection is slightly longer, it is made up of only two sentences. Both passages are correct grammatically, yet the effect in each is utterly different.

Each style is appropriate for the kind of story it introduces. Robert Fox in "A Fable" presents a fantasy in straightforward, direct style. The terseness of style provides an effective contrast with the dreamlike content. It has some of the effect of telling a funny story with an absolutely straight face.

"The Nightingales Sing" is quite a different kind of story. It starts out by setting a mood of mystery. Then it portrays the lifestyles of its characters and reveals the reactions of the protagonist with great detail. Creating mood and defining character with high realism both seem to call for a more intricate, complex sentence structure.

But before we go too far in linking a particular style with an appropriate subject matter, we have to recognize another factor: author's preference. If you read other stories by Robert Fox (see *Destiny News*, December Press), you will see that he prefers terse tales written in a terse style. They are not always as unadorned as the passage above, but they are quite distinct from, say, stories by Elizabeth Parsons (see *An Afternoon*, Viking).

This is true of many authors. Ernest Hemingway is known for his sparse, unadorned syntax, while Faulkner's sentence structure tends to be long. Length is only one of several variables in syntax; internal structure can also be quite different. Faulkner's lengthy sentences tend to be loose, occasionally rambling, while those of Thomas Wolfe are often rhythmic. Punctuation is another variable. Although most authors are fairly conventional, those who echo the spoken language may use an informal system with, say, frequent use of dashes.

Having an identifiable approach to syntax is in no way a necessity. In fact, a majority of stories in print are closer to what is sometimes called a neutral style. If you struggle to achieve a clearly defined style too soon, you may find you are only imitating someone you admire. But it is a good idea to examine the syntax of every first draft. Make sure the pattern you have selected unconsciously is appropriate for that particular story. And avoid monotony by varying the length of your sentences.

The third method of influencing your style in fiction is the balance of *narrative modes*. I am using *mode* in the special sense introduced at the beginning of the fiction section: dialogue, thoughts, action, description, and exposition.

A particular sentence may contain two or more modes, but usually one will dominate. The concept becomes helpful when a scene or a whole story stresses one mode more than the others. This is not necessarily bad; it may produce just the style you want. But be aware of how you are affecting your style.

Depending heavily on dialogue, for example, may be entirely appropriate if that mode is used effectively to develop theme and characterization. "Graveyard Day" is a good example. It depends more on dialogue than the other stories in this volume. Much of what we learn about Waldeen comes through what she says. If you try such an approach, however, be careful that your work doesn't become "talky." That usually means that the dialogue isn't revealing enough. It has become padding.

When fiction is dominated by thoughts, the style may become heavy and slow. This is due to the significant difference between thoughts and dialogue: When characters talk, they interact with others, but when they think, they are in isolation. An extended passage of thoughts is a monologue within the mind. All too easily it begins to sound like exposition—an author's analysis. When a character thinks to himself, "I've been too selfish about this whole thing," the reader may have the feeling that what is being presented as thoughts is really just a poorly disguised form of exposition. An extended passage in this vein will make the style heavy, slow, and possibly boring. Often you can correct this by presenting those thoughts through a more active mode like dialogue or action. It's far more effective to have a character jump into a pile of leaves than to think, "Yes, I really do want to marry Joe McClain."

Action tends to enliven your style, but too much may give the piece a breathless effect. The story may seem superficial. Description and exposition are stylistically opposite to action. They can provide valuable information, but they add weight to your style. If overused, they can make a story seem sluggish.

The balance of modes is, like other aspects of style, something that comes naturally in first-draft writing. The time to examine it is when you have a story on paper. There is no reason whatever not to favor one mode over the others in a particular story, but try to judge as objectively as you can how this has affected your style. A few revisions at that stage may make a major difference in the overall effect.

The matter of *tense* has become a major controversy in the past decade. Traditionally, most short stories and novels were written in the past tense. Starting in the early '80s, however, an increasing number of authors began using the present tense. Some people take this very seriously. An article in the *New York Times Book Review* attacked the practice on principle, and at least one editor refuses to print present-tense stories regardless of worth. On the other hand, the number of present-tense stories in print continues to increase.

The effect of the present tense on style is highly subjective and difficult to judge. For some, it seems illogical and therefore disruptive to imply that events are occurring at the time of the telling. This is particularly bothersome in scenes of dramatic action. Out of context, it seems a bit odd to have a first-person narrator write, "She slaps me across the face and I am left speechless." This surely is an odd time to be writing a diary entry.

The counterargument is that you really don't respond to stories like these as if they are diary entries. Readers lose themselves in the action, and after the first paragraph the matter of tense is largely forgotten. Can you, for example, recall which one of the four stories in this volume is written in the present tense?

Present-tense enthusiasts often claim that fiction is livelier and more immediate in that tense. But if this were so, past-tense writing would not have dominated fiction for over a century.

There is one good technical reason for adopting the present tense. If a story in the past tense contains a number of flashbacks, the author must cue the reader with the past perfect each time: "She had been an excellent lawyer in her thirties," for example. The flashback itself, you remember, reverts to simple past tense. But if the main part of the story is written in the present tense, the author can signal the start of those flashbacks simply by shifting to the past tense and staying there: "She was an excellent lawyer. . . ." It is simpler both moving into the flashback and coming out of it.

But this does not account for more than a few present-tense stories. In answer to the question I posed above, "Graveyard Day" is written in the present tense. For most readers, it feels right in that tense, but if you type out a page of that story in past tense, it is hard to say why that wouldn't have worked too. The story comes from a collection of Mason's work called *Shiloh* (Harper & Row). It contains sixteen of her stories, and ten of these are in the present tense. They are excellent stories, but I suspect that if they had been written fifteen years ago, they all would have been in the past tense.

It is odd that while the choice of tense is one of the most debated aspects of style today, its effect on fiction is almost entirely subjective. If you are uncertain which to use with a particular story, try an opening half page first in past tense and then in present. One will seem better than the other; you can invent a good explanation later.

These four literary concerns—theme, tone, symbol, and style—are enormously important, but don't let them distract you when starting a new work. You can suffer a serious case of writer's block if you stare at a blank piece of paper (or a computer screen) worrying about your options. As I have urged before, let the story develop. Have faith in your initial vision. Once you have a rough draft safely down on paper, then turn critic and examine these literary aspects.

Remember, too, that this chapter is largely a distillation of abstract concepts. For a real appreciation of what you can do with theme, tone, symbol, and style, you have to read a lot of fiction. This chapter will help you identify and evaluate those literary elements, but your continuing growth and development over the years will come from fiction itself.

24 Developing as a Writer of Fiction

The importance of revision; six critical questions to be asked about
a work of fiction regarding characterization, plot construction,
tensions, theme, setting, and tone; *learning from published
fiction* in story collections and magazines.

If you are going to develop as a writer of fiction, you will have to spend a
great deal of your time revising. You will also have to study published fiction
carefully enough and regularly enough so that the authors become your teachers in a process of growth that will never stop.

You will find that the more time you spend writing fiction the more
emphasis you will place on revision. It is true that this is difficult when taking
a writing course. An academic term is relatively short, and the effectiveness
of a course requires a high output of new material. Rewriting cannot in most
cases be given as much credit as new writing. But when you are working on
your own or as a member of an informal writing group, you will not have
that kind of pressure and you will find that a far greater percentage of your
time will go into the revisions than was spent on the original draft.

As with poetry, it is very helpful to receive a critical reaction from
those who are familiar with the genre. But unless you are taking a course, it

will be difficult to find qualified individuals who have the time. Writers of fiction are thrown on their own rather abruptly. For this reason, it is all the more important to acquire an ability to criticize your own work as soon as possible.

Six Critical Questions

Discussions about a story or novel tend to cover six general areas. If you are working on your own, these are the critical questions you should ask yourself as you begin to plan your revisions.

I list them here in the order in which they frequently are raised. There is a tendency, for example, to discuss characters and scene construction before the theme because they are in some respects more visible, more immediately available. Setting and tone, on the other hand, are often brought up toward the end of a discussion since they depend on what the thematic concerns are.

But it would be a great mistake to insist on any particular order. A good discussion is in a sense an organic development: It should move in whatever direction appears productive. The point of this list is not to restrict or direct discussion but to encourage as broad a range of analysis as possible.

First, *are the primary characters convincing or, in the case of satire, effective?* Stories that develop characters fully should give readers the feeling they have actually met someone and come to know them in some insightful way. Satiric fiction like "A Fable" has a different goal since the characters being satirized usually represent types, not realistic individuals. In such cases the characters are not necessarily convincing, but they should illustrate the type with some ingenuity. That is, they must be effective.

If a character does not seem to be developed properly, consider the possibility of changing the viewpoint. You may be too close to the character to maintain fictional control, or the character you thought was central may not have as much fictional potential as another.

Secondary characters don't have to meet the same standards, but they still should have a purpose. As we have seen, minor characters sometimes offer commentary, serve as foils, or provide comic contrast. Even though they are "flat" (seen only in one dimension), make sure they really contribute to the story as a whole.

In analyzing characters, don't rely entirely on general impressions. Look closely at the narrative modes that have been used. Is the dialogue convincing? Do we enter the inner world of thoughts? Do we see the character *doing* enough? And most important of all, has exposition been used too heavily to develop character? Are there ways some of those aspects can be shown through another mode, like action or dialogue?

If you are looking over your own story without benefit of an objective reader, you will have to ask the same questions. It helps if you can set the story aside for a few days between finishing the first draft and planning your second.

Second, *is the story constructed successfully?* It is often helpful to analyze just how many scenes there are before beginning to evaluate how they are handled. Once this is done, it is natural enough to discuss which scenes seem to be the most successful ones. Some may be too brief to provide the reader with a sense of being present; others may seem to drag. Frequently, a scattering of scenes may be combined to give the story a more solid base.

After discussing the scenes individually, examine the order: Is this the most effective sequence? If the opening is slow, for example, it might be worth starting with a livelier scene and returning to the original situation at a later point in the story. If the order is complicated with a storyteller or with numerous flashbacks, consider whether the advantage of such a sequence is worth the risk of confusion and distraction. Keep in mind that while there is no "right" way for any one story, every approach has both advantages and disadvantages—and in different proportions. The critic's job is not to make pronouncements like, "You can't write a story that way," but, rather, to describe what seems to be successful from the reader's point of view and what is confusing or dull. Frequently, such reactions stem from the handling of the plot.

Third, *does the story contain the type of tensions that keeps fiction alive and interesting?* It is all too easy to say that a story is slow or that "It's just plain dull." But a critic who is helpful moves directly to the problem of determining what kinds of tensions might be established. In some cases this may be a matter of creating a conflict between the protagonist and another character or some other force. This could mean basic revisions in plot. In other cases it might be solved by adding some kind of dramatic question to arouse the curiosity of the reader.

Fourth, *what is the theme, and is it sophisticated enough to be fresh and evocative?* You may have started with a clear idea of what your central concern was, but look at the finished story objectively to see if your aim has shifted. If your work is being discussed by a group, let them talk about what they see as the theme before you say anything. Ask them to be specific.

When dealing with theme, make sure that every scene and most of the small details contribute in some way to that central concern. Sometimes elements in a story remain merely because they were a part of the original experience or an earlier draft of the story. In those cases, careful cutting is needed.

Fifth, *is the setting vivid, and does it contribute to the theme?* As we have seen, setting is not always a highly visible factor in fiction, but look closely at what you have and see if it does all you want it to. Could the same plot be moved to a place that would make more of an impression on the reader?

Don't reach for the exotic, however, since that makes the setting an end in itself. Your goal is to place the story in an environment that contributes to the theme.

Although short-short stories are usually limited to a single setting, longer ones can easily afford two or more. Consider the possibility of contrasting two settings, as was done in "Sausage and Beer" and "The Nightingales Sing."

Finally, *is the tone effective?* If your story is unrelentingly dark and brooding, could it use an occasional light touch? On one level, this is simply a stylistic concern. But on a deeper level it may mean revising your attitude toward your material. Try to view your story with some perspective.

Occasionally the tone may be bland and without variation. If so, you might consider the value of providing dramatic questions to hold the reader's interest. At the other extreme, some stories have too much drama. Has action drowned out subtleties of characterization and theme? If this is the case, consider muting the action and at the same time developing insights into your characters and your theme.

The two greatest dangers in the area of tone are sentimentality and melodrama. In the first, the story appears to make an unjustified appeal to emotions such as pity or love. In the second, drama is pushed too far and becomes blatant and unconvincing. Group response is very helpful in determining whether you have moved in either of these directions. But if you have no critics available, you will have to make a special effort to read your own work as objectively as possible.

Learning from Published Fiction

Writing courses are valuable because they encourage you to produce a great deal in a short period of time and because they offer you a lot of feedback on your work. An occasional writers' conference (listed in *Literary Market Place* *(LMP)*, available at most libraries) may be useful because it will introduce you to many other writers, at least some of whom are serious about their craft. But in the long run your best teachers will be authors speaking to you through their fiction.

The word *reading* refers to two quite different activities. The first, *passive reading*, is a form of entertainment. It is enjoyable recreation for many. Passive or recreational reading is relatively inexpensive, legal, and has no dangerous side effects. The second, *active reading*, is what writers do. For them, reading also has its rewards, but much of the time it is a professional activity. Some writers, for example, cannot read without a pencil in hand; others keep notes on stories and novels they have found effective. Unlike recreational readers, they are often willing to study work they don't really enjoy if a technique is being used that seems interesting or valuable. This does not mean there is no pleasure in reading; it means that much of the pleasure stems from personal growth rather than the immediate experience.

At first, writers of fiction, like poets, have a problem knowing what to read. Anthologies provide a good initial step. They will introduce you to the best of the past 30 or so years. It will help if you keep a literary journal and record at least briefly your impressions (and a bit of the plot) of stories you found effective. Be sure to include where the stories were published so that you can refer to them later.

More recent short stories can be found in two annual collections, the *O. Henry Prize Stories* and *The Best American Short Stories*. These can be found in almost every library and can be ordered through your bookstore. In addition, the University of Illinois Press has been publishing four volumes of paperback collections (one author to each collection) annually since 1975. A list of these can be obtained by writing to the publisher, and individual volumes can be ordered directly or through your bookstore.

As for magazines, there are two large-circulation publications that include fiction in every issue: *The New Yorker* (two stories almost every week) and *The Atlantic*, a monthly. There are also about 100 little magazines, many of them quarterlies, which publish stories along with poems, articles, and reviews. Some, like *The North American Review* and *Fiction Network* specialize in fiction. More titles are listed in Appendix B.

How do you find them? Start by reading whichever magazines are available in your library. Then select one or two and subscribe. As I have mentioned before, the cost is less than many record albums. When you have your own copy of the magazine you will be sure to read it, will feel free to mark it up, and will have it for future reference.

Writers of fiction are even more isolated than poets. They do not take part in most poetry readings, and they have difficulty finding individuals who are willing to read and criticize their work. But they are in touch through their published work.

If you decide to invest your time and energy in writing fiction, make sure you invest at least as much time in reading what others have written. If you value fiction, you will not find the cost of books and subscriptions excessive. Your development as a writer will depend in large measure on how active and perceptive you are as a reader.

25 THEATER: A LIVE PERFORMANCE

> Drama as a *live performance;* the *special attributes* of *drama:* its
> *dramatic impact, visual* quality, its appeal to the *ear,* the fact
> that it is *physically produced* and is a *continuous art* performed
> for *spectators;* getting started with a *concept,* primary *characters,*
> and an outline of *plot.*

The transition from writing fiction to writing plays is not as great as one might
think. Both depend heavily on plot. Both reveal character through action and
dialogue. Both are presented with a distinctive tone and are unified with some
kind of central concern or theme.

The primary difference, however, is that a play is a live performance.
It is produced physically in front of an audience and is performed by actors.
This is theater's greatest asset and explains why it is flourishing today in spite
of competition with film and television.

Ever since the first "talking movie," critics have predicted the end of
legitimate theater. But not even the competition of television has slowed the
constant growth of new theaters. Many middle-sized cities have resident
companies that have been formed within the past ten years, and this activity
has been augmented with university theater programs of high quality. It is
clear that there is a genuine need for performances given by actors on a stage.

Every genre has its special attributes—qualities that distinguish it fundamentally from other forms of writing. It is a mistake to think of a play as fiction acted out on the stage or as a poem performed or as a low-budget version of film. It is none of these things. Before you begin writing your first play script, consider carefully what the special characteristics of the genre are.

The Special Attributes of Drama

The unique qualities of drama stem from the fact that the genre is intended to be a live performance. You will be able to find plays that do not contain one or two of the following characteristics, just as you can find some poems that make little use of rhythm and some stories without dialogue. Clearly these are not rules; they are merely recurring characteristics. Most playwrights consider them the assets of the genre.

First, drama is by definition a *dramatic art*. That is, it generally has an emotional impact or force. In the case of comedy, we call it vitality. This is not just a tradition; it is a natural aspect of an art form that requires an audience to give its undivided attention for two-and-a-half to three hours.

This impact is often established early in a play with a *dramatic question* which seizes the attention of the audience long before the theme becomes evident. Dramatic questions are usually blunt and simple: Is this stranger a threat? Whom are they waiting for? Why do these characters hate each other? In most cases, these initial questions develop into specific conflicts. Although the need for tension like this is not as strong in very short plays and in comedies, it is usually greater in drama than in either fiction or poetry.

As in fiction, irony and satire often add to the dramatic aspect of a play. And still another device is the use of shock. Unusual or violent situations can explode where the audience least expects them.

Dramatic impact is hard to sustain, however. For this reason, most plays work up to a series of peaks, allowing the emotions of the audience to rest in between. This system of rising and falling action does not follow any prescribed pattern and is often intuitive on the part of the playwright—just as it is in the writing of short stories. But the need for such structure tends to make drama more sharply divided into scenes and acts, divisions that help to control the dramatic impact.

Second, drama is a *visual art*. Action on the stage is usually a significant and organic part of the whole production. It is not enough in the twentieth century to have characters simply walk back and forth reciting poetry as they did in the highly stylized tradition of Greek theater. In most cases, the movement of characters on the stage is as important as the lines themselves.

And the visual concern extends beyond the characters. The set itself is often another important part of the production. Sophisticated lighting boards can convert the set from a static backdrop to a dynamic factor in developing the moods of each scene. The addition of projected images and even movie sequences—experiments in mixed media—offers one more appeal to the visual aspect of theater.

Third, drama is an *auditory art*. It appeals to the ear. Except for stage directions, every word is dialogue and intended to be spoken out loud. The sound of those lines becomes very important. In some respects, this brings playwrights closer to poets than to writers of fiction. Playwrights often read their lines out loud or have others read them, listening to the composition rather than studying it on the page.

This special attention to the sound of language applies as much to plays that are in the tradition of realism as to those that create the dreamlike distortions of expressionism. Not only are the sounds important, but the space between the lines can be utilized. In theater, silence can have as much dramatic impact as a shout.

Fourth, drama is a *physically produced art*. This is sometimes difficult to remember for those who have been writing fiction. Since sets have to be constructed with wood and nails, there is not the freedom to shift from scene to scene the way one can in a short story. Scriptwriters should keep in mind just what kinds of demands they are placing on set designers and stage crews.

At first this may seem like a limitation, but there are compensating assets. Playwrights have an intense, almost personal contact with their audiences which is entirely different from the indirect connection fiction writers have with their readers. And the constraints of the stage often stimulate the imagination. For many playwrights these aspects outweigh any disadvantage.

Fifth, drama is a *continuous art*. Members of the audience, unlike readers of fiction or poetry, must receive the play at whatever pace the playwright sets. They cannot linger on a sage observation or a moving episode. They cannot turn back a page or review an earlier scene. If you are shifting from writing fiction to drama, you can be more blatant with your themes and can, as we will see, make use of refrains to repeat your key themes.

As you get into play writing you will find that the flow of drama is an aspect you can utilize. There is a momentum to a play which you can control. With practice you can make one portion of a scene move rapidly and another more slowly. Fiction writers can't maintain quite this kind of control over their readers.

The other side of this same coin is the concern a playwright must have about pacing. A slow scene that is extended just a bit too long can do real damage.

Finally, and closely connected, is the fact that drama is a *spectator art*. Even more than with spectator sports, audience reaction is important. Poets are relatively far removed from such concerns. It is rare indeed for poets to change lines of their verse because of critical reviews or poor public response. Novelists are slightly more susceptible to "audience" reaction. Their circle of readers is potentially larger than a poet's, and authors tend to be aware of this. Many novelists will make fairly extensive revisions on the basis of their editors' suggestions. Usually, however, the publication of the work marks the end of the revisions process.

Not so with plays. Playwrights often revise when their work is in rehearsal and after the opening-night reviews and even later if changes seem necessary. They frequently base their revisions on audience reaction—those awful moments when it laughs at the wrong moment or squirms with boredom.

This does not mean that dramatists are slaves to the reactions of audiences and critics. In most cases playwrights have a basic conception of the work which remains unalterable. But there is a direct and dynamic relationship between playwrights and their audiences. For many, this is one of the real pleasures in writing for the legitimate stage.

Getting Started

Poems frequently begin with an image and stories with a character in a situation. Plays more often begin with what is called *a concept.*

A dramatic concept includes a basic situation, some type of conflict or struggle, and an outcome, all in capsule form. You can, of course, start a play as tentatively as you might begin a story, hoping to shape and develop the plot as you work through the first draft. But such an approach is generally not as successful in playwriting because so much depends on the whole dramatic structure.

Plays, like stories, often evolve from personal experience, but the need to create a dramatic situation involving conflict or struggle between two or more people often requires metamorphosing of the original episode from the start. Although this is a risky generalization, it is probably fair to say that plays tend to be less closely tied to direct personal experience than stories. In any case, you should feel free to explore newspaper stories and accounts told to you about individuals you have not met, as long as the situation is familiar enough for you to make it appear authentic.

If you keep a literary journal, it helps to jot down a number of possible concepts. If one seems to take shape in your mind, add the name and a brief description of one or two characters. Actually giving these characters names at the outset will help stimulate your imagination.

Next, try some sample dialogue. It helps if you can begin to hear two characters interact. See if you can create a little scene which at least roughly contributes to the concept you have in mind. Read the lines out loud. Imagine actors (male or female) saying those lines. Close your eyes and visualize the scene.

If you have done all this and you still feel that the concept has potential, begin to block out the action. This may be quite different from the approach you used in fiction. Needless to say, there is no one technique and whatever works is fine; but the reason many playwrights block out the action at this point has a good deal to do with the nature of the genre.

Even if you are writing a one-act play with a single set—which is a good pattern to start with—you will want to think in terms of *scenes*. I will have more to say about this in the chapter on plot (Chapter 27), but essentially a dramatic scene is a unit of action and dialogue that begins and ends with a character coming on stage or leaving. Some short plays have been written without these subtle yet important divisions, but they are rare. *Hello Out There*, which is presented as the next chapter, uses eight such scenes. When you read it, mark these divisions and see how they provide structure for the read it, mark these divisions and see how they provide structure for the play.

As for the form of the script, follow the pattern used by the plays included in this volume. At first it may seem monotonous to repeat the name of each speaker, but it is the customary practice, one that actors depend on in rehearsal. Stage directions are written in italics (underlined when you are typing). Place them in parentheses when they are short. It is helpful to include names of characters after the title, listing them in order of appearance.

There are two plays included in this section. The first is serious, realistic, and highly dramatic; the second is dreamlike and partially satiric. They represent two entirely different approaches to drama. They are a good indication of what an enormous latitude you have in tone and treatment.

Getting started, then, involves finding a good concept, creating vivid characters, fleshing them out with some samples of dialogue, and then blocking out the action by outlining a plot in the form of scenes. Keep in mind that what you are writing down is not primarily a work to be read on the page. You are creating a live performance for members of a live audience. Make their experience a memorable one.

26 A Play by William Saroyan

Hello Out There

for George Bernard Shaw

> *Characters:* A YOUNG MAN
>
> A GIRL
>
> A MAN
>
> TWO OTHER MEN
>
> A WOMAN

Scene: There is a fellow in a small-town prison cell, tapping slowly on the floor with a spoon. After tapping half a minute, as if he were trying to telegraph words, he gets up and begins walking around the cell. At last he stops, stands at the center of the cell, and doesn't move for a long time. He feels his head, as if it were wounded. Then he looks around. Then he calls out dramatically, kidding the world.

YOUNG MAN: Hello—out there! (*Pause.*) Hello—out there! Hello—out there! (*Long pause.*) Nobody out there. (*Still more dramatically, but more comically, too.*) Hello—out there! Hello—out there!

A GIRL'S VOICE *is heard, very sweet and soft.*

THE VOICE: Hello.

YOUNG MAN: Hello—out there.

THE VOICE: Hello.

YOUNG MAN: Is that you, Katey?

THE VOICE: No—this here is Emily.

YOUNG MAN: Who? (*Swiftly.*) Hello out there.

THE VOICE: Emily.

YOUNG MAN: Emily who? I don't know anybody named Emily. Are you that girl I met at Sam's in Salinas about three years ago?

THE VOICE: No—I'm the girl who cooks here. I'm the cook. I've never been in Salinas. I don't even know where it is.

YOUNG MAN: Hello out there. You say you cook here?

THE VOICE: Yes.

YOUNG MAN: Well, why don't you study up and learn to cook? How come I don't get no jello or anything good?

THE VOICE: I just cook what they tell me to. (*Pause.*) You lonesome?

YOUNG MAN: Lonesome as a coyote. Hear me hollering? Hello out there!

THE VOICE: Who you hollering to?

YOUNG MAN: Well—nobody, I guess. I been trying to think of somebody to write a letter to, but I can't think of anybody.

THE VOICE: What about Katey?

YOUNG MAN: I don't know anybody named Katey.

THE VOICE: Then why did you say, Is that you, Katey?

YOUNG MAN: Katey's a good name. I always did like a name like Katey. I never *knew* anybody named Katey, though.

THE VOICE: *I* did.

YOUNG MAN: Yeah? What was she like? Tall girl, or little one?

THE VOICE: Kind of medium.

YOUNG MAN: Hello out there. What sort of a looking girl are *you?*

THE VOICE: Oh, I don't know.

YOUNG MAN: Didn't anybody ever tell you? Didn't anybody ever talk to you that way?

THE VOICE: What way?

YOUNG MAN: You know. Didn't they?

THE VOICE: No, they didn't.

YOUNG MAN: Ah, the fools—they should have. I can tell from your voice you're O.K.

THE VOICE: Maybe I am and maybe I ain't.

YOUNG MAN: I never missed yet.

THE VOICE: Yeah, I know. That's why you're in jail.

YOUNG MAN: The whole thing was a mistake.

THE VOICE: They claim it was rape.

YOUNG MAN: No—it wasn't.

THE VOICE: That's what they claim it was.

YOUNG MAN: They're a lot of fools.

THE VOICE: Well, you sure are in trouble. Are you scared?

YOUNG MAN: Scared to death. (*Suddenly.*) Hello out there!

THE VOICE: What do you keep saying that for all the time?

YOUNG MAN: I'm lonesome. I'm as lonesome as a coyote. (*A long one.*) Hello—
out there!

> THE GIRL *appears, over to one side. She is a plain girl in plain clothes.*

THE GIRL: I'm kind of lonesome, too.

YOUNG MAN (*turning and looking at her*): Hey—No fooling? Are you?

THE GIRL: Yeah—I'm almost as lonesome as a coyote myself.

YOUNG MAN: Who *you* lonesome for?

THE GIRL: I don't know.

YOUNG MAN: It's the same with me. The minute they put you in a place like
this you remember all the girls you ever knew, and all the girls you
didn't get to know, and it sure gets lonesome.

THE GIRL: I bet it does.

YOUNG MAN: Ah, it's awful. (*Pause.*) You're a pretty kid, you know that?

THE GIRL: You're just talking.

YOUNG MAN: No, I'm not just talking—you *are* pretty. Any fool could see that.
You're just about the prettiest kid in the whole world.

THE GIRL: I'm not—and you know it.

YOUNG MAN: No—you are. I never saw anyone prettier in all my born days,
in all my travels. I knew Texas would bring me luck.

THE GIRL: Luck? You're in jail, aren't you? You've got a whole gang of people
all worked up, haven't you?

YOUNG MAN: Ah, that's nothing. I'll get out of this.

THE GIRL: Maybe.

YOUNG MAN: No, I'll be all right—*now.*

THE GIRL: What do you mean—now?

YOUNG MAN: I mean after seeing you. I got something now. You know for a
while there I didn't care one way or another. Tired. (*Pause.*) Tired of
trying for the best all the time and never getting it. (*Suddenly.*) Hello
out there!

THE GIRL: Who you calling now?

YOUNG MAN: You.

THE GIRL: Why, I'm right here.

YOUNG MAN: I know. (*Calling.*) Hello out there!

THE GIRL: Hello.

YOUNG MAN: Ah, you're sweet. (*Pause.*) I'm going to marry *you*. I'm going away with *you*. I'm going to take you to San Francisco or some place like that. I *am*, now. I'm going to win myself some real money, too. I'm going to study 'em real careful and pick myself some winners, and we're going to have a lot of money.

THE GIRL: Yeah?

YOUNG MAN: Yeah. Tell me your name and all that stuff.

THE GIRL: Emily.

YOUNG MAN: I know that. What's the rest of it? Where were you born? Come on, tell me the whole thing.

THE GIRL: Emily Smith.

YOUNG MAN: Honest to God?

THE GIRL: Honest. That's my name—Emily Smith.

YOUNG MAN: Ah, you're the sweetest girl in the whole world.

THE GIRL: Why?

YOUNG MAN: I don't know why, but you are, that's all. Where were you born?

THE GIRL: Matador, Texas.

YOUNG MAN: Where's that?

THE GIRL: Right here.

YOUNG MAN: Is this Matador, Texas?

THE GIRL: Yeah, it's Matador. They brought you here from Wheeling.

YOUNG MAN: Is that where I was—Wheeling?

THE GIRL: Didn't you even know what town you were in?

YOUNG MAN: All towns are alike. You don't go up and ask somebody what town you're in. It doesn't make any difference. How far away is Wheeling?

THE GIRL: Sixteen or seventeen miles. Didn't you know they moved you?

YOUNG MAN: How could I know, when I was out—cold? Somebody hit me over the head with a lead pipe or something. What'd they hit me for?

THE GIRL: Rape—that's what they *said*.

YOUNG MAN: Ah, that's a lie. (*Amazed, almost to himself.*) She wanted me to give her money.

THE GIRL: Money?

YOUNG MAN: Yeah, if I'd have known she was a woman like that—well, by God, I'd have gone on down the street and stretched out in a park somewhere and gone to sleep.

THE GIRL: Is that what she wanted—money?

YOUNG MAN: Yeah. A fellow like me hopping freights all over the country, trying to break his bad luck, going from one poor little town to another, trying to get in on something good somewhere, and she asks for money. I thought she was lonesome. She *said* she was.

THE GIRL: Maybe she was.

YOUNG MAN: She was *something*.

THE GIRL: I guess I'd never see you, if it didn't happen, though.

YOUNG MAN: Oh, I don't know—maybe I'd just mosey along this way and see you in this town somewhere. I'd recognize you, too.

THE GIRL: Recognize me?

YOUNG MAN: Sure, I'd recognize you the minute I laid eyes on you.

THE GIRL: Well, who would I be?

YOUNG MAN: Mine, that's who.

THE GIRL: Honest?

YOUNG MAN: Honest to God.

THE GIRL: You just say that because you're in jail.

YOUNG MAN: No, I mean it. You just pack up and wait for me. We'll high-roll the hell out of here to Frisco.

THE GIRL: You're just lonesome.

YOUNG MAN: I been lonesome all my life—there's no cure for that—but you and me—we can have a lot of fun hanging around together. You'll bring me luck. I know it.

THE GIRL: What are you looking for luck for all the time?

YOUNG MAN: I'm a gambler. I don't work. I've *got* to have luck, or I'm a bum. I haven't had any decent luck in years. Two whole years now—one place to another. Bad luck all the time. That's why I got in trouble back there in Wheeling too. That was no accident. That was my bad luck following me around. So here I am, with my head half busted. I guess it was her old man that did it.

THE GIRL: You mean her father?

YOUNG MAN: No, her husband. If I had an old lady like that, I'd throw her out.

THE GIRL: Do you think you'll have better luck, if I go with you?

YOUNG MAN: It's a cinch. I'm a good handicapper. All I need is somebody good like you with me. It's no good always walking around in the streets for anything that might be there at the time. You got to have somebody staying with you all the time—through winters when it's cold, and springtime when it's pretty, and summertime when it's nice and hot and you can go swimming—through *all* the times—rain and snow and all the different kinds of weather a man's got to go through before he dies. You got to have somebody who's right. Somebody who knows you, from away back. You got to have somebody who even knows you're wrong but likes you just the same. I know I'm wrong, but I just don't want anything the hard way, working like a dog, or the *easy* way, working like a dog—working's the hard way and the easy way both. All I got to do is beat the price, always—and then, I don't feel lousy and don't hate anybody. If you go along with me, I'll be the finest guy anybody ever saw. I won't be wrong any more. You know when you get enough of that money, you *can't* be wrong any more—you're right because the money says so. I'll have a lot of money and you'll be just about the prettiest, most wonderful kid in the whole world. I'll be proud walking around Frisco with you on my arm and people turning around to look at us.

THE GIRL: Do you think they will?

YOUNG MAN: Sure they will. When I get back in some decent clothes, and you're on my arm—well, Katey, they'll turn around and look, and they'll see something, too.

THE GIRL: Katey?

YOUNG MAN: Yeah—that's your name from now on. You're the first girl I ever called Katey. I've been saving it for you O.K.?

THE GIRL: O.K.

YOUNG MAN: How long have I been here?

THE GIRL: Since last night. You didn't wake up until late this morning, though.

YOUNG MAN: What time is it now? About nine?

THE GIRL: About ten.

YOUNG MAN: Have you got the key to this lousy cell?

THE GIRL: No. They don't let me fool with any keys.

YOUNG MAN: Well, can you get it?

THE GIRL: No.

YOUNG MAN: Can you *try?*

THE GIRL: They wouldn't let me get near any keys. I cook for this jail, when they've got somebody in it. I clean up and things like that.

YOUNG MAN: Well, I want to get out of here. Don't you know the guy that runs this joint?

THE GIRL: I know him, but he wouldn't let you out. They were talking of taking you to another jail in another town.

YOUNG MAN: Yeah? Why?

THE GIRL: Because they're afraid.

YOUNG MAN: What are they afraid of?

THE GIRL: They're afraid these people from Wheeling will come over in the middle of the night and break in.

YOUNG MAN: Yeah? What do they want to do that for?

THE GIRL: Don't *you* know what they want to do it for?

YOUNG MAN: Yeah, I know all right.

THE GIRL: Are you scared?

YOUNG MAN: Sure I'm scared. Nothing scares a man more than ignorance. You can argue with people who ain't fools, but you can't argue with fools—they just go to work and do what they're set on doing. Get me out of here.

THE GIRL: How?

YOUNG MAN: Well, go get the guy with the key, and let me talk to him.

THE GIRL: He's gone home. Everybody's gone home.

YOUNG MAN: You mean I'm in this little jail all alone?

THE GIRL: Well—yeah—except me.

YOUNG MAN: Well, what's the big idea—doesn't anybody stay here all the time?

THE GIRL: No, they go home every night. I clean up and then I go, too. I hung around tonight.

YOUNG MAN: What made you do that?

THE GIRL: I wanted to talk to you.

YOUNG MAN: Honest? What did you want to talk about?

THE GIRL: Oh, I don't know. I took care of you last night. You were talking in your sleep. You liked me, too. I didn't think you'd like me when you woke up, though.

YOUNG MAN: Yeah? Why not?

THE GIRL: I don't know.

YOUNG MAN: Yeah? Well, you're wonderful, see?

THE GIRL: Nobody ever talked to me that way. All the fellows in town—(*Pause.*)

YOUNG MAN: What about 'em? (*Pause.*) Well, what about 'em? Come on—tell me.

THE GIRL: They laugh at me.

YOUNG MAN: Laugh at *you?* They're fools. What do they know about anything? You go get your things and come back here. I'll take you with me to Frisco. How old are you?

THE GIRL: Oh, I'm of age.

YOUNG MAN: How old are you?—Don't lie to me! Sixteen?

THE GIRL: I'm seventeen.

YOUNG MAN: Well, bring your father and mother. We'll get married before we go.

THE GIRL: They wouldn't let me go.

YOUNG MAN: Why not?

THE GIRL: I don't know, but they wouldn't. I know they wouldn't.

YOUNG MAN: You go tell your father not to be a fool, see? What is he, a farmer?

THE GIRL: No—nothing. He gets a little relief from the government because he's supposed to be hurt or something—his side hurts, he says. I don't know what it is.

YOUNG MAN: Ah, he's a liar. Well, I'm taking you with me, see?

THE GIRL: He takes the money I earn, too.

YOUNG MAN: He's got no right to do that.

THE GIRL: I know it, but he does it.

YOUNG MAN (*almost to himself*): This world stinks. You shouldn't have been born in this town, anyway, and you shouldn't have had a man like that for a father, either.

THE GIRL: Sometimes I feel sorry for him.

YOUNG MAN: Never mind feeling sorry for him. (*Pointing a finger.*) I'm going to talk to your father some day. I've got a few things to tell that guy.

THE GIRL: I know you have.

YOUNG MAN (*suddenly*): Hello—out there! See if you can get that fellow with the keys to come down and let me out.

THE GIRL: Oh, I couldn't.

YOUNG MAN: Why not?

THE GIRL: I'm nobody here—they give me fifty cents every day I work.

YOUNG MAN: How much?

THE GIRL: Fifty cents.

YOUNG MAN (*to the world*): You see? They ought to pay money to *look* at you. To breathe the *air* you breathe. I don't know. Sometimes I figure it never is going to make sense. Hello—out there! I'm scared. You try to get me out of here. I'm scared them fools are going to come here from Wheeling and go crazy, thinking they're heroes. Get me out of here, Katey.

THE GIRL: I don't know what to do. Maybe I could break the door down.

YOUNG MAN: No, you couldn't do that. Is there a hammer out there or anything?

THE GIRL: Only a broom. Maybe they've locked the broom up, too.

YOUNG MAN: Go see if you can find anything.

THE GIRL: All right. (*she goes.*)

YOUNG MAN: Hello—out there! Hello—out there! (*Pause.*) Hello—out there! Hello—out there! (*Pause.*) Putting me in jail. (*With contempt.*) Rape! Rape? *They* rape everything good that was ever born. His side hurts. They laugh at her. Fifty cents a day. Little punk people. Hurting the only good thing that ever came their way (*Suddenly.*) Hello—out there!

THE GIRL (*returning*): There isn't a thing out there. They've locked everything up for the night.

YOUNG MAN: Any cigarettes?

THE GIRL: Everything's locked up—all the drawers of the desk, all the closet doors—everything.

YOUNG MAN: I ought to have a cigarette.

THE GIRL: I could get you a package maybe, somewhere. I guess the drug store's open. It's about a mile.

YOUNG MAN: A mile? I don't want to be alone that long.

THE GIRL: I could run all the way, and all the way back.

YOUNG MAN: You're the sweetest girl that ever lived.

THE GIRL: What kind do you want?

YOUNG MAN: Oh, any kind—Chesterfields or Camels or Lucky Strikes—any kind at all.

THE GIRL: I'll go get a package. (*She turns to go.*)

YOUNG MAN: What about the money?

THE GIRL: I've got some money. I've got a quarter I been saving. I'll run all the way. (*She is about to go.*)

YOUNG MAN: Come here.

THE GIRL (*going to him*): What?

YOUNG MAN: Give me your hand. (*He takes her hand and looks at it, smiling. He lifts it and kisses it.*) I'm scared to death.

THE GIRL: I am, too.

YOUNG MAN: I'm not lying—I don't care what happens to me, but I'm scared nobody will ever come out here to this Godforsaken broken-down town and find you. I'm scared you'll get used to it and not mind. I'm scared you'll never get to Frisco and have 'em all turning around to look at you. Listen—go get me a gun, because if they come, I'll kill 'em! They don't understand. Get me a gun!

THE GIRL: I could get my father's gun. I know where he hides it.

YOUNG MAN: Go get it. Never mind the cigarettes. Run all the way. (*Pause, smiling but seriously.*) Hello, Katey.

THE GIRL: Hello. What's *your* name?

YOUNG MAN: Photo-Finish is what they *call* me. My races are always photo-finish races. You don't know what that means, but it means they're very close. So close the only way they can tell which horse wins is to look at a photograph after the race is over. Well, every race I bet turns out to be a photo-finish race, and my horse never wins. It's my bad luck, all the time. That's why they call me Photo-Finish. Say it before you go.

THE GIRL: Photo-Finish.

YOUNG MAN: Come here. (THE GIRL *moves close and he kisses her.*) Now, hurry. Run all the way.

THE GIRL: I'll run. (THE GIRL *turns and runs. The* YOUNG MAN *stands at the center of the cell a long time.* THE GIRL *comes running back in. Almost crying.*) I'm afraid. I'm afraid I won't see you again. If I come back and you're not here, I—

YOUNG MAN: Hello—out there!

THE GIRL: It's so lonely in this town. Nothing here but the lonesome wind all the time, lifting the dirt and blowing out to the prairie. I'll stay *here.* I won't *let* them take you away.

YOUNG MAN: Listen, Katey. Do what I tell you. Go get that gun and come back. Maybe they won't come tonight. Maybe they won't come at all. I'll hide the gun when they let me out you can take it back and put it where you found it. And then we'll go away. But if they come, I'll kill 'em! Now, hurry—

THE GIRL: All right. (*Pause.*) I want to tell you something.

YOUNG MAN: O.K.

THE GIRL (*very softly*): If you're not here when I come back, well, I'll have the gun and I'll know what to do with it.

YOUNG MAN: You know how to handle a gun?

THE GIRL: I know how.

YOUNG MAN: Don't be a fool. (*Takes off his shoe, brings out some currency.*) Don't be a fool, see? Here's some money. Eighty dollars. Take it and go to Frisco. Look around and find somebody. Find somebody alive and halfway human, see? Promise me—if I'm not here when you come back, just throw the gun away and get the hell to Frisco. Look around and find somebody.

THE GIRL: I don't *want* to find anybody.

YOUNG MAN (*swiftly, desperately*): Listen, if I'm not here when you come back, how do you know I haven't gotten away? Now, do what I tell you. I'll meet you in Frisco. I've got a couple of dollars in my other shoe. I'll see you in San Francisco.

THE GIRL (*with wonder*): San Francisco?

YOUNG MAN: That's right—San Francisco. That's where you and me belong.

THE GIRL: I've always wanted to go to *some* place like San Francisco—but how could I go alone?

YOUNG MAN: Well, you're not alone any more, see?

THE GIRL: Tell me a little what it's like.

YOUNG MAN (*very swiftly, almost impatiently at first, but gradually slower and with remembrance, smiling, and* THE GIRL *moving closer to him as he speaks*): Well, it's on the Pacific to begin with—ocean water all around. Cool fog and seagulls. Ships from all over the world. It's got seven hills.

The little streets go up and down, around and all over. Every night the fog-horns bawl. But they won't be bawling for you and me.

THE GIRL: What else?

YOUNG MAN: That's about all, I guess.

THE GIRL: Are people different in San Francisco?

YOUNG MAN: People are the same everywhere. They're different only when they love somebody. That's the only thing that makes 'em different. More people in Frisco love somebody, that's all.

THE GIRL: Nobody anywhere loves anybody as much as I love you.

YOUNG MAN (*shouting, as if to the world*): You see? Hearing you say that, a man could die and still be ahead of the game. Now, hurry. And don't forget, if I'm not here when you come back, get the hell to San Francisco where you'll have a chance. Do you hear me?

THE GIRL *stands a moment looking at him, then backs away, turns and runs. The* YOUNG MAN *stares after her, troubled and smiling. Then he turns away from the image of her and walks about like a lion in a cage. After a while he sits down suddenly and buries his head in his hands. From a distance the sound of several automobiles approaching is heard. He listens a moment, then ignores the implications of the sound, whatever they may be. Several automobile doors are slammed. He ignores this also. A wooden door is opened with a key and closed, and footsteps are heard in a hall. Walking easily, almost casually and yet arrogantly, a* MAN *comes in.*

YOUNG MAN (*jumps up suddenly and shouts at* THE MAN, *almost scaring him*): What the hell kind of jailkeeper are you, anyway? Why don't you attend to your business? You get paid for it, don't you? Now, get me out of here.

THE MAN: But I'm not the jailkeeper.

YOUNG MAN: Yeah? Well, who are you, then?

THE MAN: I'm the husband.

YOUNG MAN: What husband you talking about?

THE MAN: You know what husband.

YOUNG MAN: Hey! (*Pause, looking at* THE MAN.) Are you the guy that hit me over the head last night?

THE MAN: I am.

YOUNG MAN (*with righteous indignation*): What do you mean going around hitting people over the head?

THE MAN: Oh, I don't know. What do you *mean* going around—the way you do?

YOUNG MAN (*rubbing his head*): You hurt my head. You got no right to hit anybody over the head.

THE MAN (*suddenly angry, shouting*): Answer my question! What do you mean?

YOUNG MAN: Listen, you—don't be hollering at me just because I'm locked up.

THE MAN (*with contempt, slowly*): You're a dog!

YOUNG MAN: Yeah, well let me tell you something. You *think* you're the husband. You're the husband of nothing. (*Slowly.*) What's more, your wife—if you want to call her that—is a tramp. Why don't you throw her out in the street where she belongs?

THE MAN: (*draws a pistol*): Shut up!

YOUNG MAN: Yeah? Go ahead, shoot—(*Softly.*) and spoil the fun. What'll your pals think? They'll be disappointed, won't they. What's the fun hanging a man who's already dead? (THE MAN *puts the gun away.*) That's right, because now you can have some fun yourself, telling me what you're going to do. That's what you came here for, isn't it? Well, you don't need to tell me. I *know* what you're going to do. I've read the papers and I know. They have fun. A mob of 'em fall on one man and beat him, don't they? They tear off his clothes and kick him, don't they? And women and little children stand around watching, don't they? Well, before you go on *this* picnic, I'm going to tell you a few things. Not that that's going to send you home with your pals— the other heroes. No. You've been outraged. A stranger has come to town and violated your women. Your pure, innocent, virtuous women. You fellows have got to set this thing right. You're men, not mice. You're homemakers, and you beat your children. (*Suddenly.*) Listen, you—I didn't know she was your wife. I didn't know she was anybody's wife.

THE MAN: You're a liar!

YOUNG MAN: Sometimes—when it'll do somebody some good—but not this time. Do you want to hear about it? (THE MAN *doesn't answer.*) All right, I'll tell you. I met her at a lunch counter. She came in and sat next to me. There was plenty of room, but she sat next to me. Somebody had put a nickel in the phonograph and a fellow was singing *New San Antonio Rose.* Well, she got to talking about the song. I thought she was talking to the waiter, but *he* didn't answer her, so after a while *I* answered her. That's how I met her. I didn't think anything of it. We left the place together and started walking. The first thing I knew she said, This is where I live.

THE MAN: You're a dirty liar!

YOUNG MAN: Do you want to hear it? Or not? (THE MAN *does not answer.*) O.K. She asked me to come in. Maybe she had something in mind, maybe she didn't. Didn't make any difference to me, one way or the other. If she was lonely, all right. If not, all right.

THE MAN: You're telling a lot of dirty lies!

YOUNG MAN: I'm telling the truth. Maybe your wife's out there with your pals. Well, call her in. I got nothing against her, or you—or any of you. Call her in, and ask her a few questions. Are you in love with her? (THE MAN *doesn't answer.*) Well, that's too bad.

THE MAN: What do you mean, too bad?

YOUNG MAN: I mean this may not be the first time something like this has happened.

THE MAN (*swiftly*): Shut up!

YOUNG MAN: Oh, you know it. You've always known it. You're afraid of your pals, that's all. She asked me for money. That's all she wanted. I wouldn't be here now if I had given her the money.

THE MAN (*slowly*): How much did she ask for?

YOUNG MAN: I didn't ask her how much. I told her I'd made a mistake. She said she would make trouble if I didn't give her money. Well, I don't like bargaining, and I don't like being threatened, either. I told her to get the hell away from me. The next thing I knew she'd run out of the house and was hollering. (*Pause.*) Now, why don't you go out there and tell 'em they took me to another jail—go home and pack up and leave her. You're a pretty good guy, you're just afraid of your pals.

THE MAN *draws his gun again. He is very frightened. He moves a step toward the* YOUNG MAN, *then fires three times. The* YOUNG MAN *falls to his knees.* THE MAN *turns and runs, horrified.*

YOUNG MAN: Hello—out there! (*He is bent forward.*)

    THE GIRL *comes running in, and halts suddenly, looking at him.*

THE GIRL: There were some people in the street, men and women and kids— so I came in through the back, through a window. I couldn't find the gun. I looked all over but I couldn't find it. What's the matter?

YOUNG MAN: Nothing—nothing. Everything's all right. Listen. Listen, kid. Get the hell out of here. Go out the same way you came in and run— run like hell—run all night. Get to another town and get on a train. Do you hear me?

THE GIRL: What's happened?

YOUNG MAN: Get away—just get away from here. Take any train that's going— you can get to Frisco later.

THE GIRL (*almost sobbing*): I don't want to go any place without you.

YOUNG MAN: I can't go. Something's happened. (*He looks at her.*) But I'll be with you always—God damn it. Always!

    He falls forward. THE GIRL *stands near him, then begins to sob softly, walking away. She stands over to one side, stops sobbing, and stares out. The excitement of the mob outside increases.* THE MAN, *with two of his pals, comes running in.* THE GIRL *watches, unseen.*

THE MAN: Here's the son of a bitch!

ANOTHER MAN: O.K. Open the cell, Harry.

> *The* THIRD MAN *goes to the cell door, unlocks it, and swings it open. A* WOMAN *comes running in.*

THE WOMAN: Where is he? I want to see him. Is he dead? (*Looking down at him, as the* MEN *pick him up.*) There he is. (*Pause.*) Yeah, that's him.

> *Her husband looks at her with contempt, then at the dead man.*

THE MAN (*trying to laugh.*): All right—let's get it over with.

THIRD MAN: Right you are, George. Give me a hand, Harry.

> *They lift the body.*

THE GIRL (*suddenly, fiercely*): Put him down!

THE MAN: What's this?

SECOND MAN: What are you doing here? Why aren't you out in the street?

THE GIRL: Put him down and go away.

> *She runs toward the* MEN.
>
> THE WOMAN *grabs her.*

THE WOMAN: Here—where do you think *you're* going?

THE GIRL: Let me go. You've no right to take him away.

THE WOMAN: Well, listen to her, will you? (*She slaps* THE GIRL *and pushes her to the floor.*) Listen to the little slut, will you?

> *They all go, carrying the* YOUNG MAN'S *body.* THE GIRL *gets up slowly, no longer sobbing. She looks around at everything, then looks straight out, and whispers.*

THE GIRL: Hello—out—there! Hello—out there!

CURTAIN

27 THE DRAMATIC PLOT

Starting with a *concept; the scene* as the basic unit of drama; providing *dramatic questions* throughout the play; controlling the *pace* in traditional and nontraditional ways; the plot in *comedy*.

A good dramatic plot starts with a good concept. As I explained in Chapter 25, a concept includes a basic situation, some type of conflict or struggle, and an outcome. It is far more fruitful to think in terms of a situation involving specific characters than it is to begin with abstract ideas because drama, even more than fiction, depends on events.

We can be fairly certain, for example, that in *Hello Out There*, William Saroyan did not start out with a determination to reveal aspects of hypocrisy in society and the fundamental need for individuals to make contact with one another. More likely he began with a concept that might be described like this: "A drifter is held in a small-town jail on a false rape charge. He almost manages to escape with the help of a young woman who is as lonely as he, but a mob, filled with a hypocritical sense of justice, reaches him first and kills him."

Turning from concept to the characters, brief descriptions might read like this: "Young man is a drifter and is genuinely lonely. Has always taken chances (named Photo-Finish). Appears to take advantage of girl to get out of jail, but is sincerely concerned about the plight of her life as well. Does his best to get her to leave town before he is killed."

These are the raw materials of a play. Once you have them down on paper, you are ready to start outlining the plot.

The Scene as Basic Unit

In full-length plays the word *scene* is generally used to describe subdivisions of *acts*. Often they are written into the program notes and may involve a lapse of time or even a change of setting. In some cases they replace acts altogether.

For dramatists, however, the word *scene* also refers to each unit of action that begins with an entrance or an exit and ends with the next shift of characters on the stage. To avoid confusion, think of these as *secondary scenes*. They are the essential and basic units of action for the playwright, the actors, and the director as well.

Occasionally, a secondary scene may have a strong dramatic unity. It may build to a climax that is dramatically punctuated by the departure of one or more characters. Often, the unity is more subtle. It establishes the almost unnoticed rise and fall of action that distinguishes the play which is "dramatic" from the play that appears to be "flat" or "dull."

Hello Out There is an excellent example. It is a one-act play presented in one primary scene. There is one stage set and one apparently uninterrupted flow of action. But from a playwright's point of view, the work is divided into eight secondary scenes. Each of these is marked by an exit or entrance, and each has an influence on the rise and fall of dramatic impact.

Here are the scenes listed in the kind of outline some playwrights find helpful when planning a new play. The word *girl* is used rather than the more contemporary *young woman* simply to conform with Saroyan's script.

1. Man alone on stage; talks to girl offstage
2. Girl enters; they get to know each other
3. Girl exits; man gives brief monologue
4. Girl returns; they make pact
5. Girl exits; husband enters, argues, shoots
6. Husband exits, girl returns
7. Husband and pals return, drag body out
8. Girl alone on stage; repeats refrain

This sparse outline demonstrates how many separate units will be involved, but it doesn't indicate which are major scenes and which are minor, which are highly dramatic and which merely develop relationships. Each of these secondary scenes deserves a closer look.

Although the opening scene has only one actor on the stage, it is far from static. Notice that the man is neither musing philosophically to himself nor addressing the audience. His first lines call out for contact with someone else, and then almost at once he is interacting with the young woman, even before she is on stage. This is no prologue. Psychologically, the play begins as soon as these two characters are in voice contact.

The second scene begins when the young woman actually appears. If one merely reads the script on the page as if it were fiction, her entrance may not seem significant. But a playwright always keeps the visual aspect in mind, imagining the action from the audience's point of view. In production, her arrival on stage is the psychological start of a new scene.

This second scene is the longest in the play. Saroyan has to fill in a great deal of background and, in addition, draw these two strangers together convincingly. It would have been possible to have Emily on stage from the start, but postponing her entrance helps to keep that long second scene from becoming even longer.

The third scene is very brief. She goes out to look for tools, and he is left on the stage alone. But it is important because it allows him to lash out vehemently against what he sees as injustice. The fact that he is alone on the stage indicates to the audience that he is speaking his inner conviction. Were it not for this little scene, we might feel that he was cynically lying to the girl simply to save himself.

The fourth scene is one in which Emily and Photo-Finish make the pact to meet in San Francisco. Notice that their relationship has grown with surprising speed. In a story, one might be tempted to spread the action out over the course of a day or so; but Saroyan's dramatic sense leads him to keep the action continuous.

Emily leaves, ending the fourth scene, and there is only a moment of sound effects before a new character suddenly appears on the stage. The tension mounts as we learn that this is the angered husband. An argument pushes the dramatic impact to new levels, and the husband draws his gun. The scene culminates with three shots.

In the sixth scene the husband has fled and Emily returns. The dying hero and heroine are alone on the stage. If this were opera, it would be the point where the final duet is sung. As realistic drama, it is a brief, terse, yet tender moment.

But a problem arises here. How is the playwright going to maintain dramatic interest in that brief yet important section which follows the death of the protagonist? Once again, a new secondary scene is prepared for—the seventh. First the audience hears activity building off stage. Saroyan is careful to include this in his stage directions: "The excitement of the mob outside increases." The husband, two friends, and then the wife all burst on the stage. Emily demands that they put the body down—what we can assume is the first dramatically assertive act of her life. She is slapped to the floor.

The last of these secondary scenes is so brief that it consists of only one line. But to understand just how powerful the device is, imagine the girl delivering that last line with the other characters still on stage, struggling to drag the body off. Emily would be literally upstaged. In addition, her line would be a mere continuation of the preceding dialogue. Having her alone on the stage, probably with a single beam of light on her, isolates the final words. Her plight—now matching that of Photo-Finish at the very beginning of the play—becomes the focal point of the play.

When one first reads a play like this, it is easy to assume that it is one continual flow of action from beginning to end. Such an approach would, of course, be possible. But it would be far more difficult to hold the audience's emotional involvement for that length of time. Exits and entrances in this play provide the basic organizational structure with which the dramatic impact is heightened and lowered and then heightened again in regular succession, holding the audience from beginning to end.

Because most of us have seen more films than plays, it is easy to be influenced by the rapid pace of their scenes. The camera not only can blend extremely brief units of action into an apparently smooth flow, it can shift setting without a break. Changing the set on the stage is time-consuming and tends to break the illusion of reality. For this reason, many full-length plays and almost all one-act plays maintain a single set. In addition, very short scenes such as the ones Saroyan uses to reveal Photo-Finish alone on the stage are kept to a minimum.

In judging the length of your secondary scenes, keep imagining the effect on your audience. Too many short scenes will make the action seem choppy; lengthy scenes may create monotony and slow the pace. You can make these decisions more easily if you have a chance to hear your script read aloud or, best of all, to see it in production.

Providing Dramatic Questions

How are you going to hold your audience in their seats? When you write fiction, this is less of a problem. A story or novel can be read in installments. But when you produce a play you are asking an audience to give it their uninterrupted attention—often while sitting on uncomfortable seats.

Because of this, most plays are energized with a series of dramatic questions. They are like lures to hold the interest of the audience. We have already seen how fiction also makes use of dramatic questions (Where are we going? What will this stranger be like?), but plays depend on them to a far greater degree.

Looking at the full range of drama from Sophocles to our own decade, there are certain dramatic questions that recur frequently. This does not make the plays redundant; one hardly notices the similarity. But their widespread use does suggest just how important the dramatic question is.

1. *Will he come?* Shakespeare charged the first act of *Hamlet* with this question, applying it to the ghost. More recently, it has been broadened to cover the full length of plays. Clifford Odets' *Waiting for Lefty*, written in the '30s, Samuel Beckett's *Waiting for Godot*, and Harold Pinter's *The Dumb Waiter* all rely heavily on anticipation of a character who never appears. And to some degree, the question is a factor in *Hello Out There* as soon as the threat of a lynching is raised.

2. *Who did it?* This is, of course, the literary version of "Whodunit?" We find it running the full length of drama from *Oedipus Rex* to Tennessee Williams' *Suddenly Last Summer*. The trial scenes in *The Caine Mutiny Trial* and, in a loose sense, *Tea and Sympathy* and *The Crucible* are simply variations of this. In many cases the audience knows who is guilty; the dramatic question arises out of the attempt on the part of the *characters* to determine guilt. It is a highly variable device, though the trial scene has become overused.

3. *Will he or she succeed?* This is by far the most used of all dramatic questions. It has been applied both to noble and evil characters alike.

4. *Will he or she discover what we know?* The classic example is *Oedipus Rex*, in which the audience is held by the drama of a character gradually discovering terrible truths about himself. It is also a factor in *Othello*. And it has more recently been adapted in plays of psychological self-discovery such as Arthur Miller's *Death of a Salesman*.

5. *Will a compromise be found?* This question has held audiences in such varied plays as *Antigone*, John Galsworthy's *Strife*, and more subtly in Tennessee Williams' *A Streetcar Named Desire*. In all three of these examples, by the way, the dramatic question is merged with the theme itself—a connection none of the other questions have.

6. *Will this episode end in violence?* This is frequently used in contemporary drama. In fact, it is one of the final questions in *Hello Out There*. Even though almost every indication points to a tragic ending, we are still deeply concerned.

7. *What's happening?* This is the question most frequently asked of plays in the absurdist tradition. Like dream fiction, these works plunge the audience into a confusing, often inexplicable environment. Playwrights like Pinter, Beckett, Ionesco, and occasionally Albee utilize ambiguity as a dramatic question.

    This is, however, a risky device for the novice. Like free verse, it seems easy at first but often slides into meaninglessness. It requires wit or ingenuity of thematic suggestion to keep the play alive. In short, a dull play is not improved by making it an obscurely dull play.

The opening dramatic question is often referred to as the *hook*. It arouses interest from the start. But most plays move from one dramatic question to the next so that the audience is kept wondering about immediate outcomes as well as what the ultimate resolution will be. *Hello Out There* is a good example of how one can create a new question just as an old one has been resolved.

The play begins with a man in jail, and the audience immediately wonders why he is there. What did he do? Should we sympathize with him?

Through the girl we begin to get answers to these questions, but at the same time a new cluster of dramatic questions is forming: Will she help him? And if she does, will they succeed? Toward the end of the play, we have a sense of foreboding: It is not likely that the outcome will be happy. But as in all tragedies, we still concern ourselves with the survival of the protagonist. There is for most members of the audience a lingering hope that he will live up to his nickname and win by a photo-finish.

Don't confuse these questions with the theme. Saroyan's thematic concern is with the loneliness of individuals; he is comparing life in a small and hostile town with being in jail. I will return to various aspects of theme in later chapters. My concern here is for the basic technique of generating dramatic questions. They are truly theatrical devices and essential if a play is to hold the attention of the audience.

Controlling the Pace

Pace is all-important in a play. Scenes that appear to drag are revised well into production. Although one rarely hears about a play in which the pace is too rapid, it is possible to race too quickly through scenes that should unfold character or clarify aspects of the plot. And too much dramatic voltage at the beginning of a play can create a slump later on.

Traditional terms are helpful if we remember that they apply mainly to the plots of traditional plays. *Rising action,* for example, accurately describes the mounting complication with which many plays from all historical periods are begun. In full-length dramas, problems may be compounded with subplots involving secondary characters acting as *foils* to highlight or set off the major characters. The crisis is not the very end but the turning point at which the protagonist's fortunes begin to fail. From there on we have *falling action,* which in tragedies results in a *catastrophe*—often the death of the hero.

Sound old-fashioned? True, Aristotle described drama in those terms. True, they apply to Greek and Elizabethan tragedies. But they also apply to many modern works by such playwrights as Eugene O'Neill, Arthur Miller, and Tennessee Williams. In condensed form, they can be seen in William Saroyan's *Hello Out There* as well.

The rising action involves the young man meeting an ally and planning an escape. The crisis occurs when the enraged husband returns. From there on it is falling action through to the death of the protagonist. Although the play is brief and in one act, the plot structure is similar to a traditional three-act play or an Elizabethan tragedy of five acts.

This plot form continues to be popular not because playwrights who use it are imitative but because it is good theater. It lends itself to a variety of situations and it holds audiences.

This is, however, only one way to handle the pacing of a dramatic plot. Another focuses on characterization and is sometimes referred to as the onion approach: A series of scenes exposes the inner life of a character or a couple like peeling the layers of an onion. Eugene O'Neill's *The Iceman Cometh* reveals a single character this way; Edward Albee's *Who's Afraid of Virginia Woolf?* exposes the illusions of a couple with equal intensity.

Another type of loose plotting is sometimes called the *Grand Hotel* pattern, though the title refers to a novel by Vicki Baum, not a play. The novel brings together a number of different characters to portray European society in the 1920s. This approach weaves together many parallel plots and lends itself to longer plays. A good contemporary example is *(H)otel Baltimore* by Lanford Wilson. Once again a hotel (this one not so grand) is used to link characters, and the plot is episodic. Arthur Miller's relatively short *A Memory of Two Mondays* deals with the men who work in the shipping room of an auto-parts warehouse. It is concerned almost equally with all the characters. The pace in plays like this is controlled not by the rise and fall of a protagonist, but by a series of dramatic questions based on the problems faced by a number of different characters.

Some plays control the pace without following any classifiable plan. In Edward Albee's *The Sandbox*, for example (included as Chapter 29), the opening scenes are a biting satire of how some people treat their aging parents. Then the playwright drops the satiric mood and treats the grandmother herself with great compassion. As we will see, the pace is controlled more by this unusual tonal shift than by action.

As we examine the variety of approaches available, it becomes clear that we cannot talk about "rules" for constructing plots. You are free to make good use of certain traditional patterns, and you are also free to strike out with a new approach. But this doesn't mean that anything goes. You must control the pacing in some way. If you don't make use of rising and falling action, consider some type of unfolding to replace it. Low-key scenes must be alternated with dramatic ones effectively enough to maintain interest. If you ignore these basic requirements of pacing, your audience will be quick to let you know.

The Plot in Comedy

Comedy also has plot. And it must also hold an audience. It helps to distinguish three closely related and frequently overlapping types: *humor, wit,* and *satire.*

Humor tends to be warm and appreciative and usually focuses on character. The playwright adopts a fond tone and the audience in a sense laughs *with* the characters rather than *at* them.

Gently humorous plays are often nostalgic, presenting a slightly (and sometimes not so slightly) sentimental view of an earlier or idealized time.

The protagonists of such plays are often rather incompetent—a recent divorcé or divorcée, a kindly alcoholic, or aging spinster sisters. The plots focus on their humorous efforts to straighten out their lives. The outcome is almost always positive, since our concept of comedy is one in which disorder is finally remedied and order is reestablished.

Such plays tend to be rather simple in terms of thematic suggestion and characterization, but they are popular fare both on Broadway and in summer stock. The greatest danger of these comedies (aside from not being funny) is slipping into outright sentimentality or banality.

There is no sharp line dividing humor and wit, but the latter tends to have more bite. It is sharper and often more ingenious. Frequently it stems from the lines themselves rather than situation or character. Playwrights who employ wit are closer to stand-up comics since they depend so heavily on phrasing.

Satire is a form of wit. It involves two basic elements: exaggeration and ridicule. Drama is an excellent medium for satire since the group response of an audience is infectious.

The plot of a satiric play requires special thought. Consider first just what it is that you are satirizing. Is it a personality type or some kind of institution? Once you have defined your intent, list all the characteristics of the subject that you find objectionable. With this kind of precise information, you are ready to create both characters and plot that ridicule those elements.

Keep in mind that there is a wide range between mild satire, which tends to be subtle and often kindly and, on the other hand, bitter or corrosive satire, which is frequently presented in plots that are wildly exaggerated and farcical. Your play will be more effective if the level of satire remains consistent.

Just as serious drama depends on dramatic questions and careful plotting to hold the attention of an audience, a comedy depends on the regular unfolding of a humorous situation or satiric attack. You will have to keep inventing new material to sustain the comedy and gradually increase the tempo toward the end. Be careful not to peak too early. If the material midway seems more effective than your last scene, see if you can shift the stronger episode to the end so as to strengthen the climax. Pacing is just as important as in tragedy.

In addition to the varieties of comedy, consider the value of comic relief in otherwise serious plays. Light touches here and there or, in longer plays, comic characters used as contrast with the protagonist are often highly effective. Such comic elements are one of the best ways to counter the risk of melodrama in a highly dramatic plot. They also take the pressure off temporarily and keep a play from seeming to peak too early.

When you read Albee's *The Sandbox* (Chapter 29), notice how the playwright fuses a bitter-comic satire with a tender and moving tribute to a dying woman at the end. It is most unusual to find a short play that brings together two such disparate tones. You may not wish to attempt such an extreme split, but the play should encourage you to shift the tone occasionally as a method of controlling the pace of your plot.

Although plot is important in fiction, it is crucial in drama. The importance of plot is somewhat softened in a story by the fact that you can occasionally use exposition and slip into the inner thoughts of a character. But a play is all right out there: Action and dialogue are all you have to work with. A lapse in plot development will be painfully evident in production.

But don't let this deter you. On the positive side, plot gives you an opportunity to attract and hold the attention of your audience from start to finish. This direct and charged contact between artist and viewer is one of the special rewards for the playwright.

28 CONFLICT

The limitation of *simple conflicts;* creating a *system of interrelated conflicts; inner conflicts* and how to reveal them through monologues, dialogue, and action; *triangular conflicts,* hackneyed versus fresh; the *individual* against *society.*

Simple dramas have simple conflicts. Such conflicts usually erode characterization, reducing the work to a combat between good and bad. In such plays, the loyalties of the audience are fixed from start to finish. It's our team versus theirs. We see this pattern so often in popular film and television dramas that we sometimes discount the real potential of conflict.

Conflict is, however, the primary energizing force in drama. When we say that work is "dramatic" or "powerful," we are implying that conflict has been used convincingly. Dramatic questions, described in the previous chapter, arouse curiosity. Conflict evokes fear, excitement, anger, commitment. It pumps adrenalin.

There are ways to use conflict without turning your play into a simple slugfest. The best approach is to create a network of related conflicts. One should also consider inner struggles, triangles, and conflicts with society. We can examine these in the abstract, but remember that selecting a type of conflict is not a good way to start a new play. As I have suggested before, start with a specific character or a group of characters already involved in an ongoing situation. Once you have that as a base, consider what types of conflict arise naturally from that situation and which of these might be developed.

Multiple Conflicts

At first glance, the conflict in many plays—even highly sophisticated works—appears to be a basic struggle between two characters. It is easy enough in most cases to pick out the protagonist (central character) and the antagonist (his or her opponent). But if there are more than two characters, this struggle may well be a part of what is really a system of interrelated conflicts.

In full-length plays this pattern of conflict may be dramatized through one or more *subplots* involving secondary characters who echo, amplify, or contrast the conflicts of the main plot. Although there is rarely time to construct a subplot in a one-act play, you can still develop a cluster of conflicts rather than relying entirely on a single struggle.

Hello Out There is a good example. When the play opens, there is no antagonist in sight. The first major conflict to be developed is a man against a hostile town. The enemy is "they"—a vague notion of forces outside that jail. This conflict, man against society, is highlighted when we learn that the name of the town is Matador. He is the bull in the arena.

We soon see that Emily is also pitted against this town. Her life is not threatened, but her spirit is. She is not just lonesome, she is alienated. The men in town, she reports, laugh at her. Her father takes what little money she earns. She is willing to take great risks to escape.

Their conflict with this oppressive town is soon overshadowed by the direct confrontation between Photo-Finish and the husband. But the town remains an antagonist right through to the end of the play. The avenging husband is not pictured as a totally evil character. We can see from his responses that he is increasingly aware that his wife is a tramp. We are told in the stage directions that he is "very frightened" even before he has committed the murder. To a significant degree he is being driven by pressures from his wife and friends. "You're a pretty good guy," Photo-Finish says, "you're just afraid of your pals." Here is another level of conflict. Even though the killing takes the outward form of a simple television drama, the play is not simply an all-good hero pitted against an evil antagonist. The killing is a tragic result of a network of conflicts.

It may seem difficult at first to generate a multiplicity of conflicts in the very limited time frame of a short one-act play. But if you have well-rounded characters, conflicts often develop naturally. I will return to characterization in Chapter 30, but it is worth pointing out here that plays that depend too heavily on a single, simple conflict almost always suffer from characterization which is also simple.

Inner Conflict

Inner conflicts are another effective method of achieving subtlety. The very phrases with which we describe such indecision suggest dramatic tension: a character is "of two minds," "struggling with himself," or even "at war with herself." Such individuals are torn between love and fear, courage and timidity, anger and affection. Or they may be attracted to two different people, two opposing ethical positions, two sexual identities. Inner conflict is a part of the human condition.

But how is one to reveal what goes on in the mind of a character in a genre that depends almost entirely on dialogue and actions? If you have been writing fiction, your first inclination may be to consider monologues. After all, Shakespeare used them. The soliloquies of Hamlet and Lady Macbeth are among the most quoted dramatic lines in the language. But remember that those monologues were embedded in five-act plays. If we hadn't heard those monologues so often and studied them so carefully out of context they would blend into the work as a whole. In addition, Elizabethan drama accepted the convention of major characters expressing their inner conflicts eloquently in blank verse. In a contemporary, realistic play that is intended to reflect more closely the behavior and speech of daily life, the inner debate expressed through a monologue may seem artificial.

In spite of these risks, monologues are used from time to time in contemporary drama. Saroyan's first scene begins with a brief one, and he repeats the device by having Photo-Finish alone on the stage in that abbreviated third scene. This second monologue is particularly important because it is the only hard evidence the audience has that Photo-Finish really is fond of Emily and is not just using her for escape. Although Emily's two lines at the very end of the play take only a moment, they effectively reveal her inner lament.

During the 1960s and '70s there was a certain vogue for long monologues among playwrights in the absurdist school. Their plays were often dreamlike, philosophical, and talky. They frequently contained lengthy pronouncements. The best of them held interest through flashes of insight and wit, but the approach was short-lived. It takes remarkable skill on the part of both playwright and actor to maintain the interest of an audience with thought alone.

To avoid the static quality of monologues, consider the possibility of providing your protagonist with a confidant—a personal friend who is not quite central to the action. In some cases, this may turn out to be a foil—a character who sets off some of the characteristics of your protagonist by contrast. If you are working with two couples, the two women or the two men can sometimes reveal to each other inner conflicts that they are reluctant to share with their partners.

Another approach is using action. People often reveal their inner conflicts through the way they behave—often quite unconsciously. It is not difficult to have your characters do the same. There is a small example in *Hello Out There* which is easily missed, but it represents a well-used device. Emily is struggling between the desire to do whatever she can for Photo-Finish and, on the other hand, the fear of leaving him for a minute. When he asks her to go and look for cigarettes, she leaves, running, and then comes running back in without the cigarettes almost at once. Alternating behavior like this can be used in more significant scenes as well. A character starts to do one thing, then abruptly does another. Often no lines are needed to spell out the inner conflict.

Inner conflicts or debates with oneself are almost always linked in some way to outer conflicts. Such indecision is one of the best ways of keeping your major conflict from becoming wooden and unconvincing.

Triangular Conflicts

To this point we have been examining conflicts that pit a single element against another. Triangles provide an additional dimension.

The first pattern that comes to mind is the couple threatened by a third party. It has a venerable tradition. Medea's betrayal by her husband, Jason, who fell in love with another woman has been told and retold from the tragedy of Euripides to the modern verse play of Robinson Jeffers. The same pattern of betrayal and revenge is repeated endlessly in contemporary play and film scripts, both on serious and comic levels. Sometimes the malevolent agent is not another lover but simply an evil force, as in the case of Iago in Shakespeare's *Othello*.

If you consider a love triangle as the basis of conflict in a one-act play, you will have to work hard to achieve originality. The sexy baby-sitter and obliging secretary are stereotypes. But triangles do continue to exist in life, and in some cases the unique circumstances of an actual case will suggest a fresh dramatic situation.

Remember too that not all triangles involve a third person. Both husbands and wives have been known to become seduced by professional commitments. A married person's involvement with a political cause, a new religious faith, or a physically disabled child can have the impact of an infidelity. Here too there are situations that have been overdone. The marriage that is threatened by a husband's preoccupation with his business can, if not done in a fresh manner, become as hackneyed in drama as in fiction. As I mentioned in the fiction section, merely reversing the sexes doesn't add much if the characters are still cardboard. And there should be a moratorium on drama plots based on painters who wreck their marriages for the sake of art. But even setting these aside, there are enough triangulations left to serve future dramatists for some time to come.

It is not enough merely to select or invent a triangular pattern of conflict and fill in the blanks. Remember that if you are writing serious drama you are dealing with people in pain. If you consider the situation carefully, you will see inner conflicts as well as the more obvious outer ones. In short, the triangle is only a frame. The worth of your play will depend on how successfully you can humanize that structure with credible characters.

The Individual Against Society

Conflict between individuals is often given greater resonance when it is played against a larger struggle with society. The confrontation between a small-time gambler and an irate husband in a backwater town does not in itself seem very promising. But Saroyan raises the play above the level of a minor news item by using that incident to dramatize and personalize a conflict between the individual and society as a whole.

In that broader conflict, Saroyan unmistakably takes sides. On the one hand, all the characters are treated with some compassion—even the worst of them. The husband who does the killing is described in the lines quoted earlier as frightened and mainly motivated by what others expect of him. And although the wife is seen as hard and brutal when in the company of the men at the end, she is earlier described as more pathetic than evil. Society, on the other hand, is pictured as the real culprit. Photo-Finish, musing to himself, says "This world stinks." Later, outraged at the charge of rape and also at how the town has treated Emily, he says, "Rape? *They* rape everything good that was ever born." When there is still hope of escape she asks, "Are people different in San Francisco?" "People are the same everywhere," he says. "They're different only when they love somebody. More people in Frisco love somebody, that's all." In the conflict between the individual and society as a whole, Saroyan clearly sides with the individual.

Society for Saroyan is a fairly general concept. But it can be viewed in much more specific terms. Some playwrights see society as the rich and powerful. Their work takes a political stance. For many black playwrights, society is the white world. I will have more to say about socially conscious drama and themes of protest in Chapter 33, Dramatic Themes. What concerns us here is the way in which society can be seen as the opposing force, creating a conflict that almost always is repeated in the form of individual against individual.

The dramatic impact that can be generated by pitting the individual against society is enormous. If you take that route, however, be careful not to let your play turn into a sermon. Sermons have their place, but they make poor drama—except for those who already agree. The most successful plays dealing with society are the ones that can translate those relatively abstract convictions into person-to-person conflict. Even when social statement is the primary concern of the playwright, it is personal conflict between credible characters that has immediate impact.

When we use the world *dramatic*, we imply conflict. Plays that lack conflict are often described as slow, talky, tedious, lacking in vitality, or just plain dull. Fiction can afford reflective or descriptive passages if occasionally revitalized by a forward movement of the plot. But a play thrives on energy, and energy is generated through conflict.

29 A Play by Edward Albee

The Sandbox

a brief play, in memory of my grandmother (1876–1959)

The players: THE YOUNG MAN, 25, a good-looking, well-built boy in a bathing suit.

MOMMY, 55, a well-dressed, imposing woman.

DADDY, 60, a small man; gray, thin.

GRANDMA, 86, a tiny, wizened woman with bright eyes.

THE MUSICIAN, no particular age, but young would be nice.

Note: When, in the course of the play, MOMMY and DADDY call each other by these names, there should be no suggestion of regionalism. These names are of empty affection and point up the pre-senility and vacuity of their characters.

The Scene: A bare stage, with only the following: Near the footlights, far stage-right, two simple chairs set side by side, facing the audience; near the footlights, far stage-left, a chair facing stage-right with a music stand before

*it; farther back, and stage-center, slightly elevated and raked, a large child's
sandbox with a toy pail and shovel; the background is the sky, which alters
from brightest day to deepest night.*

At the beginning, it is brightest day; the YOUNG MAN *is alone on stage, to
the rear of the sandbox, and to one side. He is doing calisthenics; he does
calisthenics until quite at the very end of the play. These calisthenics, employing the arms only, should suggest the beating and fluttering of wings.
The* YOUNG MAN *is, after all, the Angel of Death.*

MOMMY *and* DADDY *enter from stage-left,* MOMMY *first.*

MOMMY: (*Motioning to* DADDY) Well, here we are; this is the beach.

DADDY: (*Whining*) I'm cold.

MOMMY: (*Dismissing him with a little laugh*) Don't be silly; it's as warm
as toast. Look at that nice young man over there: *he* doesn't think it's
cold. (*Waves to the* YOUNG MAN) Hello.

YOUNG MAN: (*With an endearing smile*) Hi!

MOMMY: (*Looking about*) This will do perfectly . . . don't you think so,
Daddy? There's sand there . . . and the water beyond. What do you
think, Daddy?

DADDY: (*Vaguely*) Whatever you say, Mommy.

MOMMY: (*With the same little laugh*) Well, of course . . . whatever I say.
Then, it's settled, is it?

DADDY: (*Shrugs*) She's *your* mother, not mine.

MOMMY: *I* know she's my mother. What do you take me for? (*A pause*)
All right, now; let's get on with it. (*She shouts into the wings, stage-left*)
You! Out there! You can come in now.

(*The* MUSICIAN *enters, seats himself in the chair, stage-left, places music on
the music stand, is ready to play.* MOMMY *nods approvingly*).

MOMMY: Very nice; very nice. Are you ready, Daddy? Let's go get
Grandma.

DADDY: Whatever you say, Mommy.

MOMMY: (*Leading the way out, stage-left*) Of course, whatever I say. (*To
the* MUSICIAN) You can begin now.

(*The* MUSICIAN *begins playing;* MOMMY *and* DADDY *exit; the* MUSICIAN,
all the while playing, nods to the YOUNG MAN)

YOUNG MAN: (*With the same endearing smile*) Hi!

(*After a moment,* MOMMY *and* DADDY *re-enter, carrying* GRANDMA. *She
is borne in by their hands under her armpits; she is quite rigid; her legs are
drawn up; her feet do not touch the ground; the expression on her ancient
face is that of puzzlement and fear*)

DADDY: Where do we put her?

MOMMY: (*The same little laugh*) Wherever I say, of course. Let me see . . . well . . . all right, over there . . . in the sandbox. (*Pause*) Well, what are you waiting for, Daddy? . . . The sandbox!

(*Together they carry* GRANDMA *over to the sandbox and more or less dump her in*)

GRANDMA: (*Righting herself to a sitting position; her voice a cross between a baby's laugh and cry*) Ahhhhhh! Graaaaa!

DADDY: (*Dusting himself*) What do we do now?

MOMMY: (*To the* MUSICIAN) You can stop now.

(*The* MUSICIAN *stops*)

(*Back to* DADDY) What do you mean, what do we do now? We go over there and sit down, of course. (*To the* YOUNG MAN) Hello there.

YOUNG MAN: (*Again smiling*) Hi!

(MOMMY *and* DADDY *move to the chairs , stage-right, and sit down. A pause*)

GRANDMA: (*Same as before*) Ahhhhhh! Ah-aaaaaa! Graaaaaa!

DADDY: Do you think . . . do you think she's . . . comfortable?

MOMMY: (*Impatiently*) How would I know?

DADDY: (*Pause*) What do we do now?

MOMMY: (*As if remembering*) We . . . wait. We . . . sit here . . . and we wait . . . that's what we do.

DADDY: (*After a pause*) Shall we talk to each other?

MOMMY: (*With that little laugh; picking something off her dress*) Well, *you* can talk, if you want to . . . if you can think of anything to *say* . . . if you can think of anything *new*.

DADDY: (*Thinks*) No . . . suppose not.

MOMMY: (*With a triumphant laugh*) Of course not!

GRANDMA: (*Banging the toy shovel against the pail*) Haaaaaa! Ah-haaaaaa!

MOMMY: (*Out over the audience*) Be quiet, Grandma . . . just be quiet, and wait.

(GRANDMA *throws a shovelful of sand at* MOMMY)

MOMMY: (*Still out over the audience*) She's throwing sand at me! You stop that, Grandma; you stop throwing sand at Mommy! (*To* DADDY) She's throwing sand at me.

(DADDY *looks around at* GRANDMA, *who screams at him*)

GRANDMA: GRAAAAAA!

MOMMY: Don't look at her. Just . . . sit here . . . be very still . . . and wait. (*To the* MUSICIAN) You . . . uh . . . you go ahead and do whatever it is you do.

(*The* MUSICIAN *plays*)

(MOMMY *and* DADDY *are fixed, staring out beyond the audience.* GRANDMA *looks at them, looks at the* MUSICIAN, *looks at the sandbox, throws down the shovel*)

GRANDMA: Ah-haaaaaa! Graaaaaa! (*Looks for reaction; gets none. Now . . . directly to the audience*) Honestly! What a way to treat an old woman! Drag her out of the house . . . stick her in a car . . . bring her out here from the city . . . dump her in a pile of sand . . . and leave her here to set. I'm eighty-six years old! I was married when I was seventeen. To a farmer. He died when I was thirty.

(*To the* MUSICIAN) Will you stop that, please?

(*The* MUSICIAN *stops playing*)

I'm a feeble old woman . . . how do you expect anybody to hear me over that peep! peep! peep! (*To herself*) There's no respect around here. (*To the* YOUNG MAN) There's no respect around here!

YOUNG MAN: (*Same smile*) Hi!

GRANDMA: (*After a pause, a mild double-take, continues, to the audience*) My husband died when I was thirty (*indicates* MOMMY), and I had to raise that big cow over there all by my lonesome. You can imagine what *that was like.* Lordy! (*To the* YOUNG MAN) Where'd they get *you?*

YOUNG MAN: Oh . . . I've been around for a while.

GRANDMA: I'll bet you have! Heh, heh, heh. Will you look at you!

YOUNG MAN: (*Flexing his muscles*) Isn't that something? (*Continues his calisthenics*)

GRANDMA: Boy, oh boy; I'll say. Pretty good.

YOUNG MAN: (*Sweetly*) I'll say.

GRANDMA: Where ya from?

YOUNG MAN: Southern California.

GRANDMA: (*Nodding*) Figgers; figgers. What's your name, honey?

YOUNG MAN: I don't know. . . .

GRANDMA: (*To the audience*) Bright, too!

YOUNG MAN: I mean . . . I mean, they haven't given me one yet . . . the studio . . .

GRANDMA: (*Giving him the once-over*) You don't say . . . you don't say. Well . . . uh, I've got to talk some more . . . don't you go 'way.

YOUNG MAN: Oh, no.

GRANDMA: (*Turning her attention back to the audience*) Fine; fine. (*Then, once more, back to the* YOUNG MAN) You're . . . you're an actor, hunh?

YOUNG MAN: (*Beaming*) Yes. I am.

GRANDMA: (*To the audience again; shrugs*) I'm smart that way. *Anyhow,* I had to raise . . . *that* over there all by my lonesome; and what's next to her there . . . that's what she married. Rich? I tell you . . . money, money, money. They took me off the *farm* . . . which was real decent of them . . . and they moved me into the big town house with *them* . . . fixed a nice place for me under the stove . . . gave me an army blanket . . . and my own dish . . . my very own dish! So, what have I got to complain about? Nothing, of course. I'm not complaining. (*She looks up at the sky, shouts to someone off stage*) Shouldn't it be getting dark now, dear?

(*The lights dim; night comes on. The* MUSICIAN *begins to play; it becomes deepest night. There are spots on all the players, including the* YOUNG MAN, *who is, of course, continuing his calisthenics*)

DADDY: (*Stirring*) It's nighttime.

MOMMY: Shhhh. Be still . . . wait.

DADDY: (*Whining*) It's so hot.

MOMMY: Shhhhhh. Be still . . . wait.

GRANDMA: (*To herself*) That's better. Night. (*To the* MUSICIAN) Honey, do you play all through this part?

(*The* MUSICIAN *nods*)

Well, keep it nice and soft; that's a good boy.

(*The* MUSICIAN *nods again; plays softly*)

That's nice.

(*There is an off-stage rumble*)

DADDY: (*Starting*) What was that?

MOMMY: (*Beginning to weep*) It was nothing.

DADDY: It was . . . it was . . . thunder . . . or a wave breaking . . . or something.

MOMMY: (*Whispering, through her tears*) It was an off-stage rumble . . . and you know what *that* means. . . .

DADDY: I forget. . . .

MOMMY: (*Barely able to talk*) It means the time has come for poor Grandma . . . and I can't bear it!

DADDY: (*Vacantly*) I . . . I suppose you've got to be brave.

GRANDMA: (*Mocking*) That's right, kid; be brave. You'll bear up; you'll get over it.

(*Another off-stage rumble . . . louder*)

MOMMY: Ohhhhhhhhhh . . . poor Grandma . . . poor Grandma. . . .

GRANDMA: (*To* MOMMY) I'm fine! I'm all right! It hasn't happened yet!

(*A violent off-stage rumble. All the lights go out, save the spot on the* YOUNG MAN; *the* MUSICIAN *stops playing*)

MOMMY: Ohhhhhhhhhh. . . . Ohhhhhhhhhh. . . .

(*Silence*)

GRANDMA: Don't put the lights up yet . . . I'm not ready; I'm not quite ready. (*Silence*) All right dear . . . I'm about done.

(*The lights come up again, to brightest day; the* MUSICIAN *begins to play.* GRANDMA *is discovered, still in the sandbox, lying on her side, propped up on an elbow, half covered, busily shoveling sand over herself*)

GRANDMA: (*Muttering*) I don't know how I'm supposed to do anything with this goddam toy shovel. . . .

DADDY: Mommy! It's daylight!

MOMMY: (*Brightly*) So it is! Well! Our long night is over. We must put away our tears, take off our mourning . . . and face the future. It's our duty.

GRANDMA: (*Still shoveling; mimicking*) . . . take off our mourning . . . face the future. . . . Lordy!

(MOMMY *and* DADDY *rise, stretch.* MOMMY *waves to the* YOUNG MAN)

YOUNG MAN: (*With that smile*) Hi!

(GRANDMA *plays dead.* (!) MOMMY *and* DADDY *go over to look at her; she is a little more than half buried in the sand; the toy shovel is in her hands, which are crossed on her breast*)

MOMMY: (*Before the sandbox; shaking her head*) Lovely! It's . . . it's hard to be sad . . . she looks . . . so happy. (*With pride and conviction*) It pays to do things well. (*To the* MUSICIAN) All right, you can stop now, if you want to. I mean, stay around for a swim, or something; it's all right with us. (*She sighs heavily*) Well, Daddy . . . off we go.

DADDY: Brave Mommy!

MOMMY: Brave Daddy!

(*They exit, stage-left*)

GRANDMA: (*After they leave; lying quite still*) It pays to do things well. . . . Boy, oh boy! (*She tries to sit up*) . . . well, kids . . . (*but she finds she can't*) . . . I . . . I can't get up. I . . . I can't move. . . .

(*The* YOUNG MAN *stops his calisthenics, nods to the* MUSICIAN, *walks over to* GRANDMA, *kneels down by the sandbox*)

GRANDMA: I . . . can't move. . . .

YOUNG MAN: Shhhhh . . . be very still. . . .

GRANDMA: I . . . I can't move. . . .

YOUNG MAN: Uh . . . ma'am; I . . . I have a line here.

GRANDMA: Oh, I'm sorry, sweetie; you go right ahead.

YOUNG MAN: I am . . . uh . . .

GRANDMA: Take your time, dear.

YOUNG MAN: (*Prepares, delivers the line like a real amateur*) I am the Angel of Death. I am . . . uh . . . I am come for you.

GRANDMA: What . . . wha . . . (*Then,   with   resignation*) . . . ohhhh . . . ohhhh, I see.

(*The* YOUNG MAN *bends over, kisses* GRANDMA *gently on the forehead*)

GRANDMA: (*Her eyes closed, her hands folded on her breast again, the shovel between her hands, a sweet smile on her face*) Well . . . that was very nice, dear. . . .

YOUNG MAN: (*Still kneeling*) Shhhhhh . . . be still. . . .

GRANDMA: What I meant was . . . you did that very well, dear. . . .

YOUNG MAN: (*Blushing*) . . . oh . . .

GRANDMA: No; I mean it. You've got that . . . you've got a quality.

YOUNG MAN: (*With his endearing smile*) Oh . . . thank you; thank you very much . . . ma'am.

GRANDMA: (*Slowly; softly—as the* YOUNG MAN *puts his hands on top of* GRANDMA'S) You're . . . you're welcome . . . dear.

(*Tableau. The* MUSICIAN *continues to play as the curtain slowly comes down*)

CURTAIN

30 Dramatic Characterization

The dramatic intensity of characters in drama; the impact of first impressions; depth of character as seen through multiple characteristics; characters in flux: shifts in attitudes and in the audience's perception; comic characters as satiric vehicles and foils.

On a literal level, the title of this chapter refers to the special ways characters in plays are developed. It also suggests quite correctly that such characters are often more *dramatic* than those in fiction in the sense of being vivid and slightly exaggerated. While this is not true in every case, it is a general characteristic and does apply to both the plays included in this text.

This special vividness of characters on the stage is due partly to the nature of the genre. As I pointed out earlier, drama is a continuous art. Unlike fiction, it is presented at a single sitting and at a regular rate. There is no going back to review a passage that introduced a character or to fill in some missing detail. Imagine novelists insisting that their work be read nonstop from cover to cover in some spot miles from home in the company of total strangers. It's no wonder playwrights tend to paint in bold colors!

There is a second factor that tends to make characters on the stage just a bit stagy. Writers of fiction have at their disposal a whole array of techniques with which they can develop characters. They can quote thoughts naturally and frequently without slowing the action; they can thrust a reader into a flashback at any moment; they can even comment on a character in their own voice if they wish. Not so for playwrights. Essentially they are limited to what a character says and does. True, there are ways of extending these limitations—techniques I will turn to shortly. But the basic restriction is there. Because playwrights rely so heavily on those two devices, action and dialogue, they tend to use them more boldly.

The Impact of First Impressions

When the protagonist of a play enters for the first time, what he or she does and says provides an initial impression that will linger for the length of the play. Those first few lines have a crucial influence on the audience's judgment of a character.

In the case of *Hello Out There*, Saroyan is faced with a particularly difficult challenge. How can he induce an audience to look favorably and sympathetically at a small-time gambler and drifter who has been jailed for rape? With this question in mind, take a close look at the way Saroyan handles those very first lines:

YOUNG MAN: Hello—out there! (*Pause.*) Hello—out there! (*Long pause.*) No-body out there. (*Still more dramatically, but more comically, too.*) Hello—out there! Hello—out there!

Normally, playwrights don't provide so many stage directions, since both directors and actors like to have more leeway. But in this case Saroyan is clearly concerned with creating just the right initial impression. He keeps his protagonist alone on the stage and gives him lines that establish his mood and character before revealing the actual situation.

Those very first lines are hesitant, nonthreatening, appealing. They focus on loneliness and reach out for sympathy as much as for companionship. His tone is insistent—we are encouraged to take him seriously—yet also comic. And those same qualities dominate that entire initial scene. Why is this so important? Because if the audience is not won over in the first few minutes, it will not believe him when he claims that the charge of rape is false. Deciding whether to accept as true what strangers say is based entirely on a quick judgment of character. The fact that the audiences of this play trust Photo-Finish's claim of innocence just as quickly as Emily does is a dramatic illustration of how rapidly a good playwright can establish character.

For some, there are lingering doubts about his actual feelings toward Emily. He is, after all, a street-wise character in a life-and-death situation, and Emily is no beauty. Does he really feel love for her? Or does he see her as the last chance of escape? If we read the play script as if it were a story, his sudden protestations of love seem preposterously rapid—far too quick to be taken seriously. But the play insists that you believe it. As I have pointed out before, we know that he is presenting his inner thoughts honestly in the little monologue that forms the third scene because he is speaking to himself. He refers to her as "the only good thing that ever came their way." And later when he realizes that there is practically no chance of escape, he gives her his last eighty dollars so that she can escape her own imprisonment in that town and get to San Francisco. There can be no ulterior motive in this offer. So both in lines of dialogue and in action we are assured that his love for her is genuine.

How can an aspect of character that would be hard to believe in fiction somehow work in drama? The answer lies in one of the more subtle distinctions between the two genres. As I mentioned at the beginning of this chapter, characters tend to be slightly exaggerated in drama, and their emotions are allowed to develop and shift at a faster rate. Certain aspects of character and especially changes in attitude that would be unconvincing if read on the page become credible when viewed in production.

In a sense, when you read a script you are not reading a play; you are reading lines of dialogue and a few stage directions—merely two ingredients of a full production. The rest is provided by the actors, director, set designer, costume designer—an entire team. How, then, can a writer learn to create effective dramatic characterization in a script when what appears in production is influenced by so many others? Mainly by seeing as many plays as possible in production and studying the scripts. With experience one begins to judge what is possible and how to go about creating it. Saroyan, for example, knew that he could convince an audience that a man like Photo-Finish could sincerely fall in love in what by real-life standards is only minutes because he had a sense of what works on the stage. And the continuing popularity of this play (it has become a kind of classic) demonstrates that he was right.

Important as your protagonist's first lines are, don't spend hours getting that introduction just right in your first draft. Once you have your opening scene in mind, plunge in and get it down on paper. After you have completed the first draft, however, take a second look at that opening. Have you done all you can to give your audience a "handle" on your protagonist? Read the first two minutes of dialogue and ask yourself whether that character has been individualized. With your first draft safely down on paper, you will have a clear idea of how that character is developed later, and you can then make sure that the audience has started off with just the right impression.

First impressions of characters who will be treated satirically have an entirely different function. Edward Albee's characters Mommy and Daddy are excellent examples. I will examine them more closely at the end of this chapter, but it is worth noting here that if a play is to open on a satiric note, it should do so with assurance. There is no question at the start of *The Sandbox* that these two characters are both comic and satiric. We don't expect them to be developed realistically. We accept them at once as cartoons of certain types, the type we love to hate.

Depth of Character

E. M. Forster's distinction between "round" and "flat" characters in fiction applies just as well to drama. "Round" characters are presented with depth. The audience is shown different aspects of them and ends with the sense of having met a real person. "Flat" characters are seen in one dimension, like a cardboard cutout.

"Flat" characters have important functions and are used in a variety of plays. In comedy, for example, all of the characters are relatively "flat" in that sense. In satire, that sharp and caustic form of comedy, the function of a character is to ridicule a type. Like a cartoon, satiric figures are exaggerations of particular traits. And in highly didactic plays committed to a particular political or social thesis, characters are also drawn in bold, exaggerated manner without depth. Even in plays that develop the major characters fully, the minor characters are usually "flat." They may serve a single purpose, such as delivering a message, or they may have a comic function.

The central characters in serious drama, on the other hand, are usually well rounded and carefully delineated. Achieving this effect in a short one-act play is a challenge, but it can be done. Saroyan manages to give us a good deal about Photo-Finish in only a few minutes of playing time. He is lonely but not a whiner. He has a whimsical sense of humor yet can be serious not only about practical things but about broader concerns, like what makes people so mean. There is a merry quality to the way he treats Emily, but we know almost from the start that he is genuinely scared about his position. These contrasts provide a range of characteristics and attitudes, and it is this range that gives us a sense of knowing him as an individual.

Characterization in this play is particularly important because so much depends on the audience feeling sympathy for this unsuccessful gambler and born loser. Only if we take him seriously will we respond to the theme of the play—the capacity of love to transform "little punk people" into something fine.

At first reading, one might think there is no real range of characterization in Albee's *The Sandbox*. Certainly Mommy and Daddy are cartoon figures whose whole function is to satirize dominant wives and passive, childlike husbands. Even the grandmother herself seems for a while to be a part of the satire. She bangs her toy shovel against the pail, makes infant sounds, and throws sand.

But surprisingly, Grandma is then transformed into a three-dimensional character in the second half of that play. We come to see her as opinionated ("Honestly! What a way to treat an old woman!"), spunky (a single parent since the age of 30), witty (wry cracks about Southern California and the intelligence of the young man), still lusty (she admires the young man's muscles), uncomplaining about death ("Shouldn't it be getting dark now?"), understandably alarmed at the moment of death, yet ultimately resigned and dignified. All this in less than six minutes playing time!

The second half of *The Sandbox* is an excellent example of how much can be done to develop a character in a very short space of time. Notice that Albee does this through dialogue alone. There is almost no action during the final scene. In order to achieve this he has used every line to reveal some aspect of characters. There is no wasted material.

Achieving depth of character in a play this short requires striking a delicate balance. You should provide enough variety to give the audience the sense of knowing the character, yet if you push that variety too far the character will seem implausible. One way to examine how well you have achieved this balance in your first draft is to write out a character sketch. Describe the character's personality, but don't include purely factual background. If you have trouble writing more than a few sentences, it is unlikely that you have created a well-rounded character with depth. If you are able to write a half page or so, good; but then make sure that everything you have written down will also be perceived by the audience through action or dialogue. Occasionally an aspect of character you merely assumed is not being shown to the audience. In such a case, you have some revisions to do.

Characters in Flux

Nothing is static in drama, and character is no exception. The term "character change" is handy, but it is also a bit misleading. Characters in plays rarely go through a basic personality change any more than people do in life. Only in comedies do villains finally see the light and undo the damage they have done.

There are, however, three types of "character change" that are well worth considering. One is when a character's *attitude* changes. Such occurrences are almost never complete transformations of character, but they can be dramatic or even catastrophic. In plays, as in life, people are occasionally stricken with remorse, given new hope, shattered by a crisis or strengthened by one. Friendships form between unlikely pairs, and "ideal" couples become alienated. Quite often a naive character is suddenly made aware of some aspect of life; occasionally a sophisticated character is taught how to appreciate some simple truth.

All this is fairly abstract, and plays, as I have pointed out before, are not created out of abstractions. But keep your eyes open for situations in which individuals have gone through a significant shift in attitude. Plays are less often rooted in personal experience than are stories; this may be due to the fact that for playwrights a dramatic concept is more important than the fine nuances of a personal experience.

The second type of character change is a *shift in fortune*. Traditionally, tragedies dealt with men and, less often, women of power who are brought low by the lust for more power (Macbeth, Julius Caesar), poor judgment (King Lear, Othello), turns of fate (Oedipus), or treachery (Medea). In recent times, tragedies deal more frequently with average people like Willy Loman in *Death of a Salesman*, who is brought down by the forces of society and self-delusion.

Hello Out There follows that pattern, showing the individual as a victim of social forces beyond his control. But it is not at all necessary to bring a character to the point of death in a one-act play. One can generate plenty of drama without indulging in murder or suicide, and if you take the safer route you will avoid the risk of melodrama. Melodrama pushes drama to the point where it no longer seems credible and the audience loses its sense of involvement. You can charge a short play with more voltage than a story of the same length; *Hello Out There* is a good example. But to continue that metaphor, melodrama is a short circuit. How can you tell when you have pushed dramatic intensity too far? Read the play to an audience of three or more, and if one of them giggles you have some rewriting to do.

The third type of character change is quite different. Here the character actually remains the same, but *audience perception* of that character changes. This is a standard device of simple murder mysteries, in which the character who seems least likely to be the killer is revealed in the end to be just that. In such plays, however, characterization is often reduced to a kind of shorthand. The same technique can be used in much more sophisticated dramas.

A brief example is seen in Albee's *The Sandbox*. Our first impression of Grandma is that she is indeed what her daughter and son-in-law take her to be: an old woman reduced by senility to the level of a child. But we then are introduced to a spunky, witty, opinionated, and ultimately brave woman. It is the same character. She has not changed, but our perception of her has.

One of the best-known examples in full-length plays appears in *The Country Girl* by Clifford Odets, which concerns the efforts of an older actor to make a comeback. For much of the play the audience is convinced that he is doing his best to cope with a very difficult wife. But it turns out that he is an alcoholic and she has been heroically trying to cover for him. The audience has been as misled as have the other characters, and the revelation has genuine dramatic impact.

There are all kinds of deceits that can be used in this manner. Some are the result of conscious scheming, as in the Odets play; others develop from self-deception. If you are working with this type of reversal, remember to drop small hints along the way so that when the correct view is revealed the audience will have that special sense of, "Oh, I should have seen it."

Developing Comic Characters

If there is anything more difficult than creating a comic character, it is trying to explain to a playwright why a certain character isn't funny. It seems as if the ability to write good comedy is intuitive, but actually it may depend more on how much comedy you have read.

The easiest type of comic character to create is the satiric lampoon of a particular type. Satire of a rather blunt sort is familiar to almost all students through *Mad* and *National Lampoon* magazines. Television has also produced a long series of satiric skits over the years.

The satiric character is an exaggeration both in lines of dialogue and in action. The more specific characteristics you can find and develop, the better the satire will be. Notice, by the way, that it is difficult to satirize a truly comic type of person, just as it is next to impossible to satirize a funny magazine or story, without simply imitating the object of your ridicule. The most likely sources for satiric attack are individuals who take themselves very seriously.

This certainly applies to Mommy and Daddy in *The Sandbox.* As we have seen, they are "flat" in the sense of having no depth. And like most satiric characters, they are also static. They do not change or develop. But in spite of this, they do satirize different characteristics. Mommy is excruciatingly dominant; Daddy is painfully passive. The terms with which they refer to each other become highly ironic. It is hard to imagine either of them as parents.

The main thrust of the satire, however, is the way they treat her mother. They pretend to be caring, but in fact they dump her in a sandbox as callously as some drop their parents in a rest home. This hypocrisy reaches a peak when she appears to die and they can scarcely hide their delight:

MOMMY: (Brightly) . . . Well! Our long night is over.
We must put away our tears, take off our mourning . . . and face the future. It's our duty.

In some plays, all the characters are satiric. The tone is consistently comic and critical. This play is unusual in that the two satiric characters whom we supposed at first would be central turn out to be foils to set off the true subject of the play, Grandma. They are vivid examples of how a playwright can enhance a protagonist by contrasting her or him with comic figures.

More often, the comic foil is a minor character who also has the function of easing the dramatic tension from time to time. Such characters serve as a comic relief and can in this way reduce the danger of melodrama or sentimentality.

One of the reasons good comedy is rare is that it so often slides into farce or slapstick. That kind of humor gets laughs easily but is quickly forgotten. It can become more of a skit than a true play. If you are working with satire that is serious in intent, take a close look at what you wish to attack. Then make your satiric version detailed and penetrating. If your tone is merely humorous and not biting, try to add warmth to your characters. A good comedy can be funny and memorable at the same time.

Characterization is a continuing concern at every stage of writing a play. In comedy and satire, "good" means effective. In serious drama, "good" means well rounded, insightful, penetrating. You will want the play to remain with the audience as vividly as a personal experience. To do this you will need at least one and preferably two characters who are complex and convincing. Sophisticated drama is, among other things, the illusion of getting to know total strangers very well in a very short space of time.

31 REALISTIC AND NONREALISTIC APPROACHES

Realistic and *nonrealistic* drama defined; the *illusions of life* and of *dreams* as seen in plot, motivation, characterization, setting, and time; the *two heritages* of nonrealistic drama: expressionism and theater of the absurd; *cross-fertilization* of techniques; *selecting your own approach.*

Realistic drama creates an illusion that reflects the world about us. The plot is a logical sequence of events; characters behave in ways we understand; both time and place are accounted for as they would be in realistic fiction.

Nonrealistic drama, on the other hand, is an illusion that in some ways echoes a dream. It *seems* real, just as a dream usually does, but the plot may be an illogical sequence of events or almost nonexistent, and the characters may behave in ways that lack motivation. The setting is usually detached from any identifiable geographic area, and the sense of time may be distorted.

At first glance, these two approaches appear to be entirely different. Actually they have much in common and frequently borrow techniques from each other. I will discuss them as if they were distinct, but keep in mind that they are two closely related approaches to drama.

The Illusions of Life and of Dreams

The first characteristic of realistic drama is a *logical plot*. The sequence of events may be startling or unusual, but it resembles the way things happen in everyday life.

In Saroyan's *Hello Out There*, for example, the plot is as logical as a newspaper account would be. We learn why the protagonist is in jail and soon discover why this is unjust. We are told why the young woman happens to be there after hours. We understand why it is difficult for her to obtain the key and just how long it would take her to go home and get her father's gun. When Photo-Finish is shot, we realize that he has exhausted all his possibilities of escape. A series of interlocking events has resulted in the final tragedy.

Contrast this with what could occur if this were written as a nonrealistic play. The two major characters might discover that they are trapped in that jail for eternity, that they are quite literally in hell. Absurd? This is essentially the plot of a highly successful play called *No Exit* by Jean-Paul Sartre. Or in the final scene a chariot drawn by dragons might sweep down and carry Emily off to a better world. Wild as that may seem, it is the dramatic conclusion to Euripides' play *Medea*, which has gripped audiences for over 2000 years.

These nonrealistic endings seem like preposterous ways to end *Hello Out There*, yet they are entirely acceptable when used in other plays. Why? Because the kind of imagination that will be used in a play is communicated to the audience almost at the outset. Theatergoers are assured within the first few minutes of *Hello Out There* that events will probably occur in a logical manner. In the same way, those seeing *The Sandbox* for the first time suspect that they are in some kind of dream world from the way Mommy and Daddy talk with each other, and they are sure of it when Grandma is brought in and dumped in the sandbox. Audiences are willing to accept either approach, but they expect to receive signals fairly early.

Nonrealistic plays often deal with symbolic rather than literal relationships, so what the audience sees is a representation of ideas rather than a recreation of events as they might really happen. The idea of treating older people as children and dumping them in a nursing home could be handled realistically. The set might resemble a recognizable nursing home and the Angel of Death would be replaced by a perfectly credible doctor. But Albee presents the situation with a setting and characters that are symbolic representations.

A second and closely related characteristic of realistic drama is *logical motivation*. Most of the time we know why a character is doing this or that, and when we don't, we can be fairly certain that we will find out as the play progresses. The killer in *Hello Out There* is motivated mainly by pressure from his friends, who have apparently goaded him into this "manly" response.

And Emily risks her life because she has fallen in love. If audiences remained unconvinced that she could fall in love that fast to a character like Photo-Finish, the play would be judged a failure. Success in a realistic play is measured in part by the degree to which motivation is convincing.

Not so in nonrealistic dramas. In a play called *The Lesson*, by Eugene Ionesco, a raving professor berates his young students and eventually kills them. We know nothing about this character and so can't even guess why he has done this. In a realistic play this brutal act would appear so lacking in motivation as to be completely unconvincing. But the playwright is not concerned with psychological motivation or even characterization. His theme has to do with the nature of authority and the abuses of absolute power. He has, in effect, drawn a savage cartoon to illustrate his point. Like many nonrealistic dramas, this play is designed to shock an audience, not to move it as does *Hello Out There*.

When you examine how different the two approaches are in dealing with motivation, you realize that they have fundamentally different ways of handling *characterization* as well. As I pointed out in an earlier chapter, one of the goals of realistic drama is to give the audience the sense of meeting and getting to know not just a character on the stage but a real person. For this reason, characters in realistic drama are usually given some kind of background so that we know where they came from. We have at least a rough idea, for example, how Photo-Finish has been trying to make a living and how he landed in jail.

Characters in nonrealistic plays are either specific symbols of abstractions, like the professor in *The Lesson* and the Young Man (the "Angel of Death") in *The Sandbox*, or they represent general types like Mommy and Daddy. They are rarely developed as if they were people, because that is not their function. This does not mean that they are more easily created, however. When you work with this type of character, you have to make sure the audience understands your intent. If you are too obvious, the play may turn into a simple skit; but if you are not clear enough, the audience will be too baffled to applaud.

In addition to plot, motivation, and characterization, the sense of *place* is often handled quite differently by the two approaches. Realistic drama is usually "grounded" in a particular place. The script for *Hello Out There* states that the action takes place "in a small-town prison cell." That's fairly specific to start with, and the dialogue tells us even more. From Emily we learn that this is a town called Matador in Texas. Those details give us a lot of associations to work with.

Albee's play, on the other hand, takes place in a world of its own. The stage is bare except for that sandbox and a couple of chairs. But the bare stage is not what gives the play that sense of being nowhere in particular. Bare stages can also be used effectively in highly realistic plays. What gives Albee's play that dreamlike detachment is that there is nothing in what characters say or do to link the setting with a particular geographic region.

This is true of most nonrealistic plays. Some are placed in a realistically designed room, but we have no notion of what kind of house or community. Others are more fanciful—and more symbolic. Ionesco's play *The Chairs*, for example, takes place in a castle in the middle of the sea. He calls for the realistic sound of boats moving through the water as guests arrive, but we have no idea where they are coming from. The audience does not concern itself with questions of where this might be; it accepts this dreamlike setting just as it accepts the sandbox in Albee's play.

Finally, the passage of *time* is often handled differently in realistic and nonrealistic plays. Notice how carefully Saroyan accounts for each step of his plot. Emily knows where her father's gun is, but there isn't time to get it. She has mentioned that a gang might try to get Photo-Finish, and sure enough, the husband shows up with his friends close behind. The pace is rapid, but time is accounted for in a realistic manner.

Time in *The Sandbox* is not sequential that way. Mommy and Daddy appear from nowhere and sit on what appears from the dialogue to be a beach. He wants to know what they should do, and she says "We . . . wait. We . . . sit here . . . and we wait . . . that's what we do." In symbolic terms, they are waiting for Grandma to die. But there is no precise way of determining how long it is before Daddy says, "Mommy! It's daylight!" and she says cheerfully, "Well! Our long night is over." There has been no indication of an actual night having passed, but in symbolic terms she is referring to their long wait for Grandmother to die. It could have been weeks or years. Time in nonrealistic plays is often left vague because the sequence of events is linked to ideas rather than to the illusion of a literal episode.

Two Sources of Nonrealistic Drama

When one first approaches nonrealistic drama, it sometimes appears to be literary anarchy without limits or traditions. Actually it draws from two specific sources. Although the focus of this text is on the process of writing, not literary history, a brief introduction to these two dramatic schools is an excellent way to explore the potential of nonrealistic drama.

The first of these is *expressionism*. The movement included painting, fiction, and poetry at the turn of the century and continued through the 1920s. Early examples in drama are seen in the plays of August Strindberg, a Swedish playwright. Plays like *The Dance of Death* and *The Dream Play* are readily available in translation and provide vivid contrasts with the realistic drama of the time by playwrights like Henrik Ibsen. Strindberg's plots were frequently dreamlike, his characters symbolic rather than psychologically comprehensible, and his tone often dark and pessimistic.

Another excellent example of early expressionism is the Czech dramatist Karel Čapek. His nightmarish vision of the future, *R.U.R.* is an early sample of science fiction complete with robots who revolt against their masters. More thematically comprehensible than some of Strindberg's dreamlike works, *R.U.R.* has a strong element of social protest.

For a good example of American expressionism, I would recommend Elmer Rice's *The Adding Machine,* in which the protagonist, a cipher in a highly mechanical society, is named Mr. Zero. He lives in a room surrounded by numbers. His associates are also known by numbers—all higher than his, of course. As in many dreams, costumes, set, action, and dialogue are all distorted; but also as in dreams there is an internal consistency that allows us to make sense of it. We have all had occasions when we felt as if we had been treated like a mere number.

Another excellent example is seen in Eugene O'Neill's *Emperor Jones,* a symbolic study of a deposed black leader in the Caribbean whose world is crumbling about him. The play focuses less on external events than on his inner fantasies and fears as he tries to escape through the jungle.

Varied as expressionistic plays are, they reject situations and characters that reflect in a literal way the world which we see. Instead, they explore the world we feel. They do this through symbolic representation. In addition, they often share a critical or even angry view of society as a whole. The individual is frequently seen as victim.

In the 1950s and '60s there was a new surge of interest in nonrealistic drama. It became known as *theater of the absurd* because many of the playwrights shared the existential notion that life is absurd in the sense of being without ultimate meaning. Oddly, few of them recognized the other important aspect of existential thought: that we create meaning and values by the way we act. As a result, absurdist plays tend to be pessimistic and often cynical.

The school is best represented by the works of Eugene Ionesco, whose plays *The Lesson* and *The Chairs* I have already described. Other playwrights include Samuel Beckett, Harold Pinter, and occasionally Edward Albee.

Many of the nonrealistic devices seen in expressionistic drama occur in absurdist plays as well: the avoidance of plots and characters that reflect the world about us, the dreamlike detachment from identifiable time or place. But philosophically and tonally these playwrights take a somewhat different route. Whereas many of the expressionists side with the individual as victim of an unfeeling or oppressive society, the absurdists generally offer no hope for humanity or faith in the individual. To counter the dead weight of this pessimism, many of these plays are presented with wit and satire.

To return to Ionesco's *The Chairs,* we are introduced to a couple living in a castle in the middle of the ocean. They throw a large party and plan to have an orator announce to all the guests the fundamental purpose of their lives. After a lengthy buildup, the orator turns out to be an idiot who can utter only unintelligible syllables. Both the individual and the society are seen as without meaning or purpose. *The Chairs,* like many absurdist dramas, is darker in vision than many expressionist plays, though the tone is enlivened with wit and satire.

Cross-fertilization of Techniques

Until now I have been describing realistic and nonrealistic approaches as if they were mutually exclusive. This is handy for analysis, but in practice each type of drama has enriched the other, and many plays contain elements of both.

Arthur Miller's *Death of a Salesman,* for example, is essentially a realistic play, but it makes use of an imaginary character who appears on stage. This is a nonrealistic detail based on the inner perceptions of the protagonist. In a play entitled *After the Fall,* Miller presents a realistic protagonist but handles the plot in a highly nonrealistic way. What the audience sees is a series of nonchronological scenes as if they were memories running through the mind of the protagonist.

Edward Albee is one of the few playwrights whose work ranges from fully realistic plays (*Who's Afraid of Virginia Woolf?*) to highly nonrealistic (*Tiny Alice*) and just about every gradation between. *The Sandbox* is unusual in that it draws almost equally from both approaches.

The grotesquely satiric characters of Mommy and Daddy, the Young Man described as the Angel of Death, and the use of the sandbox are all in the tradition of theater of the absurd. In fact, the first half of that play serves as a good though brief example of absurdist techniques. But the detailed characterization of Grandma and the profound respect he shows for her are complete departures from both the tone and the philosophy of absurdist drama. Paying high tribute to a character and developing him or her as a true individual and not a type is almost exclusively limited to realistic drama. *The Sandbox* is an unusual example of how the two approaches can be blended into a single, unified play.

Selecting Your Own Approach

The decision of how realistic and how nonrealistic to make a play is never simple. It depends on three factors: your own preferences, what kind of plays you have read, and the needs of the particular dramatic concept you have in mind.

The first two of these factors are a part of the same process. You cannot really have preferences until you have read or, better yet, have seen a large number of plays. The analysis in this text and the two sample plays are intended only to give a notion of what to look for in future reading and viewing. How many plays should you read and see? Four is better than two, and forty is better than four. To be reasonable, though, if you are starting out and are taking a course, you will only be able to read a few additional short plays. But if you are at the point of writing drama with more than an exploratory concern, it is essential that you read and see as many plays as time and funds will permit.

The approach you adopt will be determined not only by your own preferences, but by the material you have in mind. Some concepts lend themselves to realistic treatment, and you shouldn't feel that this approach is in any way not "modern." Whatever survey you wish to make—Broadway, off-Broadway, repertory companies, or universities—you will find that realistic drama is as well represented as the varieties of nonrealistic.

Some drama ideas, on the other hand, will come to you in highly symbolic or dreamlike form. When that happens, see if there are ways to organize and shape the material so that the audience will see it as an artistic whole.

Each approach has its assets and its liabilities. Try to weigh these in terms of a specific drama idea and see which is appropriate.

The greatest danger when working with realistic drama is making use of stock characters, hackneyed dialogue, and conventional situations. Many of the clichés I warned against in the section on fiction appear in drama as well. Be consciously aware of all those worn-out television plots that may be floating around in the back of your mind.

The advantage of realistic drama, on the other hand, is that it is rooted in character. The audience comes to believe in a carefully developed character more fully than is possible in nonrealistic plays. And the plot—whether serious or gently humorous—can seize hold of the audience as deeply as an important episode in life itself. This emotive potential is extraordinary.

There are two common faults you should guard against if you are working with nonrealistic drama. The first is total fragmentation. If your audience can't see any coherent pattern, it will simply walk out. You can't depend on novelty value the way playwrights could in the 1950s. And you can't draw on the emotional appeal of characterization the way realistic drama can because your approach is necessarily idea-oriented. For these reasons you should be sure that the ideas you are working with hold together and make a statement that is both logical and compelling.

Martin Esslin puts it this way in *The Theatre of the Absurd:*

> Mere combinations of incongruities produce mere banality. Anyone attempting to work in this medium simply by writing down what comes into his mind will find that the supposed flights of spontaneous invention have never left the ground, that they consist of incoherent fragments of reality that have not been transposed into a valid imaginative whole.

The other danger is lack of humor. The dead weight of someone else's unpleasant dream is often hard to take. Plays like *The Chairs* would be unendurable if it were not for a good deal of satire and wit. True, some nonrealistic plays are essentially humorless, but they are exceptions and are less frequently produced today for that reason. Even the most pessimistic playwrights in the absurdist school tend to keep their works afloat with wit, humor, and satire.

Remember that as you reduce the pulling power of a dramatic plot and a realistic situation, you must provide some other attraction for the audience. Shock is one alternative and was used a good deal in the 1970s, but it has a limited appeal and is difficult to sustain. Wit—even if caustic—is a natural leavening for nonrealistic drama.

In spite of these risks, however, there are distinct assets to nonrealistic drama. It is a particularly tempting approach if your theme is more important to you than your characters. You can cut through to the heart of your statement in a bold and imaginative manner without having to create credible characters or construct a plausible plot. You are working with a medium which, like the political cartoon and the poster, lends itself to strong statements. As for form, you can let your imagination take flight. Like free verse, nonrealistic drama offers freedoms and also the obligation to find new and effective structures.

Your reading and your experiences as a theatergoer will influence your feelings about realistic and nonrealistic approaches. But let the needs of your projected play have a voice too. And don't forget your audience. No matter what approach you take, the world you create on the stage is one you will want to share with them.

32 VISUAL IMPACT

Three types of *stage sets:* realistic (including distortion for
effect), symbolic, and bare; *lighting* for emphasis and symbolic
suggestion; *costumes; action:* exits, entrances, movement, stage
business, confrontations; *seeing the scene* as you write.

The visual aspect of a play can have a major impact on the audience. When
we read play scripts we can easily forget that words on the page are only a
small portion of the total dramatic experience. The degree to which drama
depends on visual elements is reflected in the way we describe a theatrical
experience: "I *saw* a good play," we say, whereas we are more apt to say, "I
went to the opera."

What the audience sees is made up of several different elements.
There is the physical set, the lighting, the costumes, and the action of actors.
Although directors, set designers, and actors all need some latitude, they
need a play that gives them the opportunity for visual impact. This chapter
has one urgent message which I will repeat several times: When you write
any type of play script, maintain a mental picture of what your stage looks
like scene by scene, moment by moment.

Three Types of Stage Sets

The term *set* includes everything the audience sees except for the actors themselves. Although each set designer will approach a play slightly differently, playwrights usually specify what that locale is and which properties are essential. These general suggestions often classify the set as falling into one of three loosely defined types: realistic, symbolic, or bare.

The realistic set is so common today that we tend to think of it as the traditional approach. Actually it is a fairly recent development—less than 200 years out of the 2500-year-old tradition of Western drama. In large degree, highly realistic details on the stage had to wait until the introduction of electric lights. When Ibsen's plays were first introduced to England in the late nineteenth century, audiences gasped with amazement at the sight of a perfectly reproduced living-room scene complete with real books in bookcases, portraits on the walls, and doors that opened and shut. Soon the stage directions for the plays of Barrie and Shaw began to reflect this new realism by including the most minute descriptions—even to the title of a book left "carelessly" on a coffee table.

We can no longer depend on that kind of naive wonder, of course. Film and television have made realism commonplace. But when a realistic set is constructed with skill and imagination, it still has enormous impact. Even today, highly effective sets presented on traditional stages are occasionally greeted with applause even before the first character appears on stage.

How much detail should a script include? There is no standard policy, but the tendency now is to be brief. One reason is that there is such a variety of stages today that playwrights can no longer be sure of just how their work will be presented. The traditional stage has what is known as a proscenium arch, which forms a picture frame for the action, and a curtain, which signals the beginning and closing of the dramatic illusion. But an increasing number of stages now have no arch and no single-picture effect because they are open on three sides. The design allows more of the audience to sit close to the action. In such theaters, the use of lights replaces the curtain. Theater in the round, or *arena stage*, extends this concept further by having the audience encircle the playing area as it does in a circus tent. The playwright's description of the set in the script should be flexible enough to allow set designers to adapt to a wide variety of stages.

In *Hello Out There*, for example, Saroyan merely states that this is to be "a small-town prison cell." On a traditional stage, this might be handled quite literally. But on a stage that is surrounded on all sides by the audience, the cell will more likely be suggested by a few bars. A good deal will have to be left to the imagination of the audience.

Remember that even the most highly realistic and detailed set is an illusion. A living room on the stage, for example, has no third wall. In a play called *Period of Adjustment* by Tennessee Williams the focal object is a television set. Because it is often on, it is placed with its back to the audience upstage center. The set in the Broadway production was meticulously realistic, yet from a literal point of view the audience was impossibly wedged between the back of the television set and where the wall should be. In other plays, the audience finds itself behind fireplaces. Oddly, this kind of distortion in no way detracts from the notion that the set is "realistic."

The significance of this for playwrights is that one can use a high degree of distortion to achieve a realistic effect. Audiences are used to these tricks and are willing to exercise their imaginations. This is particularly helpful in plays that include both indoor and outdoor scenes. A yard may be separated from the interior of, say, a kitchen by a low board; a door may be used to suggest the division between two areas without adjoining walls. The same applies to the second story of a house suggested only by a flight of stairs. If the actors treat these divisions as real, the audience will perceive them this way too.

In Arthur Miller's *Death of a Salesman*, for example, the script calls for an upstairs room, two rooms downstairs, and a portion of the yard outside. It is realistic in that the entire set is treated as if it were a real house and yard, yet it requires an act of imagination to separate what is outside from what is inside. An *actor* in the kitchen can obviously see what another actor is doing outside; but it is soon made clear that a *character* must open the door in order to see. This is not as extraordinary as it seems when you recall how children at the beach can create the same sort of illusion playing house with various rooms merely marked in the sand. It's no accident that we call drama a *play*.

Another ingenious use of realistic design is seen in William Ritman's set for Harold Pinter's *The Collection*. Working closely with the director and the playwright, Ritman managed to present the illusion of three entirely unconnected separate settings on the relatively small stage of the Cherry Lane Theatre in New York. It has been duplicated on larger stages since then. As the action shifts from one area to the next, the lights on the other two are dimmed. The illustrations (drawn by Richard Tuttle) appear on page 301. Turn to them now and notice how the illusion of where one is shifts in each case.

The great advantage of a set like this is that the playwright does not have to stop the action in order to change a set. As I have mentioned before, dropping the curtain or even dimming the lights breaks the illusion and returns the audience to the theater itself. If in addition you ask a stage crew to scurry about in the dark and change a set, that break becomes even lengthier and more distracting. A set divided into different playing areas allows a playwright to maintain a steady flow of action.

A word of warning, however. If you, like most people, have watched more television and films than plays you may unwittingly suggest an impossibly complex set. Remember that whatever you call for in the script will

The Collection, showing emphasis on the modern apartment, with the other areas dark.

The Collection, showing emphasis on the telephone booth, which is, in the play, some distance from either home.

The Collection, showing emphasis on the ornate apartment, with the other areas dark.

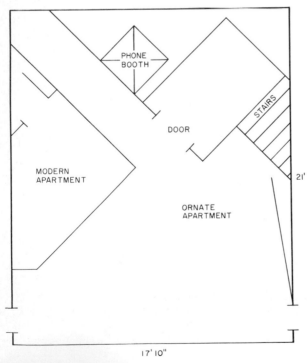

PHONE
BOOTH

STAIRS

DOOR

MODERN
APARTMENT

21'

ORNATE
APARTMENT

17' 10"

The Collection: a diagram of the stage, showing the technique of representing three entirely different scenes simply by shifts in lighting. Note how the unusual angles add both variety and depth even on a small stage.

have to be built with wood and held together with nails. The set I described for *Death of a Salesman* is about as complex as you can get even on a big stage. It is a serious challenge in a small space. The three-part set for *The Collection* has the advantage of being on one level, but on a small stage it comprises about as many separate playing areas as you can manage.

These sets are realistic because no matter how much imagination the audience has to use, the setting is perceived as representing life as we see it. *Symbolic sets,* on the other hand, are fundamentally different in that they represent ideas rather than literal scenes.

We have already touched on the ways in which the set of Edward Albee's *The Sandbox* is symbolic. A beach is identified not in the stage direction but through the dialogue. Mommy says, "There's sand there . . . and the water beyond." Midway in the play it is clear that they are waiting for Grandma to die in the same vacuous way some people sit for hours on the beach. And the sandbox, the central symbol of the play, suggests the kind of demeaning environment to which many elderly people are consigned. The audience sees this setting not in literal terms but as symbolic representations.

In the last chapter I also described Elmer Rice's play *The Adding Machine* as a good example of expressionism. Nonrealistic plays occasionally specify realistic sets, and this one could have been produced that way. Even with the symbolic names and nonrealistic plot, Mr. Zero's bedroom could have resembled those we are familiar with. But Rice extends his use of symbol to small visual details as well: Mr. Zero's room is wallpapered with a vast collection of numbers ready for addition, subtraction, or division. The room is pictured not as we would see it, but as Rice imagines it.

The bare stage can be used either for realistic or for nonrealistic plays. Thornton Wilder's play *Our Town,* for example, contains realistic segments from the American scene, yet the only stage properties are a couple of folding chairs, two ladders, and a plank.

When that play was first produced in 1938, the use of the bare stage was considered innovative. Yet no one was baffled. The two stepladders and the board connecting them suggested a house, and the audience quickly adjusted to having a "stage manager" sit to one side and talk to the audience as the play unfolded. Although this presentation requires imagination, the characters and most of the scenes are realistic.

Like many experiments in theater, it was based on a very old tradition. Elizabethan audiences were required to use their imaginations to visualize the rapid succession of scenes in Shakespearean plays. If this approach interests you, examine closely how Shakespeare identifies the setting through the dialogue at the beginning of each new scene.

Albee's script calls for "a bare stage," though he then adds a few properties. The way he suggests a beach "and the water beyond" through the dialogue is reminiscent of Shakespeare's technique of placing the audience with words rather than with props.

Although you will not want to spend more than a paragraph or so describing your set, you should have it clearly in your own mind as you write. This is the space your characters will inhabit, and it is also the space within which your imagination should flourish.

Here are some suggestions for making the best use of your set:

- Regardless of whether your play will be realistic or nonrealistic, determine whether it will be best served by a set that is realistic, symbolic, or essentially bare.

- Consider ways in which the set can have an impact right from the start. Think twice before you place a new play in that standard living room set with the stairs on one side and the front door on the other—this is the set of endless sit-com television programs.

- Be practical. Remember that some stages are small and there are limits to what one can build. You don't have to tell the set designers precisely how to proceed, but don't make impossible demands.

- Above all, keep your set in mind as you write. Make sure you know where your characters are. Make use of your stage properties.

Lighting for Effect

Lighting is the newest of all dramatic techniques. The Greeks depended on the sun, as did the Elizabethans. And from the time of the first enclosed theaters in the late sixteenth century until 1914, lighting consisted of a row of footlights designed simply to illuminate actors.

In 1914 the first spotlights were hung on the balcony rail of Wallack's Theater in New York. That was a radical improvement. But the progress made in the past twenty years with modern lighting boards is a quantum leap forward for drama. Although some playwrights leave lighting cues entirely to the director, others see lighting as an integral part of the whole effect and write basic instructions into the script.

Albee's stage directions at the opening of *The Sandbox* are a good example of how some playwrights keep the effect of lighting in mind. He states that ". . . the background is the sky, which alters from brightest day to deepest night." At the opening it is "brightest day." As Grandma begins to face death she asks, "Shouldn't it be getting dark now?" and the stage directions call for the lights to dim. Later as she deals directly with the Angel of Death, the lights come up again "to brightest day."

When lighting is used to this extent and written into the script, it turns the setting from a static element to one in constant flux. Although Albee refers to "day" and "night" in the stage directions, the play is not divided in any literal way by the time of day. He is really referring to tonal shifts within the play. When used in this manner, lighting becomes a fundamental dramatic device like exits and entrances.

In addition to overall dimming and raising of the lights for tonal effect, there is also the technique of lighting a single area of the stage while leaving other areas dark. As you can see from the illustrations of the three-part setting for *The Collection*, lighting effectively directs the audience's attention from one portion of the stage to another. In effect, selective lighting has the power to change the set.

In Arthur Miller's *After the Fall*, a play I described earlier as having the illusion of a sequence of memories, lighting becomes essential to achieve the desired effect. Miller states in the script that his characters must "appear and disappear instantaneously, as in the mind; but it is not necessary that they walk off the stage." The effect is normally achieved through a complex series of lighting shifts. This technique is well worth considering if you have many scenes. It allows you to use a variety of sets without the distracting break in illusion caused by conventional scene shifts.

Lighting can also place a special emphasis on a character or highlight a key speech the way music occasionally does in film. Although Saroyan doesn't provide light cues in *Hello Out There*, it would seem altogether appropriate to isolate Emily at the very end with a single overhead spot in an otherwise darkened stage. This effect might repeat a similar one for Photo-Finish at the beginning of the play, drawing those two scenes together visually just as they are connected in dialogue.

Costumes

Like the lighting, the costumes create a visual effect which in some cases is left to the director but in other cases is written into the stage directions. In realistic plays with a contemporary setting there usually is no mention of costumes in the script. But if a play is nonrealistic, costumes may take on a symbolic significance. In such cases, playwrights sometimes become very specific.

Occasionally a nonrealistic play may call for realistic costuming for effect. In a thoroughly absurdist play, *The Bald Soprano* by Eugene Ionesco, for example, the hero is described with comically realistic detail as "an Englishman, seated in his English armchair and wearing English slippers, is smoking his English pipe and reading an English newspaper, near an English fire." (Ionesco, incidentally, is French.) In the same way, both Mr. Zero in Elmer Rice's *The Adding Machine* and the characters in *The Sandbox* are dressed conventionally in spite of the nonrealistic quality of the plots.

On the other hand, some nonrealistic plays specifically call for costuming that is as bizarre and symbolic as the plot. In Adrienne Kennedy's dark nightmare of a play, *A Rat's Mass*, the setting is simply described as "The rat's house." But the costumes are described in more detail:

> *Brother Rat has a rat's head, a human body, a tail. Sister Rat has a rat's belly, a human head, a tail. Rosemary wears a Holy Communion dress and has worms in her hair.*

She uses somewhat the same technique in *A Lesson in Dead Language*, a short and bitter play set in a school classroom. The pupils are all in "white organdy dresses"—a gentle symbolic suggestion of their conformity and innocence. The real distortion is the teacher, who is costumed as an enormous white dog. Kennedy is working in dead earnest with both religious and racial themes in this play, and the result is a grotesque, relentless fantasy in which the costumes play an important role.

Action

As I described in the chapter on plot, most plays are divided into a number of secondary scenes. Those units are begun and ended by entrances and exits. On this basic level, then, the very structure of a play depends on action.

For this reason, most playwrights outline their plays by scene and think of the whole drama in terms of these relatively short units. If a scene goes on too long, it may lose visual impact and appear to sag. It can either be cut a bit or it can be broken into two scenes by having another entrance or exit.

The action you provide within each scene is equally important. To some degree, good directors can enliven a static scene by adding "stage business," minor activity like crossing the stage, opening a window, pacing up and down. But there are limits to this. And occasionally you may find that you have made matters even more difficult for the director by specifying that your characters sit while they talk.

Once again, it is essential that you visualize what is happening on the stage while you write. What is the speaker doing as he or she speaks, and what are the others doing as they listen? If you prefer to give only minimal stage directions, make sure your actors are not trapped into immobility. Saroyan, for example, provides only brief directions to the actors in *Hello Out There* and those only during periods when there is no dialogue (". . . he turns away from the image of her and walks about like a lion in a cage"). But one can visualize the action in each scene—moving to the bars of the jail, backing off, turning to shout "Hello out there," drawing together again. Those two characters are never static. There is a restless energy in that play from beginning to end.

In *The Sandbox* there is less opportunity for moving about on the stage.

But Albee has divided the play into six scenes (including musical interludes) and has added some important stage business which one might easily miss when reading the play in script. Throughout the play until almost the end the Young Man does calisthenics. "These calisthenics, employing the arms only, should suggest the beating and fluttering of wings." All this reminds us that he is the Angel of Death, but it also serves a larger purpose. Although his important lines do not come until the end of the play, we are made aware of "Death's" presence from the very beginning because of his constant motion.

Plays that have strong conflicts frequently dramatize them with a burst of violence toward the end. Audiences will accept intense dramatic action; but if it is not well motivated, it will seem hackneyed and melodramatic. The confrontation between Photo-Finish and the husband in *Hello Out There* comes close to the mob-versus-individual fights we have seen in standard television fare, but it is given stature partly by the character of the victim and partly by the mixed motives we are allowed to see in the murderer.

If your play is short, and the kind of action that concludes it seems too strong, remember that any confrontation can be muted a bit. Murders can become nonlethal fights; fights themselves can be downgraded. Action is important, but don't forget that action without convincing characterization and credible motivation can easily turn into melodrama.

One way to determine whether you have created enough action in your play is to write a description of each scene without quoting any of the dialogue. If you have scenes summarized with statements like "They sit on the couch and blame each other for the state of their marriage," you may have identified a visually static scene.

Seeing the Scene As You Write

If you have been writing fiction and are turning to drama for the first time, it may take a while to visualize the action as you work on a script. Keep in mind, however, that a reader of fiction moves at five times the speed at which the audience will observe your play. In fiction, three pages of an argument will flash by in two minutes; the same scene spoken out loud by characters sitting in two chairs may seem to take forever. If you are visualizing the action as you write, you might consider having them move about, throw things, or wake the neighbors, whose entrance immediately initiates a new scene.

If you are serious about drama and have a chance to see plays in production, you will find it helpful to see a play twice. To avoid the high cost, consider student productions. The first time you may be too caught up with the characters and the plot to be analytical. But if you see the same play the following night, you can analyze aspects like scene construction, entrances and exits, and stage business. Some of this can be observed in the written script, but a good deal of the action within a scene will have been devised by the director or the actors themselves. Try to judge whether there is enough, whether it is effective, and how you would have done it differently. In this second viewing, whether you like the play or not is less important than what you can learn from it.

When we say a play is talky, slow, or lacks punch, we usually mean that there was not enough going on to catch the eye. A good play maintains vitality through its visual impact.

33 DRAMATIC THEMES

Theme defined as the central concern; themes in *Hello Out There;* themes in *The Sandbox; highlighting* thematic concerns through repetition of lines, visual repetition, and symbolic names; *social and political themes* seen in *black theater* and plays by women; finding your *own themes.*

At the heart of most plays there is a *theme* or central concern. This is similar to a theme in fiction except that frequently it is presented in ways that are bolder and more vivid—that is, more dramatic.

As in fiction, what appears at first to be a single theme is often made up of a number of different but closely related concerns. The longer and more intricate a play, the more thematic suggestions it may contain. But as we will see, even short plays can contain several concerns.

Themes do not generally provide answers to the questions a play raises. *Hamlet* doesn't tell you precisely how to deal with stepfathers, and *Hello Out There* is hardly good advice on how to deal with a lynch mob. Although there are plays that do take very specific positions on political and social issues, these are said to present *theses* rather than dealing with themes. A thesis is a specific argument. The function of such plays is to persuade or convert, not to explore. I will return to that approach later in this chapter.

Both the plays included in this text deal with a cluster of related themes. The plays are helpful models for your own work because they manage to suggest a good deal in a very short space. As we examine them, however, keep in mind that the complexity of thematic suggestion that you see in a published play is not usually what came to the playwright in the first draft. Themes often develop slowly as the writer moves through successive drafts.

Thematic Suggestion in *Hello Out There*

This play is remembered by theatergoers mainly for its dramatic impact. But if it had nothing more to offer than that, it would be a melodrama. The terror of an individual facing a lynch mob has been repeated frequently in film and television dramas. The elevation of the play above the level of a simple thriller is partly achieved through characterization; but the real complexity lies in its thematic suggestion.

Even a rapid reading of the play suggests that the theme deals with the loneliness of individuals and the need to reach out in friendship or love. The protagonist is held in jail, and the girl is trapped in a small town which seems to be no better than a jail. It appears that they might escape together; but in the end his luck runs out. The girl may still have a chance.

Perhaps that is all the casual reader will ever know about the play. But a writer has to examine the technique more closely. Saroyan has used three devices in this play to dramatize his thematic concerns to the point where they are unmistakable: repetition of certain key words throughout the length of the play like refrains, reiteration of the same words in "runs" or clusters, and the use of symbolic names.

The most pronounced use of the refrain is "hello out there." No one could miss the fact that this key phrase is used in the title, at the opening, and again at the closing of the play. More significant, however, is the fact that it is repeated a total of twenty-five times!

This is no accident. If you check the first twelve uses (all of which occur before the girl appears on stage), you will see how Saroyan has established the refrain early with a "run" or cluster of three and then spaced them increasingly farther apart. After the girl appears, they occur only occasionally. The next "run" occurs when the man is left alone in the cell again. He repeats it five times in the course of one short monologue. Once again the phrase is used sparingly until the very end when the girl, trapped and alone, repeats it twice as the curtain descends.

A second series is made up of the two words "scared" and "afraid." They are used interchangeably. They are repeated sixteen times and are used to apply not only to the young couple but to the men in the town and to the husband who eventually kills Photo-Finish. Notice the redundancy in the following "run":

THE GIRL: . . . They were talking of taking you to another jail in another town.

YOUNG MAN: Yeah? Why?

THE GIRL: Because they're afraid.

YOUNG MAN: What are they afraid of?

THE GIRL: They're afraid these people from Wheeling will come over in the middle of the night and break in.

YOUNG MAN: Yeah? What do they want to do that for?

THE GIRL: Don't *you* know what they want to do it for?

YOUNG MAN: Yeah, I know all right.

THE GIRL: Are you scared?

YOUNG MAN: Sure I'm scared. Nothing scares a man more than ignorance.

First he uses "afraid" in a string of three successive lines, and then he uses "scared" three times in an almost poetic sequence.

There are two other refrains in this play which, though they are not as pronounced, still serve to dramatize the thematic concerns. One is "lonesome." It is used a total of twelve times, six of which occur in a "run" just before and just after the girl appears for the first time. Finally, there is "luck," which turns up ten times, six of which are in a cluster in about as many consecutive lines.

These, then, are five phrases or words that are repeated throughout the play and also bunched in clusters: "hello out there," "scared/afraid," "lonesome," and "luck." They also lie at the heart of what the playwright is working with: the loneliness and fear we all experience, the reaching out, and the element of luck with which we must always deal.

How does Saroyan get away with so much redundancy? He has, after all, violated a basic "rule" that is still generally honored in the writing of exposition and most fiction. This shows how far the technique of playwriting is from other types of prose.

Saroyan's approach here is actually closer to that of free verse. The use of repeated words and phrases either scattered or in clusters is, as I pointed out in Chapter 7, one of the characteristics found in the Bible, in the works of Walt Whitman, and more recently in the poetry of Allen Ginsberg, Lucille Clifton, and others.

A second device found in *Hello Out There* is the rather direct use of symbolic names. The town where the protagonist is about to meet his death is called "Matador." And the town from which the freewheeling, irresponsible men come is "Wheeling." Saroyan makes sure that the audience does not miss these names by repeating each one twice—a recognition of the fact that drama is a "continuous art form" that does not permit any hesitation.

He puts the same care into the young man's nickname, "Photo-Finish." Through the character's own dialogue we learn exactly what it means and how it is linked with the central theme of luck.

More subtle than the name is the symbolic action. The play begins with an isolated, frightened individual crying out for contact with someone—anyone. It turns out that this same longing for companionship was what got him into this spot in the first place. Ironically, it is fear rather than rage that leads the husband to commit murder. And in the end, the girl has taken the role of the isolated, frightened individual crying out for contact with someone—anyone.

When one looks closely at these devices of repetition and symbolic details, they appear extraordinarily blatant. This is often true of drama. Remember that what one is analyzing here line by line is the written version of a performance that will slide through the consciousness of an audience in about twenty-eight uninterrupted minutes. For this reason, playwrights often repeat key phrases; and when they develop a symbol, they return to it at least once and at times frequently. Drama, more than any other genre, thrives on reiteration.

Thematic Concerns in *The Sandbox*

The first half of this play seems to suggest a negative theme similar to many in the absurdist tradition: that people are without inner resources and live empty, meaningless lives.

Our introduction to Daddy suggests the passive American male who is forever being satirized in drama, fiction, and even the comics. He is a cartoon figure. But we soon see in him some thematic suggestions that go beyond the cartoon level. "What do we do now?" he asks. Then he repeats the question, "What do we do now?" The repetition is almost a refrain, similar to the one in *Hello Out There*. After a pause he asks, "Shall we talk to each other?" But he can't think of anything to talk about. Like characters in the most pessimistic absurdist plays, he seems to be asking what one should do with one's life, and the only answer is Mommy's: "We wait." In the short run they are waiting for Grandma to die, but in a broader sense they seem to have nothing to do but wait for their own lives to end. There is humor there, but it is dark indeed. They are spiritually as empty as any character produced in the absurdist tradition.

The portrait of Mommy is no more positive. Not only is she the epitome of the domineering wife, she is the insensitive boss of her mother as well. As Grandma explains:

> They took me off the *farm* . . . and moved me into the big town with *them* . . . fixed a nice place for me under the stove . . . gave me an army blanket . . . and my own dish . . . my very own dish!

Mommy pretends to love her mother, but she treats her like an old cat.

Mommy is also a master of clichés, as we see when she deals with her mother's death: "We must put away our tears . . . face the future. . . . It's our duty." And of Grandma, "She looks so happy." If Mommy and Daddy were the only characters in this play, the theme would be a bitter, derisive attack on human nature.

But in spite of that dark vision, the dominant theme of the play turns out to be resoundingly positive. We begin to see this counterstatement as soon as we hear Grandma talk. She dominates the second half of the play, and as I pointed out in the chapter on characterization, she is portrayed as a woman with humor and courage.

How can a play have two such different views? Actually the two thematic elements blend and support each other. In abstract terms, the play suggests that while many people lead empty, selfish lives marked with hypocrisy, there are some who maintain a sense of dignity and of worth even under demeaning circumstances. What begins as a highly satiric, apparently cynical view of the world turns out ultimately to be a strong affirmation of the human spirit.

Albee also makes a number of observations about the nature of death in this play. The character known as the Young Man is identified as the Angel of Death in the stage directions at the outset, but he is far from the conventional cartoon figure of an old man with a scythe. Albee's version is a complex symbolic figure. He is continually present (as is death) but nonthreatening to those who do not recognize him. He says "Hi!" to Mommy and Daddy twice, but they see nothing ominous about him. (We are "blind" to death until we are introduced.) He continues to do his calisthenics. (Death never rests.) His name is still uncertain (we tend to use euphemisms); he has "been around for a while" (actually from the beginning); he flexes his muscles (death is powerful); he is an actor (death comes in many guises) and is not very bright (death is arbitrary). In the end he is kind and gives comfort as death sometimes does for the very old. As Grandma says, "You've got a quality."

Highlighting Thematic Concerns

Because drama is continuous, flowing by the audience without pausing to allow for reflection, themes have to be stressed. There are certain techniques for doing this that lend themselves particularly well to drama.

The first of these is repetition. As we have already seen, the phrase "hello out there" is used as a recurring refrain in Saroyan's play—from title to the concluding lines. It reminds the audience repeatedly of the central theme, dealing with the need people have for other people. Repetition of the words "afraid" and "scared" is less noticeable, but it too works thematically to reinforce the suggestion of how fear influences us. As you remember, even the killer is described as being scared.

Repeating a phrase twice does not quite constitute a refrain, but it draws attention to whatever is being expressed. We have seen the effectiveness of this in Daddy's lines. The same technique is effective with plays that are entirely realistic. What might appear redundant in the dialogue of fiction often serves as a useful device in drama.

Repeating a visual pattern works the same way. The opening and closing scenes of *Hello Out There* provide a classic example—the plight of those two individuals compared not just in dialogue but in the way they stand alone on the stage staring out at the audience. It is the kind of visual repetition one sees frequently in ballet.

Using symbolic names of characters and places is another device for highlighting thematic elements. Be careful, however, not to make them so obvious that the audience senses the heavy hand of a playwright at work. If the last name of a character is unmistakably symbolic, the play will lose verisimilitude. Suppose, for example, the protagonist of *Hello Out There* was called *Hy Risk*. That's clearly too obvious for a realistic play. But you can get away with a good deal by using nicknames, since they are knowingly selected to describe some aspect of the character. Photo-Finish explains why he is called this and we accept it as entirely plausible.

Watch out for Adams and Newman for characters who are in some way living in an Eden or starting new lives. But it is possible to find names that are thematically suggestive without hitting the audience with the implication. Many people have read or seen Miller's *Death of a Salesman* without noticing that the protagonist, a man who is low in the social order, is appropriately named Willy *Loman.*

As you read other plays, look for ways in which dramatists repeat key lines or significant action or employ symbolic names. In many cases, these theatrical devices will not be easy to spot when a play is first seen in performance, but if you read the script analytically you will be able to identify the techniques and learn from them.

Social and Political Themes

Drama has always been associated with social statement and political protest. Medieval miracle plays were originally intended to teach biblical stories to illiterate peasants, but some became vehicles for satire. Vehement political statements were made through plays in the 1930s, and the Vietnam War continues to be a charged issue.

Today, black theater is a dynamic force in drama. Some plays develop themes of black identity, sharing the black experience with the whole society. Others present a specific thesis—a protest and a demand for reform.

The development of black theater is surprisingly recent. With a few rare exceptions, theater was a white art form until well into the 1960s. Black playwrights like Langston Hughes, Ossie Davis, and Lorraine Hansberry are known to most for one successful play each, but few white theatergoers can name the others they wrote. Langston Hughes alone turned out more than twenty plays. As a result, black playwrights, as well as black directors and actors, have been deprived of audiences and of the training that comes from regular production. This backlog of artistic frustration amplifies a deep sense of social injustice, to produce themes of bitter denunciation.

The harshest of these are written consciously and directly to a white audience. Plays like *The Toilet* by Amiri Baraka (LeRoi Jones) are intentionally designed to shock white, middle-class theatergoers. Rather than themes, these plays present theses—strong statements that often recommend specific social action.

Paul Carter Harrison's *Tabernacle* is another fine example. The play, described in his subtitle as *A Black Experience in Total Theater*, is a conglomerate of, in his words, "role playing, dance movement, choral chants, animism of masks, pregnancy of light and silence—integrated in such a manner as to create concrete images of a unique quality of Black expression."

The plot is based on a trial that took place after the Harlem riots of 1964. For all the varied techniques used in this play, it too is aimed primarily at a white audience. This is clear from the start when a preacher addresses members of the audience directly, telling them that they are about to "witness all the infernal ashes of Cain poured down on our souls." And at the end of this extraordinarily powerful and biting play this same preacher lambastes the audience for sitting in stunned silence. By convention, theatergoers withhold their applause until after the action of the play is over; Harrison has utilized this convention as what he describes as a "pregnant silence," turning it into a metaphor for the political inaction on the part of whites and many middle-class blacks. Like Baraka, Harrison deals with strong arguments, and he thrusts them directly at a particular audience.

Conscious appeal to a white audience is also found in plays that are thematic and less accusatory. In Charles Gordone's *No Place to Be Somebody*, for example, the plot of the play is stopped twice for lengthy monologues delivered like prose poems from the center of the stage. One of these is formally titled "There's More to Being Black than Meets the Eye." The other is a verse narrative of what it is like for a black to try living like white suburbanites, suffering the scorn of both urban blacks and white neighbors.

Other plays address themselves more specifically to black audiences. The seven plays selected originally by the Free Southern Theater group for their pilot program are good examples: *Purlie Victorious* by Ossie Davis, *Do You Want to Be Free?* by Langston Hughes, *Lower Than the Angels* by John O. Killens, *Day of Absence* and *Happy Ending* by Douglas Turner, *Great Gettin' Up Morning* by Ann Flagg, and a modern adaptation of *Antigone*. To this list should be added Martin Duberman's *In White America*, which was actually this group's first production.

Only a few plays in the black theater movement are unmistakably written for white audiences. A larger proportion are concerned with black awareness and black identity. But perhaps a majority of plays deal with themes that are significant to all audiences. They tend to be thematic rather than thetic.

Goin' a Buffalo by Ed Bullins and *Ceremonies in Dark Old Men* by Lonne Elder III are two excellent examples. So also is *Fences*, a powerful play by August Wilson whose previous Broadway hit was *Ma Rainey's Black Bottom.* All these plays dramatize the problems of black identity, economic survival, and moral corruption in urban life. They are unmistakably about aspects of the black experience, but they do not propose solutions. Instead, they develop a tragic view of men and women caught in a highly destructive society.

Women have also had a significant impact on drama in the past decade. As with black drama, plays by women vary from those that explore the woman's experience to those that make strong social or political statements. One of the more innovative playwrights is Ursule Molinaro, whose works vary from brief, nonrealistic plays in the absurdist tradition to full-length works. In one, *Breakfast Past Noon,* a mother and daughter have a series of arguments without ever addressing each other directly. They refer to each other consistently in the third person. The effect is like two antagonists who refuse to make eye contact. The play is a highly effective dramatization of a hopelessly alienated relationship.

This play and others by women have been collected in an anthology called *The New Women's Theatre,* edited by Honor Moore. For a retrospective collection that gives historical perspective I would recommend *Plays By and About Women,* edited by Victoria Sullivan and James Hatch.

Finding Your Own Themes

If the thematic core of your play does not genuinely reflect your convictions, the play will probably not ring true. Further, you may find that this occasionally unconscious insincerity will result in characters that are stereotypes and situations that are hackneyed.

On the other hand, don't feel that if you do not have a social cause to defend you should turn to another genre. What you need is a situation that is potentially dramatic and involves characters whose lives are somewhat like the lives of people you know.

In some respects, your search will be similar to finding material for fiction, but the themes tend to be broader. It may strike you that Thornton Wilder's *Our Town* is a very mild piece of drama. The lives of reasonable and kindly people are depicted in episodic fashion. But there is drama in the way the tragedy of death in childbirth is finally resolved as a part of a universal harmony. Domestic situations make good plays if you can find a way of drawing a larger truth from them in a fresh and convincing way.

Don't forget your own roots. If you have a distinctive racial or national background, there will be tensions and perhaps successes and defeats associated with it. If your own life has been secure, what of your parents'?

Your life style is also a source. Whether you live in a city apartment or on a farm, your experiences are in some ways unique. Do they have dramatic potential? Even if you see your environment as a "typical American suburban home," look again. When it comes to specific families (or individuals), there is no such thing as "typical." Each is individual.

Finally, draw on drama itself. What you read and what you see in production will suggest themes. And the play does not have to be contemporary. *Oedipus Rex* is about sons and parents in any age; *Antigone* is about the conflict between a woman's personal values and the laws of the society; *Othello* raises questions of trust and honesty in those who mean the most to us; *Hamlet* explores, among other things, the uneasy relationship between young men and their stepfathers.

Costumes change. Language changes. Theatrical conventions change. But themes remain so constant that we still feel emotionally involved with works written more than 2000 years ago. Whenever you feel this emotional pull, stop and ask what that play has revealed about your own situation, your own life, and your own society. You won't be borrowing a theme; you will be allowing another work of art to stimulate your own artistic imagination.

34 WRITING FOR FILM

The transition from play writing to script writing; film as a
highly visual medium; a new approach to *scene formation;*
patterns in *dramatic structure; adaptations* versus *original scripts;*
the *mechanics* of the script itself, including basic terms.

Shifting from play writing to script writing for television or motion pictures
is in some ways like shifting from one musical instrument to another. Much
of the basic approach is similar, but there are specific differences that are
more significant than you might expect.

Starting with the similarities, everything you have learned about creating dramatic impact applies to script writing. In some respects, dramatic
impact becomes more important since your audience is more easily distracted.
It is far easier to turn a dial than to leave a theater. So there is an even greater
need for an initial hook to capture interest and a series of dramatic questions
to hold it through to the end. If you have had practice writing drama for
stage, all this will be familiar to you when you turn to script writing.

If you choose to write comedy, the approaches to creating a humorous
situation or employing the sharper impact of wit and satire are essentially
the same. And comic relief in more serious scripts is just as important as it
is on the stage.

Characterization is also the same. Whatever skills you have developed in that area will serve you as well as a scriptwriter. You still must depend on action and dialogue. Individuality is just as important, and you will have to maintain enough consistency to make your characters credible. As with a play script, your central characters will be developed ("round"), and your minor characters or those providing comic relief will be presented in less detail ("flat").

At first it may seem that the script itself will be the major hurdle. It *is* different. But getting used to the new format is surprisingly easy. The sample script that appears in the next chapter will help you to make the transition without trauma.

This script format, incidentally, is a fairly standard style. Since most dramatic television projects are shot on film, the script is essentially the same as a motion picture screenplay. What I have to say about writing for film will in almost every case apply to both media. Mastering the form is not a major problem.

There are, however, two fundamental differences that distinguish film writing of either sort from play writing. The first is a heightened concern for the visual element. The second is a different concept of *scene*, which significantly affects the way you think about your material and the way you compose. These differences can be explained in principle, but only through practice will they become an automatic part of your approach to the genre.

Film as a Highly Visual Medium

In the drama section of this text I emphasized the importance of knowing what your characters are doing as you write. As you shift to film writing, this concern becomes central. Each scene is a visual unit, and the process of writing requires that you move from one picture to the next.

Foreign films with captions demonstrate how important the visual aspect is. If you do not know the language, your understanding of the dialogue is limited to those telegraphic captions. They are brief and are read hastily as your eyes quickly return to the scene, yet they are all you need. Comprehension is not lost. In fact, if you are able to buy a translation of the script, you will be surprised at how little you have missed. The major portion of the experience has been visual, not auditory.

Film schools stress this concern for the visual. At the University of Southern California, for example, graduate students begin their program by directing and producing three short films, all without any sound at all.

Does this make the film script less important than the play script? Yes and no. Partly because the genre is so heavily visual (and also because it requires such a complex technical process to produce), the original script is often quite different from the completed work. Producer and director Tony Bill describes the process as consisting of three different films: First is the original script—the manuscript we are describing here. Second, there is the heavily revised shooting script, which includes all the detailed instructions for camera, focus, lighting, and acting. Third, there is the edited film, which has been pieced together from actual footage. When you buy "the script" of a film, you are reading a transliteration of the film as it is finally shown. What we are examining in this chapter is the very first stage of this process. Once a film is produced, that original script is all but forgotten and probably won't even be published. It has been shed and discarded like a snake's skin.

On the other hand, the original script is absolutely essential. It begins the process. Once you are beyond the apprentice stage, you are writing for a select audience of professionals: agents, directors, producers. This is not a mass readership, this is an audience of highly knowledgeable individuals.

One reason film scripts are so visual is that the genre by its very nature calls for this kind of emphasis. The viewer is even more directly in the center of the action than when seeing a play. And the opportunities for visual effects—both symbolic and highly realistic—are increased a hundredfold.

In addition to this, a film script is actually read differently. Whereas a play may be published and read like a short story, a film script has the primary task of capturing the imagination and enthusiasm of someone who is looking for material that will make a good film. These readers are "seeing" the script scene by scene. The verbal concerns that are so important in a story or novel may seem like dead weight in a film script. This does not mean a film cannot have intellectual content. The recent proliferation of small studios and excellent low-budget films provides a real opportunity for those who want to work with sophisticated concepts. On the other hand, the themes of a film are more deeply rooted in what the audience sees than what it hears.

One way to train yourself in this new emphasis on the visual is to imagine how you would present a particular topic as a silent film. Start with an overall view by identifying the visual opportunities of your basic story line. Can they be highlighted? Then turn your attention to individual scenes. How can you show your audience what you have in mind without resorting to dialogue? Once you have done that, you are ready to add the spoken word.

A New Approach to Scene Formation

A film *scene* is a unit of action (with or without dialogue) that occurs in a single place and time. Don't confuse it with a *take*, which refers to a run of the camera. (A single scene may have many takes, from which a final *shot* will be selected.) The scene is the basic unit that concerns the scriptwriter.

Film scenes differ from those in drama in that they shift every time the audience's view changes. If, for example, two characters in a play are talking, the audience's view remains constant and the scene will continue until a character leaves the stage or another one enters. But in film a new scene is begun every time the camera shifts from one face to the other.

This is reflected in the script itself. Each scene in a film script is given a new heading. A sample of this form appears in the next chapter. More fundamental than that, however, is the effect this concept of scenes has on the act of writing. One tends to think in short, highly visual units. The rhythm of writing is entirely different.

These scenes may be extended to several minutes during, for example, a lengthy speech. But often they may be as short as three seconds. Most scriptwriters avoid long scenes, especially in 30-minute shows. The passive viewer of a television program may have the impression of long, unbroken sequences of action, but the script was probably made up of surprisingly short units.

Although you should keep your stage directions to a minimum, it is essential that you visualize each separate scene as you write your dialogue. Keep your background in mind as well as the foreground, and make use of them whenever you can. Once you are used to the script format, you will find that your writing will move from scene to scene as if you were visualizing a series of still shots. You can train yourself by watching television dramas in the same way, scene by scene, rather than viewing the action as an apparently uninterrupted flow.

Although most scenes contain dialogue, remember the value of the visual impression with no spoken words: the close-up of a character's face, a visual impression of a house or neighborhood, a minute detail like a character's hands or a leaf falling.

Dramatic Structure

When writing for the stage, we think of a full-length production as being between two and three hours and a "one act" as anywhere from ten minutes to an hour. Total length is highly flexible, and the division of acts and scenes is determined mainly by the material itself. With television writing, on the other hand, there are more conventional lengths that are designed to fit the half-hour modules of the medium. These have resulted in a more regular pattern of rising action and periodic climaxes.

If you are planning a standard 30-minute show, think of it as a two-act production. Each act will come to about thirteen or fourteen typewritten pages, though of course you should calculate the playing time by giving the script a dramatic reading. Be sure to allow for action that has no accompanying dialogue.

The first act frequently ends with some kind of dramatic event or statement. Although this initial climax shouldn't overshadow the conclusion of the drama, it may provide a fresh insight or create an unexpected twist in the plot to serve as a hook to bring your audience back after the break.

In comedy it is important to end the first act with a good line or unit of action. Be careful not to muffle it by a closing line like "See you tomorrow" or "Drive carefully." Let your comic line be the very last one for best impact.

This two-act form is less rigid in public television, which is not punctuated by commercials, but it provides a structure that many scriptwriters find valuable.

A 60-minute show is divided into four acts. They are each about the same length and frequently have the same type of climax or peak of interest. With the 90-minute show you increase the number of acts to six.

If you are just starting out, the 30-minute format is a good one to work with. You can train yourself to think in the short units of the filmed scene and still keep in mind the longer cycle of rising action that gives dramatic structure to each act.

Adaptations versus Original Scripts

Consider carefully whether you wish to start off with an adaptation of a story or an original screenplay. The advantage of an adaptation is that you can concentrate on the script and the individual scenes. It is best to select a fairly short work and one in which there is visual potential. You will want to outline your approach since significant changes may have to be made. But you can begin the actual writing sooner than if you are developing your own plot and characters. You can use any published work as long as you do not reproduce it or submit it for production. If you do plan to enter it in a contest or send it to a producer, be sure to secure permission in writing from the author first. Many authors will grant you permission to develop an adaptation in return for an agreed-upon payment to be made if and when the script is accepted for production.

The next chapter consists of a sample script based on the first third of the short story "Sausage and Beer." It is designed to illustrate the mechanics of a script, but it is only an opening fragment. You may find it helpful to complete that script, drawing on the story itself, which appears as Chapter 14 of this text. If you are able to do this in a group or in a writing class, you can learn a good deal by comparing various approaches to the same fictional scenes.

If you prefer to create an original script, begin with an outline that includes the characters and the basic plot. Keep in mind all the special needs of a theatrical performance and add to that the mobility and the pacing of film. Remember that while you were doing your best to make imaginative use of a single set for the stage, you are now working with a medium that lends itself to a constantly shifting environment. Don't trap your characters in a single room or a car. Take advantage of your freedom.

The Mechanics of a Film Script

You may wish to read a page or two of the sample script in the next chapter before you study the following details. The actual layout of the script is relatively simple.

The title page is a separate sheet with the title of your project typed in capital letters and underlined. Below that, describe the project briefly—"A 30-minute Television Drama," "A 60-minute Situation Comedy," or the like. Your name goes below that. On the lower half of the page you may write "First Draft" or "Final Draft" on the left, and it is essential that you place your *contact address* (your home, agent, or office) on the right.

The first page of your script begins with your title again—in capital letters and underlined. The first words are "<u>FADE IN:</u>" typed at the left margin. The script will end with "<u>FADE OUT</u>" typed on the right after the last line. The sample script does not have this since it is only a portion of a full script.

Assuming that you are using pica type (preferred for play scripts and fiction as well), set your left margin at 20 spaces (2 inches) for stage directions. Dialogue begins at 30 spaces, and the name above each unit of dialogue begins 40 spaces in. For convenience, set these tabs on your typewriter.

Each new scene begins with "EXT." if it is an exterior shot or "INT." if it is an interior. It should also be identified the first time as "DAY" or "NIGHT." This information with a very brief phrase or word of identification is called a *slug line*. It will look like this:

    INT. KITCHEN--DAY

or

    EXT. WOODS--NIGHT

Once you have identified the action as interior or exterior and as day or night, you don't have to repeat this information until there is a complete shift to a new location.

If you shift from, say, the interior of a car to an exterior view and then return to the same interior, you can indicate this as "BACK TO SHOT."

After your slug line, double-space and describe the setting and characters in single space, using the 20-space margin (see p. 326). Keep this material fairly brief and be careful not to overdirect. If your work goes into production, a *shooting script* will be developed with much more technical advice. That is when the scenes will be numbered and certain revisions may be made by the director. He or she is the camera expert; your job is to provide an effective, playable script.

The name of each new speaker is placed in capital letters that start

40 spaces in. This is much easier than trying to center each name. Brief directions regarding tone or gesture can be placed below the name, but usually this will be unnecessary. As with a play script, most lines can and will be interpreted by both the director and actors.

If a speaker is *off screen* but physically nearby, put "(O.S.)" after the name. If the speaker's voice is a memory of someone else's voice, commentary (as in introductions), or thoughts, use "(V.O.)" for *voice over*.

Here are a few more abbreviations you may find helpful. All are used in the sample script that follows.

BEAT	a pause in dialogue
cont.	continued; place at top of each page after the first
CU	close-up shot
MED SHOT	medium shot (use camera instructions sparingly)
P.O.V.	a scene shot from a character's point of view; that is, what he or she sees
f.g.	foreground
b.g.	background

Try not to let the terminology and the somewhat different format distract you from the essential fact that you are writing a dramatic script. If you study the sample in the next chapter and continue it for practice, following the story line printed in the fiction section, you will find that the mechanics will soon become almost automatic. When this occurs, you are ready to strike out on your own with a fresh adaptation or an original script.

35 A FILM SCRIPT

ASYLUM

(A partial adaptation of "Sausage and Beer" by Stephen Minot as a 30- minute television drama)

by
Stephen Minot

FIRST DRAFT

c/o Prentice-Hall
Englewood Cliffs, NJ 07632

<u>ASYLUM</u>

<u>FADE IN</u>:

INT. CAR--DAY

Profile of a boy, 12, in the passenger seat of an old-model car. b.g. through window of the moving car shows New England winter farm land with patchy snow, a bleak scene. Boy watches farm land roll by, absolutely expressionless. Occasionally he rubs his hands or tries to warm them under his armpits.

NEW ANGLE

Profile of father, driving. He is lean, gray, and also expressionless.

BACK TO SHOT

Boy takes a furtive look at his father, then back to the scene ahead.

          BOY
      Is it very far?

          FATHER (O.S.)
      We're about halfway now.

Long silence again. Boy takes furtive look at his father just like the first one, then turns to the view out front and speaks without looking at his father.

          BOY
      I didn't know I had an Uncle
      Theodore.

          FATHER (O.S)
        (voice flat)
      He's my brother.

EXT. BOY'S P.O.V. DOWN THE ROAD

          BOY (O.S.)
        (musing silently to self)
      How can anybody have a
      brother and not talk about him?
      Maybe he's a hermit.

                                     CUT TO

cont.

EXT. SHACK IN FOREST--DAY

Fantasy: Imaginary uncle played by father steps out of shack and smiles warmly, waving a greeting to unseen visitors.

BACK TO SHOT

> BOY (O.S.)
> (still as if thinking)
> No. They wouldn't keep that a
> secret. This Theodore's done
> something terrible.

CUT TO

INT. CELL BLOCK IN PRISON--DAY

Fantasy: Imaginary uncle played by father again is in prison uniform but smoking a cigar. He waves a "tough-guy" greeting to unseen visitors.

CUT TO

INT. CAR--CU BOY

> BOY (O.V.)
> (thinking)
> A real gangster! That's it--"my
> Uncle Ted, you know, the cop
> killer."

Just the hint of a smile crosses his face.

EXT. HIGH ANGLE

From an AERIAL SHOT, we see the car make its way along a deserted road. Patchy snow of fields and scrub land give a look of isolation and desolation.

INT. IN CAR

f.g. father and son as seen from back seat. b.g. view of long, bleak institutional buildings. Old man in a gray, nondescript uniform seen pushing a two-wheeled cart. Car moves slowly by several such buildings.

cont.

> BOY
> (awed)
> Where are all the guards?

> FATHER
> They don't have guards in a
> hospital.

> BOY
> Hospital?

> FATHER
> A kind of hospital.

CUT TO

EXT. FRONT STEPS

CU large, somewhat unshaven face of ATTENDANT who looks threatening at first.

MED SHOT shows ATTENDANT in doorway looking less threatening.

> ATTENDANT
> Well now, Mr. Bates, you
> brought the boy, I see.

CU--FATHER who looks gray against the gray background of snow and puddles in road.

> FATHER
> I brought the boy.

MED SHOT--FATHER AND ATTENDANT

> FATHER
> How's Ted?

> ATTENDANT
> Same as when you called. A
> little gloomy, maybe, but calm.
> Those boils have just about
> gone.

cont.

>   FATIIER
> Good.
>   ATTENDANT
> Funny about those boils. I don't
> remember a year but what he's
> had trouble. Funny.

>   FATHER
> Funny.

INT. HALLWAY AND WAITING ROOM

LONG SHOT shows ATTENDANT, FATHER, and BOY pass through dark hall and
into waiting room in silence. Benches around four walls. Long table in middle.
Old men shuffling about; younger men wheeling carts of linen. Everyone moving
slowly. Dreamlike effect.

MED SHOT: Father and son sit on bench. Father looks straight ahead. Boy keeps
his head motionless but moves his eyes in quiet astonishment.

>   BOY
>   (Softly to his father)
> Smells like where we bring old
> clothes and things before
> Christmas.

>   FATHER
>   (A touch of a smile)
> The Refuge? Yes, it does smell
> like the Refuge. Sort of.

BOY'S P.O.V.--WAITING ROOM

He sees an old man stretched out on the bench beside him, one hand over his
eyes, the other resting on his crotch. He is snoring.

BACK TO SHOT

Boy inches his way farther from the sleeping man. Then looks sideways at father,
hoping his attempts weren't seen. Father stares straight ahead.

BOY'S P.O.V.

cont.

He sees another patient scratching his back on the dark-varnished door frame.

BACK TO SHOT

Boy scratches his shoulder blade. Father looks up abruptly and the son, seeing this, looks, too. Then he opens his eyes wide.

LONG SHOT--WAITING ROOM

Black attendant is leading a man in who must be Uncle THEODORE. THEODORE is a heavy, sagging man with rounded shoulders. He has a clean white shirt, no tie, and pants hung up on suspenders patched with twine. He shuffles toward the others. The attendant points out the visitors and leaves. THEODORE shuffles to within inches of his visitors, who stand.

          FATHER
      Hello there, Ted, how have you
      been?

          THEODORE
        (blank-faced)
  Been?

A BEAT. No one knows what to say.

          FATHER
      I brought the boy.

          THEODORE
      The boy?

          FATHER
      My boy. Young Will.

The boy attempts to hold out his hand, but Theodore makes no move to shake it.

          THEODORE
        (to his brother)
      But _you're_ Will.

          FATHER
      Right, but we've named our boy
      William, too.

cont.

CU THEODORE

His face lights up in a broad and genuine smile which radiates charm and dispels all uneasiness about the situation.

> THEODORE
> (chuckling)
> Well now, there's one on me.
> You know, I'd forgotten I even
> <u>had</u> a boy.

36 DEVELOPING AS A PLAYWRIGHT

Evaluating your own work through a silent reading, a spoken delivery, and a group reading; *five core questions* concerning the dramatic impact, plot, characterization, themes, and degree of originality; the importance of *embracing the medium*.

The preceding chapters on drama and script writing are designed to increase your awareness of what the genre requires and what it offers. But the actual growth process will depend, as it did with poetry and fiction, on how well you learn to evaluate and revise your own work and, on a broader level, how successfully you can learn from studying professional work.

Evaluating Your Own Work

In evaluating your dramatic scripts, the opinion of friends may be helpful—more so, in fact, than with poetry because the work is probably intended for a broader audience. The advice of teachers and the professionals you may meet at conferences will be invaluable. But ultimately *you* are the one who has to decide what revisions to make.

Begin with a silent reading. You have been doing that in the process of writing, of course; but this reading is different. Give the script your un-divided attention and don't stop to make corrections or notes.

As you read, picture all the action. Visualize each scene. Try to hear the lines as they would be spoken by actors and actresses. Don't analyze; just experience. Then, when you are through, imagine yourself the director at the end of the first dress rehearsal and write an objective critique.

That's the first step. The second is reading the script out loud. One mechanical purpose is timing. The total playing time can be estimated fairly accurately if you allow for action that occurs without lines. If it is a play divided into acts and scenes, it will be important to know how long they are. Use this information when deciding where to cut and expand. If it is a tele-vision script, see if you are fairly close to the structural pattern of acts outlined in Chapter 34. In either case, you will want to know the total playing time.

In addition to these mechanical concerns, the spoken reading is an effective way for you to judge the quality of your dialogue before anyone else hears it. Lines that looked satisfactory on the page may sound awkward or out of character. Long speeches that seemed effective when read silently sometimes seem ponderous when read out loud.

After making corrections and revisions, you are ready for the third step, an informal group reading. Your readers should be familiar with the script, but there is no need for them to memorize the lines. If possible, the reading should be taped for further study. Naturally, some of the parts will appear better or worse depending on the skills of your readers, but no matter how informal the performance may be, it will give you your first real notion of what the play might be like in full production.

It is helpful to have a small audience of friends in addition to your readers, but it is not at all essential. The real value comes from translating the written script into something close to what it is intended to become: a dramatic and convincing performance for stage or film.

If possible, allow time after the reading for a discussion of the play's dramatic impact, its theme, or any of the five critical questions suggested below. Those who have taken part in the reading are apt to have insights into the work which you may not have considered.

One note of caution: Be careful not to let such sessions deteriorate into general conversations about the issues suggested by the play. Remind your critics that the subject is the play or script itself. You may wish to reproduce the following five questions (giving credit, of course) and to use them as guidelines for the discussion.

Five Core Questions

These five questions are central to the analysis of a dramatic script. They will help to keep the discussion from digressing. They should also serve as a way of looking at your own work in the early-draft stages.

1. *Does the play have dramatic impact?* Specifically, does it present some type of hook at the outset? Is this followed by dramatic questions strong enough to hold the interest of the audience? If wit and satire are used, do they work? Is the play really funny? Which characters and which specific scenes were successfully comic and which didn't come up to that standard? Precise comparisons are usually more useful than general pronouncements.

2. *Is the structure of the plot effective?* Even if your critics are not sure what improvements to suggest, you will learn a good deal if you ask them where the high points were. If they are unable to describe the work in terms of rising action and periodic climaxes, you should take a second look at the structure of your plot.

3. *Are the characters convincing and interesting?* Since characterization depends on dialogue and action, this question will necessarily include the effectiveness of the lines and the appropriateness of what each character does. As playwright, you may have to discourage such subjective comments as "I really didn't like that character." What you have to find out is whether it was the *characterization* that failed in some way.

   The group should understand that we don't make the same demands about secondary characters or those presented for comic relief or as satiric sketches. These may not be "convincing" as fully developed characters are, but they still must serve some function and in most cases provide interest.

4. *What themes are being explored and how are they developed?* It is important to find out just which themes reached your audience. Sometimes their views will differ from what you thought was clearly suggested. In such cases, don't be too quick to explain what your intent was. Encourage your critics to explain the play as they understood it. This will help you to see it objectively.

   If your themes were too subtle, the play is not going to be improved by convincing your critics that they should have seen what you had in mind. See if you can work out actual approaches to revision that would highlight the ideas that didn't come through before. If, on the other hand, the group feels that the themes were too obvious, find out if the main ideas appeared to them hackneyed or preachy or just commonplace. Again, the most profitable approach you can take is not one of defense but exploration.

5. *Does the play or script show originality?* There is nothing wrong in having your piece reflect the work of some playwright you admire. But your treatment should be fresh. Much will depend on characterization and how you shape your thematic concerns; yet originality goes beyond that. What you hope to hear is the feeling that this is a memorable script, one that was new and convincing. But if you don't get quite that sort of support, try to find out which elements of the play were too familiar to hold full interest and which were like a new experience for your audience.

Embracing the Medium

Writing a play or film script can be valuable even if you never do it again. You will learn a good deal about the medium, and your capacity to enjoy performances will be far greater. But if you want to go on from there and develop as a playwright or scriptwriter, you will have to immerse yourself in the medium.

In playwriting, this will involve a lot of reading. While the finished production is the best teacher, your ability to see plays may be limited by what is being presented in your area and how much money you can spend. Your library, on the other hand, will have more plays than you can read in a year.

The collections of so-called best plays may not always strike you as the best, but you can learn from any script. And don't feel that you should limit yourself to recent works. The ingenuity with which Shakespeare presents a dramatic question early in his tragedies is a skill well worth studying; the cleverness with which Shaw masks highly didactic themes with wit and satire is a technique that can be used in any period.

As for seeing plays in production, do so as often as you can. Students are frequently given special rates just before opening night. If you are in college, it would be well worth volunteering your time to act or to serve on a stage crew. The mechanics of producing a play should be a part of any playwright's education.

If television or film writing is what interests you, it is important to study the best productions carefully. It may also be necessary to go where the action is. Unlike the poet, you cannot develop your talents in isolation. A good school will provide contacts, and even a nonwriting job in a studio or production agency will help . You will probably discover that less of your time will be spent in actual script writing than in the intricate process of marketing. This you will have to learn directly from the men and women who have made a success of it.

Developing as a playwright or scriptwriter has one aspect in common with the process of developing as a poet or writer of fiction: Your greatest resource is the published work in your field. Remember that there are tens of thousands of individuals who have published in the very genre you hope to master. They have faced just about every technical problem you will consider in a lifetime; they have shared many of your feelings. You bring a unique set of experiences and sensitivities to the field, but you won't know what approaches you can take unless you become familiar with what has been done by others. Your finest teachers are the works themselves. Listen to them.

Appendices

A Submission of Material for Publication

Unfounded myths about publishing; the *tests* of whether one is ready to submit material; *mechanical considerations* of the manuscript itself; *what to submit; where to* submit; the *vanity presses;* the use of *personal contacts;* the dangers of *double submissions;* the value of *agents; placing a play;* and the reasonable approach to publication.

The number of novice writers who submit material long before there is any chance of publication is matched by the number of those who are reluctant to submit even when they should enter the public market. This is due to the fact that there are so many writers who have only a hazy notion about the whole area of marketing.

First, let's clear away a number of unfounded myths about publishing. One hears, for example, that nothing is published without "pull," that neither fiction nor drama can succeed without sex, that poetry must be obscure, that agents are unreliable, that book publishers are only interested in the bottom line, and that you have to live in New York to publish a play. Equally fanciful is the claim that if a piece of writing is really good it will be published without any effort on the part of the writer.

There are two essential facts to remember: First, publication is no more fair than life itself; there will always be good works that are not accepted, as well as thoroughly rotten material that is. Second, if talent, practice, and a practical system of submission are combined, one can alter the odds in one's favor.

The test of whether you are ready to submit material is twofold. First, you should have written in that particular genre for some time. So-called "first novels" usually have been preceded by considerable practice in short stories and quite frequently by one or two unpublished novels.

During this difficult period of apprenticeship you should also be reading a good deal and familiarizing yourself with the magazines that might be interested in your work. I have repeatedly stressed the need to read carefully and regularly in the genre of your choice. Writers who do not do this are at such a great disadvantage that they eventually quit. Those who study their genre actively become perpetual students. They not only develop writing ability, they become increasingly familiar with the publications that may help them later.

If you have been writing for some time and have been an active, conscientious reader, you may be ready for the long and sometimes frustrating program of submitting material.

Mechanical Considerations

The manuscript must be typed with a dark ribbon on a good grade of standard typewriter paper. The type should be pica (not elite or the new varieties). The margins at left and at the top should be $1^1/_2$ inches, the bottom one inch, and the right roughly one inch without excessive hyphenation. All material except name and address should be double-spaced.

Place your name and address on the left, about two inches down from the top, and "Fiction" or "A Poem" on the right. Some authors add the approximate length there, but this is done less now, and publishers do not require it.

The title is normally placed in capital letters (not underlined or placed in quotation marks) about a third of the way down the page in this fashion:

Harley Q. Smith
205 Main St.   Fiction
Middletown, IL 62666

LOOKING FORWARD

The story begins two double spaces below this. Title pages on a separate sheet are used only for novels, plays, and film scripts.

The pages (after the first) should be numbered in Arabic numerals along with your last name in the *upper right* corner: Smith 2, Smith 3, and so on.

Do not place the manuscript in a folder or binder and do not staple it. A simple paper clip will do. Novels should be sent loose in a box. Covering letters are not necessary with poetry or fiction unless you have something specific to say. If the editor has added a kind word to a rejection slip or has actually written a letter, be sure to remind him or her. In any case, be brief and factual. Never defend your own work.

If all this seems rather restrictive, remember that originality belongs in the art form itself, not in the manuscript or covering letter.

For mailing, the envelope should be large enough so that the manuscript need not be folded. If one buys $9^1/_2$" $\times$ $12^1/_2$" envelopes for sending, one can include a self-addressed, stamped 9" $\times$ 12" envelope for its return. If this is too complicated, merely fold the second $9^1/_2$" $\times$ $12^1/_2$" envelope so that it can be placed inside the first with the manuscript. In either case, be sure that your address and proper postage are on it. Failure to do this not only irritates the editor but increases your chances of never seeing it again.

Poems and stories are sent first class. Novels are wrapped or boxed and sent in padded mailers marked "SPECIAL FOURTH CLASS—MANUSCRIPT" if they are to be mailed at the more economical book rate. United Parcel rates vary by zone but are often almost as inexpensive as the Postal Service book rate.

Allow about four weeks for poetry and short stories and an agonizing three months for novels. Resist that temptation to inquire about work sent until at least twice the expected time has passed.

If you know no one on the staff, merely send the manuscript to the fiction or poetry editor at the address given in the magazine. But if you have met or corresponded with an editor of even a junior reader, send it to him or her.

Keeping records is extremely important. It is impossible to remember what went out when and to which magazine if you do not keep a submissions notebook. In addition, it is invaluable to record not only which editors had a kind word or two but which magazines sent specifically worded rejection slips. The lowest level of rejection slip is merely a printed statement saying that they appreciated receiving your work and were unable to use it. In addition, most magazines have one or two special slips with wording like "this was of particular interest to us" or "we hope to see more of your work." Take these seriously. Next on the scale is the penned comment on the bottom of the slip like "good dialogue" or "try us again." These are infuriatingly brief, but they are worth recording. Be careful, however, not to inundate a magazine with weekly submissions. An editor who has commented on one poem is not going to be impressed with a flood of inferior work. Treat such individuals as potential allies who deserve only your best efforts.

The highest point on this scale is the *letter* of rejection. Even if brief, this is close to acceptance. If they suggest specific revisions that seem wise, revise and resubmit. If not, send your next really good piece. These are two situations in which you should definitely include a short covering letter.

Word Processors

Should you buy a word processor? If you spend four or more hours a week writing prose and can afford the investment, the answer is yes.

Word processors were badly oversold in the early '80s as handy for writing checks, keeping budgets, storing recipes, and the like. They *can* do those things, but not as well as paper and pencil. They are also of limited value for poets. The one genuine function of a word processor in the home is as an aid in writing prose.

It allows you to see your work on a screen before it is committed to paper, to move blocks of material around, to break up and reform paragraphs, to try different wording, to compare different versions. As a result, you compose many more drafts than you ever did as a typist. Surprisingly, most word-processor converts find that they are able to work longer hours than they did when they spent their time cutting and pasting.

There are four disadvantages that no computer magazine will warn you about. First, your typing accuracy will deteriorate. Corrections are so easy to make that you become permanently careless. Second, word processors occasionally break down. Those breakdowns are more complicated and more expensive than anything that happens to a typewriter. Breakdowns occur regardless of how much you pay for your computer. Oddly, some individual machines run flawlessly year after year, while others made by the same company give trouble. Third, once in a long time a word processor will irretrievably lose a block of material. It does not happen often, but it is an experience you don't easily forget. It is essential to make backup copies. Finally, you will bore all your friends who do not own one. Conversationally, computers are as addictive as baseball.

What kind to buy? That's a big topic, but here is a basic rule: If your primary need is word processing, don't spend extra money for equipment that can do statistical reports, cost accounting, games, and graphs in five colors. And don't be too impressed with "IBM compatibility" since you may never have a need for their programs. If words are your concern, find out what a machine will do with words and ignore capabilities you will never use. This textbook as well as a companion work, *Reading Fiction,* were prepared on a Kaypro II, one of the most portable and least expensive word processors on the market.

There are two types of printers: dot matrix and letter quality. Dot-matrix printers are faster and cheaper but slightly fuzzy. Each letter is made up of tiny dots. This type is improving in quality each year, but almost every editor polled by *Writer's Market* expressed a distinct preference for letter-quality printers. Some even refuse to read dot-matrix manuscripts.

For those who are already writing fiction, drama, or film scripts regularly, word processors are invaluable.

What to Submit

This decision must rest ultimately with you. Although the advice of other serious writers can be helpful, don't be swayed by friends who do not know what you are doing. Classmates or neighbors who never read poetry are not going to be very helpful as critics.

This does not hold for drama or television scripts, however. Since such work is designed to reach a larger audience, the advice of nonwriters may be of real value.

Poets should select a group of three or four poems. Writers of fiction should limit each submission to one story. Once the choice is made, keep sending the work out repeatedly. A single editorial rejection means absolutely nothing. A manuscript is not "dead" until it has been turned down by at least ten magazines. The best approach is to send the work out on the very day it is returned—otherwise you are apt to lose courage. As a practical matter, just as many manuscripts are accepted after six or eight rejections as after only one. This is largely due to the fact that so many nonliterary factors go into selecting a work for publication, such as the number and kind of manuscripts on hand, the balance of a particular issue, and the personal preferences of the first reader.

There is no easy rule concerning what should be sent out; but once the decision is made, stand by it until you have cumulative proof that the work is unpublishable.

Where to Submit

As I have suggested in earlier chapters, the place to start studying publications is your nearest library. Read the little magazines and quarterlies and find out which ones are printing your kind of work. Keep a file on each publication with a brief description of the works you found successful so that you will remember them and can look them up later.

You can find additional titles listed in *The International Directory of Little Magazines and Small Presses* (Dustbooks, Box 100, Paradise, CA 95969). This is by far the best directory of little magazines available. Other directories (listed in Appendix B) may prove helpful but tend to concentrate on more commercial markets.

Never submit material to a magazine on the basis of a listing alone.

Always review at least one issue of the periodical and make sure that it would be interested in your kind of work. "Blind submissions"—those made without being familiar with the publication—not only waste your time and money, they are a terrible burden for the editors, who frequently work for little or no salary.

Novels and book-length collections of poems or stories should be handled in a similar manner. The best listing of book publishers (and agents), is *Literary Market Place*, known as *LMP*. Make up a list, selecting houses that have published works similar to yours. Then keep submitting until you have sent it to thirteen or fourteen major publishers. This will take you about three years—time enough to complete the next novel or collection.

Circulating novels and book-length collections of short works raises four questions which are asked at every writer's conference. First, what about vanity presses?

A vanity press is one that charges the author a large fee for publication costs and sometimes for revisions. Many such organizations are perfectly honest, but it is rare indeed that a vanity press with its minimal system of distribution can do much with a novel that has been rejected by major publishers.

Don't confuse these commercially oriented vanity houses with small presses often run by individuals who love books and are willing to live a marginal economic life to work with them. Private presses are used less for novels, but they are a growing outlet for collections of poems and stories. The author still has to pay, but the venture is a cooperative one.

Another question raised by those submitting book-length manuscripts is whether it is appropriate to make use of a personal contact at a publishing house. Yes, it most certainly is. Even if your acquaintance is not in the editorial department, submit through him or her. Using such a connection probably won't get a bad manuscript published, but it may bypass that first reader who has a great many manuscripts to review. In the case of rejections, the writer is apt to receive a lengthier comment if the reader has some personal interest. I can testify to the fact that such personal contact is not a prerequisite for having stories or novels accepted; but it is neither unethical nor a waste of time to make use of any interested reader or publisher.

Third, should you submit copies of the same work to different publishers at the same time? No, you should not. This applies to individual stories and poems as well. Such double submissions are acceptable only from novelists who have repeatedly been on the best-seller list and who have a high-powered agent who can referee what may resemble a kind of manuscript auction. For the rest of us, it's one at a time.

Publishers assume that if they accept a novel, they are investing in an author. Standard contracts usually insist on a first refusal on whatever book-length manuscript you may submit next. This does not apply to individual stories or poems you may be circulating at the same time, but it does mean that you should not have two copies of a book-length manuscript or even two different novels circulating at the same time.

This is frustrating and, to my mind, unfair to writers who have two novels they would like to keep in circulation. As for taking a chance, remember that the publishing world is small and closely connected. It is not worth trying to violate what editors call "publishers' ethics."

Finally, what about agents? Don't even consider finding an agent if you write short stories intended primarily for little magazines or poetry of any sort. Placing material in literary quarterlies is an honor well worth struggling for, but they pay relatively little and an agent's 10 percent of that hardly covers postage. Agents, unlike writers, cannot afford to work for love alone.

On the other hand, you *should* consider looking for an agent if you have completed a mainstream novel or if you have a group of five or six potentially publishable stories that might be considered by quality magazines (*The Atlantic, The New Yorker*), the women's magazines (*Redbook, McCalls, The Ladies' Home Journal*) or the men's magazines (*Playboy, Penthouse, Esquire*). Manuscripts submitted to such magazines through agencies usually receive more careful scrutiny by readers with more editorial authority.

Most reputable agents still charge a flat 10 percent of all material sold through them and make no other charges whatever, regardless of how much postage or time they spend. In return, they expect to handle *all* your work.

A few agents are now beginning to charge 15 percent, and some are requiring a "reading fee" for unpublished writers. Don't confuse this with a "criticism fee," for which you will receive a critical report. Watch out for those who charge "overhead"—additional fees. All this may become a growing trend, but the basic 10 percent contract is still the standard.

If you are unpublished, it will be difficult but not impossible to find an agent. Some writers try to place their first book and then secure an agent to handle the contract when it is offered by a publisher. Others send query letters to many different agents (addresses in *LMP*) describing the completed manuscript they hope to place. It is perfectly all right to send out many query letters at the same time. Be sure to ask them to recommend another agent if they cannot take on your work themselves. Often they will know of younger agents who are looking for new clients.

Marketing a play requires a somewhat different approach. There are four basic techniques which can be adopted separately or together:

- *Enter play contests.* The best listings are in the *Dramatists Sourcebook* (Theater Communications Group, 355 Lexington Ave., New York, NY 10017). This annual is fully revised each August. In addition, consider *Poets and Writers Magazine* (201 W. 54th St., New York, NY 10019).
- *Submit to theaters.* Again, use the *Dramatists Sourcebook*. Another listing appears in *Writer's Market* (Writer's Digest Books). Each theater has special needs, requirements, and deadlines, so read the fine print carefully.

- *Work with a theater group.* Any theater experience will be useful. In addition, you will meet people who will guide you. Even as a volunteer you will benefit.
- *Submit to publishers of plays.* The two major publishers are Baker's Plays and Samuel French. Their addresses are in Appendix B. They accept many new plays (mostly mainstream) each year. If you are offered a contract, consider the terms carefully.

There is probably no other branch of the arts more committed to personal contact than drama. To put it bluntly, "pull" is extraordinarily valuable. If you know a producer, director, actor, or even a stagehand, write to him or her. This situation is not merely a matter of commercial corruption. The fact is that although book publishers come to know potential writers through little magazines (which they read with professional care), producers have little contact with the young playwright whose work has not yet appeared on the stage. This situation will continue until there are more little magazines willing to specialize in original plays and more low-budget stage companies in the smaller cities. Meanwhile, playwrights must struggle with the particularly difficult task of presenting their material.

Marketing television and motion picture scripts is a world unto itself. There is no art form that plunges the writer so deeply into the marketplace. There are three areas to consider, each with its own approaches: commercial television, public television, and motion-picture studios. For a clear introduction to the television world, I recommend *Television Writing* by Richard A. Blum (Communication Arts Books, Hastings House, Publishers, Inc.).

Like playwrights, scriptwriters benefit by being where the action is. Consider working in a television or film studio. Even volunteer work can be helpful. Have extra copies of your scripts handy and present them to anyone who expresses the slightest interest.

If you are serious about your art, you must be realistic when considering publication. It is naive to assume that marketing your work is crass and demeaning. Publishers have no way of discovering you if you make no effort to circulate your work. On the other hand, a mania to publish at all costs can be damaging to the creative process. If often leads to imitative and conventional work and to feelings of hostility toward editors and publishers.

To avoid these most unrewarding extremes, begin with an honest evaluation of your own work. Then follow through with a planned, long-range program of submissions. There are, of course, writers who achieve wide recognition very suddenly; but this is rare and not always a blessing. Ideally, creative work is a way of life, and the effort to publish is an important but not a central portion of that life.

B RESOURCES FOR WRITERS

General Reference Books

The following four reference books are published annually and can be found in most libraries. The most complete listing of little magazines and quarterlies is found in *The International Directory of Little Magazines and Small Presses*. A specialized directory and information book for dramatists is described in the drama section of this appendix.

- *The International Directory of Little Magazines and Small Presses*, Dustbooks. This is by far the best listing of little magazines, quarterlies, literary journals, and small presses. It devotes a paragraph to each magazine, describing what it publishes and listing names of editors, payment scale, and the like. Cross listings by subject, genre, and region. It does *not* list large-circulation magazines or major publishers. Dustbooks also offers *The Directory of Poetry Publishers*, which is handy for those working only with poetry.
- *Literary Market Place*, R.R. Bowker Co. *LMP* no longer lists magazines, but it remains the most authoritative list of book publishers, literary agents, writers' conferences, and addresses of those in publishing. It is entirely factual and does not contain articles on how to write or market your material.

- *The Writer's Handbook,* The Writer, Inc. This annual is dominated by "how-to" articles on all aspects of writing, with an emphasis on commercial markets. There is also a list of magazines.
- *Writer's Market,* Writer's Digest Books has fewer articles than *Writer's Handbook* but more listings. Many are commercial (science, sports, travel) or technical journals (hardware, real estate, toys), but there is a small listing of literary journals. All poetry titles have been moved to *Poet's Market,* also published by Writer's Digest Books.

Informative Magazines

These magazines provide information and advice for writers, poets, and to a lesser degree, dramatists. They do not generally publish fiction or poetry. Consult library copies for current subscription rates.

- *Poets and Writers Magazine,* 201 W. 54th St., New York, NY 10019. Formerly known as *CODA,* this nonprofit publication is a must for anyone who writes poetry, fiction, or dramatic scripts. It is published six times a year. Its articles deal with problems faced by all literary writers: how to find time to write when teaching, how to arrange readings, publishing translations, dealing with small presses. It is also the best source of contest and grant application deadlines, dates of conferences and readings, winners of awards.
- *The Writer,* 8 Arlington St., Boston, MA 02116. Both this monthly and *Writer's Digest,* 9933 Alliance Rd., Cincinnati, OH 45242, focus more on mass markets than does *Poets and Writers Magazine.* Articles give advice on writing and marketing a great variety of material from gothic novels to "confessionals" and from poetry to greeting card verse.
- *Publishers Weekly,* 205 E. 42nd St., New York, NY 10017. Of particular interest to those in the business end of publishing, this magazine covers what books are about to be released, who is doing what in the field, author profiles, and future trends.

Literary Journals

These magazines, also known as *quarterlies* and *little magazines,* publish fiction, poetry, reviews, and articles in varying proportions. Some devote special issues to fiction or poetry. The five listed here are only a small sampling of the great variety available. Be sure to read at least one issue before submitting. If you write regularly, you should subscribe to several.

- *Grand Street,* 50 Riverside Dr., New York, NY 10024. A relatively new but distinguished quarterly, *Grand Street* publishes a variety of fiction, poetry, reviews, and articles. Average issues contain more than 200 pages.

- *Missouri Review*, 231 Arts and Science, University of Missouri, Columbia, MO 65211. Published three times a year, this journal prints more fiction and poetry than most.
- *Paris Review*, 541 E. 72nd St., New York, NY 10021. Published four times a year, *Paris Review* prints fiction, interviews with writers and poets, and many poems. The magazine, originally published in Paris, enjoys a circulation of 10,000.
- *Ploughshares*, Box 529, Cambridge MA 02139. Relatively new, this quarterly rotates its editorship for variety. Special issues are occasionally devoted to poetry or to fiction. These special issues serve well as inexpensive anthologies for writing classes.
- *Sewanee Review*, University of the South, Sewanee, TN 37375. A quarterly, *Sewanee Review* usually prints one story and a number of poems, essays (mostly on literary topics), and reviews in each issue.

Poetry Journals

Although all the journals listed above (and most other "little magazines") publish some poetry, the following publications specialize in this genre. Each has its own literary preferences, so be sure to read several issues before submitting. If you write poetry, you will want to subscribe to at least one so that you can enjoy each issue at your leisure.

- *The American Poetry Review*, 1616 Walnut St., Rm. 405, Philadelphia, PA 19103. Printed bimonthly in tabloid form, *APR* is a relatively large-circulation (26,000) publication which contains not only new poetry but news and opinion about and by poets.
- *Beloit Poetry Journal*, Box 154, RFD 2, Ellsworth, ME 04605. Originally published in Beloit, Wisconsin, this quarterly continues to publish a wide variety of excellent work at its new location.
- *Field*, Rice Hall, Oberlin Hall, Oberlin, OH 44074. Published twice a year, *Field* publishes both poetry (including translations) and reviews of new collections.
- *Poetry*, P.O. Box 4348, Chicago, IL 60680 Known as "Poetry Chicago," this distinguished monthly was established in 1912 and has a circulation of about 8000.
- *Poetry East*, Rt. 1, Box 50, Earlysville, VA 22936. This journal is published three times a year.
- *The Poetry Miscellany*, English Department, University of Tennessee, Chattanooga, TN 37403. Like an increasing number of journals, *The Poetry Miscellany* is published only twice a year. It offers a distinguished variety of poetry and translations.
- *Poetry Northwest*, 4045 Brooklyn NE, University of Washington, Seattle, WA 98105. This quarterly was founded in 1960.

Poetry Anthologies and Collections

The following anthologies will serve to introduce you to a wide variety of contemporary poets.

- *Contemporary American Poetry*, A. Poulin Jr., ed., Houghton Mifflin (paperback). This extensive paperback collection offers a good variety of poets. Women and black poets are well represented. It is frequently adopted for college courses.
- *The Harvard Book of Contemporary American Poetry*, Helen Vendler, ed., Harvard University Press. This is a solid collection compiled by a distinguished critic, but it is not available in paperback.
- *No More Masks! An Anthology of Poems by Women*, F. Howe and E. Bass, eds., Anchor/Doubleday. From Amy Lowell to Nikki Giovanni—a full spectrum of women poets in this century.

Magazines and anthologies are both excellent ways of discovering poets whose work you enjoy and can learn from. Collections (as opposed to anthologies) have the advantage of giving you a far greater appreciation of the work of a single poet.

Many such collections can be found in any good library. But consider buying your own copies when you can. Since most bookstores do not stock more than a few titles, the best approach is to list the poets whose work you admire and check the "Authors" section of *Books in Print* in any library or bookstore to see which poets have published collections. Then order them through your bookstore or directly from the publisher (addresses in *LMP*). The cost of each volume will be less than a single meal at a restaurant, and the rewards will be long lasting.

Listening to Poetry

There are two ways of hearing poets read their own work. First, attend poetry readings. Almost every college and university offers a series of poetry readings that are open to the public. Often colleges will place you on a mailing list if you are not a student. In addition, larger libraries and organizations like the Y.M.C.A., Y.W.C.A., and Y.M.H.A. invite poets to read their works. Attending writers conferences in the summer (listings in *LMP*) is also a good way to hear poets read their own work.

The second approach is through recordings. Many libraries have good record collections. Records and tapes may also be ordered through any music store.

Magazines That Publish Fiction

Anyone who writes fiction should make a habit of reading the stories that appear in the three big-circulation magazines:

- *The Atlantic* (one or two stories each issue)
- *Esquire* (usually one story; published fortnightly)
- *The New Yorker* (normally one light and one serious story each week)

Although most little magazines print a few stories in each issue, the following specialize in fiction. If you write stories, you should subscribe to at least one and make sure that your library receives all four.

- *Fiction Network*, P.O. Box 5651, San Francisco, CA 94101. Published twice a year, this publication prints seven or eight stories in each issue as well as a "book guide" of recent publications. It also distributes stories to newspapers, dividing payments fifty-fifty with the authors.
- *The North American Review*, University of Northern Iowa, Cedar Falls, IA 50614. The oldest quarterly in the United States, *NAR* maintains a strong commitment to new fiction. In 1981 it received the National Magazine Award for Fiction (with *The New Yorker* and *Esquire* as runners-up!)
- *Stories*, 14 Beacon St., Suite 614, Boston, MA 02108. Established in 1982, this quarterly publishes short fiction by both known and unknown authors. Foreign work in translation is well represented. There is no poetry or criticism.
- *Story Quarterly*, P.O. Box 1416, Northbrook, IL 60065. This relatively new quarterly rotates its editorship with each issue.

Fiction Anthologies and Collections

There are two widely read annual publications made up of short stories published in magazines during the previous year. While no two editors will agree on the "best" stories published in any year, these volumes provide a fine overview of good contemporary fiction.

- *The Best American Short Stories*, Houghton Mifflin Co. This volume has been published annually since 1915. Edited for 36 years by Martha Foley, the collection is still referred to informally as "the Foley collection." The editorship is now changed each year.
- *Prize Stories, The O. Henry Awards*, William Abrahams, ed., Doubleday and Co. Better known as "the O. Henry collection," this is another view of the best fiction published during the previous year. It serves as an excellent companion work to *The Best American Short Stories*.

In addition to these two annuals, there are many short-story anthologies designed mainly for college use. They offer an opportunity to discover authors you may not have read.

- *Classic Short Fiction,* Charles H. Bohner, ed., Prentice-Hall. This large (1171 pp.) paperback gives a sampling of nineteenth century fiction but focuses primarily on the major writers of our own period.
- *Editors' Choice: New American Stories,* George E. Murphy, Jr., ed. Bantam. There are several volumes under this title, all paperback. The selections were made by magazine editors.
- *Modern Short Stories,* A. Mizener, ed., W. W. Norton. A good, comprehensive collection of twentieth-century work.
- *New American Short Stories: The Writers Select Their Own Favorites,* Gloria Norris, ed. New American Library (paperback). In this strictly contemporary collection, each story has been selected by the author and is accompanied with a statement explaining why he or she chose that work. These brief commentaries are of particular interest to those who write stories.

As with poetry anthologies, these volumes will introduce you to a variety of work. But when you find an author you admire, see if he or she has published a collection of stories. In many cases you can find such volumes in your local library. But if you wish to order your own copy, turn to the "Author" section of *Books in Print* in your library or bookstore.

A number of university presses publish collections of short stories by a single author in paperback. Among the first to do this was the University of Illinois Press (Urbana, IL 61801). They have been publishing four paperback collections a year since 1975. This admirable policy has been adopted in modified forms by The Johns Hopkins University Press (Baltimore, MD 21218), the University of Pittsburgh Press (Pittsburgh, PA 15260), and a few others. Write to these publishers if you wish a list of their short-story collections and prices.

Magazines for Playwrights and Scriptwriters

- *Poets and Writers Magazine,* 201 W. 54th St., New York, NY 10019. Listed earlier for poets and writers of fiction, this bimonthly is also valuable for dramatists. It gives deadlines for drama contests and occasionally offers advice on marketing scripts.
- *Drama Review,* 51 West 4th St., Rm. 300, New York, NY 10012. This quarterly focuses on contemporary avant-garde drama. Articles are often in depth and cover a wide range of generally innovative drama: women's theater, European trends, mixed-media productions, and so on.

Books for Playwrights and Scriptwriters

- *Best Short Plays*, Chilton Book Co. (paperback edition, Applause Theater Book Publishers). This annual has been published for decades. Back issues can be found in many libraries.
- *Dramatists Sourcebook*, Theater Communications Grp., 355 Lexington Ave., New York, NY 10017. This annual is fully revised each August. It contains a wealth of current information including submission policies of many theaters, contests, and the like. It is *the* basic source of information for any playwright.
- *New American Plays*, Hill and Wang. Paperback. Each volume in this series has a different editor. It contains full-length plays. No volumes since 1971.
- *On Screen Writing*, Edward Dmytryk, Focal Press. A basic text on script writing.
- *Television Writing*, Richard A. Blum, Communication Arts Books, Hastings House, Publishers, Inc. A brief, practical introduction to writing and marketing television scripts.
- *Twenty-Four Favorite One-Act Plays*, Catmell and Cerf, Doubleday. This paperback collection contains a variety of fairly traditional plays, from serious to light.

Publishers of Play Scripts

These publishers buy, print, and sell play scripts—both one-act and full-length. Since they deal largely with schools and regional companies, their selections tend to be conservative and easily playable. Each publisher puts out a catalogue describing its plays briefly.

- *Baker's Plays*, 100 Chauncy St., Boston, MA 02111. In business since 1845, Baker's Plays offers not only a great many rather light comedies and mysteries, but also a number of serious dramas that have had Broadway success. Their scripts are relatively inexpensive and offer a good way to study plays not found in drama anthologies.
- *The Dramatic Publishing Co.*, 4150 N. Milwaukee Ave., Chicago, IL 60641. Established in 1885, this company prints from 40 to 60 titles a year.
- *Samuel French, Inc.*, 25 W. 45th St., New York, NY 10036. The oldest (1830) of these three venerable publishing houses, Samuel French, Inc. has branches in England and Canada and publishes about 50 titles a year.

In addition to these publishers specializing in drama, many other houses print paperback editions of plays. They may be difficult to find, however, because few bookstores stock more than a sampling. The best solution is the same as it is for poetry and fiction: Start with the card file in your library. If you want to order a copy, turn to the "Authors" section of *Books in Print* and order through your bookstore or directly from the publisher (address in *LMP*).

Remember, finally, that whether your interest is in theater, television drama, or film, it is essential that you see as many productions as you can. Whenever possible, combine your study of the script with the experience of seeing the work performed. Each approach will provide insights the other cannot.

C GLOSSARY-INDEX

This appendix may be used both for quick review of literary terms and as an index. The explanations are limited to the way terms are used in this text. Numbers refer to pages; those in italics indicate lengthier treatment. Words in small capitals indicate cross-reference either in the same or a closely related form, e.g., METERED may be found under **meter,** RHYMING under **rhyme.** Items marked *ff* are continued on the next page.

Abstraction, 13, *28.* A word or phrase which refers to a concept or state of being. It is at the opposite end of a scale from *concrete* words which refer to objects we can see and touch. *Peace* is an abstraction; *dove* is a concrete word.

Absurdist, 294. See THEATER OF THE ABSURD.

Alliteration, 43. See SOUND DEVICES.

Ambiguity, 90. That which suggests two or more different meanings. Ambiguity in THEME which is not resolved frequently leads to obscurity. But ambiguities can be effective when the two alternative meanings join to make a broader, more profound suggestion.

Ambivalence, *16,* 76, 192. Conflicting or contrasting emotions which are held at the time time. Lack of ambivalence sometimes results in SIMPLE WRITING.

Anapestic foot, 56. See METER.

Anecdote, 217. A clever, sometimes humorous account usually told in conversation rather than written. Anecdotal FICTION tends to be SIMPLE, depending more on a twist of events (PLOT) than on CHARACTERIZATION.

Archaic diction, 29. Words which are primarily associated with an earlier period and are no longer in general use.

Arena stage, 299. See STAGE DESIGNS.

Assonance, 43. See SOUND DEVICES.

Automatic writing, 127. See STREAM OF CONSCIOUSNESS.

Ballad, 87. A NARRATIVE POEM often written in quatrains (see STANZA) of alternating iambic tetrameter and trimeter RHYMING *abcb*. *Folk ballads* are often intended to be sung and are relatively SIMPLE. *Literary ballads* are a SOPHISTICATED use of the old form.

Beat, 324. A pause in a LINE of DIALOGUE in a television or film script.

Black theater, *314 ff.* Plays written by black Americans. Although playwrights like Langston Hughes and Ossie Davis wrote hundreds of works in the 1930s and 40s, the term is most frequently used to refer to those who have come into prominence since the 1960s such as Amiri Baraka (LeRoi Jones), Paul Carter Harrison, Lonne Elder III, Adrienne Kennedy, and August Wilson.

Black verse, 12, 74. VERSE written by black Americans like Lucy Smith, David Henderson, Conrad Kent Rivers (p. 105), Lucille Clifton (p. 106), Maya Angelou (p. 98), Gwendolyn Brooks (p. 98), and Nikki Giovanni (p. 109).

Blank verse, 57. Unrhyming iambic pentameter (see VERSE and METER).

Breath units, 68. See RHYTHM.

Caesura, 53. A pause or complete break in the RHYTHM of a LINE of VERSE frequently occurring in the middle. It is particularly noticeable in Old English alliterative verse (see SOUND DEVICES) such as *Beowulf*. It is also found in METERED VERSE.

Canto, 86. A relatively lengthy unit, often numbered, found in both METERED and FREE VERSE. It may consist of several STANZAS.

Central concern, *222ff.* See THEME.

Characterization, *184ff., 282ff.,* 292. The illusion in FICTION or DRAMA of having met someone. The illusion depends on consistency of details, complexity of insight, and on individuality. SIMPLE characterization stresses consistency at the expense of complexity and often results in a STOCK CHARACTER, a form of SIMPLE WRITING.

Cinquain, 85. See STANZA.

Cliché, *25ff.* A METAPHOR or simile which has become so familiar from overuse that the vehicle (see METAPHOR) no longer contributes any meaning whatever to the tenor. It provides neither the vividness of a good metaphor nor the strength of a single, unmodified word. "Good as gold" and "crystal clear" are clichés in this specific sense. The word is also used to describe overused but nonmetaphorical expressions such as "tried and true" and "each and every."

Comedy, 266*ff.*, 288. DRAMA which is light in TONE and ends happily. Such plays are usually characterized by humor, wit, and occasionally *satire.*

Commercial fiction, 120. FICTION which is SIMPLE and conforms to certain rigid CONVENTIONS of PLOT and CHARACTER usually for the sake of publication and profit. Forms include the "pulps" (confessionals such as *True Romance*) and the "slicks" (*McCalls, Redbook,* and the like). The so-called slick magazines, however, have also published some sophisticated *fiction.*

Concrete poetry, 63. VERSE in which TYPOGRAPHY is employed in an extreme fashion to make the words and word fragments suggest a shape or picture which becomes of greater importance than RHYTHM or sound. Also called *shaped poetry.*

Concrete words, 13. See ABSTRACTION.

Conflict, 202 *ff.*, 269*ff.* See TENSION.

Connotation, 21, 72. The unstated suggestion implied by a word, phrase, passage, or any other unit in a literary work. This term includes everything from the emotional overtones or associations of a word or phrase to the symbolic significance of a character, setting, or sequence of actions. It is contrasted with *denotation,* the literal meaning.

Consonance, 44. See SOUND DEVICES.

Convention, 9, 86, 126*ff.* Any pattern or device in literature that is repeated in a number of different works by a number of different writers. It is a broad term which includes basic devices like PLOT, DIALOGUE, the division of a play into acts and SCENES, and the FIXED FORMS of POETRY like the SONNET and BALLAD. It also refers to recurring patterns in subject matter. Such conventions can be subtle or HACKNEYED. The term includes everything that is not unique in a work of literature.

Cosmic irony, 77, 208. See IRONY.

Couplet, 47, 84. See STANZA.

Creative writing, 131. Generally used to describe college courses in the writing of FICTION, poetry (see VERSE), and DRAMA, or any combination of these. It excludes courses in expository writing, assertive writing, and (usually) COMMERCIAL WRITING. Although all forms of writing require creativity in the broad sense, *creative writing* normally applies to the three more imaginative GENRES.

Dactylic foot, 56. See METER.

Denotation, 72. See CONNOTATION.

Dialogue,   *191ff.*, 271. Any word, phrase, or passage which quotes a character's speech directly. It normally appears in quotation marks to distinguish it from thoughts. *Monologue* is reserved for relatively lengthy and uninterrupted speeches. *Soliloquy* refers to monologues spoken in plays. *Indirect dialogue* is the same as *indirect discourse;* it echoes the phrasing of dialogue without actually quoting. Dialogue and thoughts constitute two of the five NARRATIVE MODES.

Diction,   30, 230. The choice of words in any piece of writing. Diction is a major factor in determining STYLE.

Dimeter,   57. See LINE.

Distance, 75,226. That aspect of TONE which describes how closely identified an author (or narrator) appears to be to his or her fictional character. Highly autobiographical and subjective works tend to have very little distance. METAMORPHOSING the PROTAGONIST or adding an IRONIC or humorous TONE increases the *distance.*

Double rhyme,   46. See RHYME.

Drama,   *242ff.* Writing intended primarily for presentation by performers speaking and acting on a stage. Drama is characterized, generally speaking, by the following: it is a "dramatic art" in the sense that it has an emotional impact or force; it is a visual art; it is an auditory art; it is physically produced on a stage; it moves continuously; and it is intended for spectators.

Dramatic conflict,   202*ff.*, 269 *ff.* See TENSION.

Dramatic irony,   77, 207. See IRONY.

Dramatic question,   205, 242, *263ff.* The emotional element in a play or work of FICTION which holds the attention of an audience or readers. An initial dramatic question is sometimes called a *hook.* Dramatic questions are usually SIMPLE emotional appeals based on curiosity or SUSPENSE. When dramatic questions are stressed at the expense of THEME or CHARACTERIZATION, the result is usually MELODRAMA.

End-stopped line,   48, 58. See RUN-ON LINE.

Epiphany,   147. A moment of awakening or discovery on the part of a FICTIONAL character, the reader, or both. Originally suggested by James Joyce, this term is generally limited to FICTION.

Expressionism,   293*ff.* See REALISTIC DRAMA.

Eye rhyme,   46. See RHYME.

Fable,   163, 209. A short tale intended to teach a lesson. It is similar to a parable except that it is less frequently religious and often deals with animals as characters. Modern fables are often SATIRIC.

Falling action,   265. See PLOT.

Falling meter,   57. See METER.

Feminine rhyme,   45*ff.* See RHYME.

Fiction,   *113ff.* Writing which tells an untrue story in PROSE. It may be SIMPLE like most COMMERCIAL WRITING or SOPHISTICATED. Fiction is also classified loosely by length: Short-short stories tend to be from three to eight pages of typed, double-space manuscript; short stories range upward to 24 or 30 pages; novellas are often in the 100-to-150-page range after which the work is considered a novel. Complexity of PLOT tends to increase with length.

Figure of speech,   *34ff.* See IMAGE.

First person narration,   *163ff.* See PERSON.

Fixed forms,   86. Traditional VERSE forms that follow certain CONVENTIONS in METER, RHYME scheme, or syllabics (see RHYTHM). Examples: the BALLAD, SONNET, and HAIKU.

Flashback,   *143ff.* See PLOT.

Focus,   *167ff.* The character or characters who are the primary concern of a story. When it is a single individual, he or she is also referred to as the PROTAGONIST. If the protagonist has an opponent (especially in drama), this character may be referred to as the *antagonist.*

Foil,   224, 271. A secondary character in FICTION or DRAMA who sets off a primary character by contrast in attitude, appearance, or in other ways.

Foot,   55. See METER.

Forewarning,   227. The technique in FICTION of preparing the reader for a shift in tone or for some turn of PLOT. Also referred to as a *pre-echo.*

Formula,   123. Popular CONVENTIONS which characterize SIMPLE FICTION and DRAMA. These conventions are usually patterns of PLOT combined with STOCK CHARACTERS. Sample: The-sincere-brunette who competes with The-scheming-blonde for the attentions of The-rising-young-executive who at first is "blind to the truth" but who finally "sees the light."

Frame story,   144. See PLOT.

Free verse,   *61ff.* VERSE which is written without meter, depending instead on RHYTHMICAL patterns derived from TYPOGRAPHY, syntactical elements, the repetition of words and phrases, SYLLABICS, or breath units. Free verse contains no regular RHYME, depending instead on SOUND DEVICES such as assonance, consonance, and alliteration.

Genre,   *1ff., 113ff., 241ff.* Any of several types of imaginative writing. In common usage, genres refer to FICTION, POETRY, and DRAMA. Classifications like "mysteries," "Westerns," and "science fiction" are often referred to as *sub-genres* or *genre writing.*

Gimmick,   188. An unusual twist of PLOT or CHARACTERIZATION. This somewhat colloquial term is generally used in a pejorative sense to describe contrived, attention-getting details.

Hackneyed language, 26. A broad term which includes CLICHÉS as well as nonmetaphorical phrases and words which have been weakened by overuse. Such language is closely associated with SENTIMENTALITY and with STOCK CHARACTERS.

Haiku, *40, 86, 106.* Originally a Japanese VERSE form. In English it is usually written as a three-line poem containing five syllables in the first LINE, seven in the second, and five in the third.

Heptameter, 57. See LINE.

Hexameter, 57. See LINE.

Hook, 264. See DRAMATIC QUESTION.

Hyperbole, 36. A figure of speech (see IMAGE) employing extreme exaggeration usually in the form of a simile or METAPHOR.

Iambic foot, *55ff.* See METER.

Image, *31ff.* Any significant piece of sense data in a poem. It may be used in a literal statement, as a SYMBOL, or in a figure of speech. A figure of speech (also called *figurative language*) uses an image in a stated or implied comparison. METAPHORS are the most common figures of speech. When several contain images which are closely related, the result is an *image cluster* (p. 36). Other figures of speech include similes, PUNS, and HYPERBOLE.

Indirect discourse, 194. See DIALOGUE.

Irony, *77ff., 206ff.* A reversal in which the literal statement or actual event is contrasted with the intended meaning or expected outcome. Irony can take three forms. The first is *verbal irony*, in which a statement by the author or a character is knowingly the opposite of the actual meaning (like saying, "Great day for a sail" during a hurricane). The second is *dramatic irony*, in which events, not words, are reversed (like the messenger in *Oedipus Rex* who says "Good news" when unknowingly he brings disastrous information). The third is *cosmic irony*, which is usually thought of as a reversal on the part of fate or chance (like the fire fighter who dies from smoking in bed).

Legitimate theater, 241. Plays performed by actors on a stage as contrasted with television DRAMA, cinema, and the like.

Line, *2ff., 55 ff.* A unit of VERSE which when printed normally appears without being broken, the length of which is determined by the poet alone. The inclusion of the line as a part of the art form rather than merely a printer's concern is one of the fundamental distinctions between VERSE and PROSE. In METERED VERSE, lines usually contain the same number of feet (see METER); in SPRUNG RHYTHM and ALLITERATIVE VERSE, lines are linked by having the same number of stressed syllables; and in FREE VERSE, the length of lines is more of a visual concern (see TYPOGRAPHY). The following represent eight types of lines used in metered verse: (1) monometer (one foot), (2) dimeter (two feet), (3) trimeter (three feet) (4) tetrameter (four feet), (5) pentameter (five feet), (6) hexameter (six feet), (7) heptameter (seven feet), (8) octometer (eight feet).

Lyric, 3, 52. Originally a Greek term referring to VERSE to be accompanied by a lyre. Today, it generally refers to a short poem which presents a single speaker expressing a strongly felt emotion. Thus, poems of love, observation, and contemplation are "lyrics" in contrast with BALLADS and other types of NARRATIVE POETRY. *Lyrical* is often used loosely to describe poetry which sounds musical because of its SOUND DEVICES and RHYTHM.

Means of perception, 159*ff.* The agent through whose eyes a piece of FICTION appears to be presented. This character is also the one whose thoughts are revealed directly. The term is synonymous with *point of view* and *viewpoint*. It is generally limited to a single character in short fiction.

Melodrama, 125, 238, 287. SIMPLE WRITING (usually DRAMA or FICTION) which is dominated by SUSPENSE and exaggerated forms of dramatic TENSION. SOPHISTICATED LITERATURE also uses conflict, but melodrama does it blatantly and at the expense of other literary concerns. It usually makes use of STOCK CHARACTERS as well.

Metamorphosis, 129*ff.* Radical transformations of an experience or of an existing draft of a story or play in order to create fresh literary work. This process can be either conscious or unconscious. It is usually employed either to clarify existing patterns or to break up patterns which appear to be too neat or contrived. It may also help a writer to regain control over an experience which is still too personal to develop in literary form.

Metaphor and **simile,** 34*ff.* A *simile* is a figure of speech (see IMAGE) in which one item (usually an abstraction) is compared with another (usually concrete) which is different in all but a few significant respects. Thus, "She fought like a lion" suggests courage but not the use of claws and teeth. The item being described is called the *tenor* (the true subject) and the one utilized is the *vehicle.* (Terms originally suggested by I. A. Richards.) A metaphor implies rather than states this same sort of comparison and so becomes a statement which is literally untrue, but when successful, figuratively stronger than a simile. "She was a lion when fighting for civil rights" is not taken literally because the reader recognizes it as a literary CONVENTION. In both cases, the base or starting point is the tenor. The reverse of this— using the vehicle as base and merely implying the tenor—is a SYMBOL ("It was the lion, not the lamb that ruled England in those years").

Meter,   54 *ff.* A system of STRESSED and unstressed syllables which creates RHYTHM in certain types of verse. The CONVENTIONALIZED units of stressed and unstressed syllables are known as *feet.* Metered verse normally contains the same number of feet in each LINE and the same type of foot throughout the poem. The effect is usually muted by occasionally substituting other types of feet. The following six feet are in common use, but the iamb is the most popular form in English. Those which end on a stressed syllable are called *rising meter;* those which end on an unstressed syllable are called *falling meter.*

iamb	(iambic)	ĕxcépt
trochee	(trochaic)	áskĭng
anapest	(anapestic)	dĭsăppoínt
dactyl	(dactylic)	háppĭlў
spondee	(spondaic)	héartbréak
pyrrhic	(pyrrhic)	ĭn thĕ

Mixed metaphor,   35. A METAPHOR which is internally confusing or illogical because the two vehicles (see METAPHOR) are contradictory. Example: "The *bitter aftertaste* of rejection *rang in my ears.*"

Modes,   117, 232*ff.* See NARRATIVE MODES.

Monologue,   271. See DIALOGUE.

Narrative modes,   117, 232*ff.* The five methods by which FICTION can be presented: DIALOGUE, thoughts, action, description, and exposition. Most writers use all five in varying proportions.

Narrative poetry,   17, 83. VERSE which tells a story. This may take the form of the BALLAD, the epic, or a tale in verse such as Hecht's "Lizards and Snakes" (p. 97).

Nonrecurrent stanzas,   86. STANZAS of unequal length. They are usually found in FREE VERSE and serve some of the same functions as paragraphs in PROSE.

Novel,   119. See FICTION.

Novella,   119. See FICTION.

Octave,   85, 87. An eight-lined STANZA in METERED VERSE. Also the first eight lines of a SONNET.

Octometer,   57. See LINE.

Off rhyme,   49. See RHYME.

Omniscient point of view,   162. The MEANS OF PERCEPTION in which the author enters the mind of all major characters. *Limited omniscience* restricts the means of perception to certain characters. Most short FICTION and a majority of novels limit the means of perception to a single character.

Onomatopoeia,   44. See SOUND DEVICES.

Orientation, 211*ff*. The sense in FICTION, DRAMA, or NARRATIVE POETRY of being somewhere specific. This includes awareness of geography, historical period, season, and time.

Overtone, 8. See CONNOTATION.

Pace, 145*ff*., The reader's sense that a story or play "moves rapidly" or "drags." This is determined by the RATE OF REVELATION and by the STYLE.

Paradox, 77. A statement which on one level is logically absurd yet on another level implies a reasonable assertion. Example from Heller's *Catch-22:* "The Texan turned out to be good-natured, generous, and likable. In three days no one could stand him."

Pentameter, 55, 57. See LINE.

Person, 163*ff*. Any of several methods of presentation by which fiction is given the illusion of being told *by* a character, *about* a character, about the *reader* and the like. The third person ("he") is the most common; the first person ("I") can be written either in a neutral STYLE or "as-if-told" style. The second person singular ("you") and the third person plural ("they") are seldom used. *Person* is *how* a story is presented; the *means of perception* is *who* appears to present it.

Persona, 24, 75. Broadly, a character in a poem, story, or play. The term is more frequently used to identify a fictitious narrator (implied or identified) in poetry.

Plot, 143*ff*., 260*ff*., 291*ff*. The sequence of events, often divided into SCENES, in FICTION, DRAMA, or NARRATIVE POETRY. This may be chronological, or it may be nonchronological in any of three ways: by flashback (inserting an earlier scene), or by multiple flashbacks (as in Vonnegut's *Slaughterhouse-Five* and Conrad's *Lord Jim*), or by using a frame (beginning and ending with the same scene). In traditional DRAMA the increasing complications are called *rising action,* the turning point is the *climax* which is followed by *falling action* which in turn leads to the final *catastrophe,* often the death of the protagonist. Contemporary DRAMA often follows modified versions of this structure.

Poetic, 1*ff*. In addition to being an adjective for "poetry" (*see* VERSE), this term is used to describe fiction or drama which makes special use of RHYTHM, SOUND DEVICES, FIGURATIVE LANGUAGE (see IMAGE), SYMBOL, and compression of meaning and implication.

Poetic diction, 30. See DICTION.

Poetry, 1*ff*. See VERSE.

Point of view, 160*ff*. See MEANS OF PERCEPTION.

P.O.V., 324, An abbreviation used in television scripts to indicate a SCENE shot from a character's point of view—that is, what the character sees.

Prose, 3. Writing in which the length of the LINES is not determined by the author and so have nothing to do with statement or form. Prose also tends to be less concerned with RHYTHM, SOUND DEVICES, and compression of statement than is VERSE.

Prose poetry,   68. Short LINES written so as to resemble poetry but usually lacking in RHYTHM, SOUND DEVICES, and figurative language (see IMAGE).

Prose rhythm,   53. See RHYTHM.

Protagonist,   169. The main character in a piece of FICTION, play or NARRATIVE POEM. This character is often opposed by an *antagonist.* The term is broader than *hero* which suggests greatness. Protagonists who are perpetual victims are sometimes referred to as *anti-heroes.*

Pun,   36. A figure of speech (see IMAGE) in which two different but significantly related meanings are attached to a single word. Most SOPHISTICATED uses of the pun are a form of METAPHOR with a vehicle (see METAPHOR) which has two meanings as in Dylan Thomas' "some grave truth."

Pyrrhic foot,   56. See METER.

Quatrain,   85. See STANZA.

Quintet,   85. See STANZA.

Rate of revelation,   145. The rate at which new information or insights are given to the reader regarding CHARACTER, THEME, or PLOT. It is one of the primary factors which determine PACE.

Realistic drama,   290*ff.* DRAMA which creates the illusion of the world about us. Costume, set, and PLOT appear to be borrowed from what we see or might expect to see in life. This is opposed to *nonrealistic drama* which creates its own world in somewhat the same manner as a dream. *Expressionism* is sometimes used as a synonym for nonrealistic drama, but more strictly it refers to a dramatic school culminating in the 1920s and 30s with the works of O'Neill, Rice, and others.

Refrain,   86, 310. A phrase, LINE, or STANZA which is repeated periodically in a poem.

Resonance,   228. That aspect of TONE in SOPHISTICATED WRITING which is created by the use of SYMBOLIC and suggestive details. It is a layering of meaning and implication not found in SIMPLE WRITING.

Rhyme,   44*ff.* A device found exclusively in VERSE and consisting of two or more words linked by an identity in sound which begins with an accented vowel and continues to the end of each word. The sounds preceding the accented vowel in each word must be unlike. This is *true rhyme. Slant rhyme* and *off rhyme* use similar rather than identical vowel sounds. *Double rhyme,* also called *feminine rhyme,* is a two-syllable rhyme as in "running" and "sunning." In an *eye rhyme,* the words look alike but sound different. *Rhyme scheme* is a pattern of rhymed endings which is repeated regularly in each STANZA of METERED VERSE.

Rhythm,   4, 52*ff.* A systematic variation in the flow of sound. In METERED VERSE this is achieved through a repeated pattern of stressed and unstressed syllables. In *alliterative* VERSE and SPRUNG RHYTHM the pattern is determined by the number of stresses in each line without regard for the unstressed syllables. In *syllabic verse,* the number of syllables in any one line matches the number in the corresponding line of the other STANZAS. In FREE VERSE, rhythms are achieved by TYPOGRAPHY, repeated syntactical patterns, and breath units. Rhythms in PROSE are achieved by repeating key words, phrases, and syntactical patterns.

Rising action,   265. See PLOT.

Rising meter,   57. See METER.

Run-on line,   48, 58. LINES in VERSE in which either the grammatical construction or the meaning or both are continued from the end of one line to the next. One function of this technique is to mute the rhythmical effect of METER. It is contrasted with *end-stopped lines,* which are usually terminated with a period or a semicolon.

Satire,   78*ff.* 208*ff.* A form of wit in which a distorted view of characters, places, or institutions is used for the purpose of criticism or ridicule. At least some measure of exaggeration (if only through a biased selection of details) is necessary for satire to be effective.

Scanning,   56. The analysis of METER in metered VERSE, identifying the various feet (see METER) and the type of LINE used.

Scansion,   56. The noun which refers to SCANNING.

Scene,   142*ff.*, 261*ff.*, 320. In DRAMA, a formal subdivision of an act marked in the script and shown to the audience by lowering of the curtain or dimming of the lights; or a more subtle subdivision of the PLOT marked only by the exit or the entrance of a character. The former are here called *primary scenes* and the latter *secondary scenes.* In FICTION, the scene is a unit of action marked either by a shift in the number of characters or, more often, a shift in time or place. In television and film scripts a scene is a unit of action (with or without dialogue) which occurs in a single place and time. As soon as the camera shifts to a different view, the scene changes. Also see TAKE.

Sentimentality,   124, 238. A form of SIMPLE WRITING which is dominated by a blunt appeal to the emotions of pity and love. It does so at the expense of subtlety and literary SOPHISTICATION. Popular subjects are puppies, grandparents, and young lovers.

Septet,   85. See STANZA.

Sestet, sextet,   85. A six-lined STANZA in METERED VERSE. Also the last six lines of the SONNET.

Set,   299*ff.* See SETTING.

Setting,   211*ff.* Strictly, the geographic area in which a PLOT takes place; but more generally, the time of day, the season, and the social environment as well. In DRAMA the setting is usually specified at the beginning of the script. What the audience sees on the stage (excluding the actors) is the *set*. Set design of *The Collection* appears on p. 301*ff*.

Shock,   206. A method of creating dramatic impact through violence or morbid surprise. When it follows naturally from PLOT and CHARACTER, it can be effective, as in the death which occurs in *Hello Out There*. But when used for its own sake or without preparation, it becomes MELODRAMA.

Short story,   118*ff*. See FICTION.

Shot,   320. See TAKE.

Simile,   34ff. See METAPHOR.

Simple writing,   *6ff., 115ff.* Writing in which the intent is made blatant, the STYLE is limited to a single effect, or the TONE is limited to a single emotion. It includes the adventure and horror story (MELODRAMA), many love stories, most greeting-card verse (SENTIMENTALITY), most patriotic VERSE and politically partisan FICTION and DRAMA (propaganda), and that which is single-mindedly sexual or sadistic (pornography). It also includes work which is so personal or so obscure that its intent fails to reach even a conscientious reader. The antonym for *simple* is SOPHISTICATED.

Slant rhyme,   49. See RHYME.

Slug line,   323. The brief identification of a SCENE in a television script. If a new scene, it begins with "EXT." (exterior) or "INT." (interior), then has a word or phrase of description, and "DAY" or "NIGHT." Example: INT. KITCHEN—DAY.

Sonnet,   87. A METERED and RHYMED FIXED FORM poem of fourteen LINES usually in iambic pentameter (see LINE). The first eight lines are known as the OCTAVE and the last six as the SESTET. The Italian or Petrarchan sonnet is often rhymed *abba, abba; cde, cde*. The Elizabethan sonnet is often thought of as three quatrains and a final rhyming couplet: *abab, cdcd, efef, gg*.

Sophisticated writing,   *6ff,* 115*ff*. Writing in which the intent is complex, having implications and ramification, the STYLE makes rich use of the techniques available, and the TONE has a range of suggestion. It is the opposite of SIMPLE WRITING. Not to be confused with the popular use of *sophisticated*.

Sound devices,   3, 43*ff*. The technique of linking two or more words by *alliteration* (similar initial sounds), *assonance* (similar vowel sounds), *consonance* (similar consonantal sounds), *onomatopoeia* (similarity between the sound of the word and the object or action it describes), or RHYME. In addition, *sound clusters* link groups of words with related vowel sounds which are too disparate to be called true samples of assonance.

Spondaic foot,   56. See METER.

Sprung rhythm,   53. A technique of RHYTHM in VERSE which is based on the number of STRESSED syllables in each LINE, disregarding those which are unstressed. It is primarily associated with the work of Gerard Manley Hopkins (see "Pied Beauty," p. 103).

Stage designs,   *299ff.* The *conventional stage* has a raised playing area which is set behind a *proscenium arch* from which a curtain is lowered between acts and SCENES. The effect is like seeing a performance in an elaborate picture frame. *Theater in the round, theater in the square,* and *arena theater* place the action in a central arena with the audience seated on all sides. Compromise designs include a variety of *apron stages* with the audience on three sides.

Stanza,   47ff., *84ff.* Normally, a regularly recurring group of lines in a poem which are separated by spaces and frequently (though not necessarily) unified by a metrical system and by rhyme. Common forms include the couplet (two lines); tercet or triplet (three lines); quatrain (four lines); quintet or cinquain (five lines); SESTET or sextet (six lines); septet (seven lines); OCTAVE (eight lines). The term is occasionally applied to irregular divisions in free verse which are used more like paragraphs in PROSE.

Stock character,   *123ff.* Characters in FICTION or DRAMA which are SIMPLE and which also conform to one of a number of types which have appeared over such a long period and in so many different works that they are familiar to readers and audiences. Their DIALOGUE is often HACKNEYED and their presence can reduce a work to the level of SIMPLE FICTION or DRAMA.

Stream of consciousness,   127. FICTION in the form of a character's thoughts directly quoted without exposition. Although wandering and disjointed, it is designed to reveal character. This is in sharp contrast with *automatic writing* in which the writer's goal is not CHARACTERIZATION (or even FICTION), but self-exploration.

Stress,   *53ff.* In metered VERSE, the relative force or emphasis placed on a particular syllable. In "awake," the second syllable is stressed. See METER.

Style,   *230ff.* The manner in which a work is written. It is determined by the author's decision, both conscious and unconscious, regarding diction (the type of words used), syntax (the type of sentences), NARRATIVE MODE (relative importance of dialogue, thoughts, action, description, and exposition), and PACE (the reader's sense of progress). It is closely connected with TONE.

Subplot,   119, 270. A secondary PLOT in a work of FICTION (usually a novel), or a play which echoes or amplifies the main plot or provides comic relief.

Substitution, 59. The technique in METERED VERSE of occasionally replacing a foot (see METER) which has become the standard in a particular poem with some other type of foot. A common form of substitution is the use of a trochee for emphasis in a poem which is generally iambic.

Suspense,   206. A heightened form of curiosity which creates excitement and a sense of drama. Too much suspense can result in MELODRAMA.

Syllabics,   66*ff*. See RHYTHM.

Symbol,   37*ff*., 227*ff*. Any verbal detail such as an object, action, or state, which has a range of meaning beyond and usually larger than itself. *Public symbols* are those which have become a part of the general consciousness—the flag, the cross, and the like. *Private symbols* are those created by individual writers and made public through a literary work or a series of works such as in the case Dylan Thomas' use of the color green. Usually the reader is first introduced to the vehicle (see METAPHOR) and then perceives the tenor as an additional or expanded meaning. This is in contrast with similes and METAPHORS, wherein the vehicle is brought into the work merely to serve as a comparison and has no other function.

Syntactical rhythm,   64*ff*. See RHYTHM.

Take,   320. The filmed version of a single SCENE before editing. Most scenes require several takes. The take which is finally selected for the edited film is a *shot*.

Tenor,   35. See METAPHOR.

Tension,   76*ff*., 202*ff*. A force and a counterforce within a work of literature. In VERSE this can take the form of thematic conflict, IRONY, or SATIRE. In NARRATIVE POETRY, FICTION, and DRAMA it may also be created through a sense of curiosity, SUSPENSE, and SHOCK. *Conflict* is that form of tension which is generated when one character opposes another character or some other force such as society or nature.

Tercet,   47. See STANZA.

Tetrameter,   57. See LINE.

Theater in the round,   299. See STAGE DESIGNS.

Theater of the absurd,   294. A somewhat loosely defined dramatic "school" in the *expressionistic* (see REALISTIC DRAMA) tradition beginning in the 1950s. Shared convictions are that life is "absurd" in the sense of lacking ultimate meaning and that the intellect cannot determine truth. Shared techniques include the use of nonrealistic situations, SATIRE, and a tendency to develop a static quality rather than a DRAMATIC

PLOT. Examples include works by Ionesco, Beckett, Pinter, and some by Albee, Genet, and Adamov.

Theme,   *222ff., 309ff.* The primary statement, suggestion, or implication of a literary work. The term is used here interchangeably with *central concern.* It does not have the moral implications of *message* nor the didactic element of *thesis.* A thesis states or clearly implies a particular conviction or recommends a specific course of action. Theses are often propagandistic. Most SOPHISTICATED WRITING is unified by a theme rather than a thesis.

Thesis,   309, 314. See THEME.

Third person narration,   *166ff.* See PERSON.

Tone,   *71ff., 225ff.* The emotional quality of a literary work itself and of the author's attitude toward the work as well. Some critics prefer to separate the two aspects of this definition, but most writers tend to think of them as two forms of the same quality. Tone, then, is described with adjectives like "exciting," "sad," "merry," "eerie," or "depressing" as well as with terms like "satiric," "sardonic," "ironic," and "dramatic."

Trimeter,   57. See LINE.

Triplet,   47, 85. See STANZA.

Trochaic foot,   56. See METER.

Truism,   7. A statement which reiterates a well-known truth. A platitude.

Typography,   *62ff.* The technique in VERSE (and particularly FREE VERSE) of arranging words, phrases, and lines on the printed page to create a RHYTHMICAL effect.

Vanity press,   342. A publisher who charges the author a part or all of the printing costs. Regular publishers assume all costs themselves and pay the author an advance and a percentage (generally between 10% and 15%) of the sales.

Vehicle,   35. See METAPHOR.

Verbal irony,   77, 206. See IRONY.

Verse,   *1ff.* That form of literary writing which is exclusively characterized by utilizing the length of the LINE as an aspect of the art, and characterized more generally by a concern for the SOUND and RHYTHM of language and by compression of statement and implication. *Verse* is occasionally used as a synonym for a LINE, a STANZA, or a REFRAIN. More frequently, it is used as a general synonym for *poetry.* Some, however, prefer that *poetry* be used only with reference to work which is truly SOPHISTICATED.

Viewpoint,   *160ff.* See MEANS OF PERCEPTION.

Villanelle, 88*ff.* A French verse form of nineteen lines divided into five tercets (see STANZA) and a final four-line STANZA with only two rhymes in this pattern: *aba aba aba aba aba abaa.* Line 1 is a REFRAIN which is repeated entirely as lines 6, 12, and 18; line 3 is repeated to form lines 9, 5, and 19. One of the challenges of this form (other than the mechanics) is to give subtly different meanings to the repeated lines.

Visual rhythm,   62. See TYPOGRAPHY.